COMPUTERS IN BUSINESS

An Introduction

DONALD H. SANDERS, Ph.D.

M. J. Neeley School of Business
Texas Christian University

McGRAW-HILL BOOK COMPANY

New York   St. Louis   San Francisco   Toronto   London   Sydney

COMPUTERS IN BUSINESS: AN INTRODUCTION

Copyright © 1968 by McGraw-Hill, Inc. All Rights Reserved.
Printed in the United States of America. No part of this
publication may be reproduced, stored in a retrieval system,
or transmitted, in any form or by any means, electronic,
mechanical, photocopying, recording, or otherwise, without
the prior written permission of the publisher.

Library of Congress Catalog Card Number 68-18553

54607

4 5 6 7 8 9 0 MAMM 7 5 4 3 2 1 0 6 9

To my patient wife, Joyce, and to my sometimes impatient children, Gary, Linda, and Craig

PREFACE

A basic objective of higher education for business is the development of potential managers and the updating of the skills of practicing managers. Students pursuing collegiate programs of study designed to prepare them for future administrative positions in such functional areas of business as marketing, finance, accounting, and management will find their future careers greatly affected by the use of electronic digital computers. Furthermore, the practicing managers of today must adapt to the changing conditions brought about by computer usage. In short, present and potential managers must prepare for a successful working relationship with computerized information processing. The primary purpose of this book is to lay the foundation for the continuing study which will produce such a working relationship.

More specifically, the objectives of this text are to: (1) provide a general orientation to the stored program computer—what it is, what it can and cannot do, and how it operates; and (2) provide an insight into the broad impact which computers have had, are having, and may be expected to have on managers and on the environment in which managers work.

Ten of the seventeen chapters are devoted primarily to the first of these objectives. Chapter 1 introduces the reader to basic data processing concepts; Chapter 2 presents the evolution of data processing; and Chapter 3 orients the reader to the information processing revolution which is getting underway. Chapter 4 is devoted to the uses and limitations of computers, while Chapters 5 and 6 deal with input/output media and devices. The emphasis in Chapters 7 and 8 is on the central processing unit; and Chapters 9 and 10 stress programming analysis and program preparation (an illustrative example is coded and explained in the COBOL programming language).

Chapters 11 through 16 focus attention on the managerial implications of computer usage (the second of the objectives stated above).

In these chapters, it is pointed out that the decision to introduce a computer into an organization has (and will have) managerial implications which go far beyond the mere acquisition of a piece of technical equipment. The reader will see in these chapters: (1) that information vital to the support of planning and control decisions is affected by the computer system which develops; (2) that the entire organizational structure may undergo stress and alteration; (3) that the nature and number of jobs are affected; (4) that the economic consequences of computer usage are often hard to predict; and (5) that the decision-making techniques which have been used by managers in the past may be changed. Thus, this volume has a somewhat broader managerial scope than most introductory business computer texts.

Computers in Business is designed for use in an introductory one-semester or one-quarter course in computer data processing offered at an early stage in an undergraduate collegiate program of education for business. No mathematical or data processing background is required or assumed; no specific computer make or model is featured. The book can be used without access to a machine. A Glossary of technical terms is included at the end of the book; and key words and phrases have been stressed throughout the text to aid the reader.

A question which generally arises concerns the depth of programming instruction which a student should receive. For many introductory courses, the programming emphasis contained in this book will be quite sufficient. However, when considerable emphasis is to be placed on the writing of programs in a specific language for a specific make and model of machine, two types of instructional materials are frequently required: (1) a basic text to add breadth to the course and (2) programming manuals available from equipment manufacturers and publishers and/or notes and materials prepared by the instructor. In such situations, this book is well-suited for use as the basic text.

Many individuals have contributed to, and have improved the quality of, this publishing effort (of course, only the author is responsible for any remaining errors). I am grateful to Dean Ike H. Harrison and to the faculty of the M. J. Neeley School of Business, Texas Christian University, for their encouragement and support. Another colleague, Dr. Alexander A. J. Hoffman, Director of the Computer Center, Texas Christian University, was most helpful in furnishing valuable reference materials.

Professor Luta P. Eaves, Coordinator of Data Processing, School of Business, Texas Technological College, and Professor Gordon B. Davis, Director of the School of Business Administration Computer Center, University of Minnesota, reviewed the manuscript and prevented me from submitting a different—and poorer—final version.

A special tribute must go to those equipment manufacturers who furnished technical materials, photographs, and other visual aids. Their individual contributions have been acknowledged in the body of the book. I am also indebted to the Data Processing Management Association, publisher of my book entitled *Introducing Computers to Small Business*, for their contractual permission to use appropriate quotations from that earlier work.

Donald H. Sanders

CONTENTS

PREFACE, vii

1 INTRODUCTION, 1

Objectives and Organization
Terminology and the Tower of Babel
Need for Data in Business
Data Processing
The Data Processing Operation
  Originating-Recording
  Classifying
  Sorting
  Calculating
  Summarizing
  Storing

Retrieving
Reproducing
Communicating
Factors behind Need for Improved Data Processing
Characteristics Desirable for Computer Processing
Objectives and Benefits
Summary
Discussion Questions
Selected References

2 THE DATA PROCESSING EVOLUTION, 13

Manual Stage
Mechanical Development
  The First Stage
  The Second Stage
  A Third Stage
Punched Card Development
  History
  The Card and the Code
  Fields

The Equipment
Computer Development
  History
  Size and Scope of Computer Market
  A Small-business Note
Summary
Discussion Questions
Selected References

3 THE INFORMATION PROCESSING REVOLUTION: AN OVERVIEW, 33

Revolutionary Environmental Changes
Revolution in Computer Technology
  Development in Hardware
  Development in Software
  Compatability Development

Computer-oriented Business Information Systems
Difficulties with Traditional Systems
Quick-response Systems
  Online Processing

Real Time Processing
Time Sharing
Broader Systems
Employment Opportunities
    Data Processing Management
    Systems Design and Analysis

Program Preparation
Computer Operation
Summary
Discussion Questions
Selected References

4 INTRODUCTION TO COMPUTERS, 55

Computer Classifications
    Analog and Digital Computers
    Special Purpose and General Purpose
    Computers
    Scientific and Business Applications
Computer Capabilities
Computer Limitations
Experiments in Learning
Computer Organization

Input
Storage
Arithmetic-Logic
Control
Output
Extensive Variety of Configurations
Summary
Discussion Questions
Selected References

5 INPUT/OUTPUT MEDIA AND DEVICES: I, 71

Some Input/Output Observations
Punched Cards
    Punched Card Equipment
    Advantages and Limitations of
    Punched Cards
Punched Paper Tape
    Tape Coding
    Input/Output Equipment
    Advantages and Limitations of

Punched Tape
Magnetic Tape
    Magnetic Tape Coding
    Magnetic Tape Equipment
    Advantages and Limitations of
    Magnetic Tape
Summary
Discussion Questions
Selected References

6 INPUT/OUTPUT MEDIA AND DEVICES: II, 95

Magnetic Ink Character Recognition
    Use and Development
    Equipment
    Advantages and Limitations of MICR
Optical Character Recognition
    Uses of OCR
    Equipment
    Advantages and Limitations of OCR
High-speed Printers
Online Terminals

Visual Communication
    Visual Input
    Visual Output
Voice Communication
Data Transmission
Buffer Storage
Summary
Discussion Questions
Selected References

7 THE CENTRAL PROCESSING UNIT: I, 123

Conceptual Storage Areas
Storage Locations
Capacity of Storage Locations

Fixed Word-length Storage
Variable Word-length Storage
A Comparison

Computer Numbering Systems
  Decimal Numbers
  Binary Numbers
  Binary Arithmetic
  Octal Numbers
Binary Coded Decimal
Computer Data Representation
Summary
Discussion Questions
Selected References

8 THE CENTRAL PROCESSING UNIT: II, 155

Properties of Storage Devices
Types of Internal Storage Devices
  Early Internal Storage
  Magnetic Core Storage
  Thin Films
  Memory Rods
Types of External Storage Devices
  Offline External Storage
Magnetic Drums
Magnetic Disks
Magnetic Cards and Strips
The Arithmetic-Logic Unit
The Control Unit
Summary
Discussion Questions
Selected References

9 PROGRAMMING ANALYSIS, 187

Introduction to Common Tools of
  Analysis
  Flowcharts
  Decision Tables
Flow Charting
  System Flowcharts
  Program Flow Charting
Benefits and Limitations of
  Flowcharts
Decision Tables
  Benefits of Decision Tables
Summary
Discussion Questions
Selected References

10 PROGRAM PREPARATION, 207

The Computer Instruction
  Command Repertoire
Computer Languages
  Machine Language
  Symbolic Language
  Procedure Oriented Language
  Common Procedural Languages
  Language Selection
Program Coding
Identification Division
Environment Division
Data Division
Procedure Division
Program Debugging and Maintenance
Programming Aids
Summary
Discussion Questions
Selected References

11 MANAGEMENT AND COMPUTERS: AN ORIENTATION, 239

Management Concepts
  Planning
  Organizing-Staffing
  Controlling
Managerial Implications in the
Introduction and Use of Computers
  Planning and Control Implications
  Organizational Implications
  Staffing Implications
Economic Implications
Implications for Decision-making
  Techniques
Systems Implications
Introducing and Using Computers
Summary
Discussion Questions
Selected References

12 THE FEASIBILITY STUDY, 253

Essential Nature of Feasibility Studies
 Reducing Economic Risk
 Avoiding Common Pitfalls
 Pointing the Way to Benefits
Study Prerequisites
 Scope and Objectives
 Appointment of Study Group
Feasibility Study Approach
 Identification of the Problem
 Gathering Data on Current Operations

Data Analysis and Determination of
 Alternatives
 Decision Making: Study Team
 Presentation of Recommendations
 Final Decision Making: Top Managers
 Follow-up on Decision
Summary
Discussion Questions
Selected References

13 PREPARING FOR CHANGE: I, 279

Technical Preparations
 Site Preparation
 Program Preparation and Conversion
 Vendor Assistance
Personnel Preparations
 Resistance Is the Rule
 Forms of Resistance

Reasons for Resistance
Employees Who Resist
Suggestions for Reducing Resistance
Summary
Discussion Questions
Selected References

14 PREPARING FOR CHANGE: II, 295

Selecting Workers for New Jobs
 New Positions Created
 Effects on Average Skill Levels
 Sources of Job Candidates
 Selection Procedures
Training Workers for New Jobs
Planning for Displacement

Distinction between Displacement
 and Unemployment
 Business Displacement Experience
Summary
Discussion Questions
Selected References

15 ORGANIZATION AND THE COMPUTER, 311

Preliminary Concepts
 Centralization or Decentralization
Organization of Data Processing
 Activities
 Trend toward Hardware Centralization
 Organizational Location of
 Computer Department
 Composition of Computer Department

The Computer's Impact on
Organization in the Future
 Centralization or Decentralization
 of Authority?
 Effects on Managers?
Summary
Discussion Questions
Selected References

16 CONTROL AND THE COMPUTER, 335

Managerial Control: A Review
The Properties of Quality Information

Accuracy
Timeliness

Completeness and Pertinency
The Nature of Internal Control
  Need for Internal Control in
  Computer Systems
  Organizational Considerations
  Internal Control and Auditing
Administrative Controls
  Systems Design Controls
  Programming Controls

Computer Operation Controls
Data Controls
  Input Controls
  Processing Controls
  Output Controls
Summary
Discussion Questions
Selected References

17 TOMORROW'S OUTLOOK, 351

The Hardware Outlook
  Trends in Input/Output Devices
  Trends in the Central Processor
  Trends in Data Communications
The Software Outlook
  Language Trends
  Trends in Applications Packages
  Growth of Software Specialists
The Outlook for Business Information

Systems
  Trend toward Quick-response Systems
  Movement toward Broader Systems
  The Growth of Time Sharing
The Outlook for Managers
Summary
Discussion Questions
Selected References

GLOSSARY, 363

INDEX, 389

1. INTRODUCTION

Computer installations are often visited by people interested in observing the machines in action. Sometimes, if the manager of the installation has been forewarned, the visitor may be treated to the sound of recognizeable tunes coming from a speaker connected to the computer. Or, if it happens to be a holiday season, the visitor may observe a printing device producing appropriate pictures, e.g., Santa Claus and his sleigh. Other snappy demonstrations are also used, and the spectator is impressed as he departs.

It requires no great amount of perception, however, for our visitor to realize that such impressive machines were not installed for their entertainment features. Magazines, newspapers, and television have informed the public of dozens of examples of how computers have been used, e.g., from guiding missiles to catching income tax cheats and from writing cake-mix recipes to monitoring elections. Indeed, our visitor may have come to the conclusion that this mysterious and baffling piece of equipment can do almost anything!

It is quite possible that our visitor is a manager in a business organization. It is also possible that the visit was to his firm's new computer installation. The impact which the computer will have on his firm (and his job) in the future is cause for personal concern. He has read articles in popular business magazines with such titles as: "Is the Computer Running Wild?," "New Tool, New World," and "The Boundless Age of the Computer." But to our visitor and to many of today's managers, the "Age of the Computer" might more appropriately be entitled the "Age of Bewilderment." The rug of familiar methods and traditional approaches to decision making has been pulled from under many managers by rapid technological change. And the computer is a prime instrument of this change. Many present managers received their formal training and initial job experience prior to the introduction of computers. Such managers must either learn to adapt their operations to this new management tool[1] or

---

[1] The author modestly recommends that the adaptation begin with a reading of this text.

1

decide to spend the remainder of their careers in a race between retirement and job obsolescence.

OBJECTIVES AND ORGANIZATION

A basic objective of education for business is the development of potential managers. Students concentrating in such areas of business as marketing, finance, accounting, or management will find their future careers greatly affected by the computer. As future managers they must prepare for a successful working relationship with computerized information processing. The primary purpose of this book, therefore, is to lay the foundation for the *continuing study* which will provide such a working relationship.

More specifically, the goals of this book are to:

1. Provide a general orientation to the stored program computer — what it is, what it can and cannot do, and how it operates.
2. Provide an insight into the broad impact which computers have had, are having, and may be expected to have on managers and on the environment in which managers work.

Chapter topics in this book will reflect these goals. Chapters 2 and 3 are orientation chapters dealing with the *evolution* of data processing and with the data processing *revolution* which is now under way. A study of the computer itself—its capabilities and limitations, its component parts, and its operation—begins with Chapter 4 and continues through Chapter 10.

In Chapters 11 to 16, attention is focused on the managerial implications of computers, on the economics of these machines, and on the managerial problems associated with their use. The final chapter attempts to project current trends a few years into the future.

TERMINOLOGY AND THE TOWER OF BABEL

In ancient Babylon a vast public works program was started by the leaders with the objective of building a tower reaching to the heavens. Obviously, a project of such magnitude required a considerable amount of managerial skill as well as the labor of thousands of workers. The book of Genesis tells us that this ambitious project was never completed. The managers had failed to plan for an unusual development. Displeased with the haughty conduct of the people, God confused their language. Foremen could not communicate with workers; workers could not even understand each other. The project came to a standstill, and the episode has been used for centuries as an example of the consequences of a communications breakdown.

The problem of lack of communication between computer specialists and business managers is a real one today. A whole new language has developed in the past decade in business data processing— a language which might be labeled "Computerese" and which must be mastered to some extent by the future manager.[2] To many of today's managers this language is a foreign one; even to computer specialists it can be confusing. Confusion results because of the lack of uniform agreement about the meaning of many of the more popular Computerese terms.

Much of the confusion, of course, comes from the rapid rate of growth of computer technology. New computers are now being installed at a rate of about 5,000 per year. Understanding suffers because the number of *new* terms and acronyms seems to be increasing at about the same rate.[3]

In the following section, and throughout the book, words are defined as they are introduced. Definitions used are the ones which appear to be most generally accepted. The reader will find that although some Computerese terms sound quite impressive and foreboding—as is often the case with technical jargon—closer inspection will prove them to be relatively simple.

NEED FOR DATA IN BUSINESS

What are data? The word "data" is the plural of "datum" which means "fact." Thus, business *data* are merely facts which may or may not be of much immediate value to managers. However, business data are the raw material input which produces meaningful managerial *information*. The main distinction between data and information is that although all information consists of data, not all data give meaningful information. Meaningful information provides managers with the means for *operating* and *controlling* a business.

For information to be meaningful to managers, the input data must have the characteristics of quality, quantity, and timeliness. If the data are inaccurate (an example of poor quality), incomplete, or out of date, the information that results will be of little value. For example, the *Statistical Abstract of the United States* for 1945 presents

---

[2] English words have taken on different meanings. For example, in dictionaries of a few years ago, a "computer" was a person who did computations. Now, a "computer" is a machine or group of machines.

[3] The reader should not despair. Rather, he should fortify himself with HADACOL (the Hope that Acceptable Definitions will Appear in Computer-Oriented Language). This is an example of an acronym — a term formed from the first letters of related words.

thousands of business facts. But these data are of little use to today's manager in making today's decisions.

Data are required to *operate* a business. For example, operating decisions must be made periodically about:

1. The firm's sales and distribution efforts, the effectiveness of these efforts, and the trends in the markets in which the firm operates
2. The quality, quantity, and cost of customer services offered
3. The quality and cost of the firm's product and the quantities to produce
4. The financial strength and weakness of the firm
5. The means for maintaining the organization's health and vitality

In dealing with these areas of decision, managers typically set standards of performance for purposes of control. For example, sales forecasts are made, sales quotas are established, and product quantities are scheduled for production. Financial budgets are prepared. Later, data are needed to check the results of operations against the planned standards. Thus, data are required in the *control* of an organization.

The *demand* for data for purposes of operating and controlling originates from managers within the organization. Data are also required, however, to meet demands originating from the environment in which the business operates. For example, tax reports are required by governmental bodies while dues reports may be expected by labor unions. Similarly, data must also be provided at the request of customers, banks, vendors, and stockholders. In short, data demand is both *internal* and *external*.

Data *sources* are also, of course, both *internal* and *external*. Internal data are produced within the business and deal with such things as costs, revenue, and production quantities. Data originating outside the organization are represented by a vendor's invoice or a bank's statement of account. External data varies in form, timeliness, and degree of accuracy and therefore is generally treated more critically than internal data.

DATA PROCESSING

We have seen that business data are the raw material input which produces meaningful managerial information. Manipulating data to create the desired information is called *data processing* (see Figure 1-1). Data processing is a broad field of study. In this book attention is focused on *business* data processing rather than one of the other data processing areas, e.g., scientific, engineering, or process control.

"Data processing" is a relatively recent phrase, but the *activity* or function is as old as writing. Long before the Greek and Roman periods of history, the Babylonians had invented cuneiform writing. Cuneiform

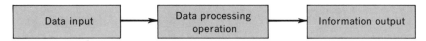

Figure 1-1

symbols were cut into damp clay, and then the clay was baked for permanence. Numerous business records on clay tablets showing such data processing outputs as sales and inventory totals have been unearthed. We no longer use clay tablets, but businesses of all sizes must still perform the data processing activity.

Data are processed for output information. The value of this information, we have seen, depends on the quality, quantity, and timeliness of the input data. Output reports, to be of value, must have these same attributes; furthermore, they must be placed in the hands of a manager who can make proper use of the information.

What information does a manager need to do his job? This fundamental question, unfortunately, can only be answered in the broadest of terms because there are no two managers whose information needs are exactly the same. The needed information includes everything the particular manager must have (1) to establish, evaluate, and adjust goals; (2) to develop plans and standards and initiate action; (3) to measure actual performance and take appropriate action when performance varies from the standard; and (4) to evaluate planning results.

Although it is impossible to specify what every manger needs in the way of information, it is less difficult to describe what he *does not* need:

1. *More information than can possibly be used.* Important information may be buried in stacks of detailed and unrefined reports. Reports will often be more pertinent if only *exceptions* to normal activity are included.
2. *Detailed information on relatively unimportant matters.* An analysis of many business inventories shows, for example, that 80 percent of the inventory value is represented by only 20 percent of the items. Control reports should (but often do not) concentrate more on the high-value items.
3. *Outdated information.* Reports are sometimes continued after they no longer serve a purpose. Battle reports may linger after truces have been signed. And information which arrives after it is too late to be used is of no value.

THE DATA PROCESSING OPERATION

All data processing, whether it be done by hand on clay tablets or by the latest electronic methods, consists of one or more of the following basic steps:

1. Originating-Recording

2. Classifying
3. Sorting
4. Calculating
5. Summarizing
6. Storing
7. Retrieving
8. Reproducing
9. Communicating

Originating-Recording

Data must be captured or originated in some tangible form for processing. The first step in the data processing operation is often to include handwritten or typed forms such as sales tickets, checks, deposit slips, and customer invoices. Data originally recorded in one form may later be converted into machine-usable form for further processing. Some recording operations produce a machine-usable output directly or as a by-product.

Classifying

Arranging items with like characteristics into groups or classes is called *classifying*. Sales data taken from a sales ticket may be classified by product sold, by location of sales point, by customer, by sales clerk, or by any other classification which the processing cycle may require.

Classifying is usually done by a shortened, predetermined method of abbreviation known as *coding*. The three types of codes used are numeric, alphabetic, and alphanumeric. Code *numbers* are used to designate persons (Social Security number, payroll number, timecard number), places (ZIP code, sales district number), and things (part numbers). *Alphabetic* codes are used to classify such diverse things as vitamins (A, B, and C), financial condition (AAA, BB, and C), and astronaut status (A-OK). Combinations of letters and numbers give such *alphanumeric* codes as military service numbers (AF17341256), further classification of vitamins (B_1 and B_2), automobile license plates (AB-1234), and mail-order catalog items (XMB2973).

Sorting

After the data are classified, it usually is then necessary to arrange or rearrange the data in a predetermined sequence to facilitate processing. This arranging procedure is called *sorting*. Sorting is done by number and by letter. Sales invoices may be sorted by invoice number or by customer name in alphabetic sequence. Numeric sorting generally requires less time than alphabetic sorting.

Calculating

Arithmetic manipulation of the data is known as *calculating*. In the calculation of an employee's pay, for example, the total of hours worked multiplied by the hourly wage rate would give the taxable gross earnings. Payroll deductions such as taxes and insurance are then computed and subtracted from gross earnings to leave net or take-home earnings. The calculating step is an important one involving a great deal of effort if done manually.

Summarizing

To be of value, data must often be condensed or sifted so that the resulting reports will be concise and effective. Reducing masses of data to a more usable form is called *summarizing*. A sales manager may be interested only in the total sales of a particular store. Thus, it would be wasteful in time and resources if he were given a report which broke sales down by department, by product, and by sales clerk.

Storing

Placing similar data into files for future reference is *storing*. In the payroll example cited above, the data on hours worked early in the pay period had to be stored until the payroll was prepared. Such a storage period, of course, is quite short. Other data may be stored for years. Storage may take a variety of forms. Storage *media* that are frequently used include paper documents, ledgers, punched cards, and magnetic and paper tapes.

Retrieving

Information should be stored only if the value of having it in the future exceeds the cost of storing it. Recovering the data when it is needed is *retrieving*. Data retrieving may be done by hand or by machine depending on the storage medium.

Reproducing

It is sometimes necessary or desirable to copy or duplicate data. This operation is known as data *reproduction*, and may be done by hand or by machine. Some machines (e.g., Xerox equipment) produce a humanly readable or *hard copy document*; others reproduce the data in machine-readable form on such media as punched cards, punched paper tape, and magnetic tape.

Communicating

As we have seen, data may go through many steps after they have been originated. The transfer of data from one operation to another for use or for further processing is known as data *communication*. The communicating process continues until the data, in a usable form, reach the final user's location. (Communication of a different nature, of course, will often result at this point.) Output data may be in the form of a vital printed managerial report; but output data can also be in the form of an electric bill on a punched card, an updated deck of payroll record cards, or an updated reel of magnetic tape. When the electric bill is paid by the customer, the card is returned and becomes the input for another processing cycle—the updating of accounts receivable records.

It should now be apparent that data processing can be a complex matter. Methods of improving processing operations have been sought for generations. Yet the need for improvement has never been greater than it is at the present time.

FACTORS BEHIND NEED FOR IMPROVED DATA PROCESSING

Businesses seek data processing improvements to remain competitive. As a competitive weapon, however, data processing techniques do not normally receive primary emphasis. Product and/or service changes and improvements, marketing efforts such as advertising and sales promotion, production economies—all of these areas are usually given attention before managerial consideration is given to data processing. Yet in United States businesses today, data processing "costs as much or more than does direct factory labor."[4]

The factors which have brought about managerial awareness of the need for improvement are:

1. *The increased paperwork volume.* Data processing capability in many firms has been strained (1) by the growth in size and complexity of the firm; (2) by the increased requirements for data from external sources such as local, state, and Federal governmental agencies; and (3) by the demand of managers for more information. It has been estimated that a million new pages of data are generated each minute of the day in our offices. This figure represents a three-fold increase in 30 years.[5]

[4] M. K. Evans and L. R. Hague, "Master Plan for Information Systems," *Harvard Business Review*, vol. 40, January – February, 1962, p. 92.

[5] See Emmet Leahy, "Don't Do It Yourself," *Systems and Procedures Journal*, vol. 14, May – June, 1963, p. 12.

2. *Demand for timeliness.* As we have seen, meaningful information is timely information. But with an increase in volume, there is often a reduction in the speed of processing. Managers demand, but often do not get, the timely information they need.

3. *Demand for quality.* Many marketing managers are responsible for supervising the sales activities of a large number of branches scattered throughout the nation. They must have accurate information if they are to control such an effort properly. But if a data processing operation is strained to and beyond the capacity for which it was originally planned (if there was an original plan), inaccuracies will begin to appear. Inadequate control will permit inadequate performance. Thus, the marketing manager will logically demand better quality in the information he receives.

4. *Pressure from outside changes.* Rapid changes are taking place in the world socially, economically, and technically. These outside changes will be discussed in some detail in Chapter 3. Such changes, however, have a significant impact on the environment in which businesses must operate, on the planning which managers must do, and on the information which they must have.

5. *Costs.* The increasing costs of clerical labor, materials, and other expenses associated with the data processing operation require eventual managerial attention. Often, when a top executive realizes the magnitude of the office expense, pressure will be exerted to get "more processing for a buck."

An improved operation can be acquired in a wide variety of ways. Better information may be obtained by using improved manual methods, noncomputer machine methods, computerized techniques, or some combination of any or all of these. This book, however, is primarily concerned with the computer. What type of operations are best suited for computer processing? The following section deals with this question.

CHARACTERISTICS DESIRABLE FOR COMPUTER PROCESSING

A computer is used most efficiently in processing operations which have one or more of the following characteristics:

1. *Large volume of input.* The greater the volume of data that must be processed to produce *needed* information, the more economical computer processing becomes relative to other possible methods.

2. *Repetition of projects.* Because of the expense involved in preparing a task for computer processing, it is frequently most economical to use the computer for repetitive projects.

3. *Desired and necessary greater speed in processing.* The greater the *need* for timely information, the greater will be the value of a computer relative to alternative (and slower) methods.

4. *Desired and necessary greater accuracy.* Computer processing will be quite accurate if the task to be performed has been properly prepared.

5. *Processing complexities that require electronic help.* In some situations
when large numbers of interacting variables are present, there is *no* alternative to the computer. For example, decision making with complex
managerial tools[6] such as linear programming and business simulation
generally requires the use of a computer. And certainly it is hard to con-
ceive of anything but a computer being used to process mission control
information for a missile while it is in flight.

The reader by now has possibly compared the characteristics outlined in this section with the factors (described in the previous section) which have caused managers to seek improved data processing
operations. Business paperwork volume is increasing, and the computer thrives on volume; speed in processing is needed, and the computer is fast. There is little wonder then that computers have been
chosen for use by many businesses. The objectives sought by businesses can often be achieved with a computer.

OBJECTIVES AND BENEFITS

In our economy, if a business is to continue in existence, it must earn
a sufficient profit. Managers are quite aware of this fact. Simply defined, profit is the difference between revenue and expenses, i.e.,
Profit = revenue − expenses.[7] A convenient way of classifying computer
objectives and benefits is by examining the effects of computer
acquisition on profit.

The profit picture can be improved in several ways, two of which
are presented here. One way to increase profit is by *reducing expenses*
while revenue remains stable. The goal of expense reduction may take
several forms, e.g., reduced labor expense, reduced supplies expense,
or reduced inventory carrying charges.

Another way the profit outlook can be improved is by *increasing
revenue* while expenses remain stable. This general objective may be
achieved (1) by having faster, more complete, and more accurate deal-
ings with present customers; (2) by making it possible (with increased
processing capacity) to expand marketing efforts to include new customers; and (3) by providing managers with more timely, more comprehensive, and more accurate information with which to improve
their operating and control decisions.

Computer benefits are sometimes classified as *tangible* (measurable)
or *intangible* (not subject to quantitative measurement). Expense-
reduction goals should lead to tangible benefits. Revenue-raising goals

[6] These tools will be discussed in Chap. 11.

[7] If this equation frequently yields a negative value for a firm, the data processing
problems, like old soldiers, may just fade away.

often produce benefits of an intangible nature. It is quite possible, of course, for a firm to seek and receive both tangible and intangible benefits from its computer.

The objectives originally sought by managers when a computer is ordered and the benefits which are ultimately received may not be the same. Some goals may not be achieved, while some unexpected benefits may appear.

SUMMARY

Future managers must prepare for a successful working relationship with computerized information processing. The objective of this text is to provide an orientation to computers and to their impact on the business community.

Data are not, strictly speaking, information. But data are the input from which information is produced. Data are needed in the operation of businesses of all sizes, from the corner grocery to the giant corporation. Data processing is an operation which takes data as input and creates information as output. This operation, in its entirety, requires nine steps. However, some steps may be omitted in specific situations.

The data processing operation, like the factory operation, needs periodic study and improvement. In recent years several factors have caused a need for such improvement. Included in these factors are an increasing volume of paperwork and an increased demand from managers for information which is more timely, more accurate, more concise, and more comprehensive.

The computer is a tool which *can* give managers such information. It is most efficiently used when large volumes of input data are required, when the tasks are repetitive, and when greater speed and accuracy in processing are needed. Its greatest contribution may lie in its ability to make possible jobs which could not otherwise be performed.

Computer benefits may be tangible or intangible; business goals generally center around the means for profit improvement. Benefits, however, are not received automatically when the computer is plugged in, as we shall see in later chapters.

DISCUSSION QUESTIONS

1 Why may there be lack of communication between computer specialists and business managers?

2 Why must data be processed?

3 (*a*) What is the difference between data and information? (*b*) Why must a manager have information? (*c*) What properties must the information possess?

4 Identify and explain the basic data processing steps.

5 Why have business managers become more aware of the importance of improved data processing methods?

6 What operations are well suited to computer processing?

7 Explain how computer acquisition may improve a company's profit picture.

8 "Revenue-raising goals often produce benefits of an intangible nature." Explain this sentence.

SELECTED REFERENCES

Raymond M. Fergus, "Educating the Non-computer Manager," *Journal of Data Management,* November, 1966, pp. 16-21.

Fred Gruenberger and Richard H. Hill, "Let's Close the Knowledge Gap at the Top," *Business Automation*, May, 1966, pp. 39-41.

2. THE DATA PROCESSING EVOLUTION

In this chapter we shall discuss the data processing *evolution*, while in Chapter 3 we shall be concerned with a survey of the information processing *revolution*. It is, of course, not change or the absence of change which distinguishes evolution from revolution, for we are interested in the process of change in both chapters. Rather, the distinction we are making is in the rapidity with which change occurs. In biology, "evolution" implies gradual change over long periods of time, and it is in this gradual change context that we are using the term. "Revolution," on the other hand, implies significant change of a much swifter nature. Thus, this chapter deals with a brief survey of data processing techniques and equipment from earliest times to about 1960. Chapter 3 presents an overview of some of the more significant developments occurring since 1960.

Four stages in the data processing evolution will be considered: (1) the manual stage; (2) mechanical development; (3) punched card development; and (4) computer development.

MANUAL STAGE

The reader will recall that there are nine steps in the data processing operation (recording, classifying, sorting, etc.). When manual methods are used, each step must usually be performed *separately*—e.g., a sales slip is written, one clerk codes it, another computes the total value, and a third enters the amount in an accounts receivable book.

For centuries all man had to work with were his fingers. They aided him in his computations, but the limited number of digits posed problems. For example, if a shepherd had a large flock and a short memory, how was he to keep control of his inventory? Problems bring solutions, and the shepherd's solution might have been to let a stone, a stick, a scratch on a rock, or a knot in a string represent each sheep in the flock. Stones and sticks, however, were not sufficient for early merchants. Our old friends the Babylonian merchants, as we have

seen, used clay tablets for their business records. And the Egyptians
made a great improvement in record keeping possible when they developed parchment or papyrus and the means for writing on it. Manual
record-keeping techniques continued to develop through the centuries
with such innovations as banking systems and budgets (the Romans)
and double-entry bookkeeping (the Italians in city-states).

An early manual calculating device was the *abacus*, which is over
2,000 years old and still being used. Its origin is unknown; it may
have indeed originated in several places, for it has appeared with
different names throughout many parts of the world. Skilled abacus
operators have won speed races in competition with clerks using desk
calculators.

In the United States, however, the abacus never became popular.
In the twenty years after the Civil War, the main tools of the data
processing trade were pencils, pens, rulers, work sheets (for classifying,
calculating, and summarizing), journals (for storing), and ledgers (for
storing and communicating).[1] The data processor was (or so the
cartoons and literature of the time would have us believe) a clerk of
unenviable status, toiling through the day in a dim corner, wearing
an eyeshade, and sitting on a tall stool.

Such methods, of course, were slow and relatively inaccurate and
could not support the rapidly expanding business and government
requirements of the time. For example, the 1880 census was not
finished until it was almost time to begin the 1890 count!

MECHANICAL DEVELOPMENT

There were two stages in the evolution of mechanical techniques. The
first stage was the improvement in performance of a *single* processing
step through the use of mechanical devices. The second, and more
advanced stage, was the development of machines which could *combine* certain steps in a single operation. A third stage is emerging
from these mechanical developments which combines computer or
electronic features with earlier mechanical developments. This third
stage defies classification-the machines are not strictly mechanical
nor are they strictly computers.

The first stage

The typewriter is a recording aid which was first introduced around
the turn of the last century and which quickly proved to be an im-

[1] One authority states that "not more than $1/100$ of 1 percent of the clerical work per-
formed seventy-five years ago [1887] was aided by the use of a clerical machine."
See A. B. Toan, Jr., "Data Processing, Accounting and Business Administration,"
The Journal of Accountancy, vol. 114, November, 1962, p. 44.

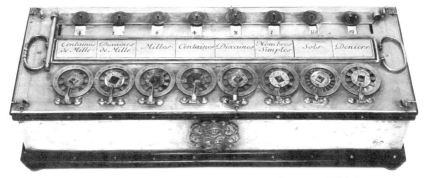

Figure 2-1. Pascal's Adding Machine (Photograph Courtesy IBM Corporation)

portant office asset. Writing speeds were doubled, and legibility was improved.

Mechanical calculating aids have a long history. In 1642, in Paris, a brilliant young (18) Frenchman named Blaise Pascal decided to help ease the computation load of his father, who was Superintendent of Taxes. Pascal's effort resulted in the world's first mechanical adding machine (Figure 2-1). Gears with one tooth for each digit from 0 through 9 were connected in a series. When one gear was rotated past the tooth representing the 9 digit, the next gear to the left would be advanced by one tooth or digit. The result was a machine which was capable of "carrying." Although this principle is used today in many mechanical office machines, it was not until well into the 1800s that the "grandfather" of present-day desk calculators was developed. In the late 1800s and early 1900s, many machines to aid in the calculating step were developed and introduced to businesses.

The second stage

Machines which calculate and print the results were first produced around 1890. They combine calculating and recording steps and produce a printed tape record suitable for storing data.

After World War I, specialized accounting machines first appeared. These machines are designed for special purposes, e.g., billing, retail sales, payroll, and they also enable an operator to combine steps. They often contain several adding *registers* or *counters* to permit the accumulation of totals for different classifications. For example, a typical supermarket accounting machine is the cash register, which will have separate registers to sort and total (summarize) the day's sales of meats, produce, and groceries. Figure 2-2 shows some of the types of modern accounting machines available.

(a)

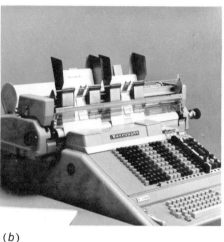
(b)

Figure 2-2. (a) Cash Register (Courtesy of the National Cash Register Company); (b) Electronic Accounting Machine (Courtesy Burroughs Corporation)

A third stage

Many of the business machines which started as pieces of mechanical equipment are now powered by electric motors and thus might be classed as electromechanical devices. Yet most of them merely use electricity to turn gears and other mechanical parts, and all of them require manual keyboards to enter the data for processing.

Office equipment manufacturers, however, have begun to take steps to ensure that accounting machines are not made obsolete by the computer. Features of accounting machines are being combined with features taken from punch card equipment and from computers to create an entirely new class of desk-size hardware—not quite as sophisticated, perhaps, as computers, but not traditional accounting or punch card machines either. These new devices (see Figure 2-3) are making it difficult to distinguish between computer and noncomputer systems.

When compared with the manual methods of the late 1800s, speed and accuracy were greatly improved by the use of the mechanical devices which we have just briefly surveyed. However, processing was still too slow and inaccurate, and the evolution continued. The census problems of 1880 led to the development of a whole family of electromechanical devices to process punched cards.

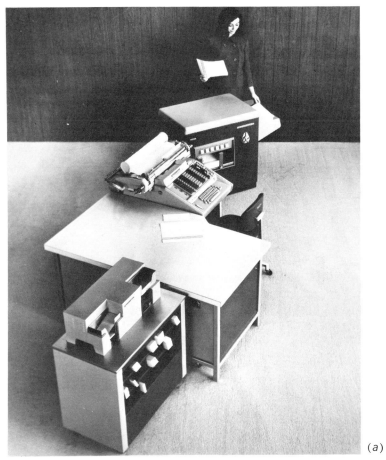

Figure 2-3. (a) Burroughs E4000 Electronic Accounting Machine (Courtesy Burroughs Corporation); (b) NCR 400 Electronic Accounting Machine (Courtesy National Cash Register Company)

Figure 2-4. The Vertical Sorter Developed by Dr. Herman Hollerith (Courtesy IBM Corporation)

PUNCHED CARD DEVELOPMENT

History

Punched card methods have been in *widespread* business use only since the 1930s. But the history of the punched card dates back to about the end of the American Revolution when a French weaver named Jacquard used them to control his looms.

Although punched cards continued to be used in process control, it was not until our 1880 census fiasco that they began to be considered as a medium for data processing. The inventor of modern punched card techniques was Dr. Herman Hollerith. He was hired by the Census Bureau as a special agent to help find a solution to the census problem. In 1887, Hollerith developed his machine-readable card concept and designed a device known as the "Census Machine." Tabulating time with Hollerith's methods was only one-eighth of that previously required. The Hollerith punched card approach was adapted for use in the 1890 count. Although population had increased from 50 to 63 million people, the 1890 census was completed in less than three years. (Of course, this would be considered intolerably slow now, but think of the alternative then!) Figure 2-4 shows an early card sorter developed by Dr. Hollerith.

In 1896, Dr. Hollerith founded the Tabulating Machine Company to make and sell his invention. Later this firm merged with others to form what is now known as International Business Machines Corporation (IBM).

By the time it became necessary to begin planning for the 1910 census, it also became obvious to officials that additional equipment would be required. James Powers was hired by the Census Bureau. He designed some new punched card machines with somewhat different characteristics, which were used in the 1910 count. The next year Powers formed the Powers Accounting Machine Company, which was later merged with Remington Rand.

The card and the code [2]

The typical punched card used in business measures $7\frac{3}{8}$ inches long by $3\frac{1}{4}$ inches wide (see Figure 2-5). Special card paper stock is used. The card is divided, from left to right, into 80 consecutively numbered vertical *columns*. Each column, in turn, has 12 horizontal positions or *rows*. By appropriate coding, each column can record one character of information, i.e., a numerical digit, a letter, or a special character. Columns 9 through 18 illustrate the digit punches. Notice that only a *single* hole is punched in each column to record the desired *number*.

When *letters* of the alphabet are recorded, *two* holes must be punched. Along the top of the card are three *zone* punching positions—the 0 row and the blank area at the top of the card which is designated as punching areas 11 and 12. A logical *combination* of zone and digit punches is required for letters. For example, letters A through I are coded by using a 12 zone punch and digit punches 1 through 9. The 11 special characters are coded by using one, two, or three holes.

Fields

Card columns are laid out in groups called *fields* for special business applications. Fields are carefully planned by the application designer

[2] In this brief exposition, we shall be concerned only with the dominant 80 column card and Hollerith code.

20

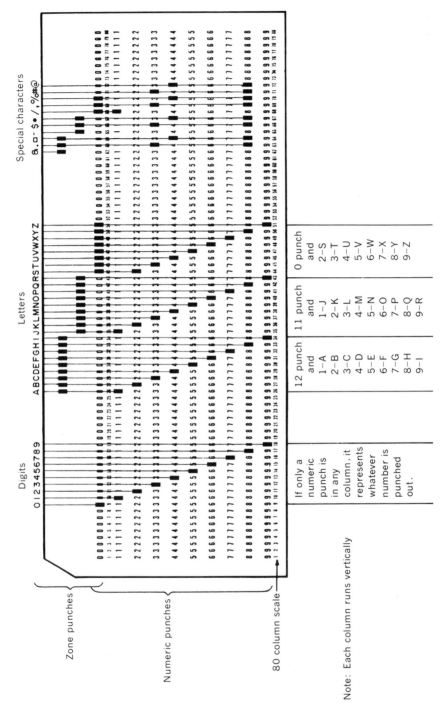

Figure 2-5. The Punched Card and the Hollerith Code (Courtesy Honeywell Electronic Data Processing)

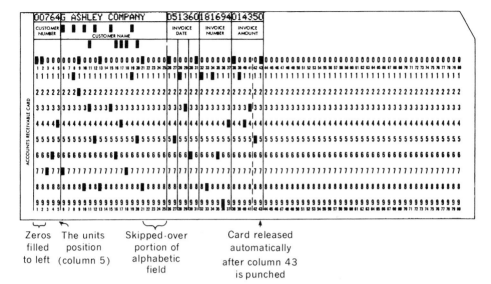

Figure 2-6. Accounts Receivable Card (Courtesy IBM Corporation)

and may be of any width from 1 column to 80. Figure 2-6 shows an accounts receivable card divided into five fields—customer number, customer name, and the date, number, and amount of the invoice. The reader can test his *understanding* of card coding by verifying the information printed at the top of the card with the hole or holes punched in the same column. Memorizing the code, however, is usually not necessary. People work with machines, and the machines know the code.

The equipment

A punched card is often referred to as a *unit of record* because data recorded in the card deal with only one business transaction. Once the data are punched, the card may be combined with many other different cards containing related data to produce a wide variety of reports.

The remainder of this section will be devoted to a brief survey of punched card (or unit record) machines. In these devices, the card passes through a *reading* station. This station is equipped with special brushes and a contact roller to convert the holes in a card into electrical impulses (see Figure 2-7). The electrical impulses are then processed by the particular machine to obtain the desired output.

Recording devices The most common way of recording data in punched card form is through the use of a *keypunch* machine (see Figure 2-8). When a key is depressed, the correct combination of holes is produced in the card. Key punching is similar, in many ways, to typing with an elec-

Card passing between roller and
brush acts as an insulator so that
no impulse is available at the brush.

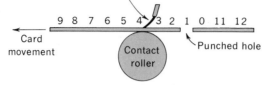

Card
movement

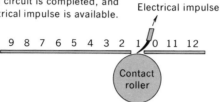

When brush makes contact with
roller, a circuit is completed, and
an electrical impulse is available.

Electrical impulse

9 8 7 6 5 4 3 2 1 0 11 12

Contact
roller

Figure 2-7. (Courtesy IBM Corporation)

Figure 2-8. The IBM 26 Printing Card Punch (Courtesy IBM
Corporation)

tric typewriter. To check keypunching accuracy, *verifiers* are used. The verifier is similar to the keypunch; but instead of punching holes, it merely senses whether or not the holes in the card being tested correspond with the key being depressed.

Data may also be recorded on cards *automatically* rather than by manual key punching. For example, a master card may be reproduced any desired number of times (*gang punching*); a group of *different* cards may be automatically duplicated (*reproducing*); cards marked with a special graphite pencil in designated places can be punched automatically (*mark sensing*); and cards may be produced automatically as by-products of other machine operations and as outputs of other activities.

Sorters Arranging the cards according to some desired order or sequence is the function of the *sorter* (Figure 2-9). The 13 pockets in the sorter correspond to the 12 rows in the card (0 through 9, 11, and 12) and a thirteenth or "reject" pocket for cards which do not belong in any other pocket (e.g., because there is no hole in the column). Sorting (which moves from the right column to the left column of the data field) is done *one* column at a time in each sorting *pass*. Thus, the sorting procedure in a data field of five digits would take five passes before the cards would be in the proper numerical sequence. Various sorters can operate during a pass at speeds ranging from 450 to 2,000 cards per minute.

Figure 2-9. The Sorter (Courtesy IBM Corporation)

Collator   The *collator* is a machine which can combine two decks of sequenced cards into a single sequenced deck (*merging*). It can also compare agreement between two sets of cards without combining them (*matching*). Other manipulations are possible with two decks of sequenced cards. The collator can check a tray of cards to determine correct ascending or descending order. After the arrangement of the cards in the proper order, they are usually then taken to a machine which can perform calculations on the data.

Calculating machines   The punched card *accounting machine* or *tabulator* (Figure 2-10) performs the steps of calculating and summarizing. It also prints reports, thus communicating the prepared information to managers. As is the case with many punched card machines, an externally wired control panel directs it in its operation. The typical accounting machine adds and subtracts and has several registers or counters for this purpose. Besides addition and subtraction, *calculators* also perform multiplication and division when needed.

Interpreter   If it is necessary to use the card for visual reference, the *interpreter* is needed to translate the machine code into humanly readable form. The machine interprets the data represented by the holes in a card and then prints the data directly on the card. The printing order need not follow the order in which the holes appear in the card—any

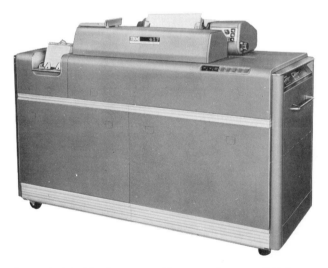

Figure 2-10. The Accounting Machine (Courtesy IBM Corporation)

desired printing sequence may be used. Generally, the data are printed at the top of the card.

From this very brief survey of punched card data processing, it is obvious that significant improvement was possible over methods previously used. Gains in speed and accuracy were made. Punch card equipment proved effective in performing many of the individual steps necessary, e.g., sorting, calculating, and summarizing. But it is still necessary to have people handle trays of cards between each step. Separate machines must be fed, started, and stopped. This *limited intercommunication* between processing stages requiring manual intervention is a major disadvantage. With the computer this disadvantage is eliminated; no manual interference between data input and information output is required. What sets the computer apart from any other type of data processing machine is the concept of storing, within the machine itself, alterable instructions which will direct the machine to perform automatically the necessary processing steps. Let us now, in the remainder of this chapter, look at the history and development of the computer.

COMPUTER DEVELOPMENT

History

The history of computer development, like any history, may be divided into arbitrary time periods. For our purposes we shall use four periods: (1) Ancient History (1833-1937); (2) the Middle Ages (1937-1954); (3) the Victorian Period (1954-1960); and (4) the Recent Period (1960-Present). The Recent Period will be discussed in Chapter 3.

Ancient history (1833-1937) In 1833, Charles Babbage, a professor of mathematics at Cambridge University in England, proposed a machine which he named the "Analytical Engine." Babbage's dream—to many of his contemporaries it was "Babbage's folly"—would have incorporated a memory unit or "store," an arithmetic unit or "mill," and a control unit which would accept instructions prepared on punched cards. In short, Babbage had designed a machine which was a prototype computer and which was a hundred years ahead of its time. His ideas were beyond the technical capabilities (and the human imagination) of the day, but he continued to work on the Analytical Engine until his death in 1871. No further progress was made until 1937.

Babbage was a very colorful and eccentric individual. His work was interrupted by feuds with organ grinders who disturbed his privacy and by disputes with neighborhood children who undoubtedly enjoyed annoying him. His life makes for very interesting reading.[3]

The middle ages (1937-1954)   Beginning in 1937, Harvard professor Howard Aiken set out to build an automatic calculating machine which would combine established technology with the punched cards of Hollerith and Powers. With the help of graduate students and IBM engineers, the project was completed in 1944. The completed device was known as the Mark I digital computer. (A *digital* computer is one which essentially does counting operations.) Internal operations were controlled automatically with electromagnetic relays; arithmetic counters were mechanical. The Mark I was thus not an *electronic* computer, but was rather an *electromechanical* one. In many respects the Mark I was the realization of Babbage's dream. However, the Mark I was nearly completed before Aiken became aware of Babbage's work—an example of a breakdown in information retrieval. Appropriately, this "medieval" machine is now on display at Harvard University.

The first *electronic* digital computer was created between 1939 and 1946 at the University of Pennsylvania's Moore School of Electrical Engineering by the team of Dr. John W. Mauchly and J. Presper Eckert, Jr. Vacuum tubes (19,000 of them!) were used in place of relays. The ENIAC (Electronic Numerical Integrator And Calculator), as it was called, weighed about 30 tons and was built for the U.S. Army for the purpose of calculating artillery trajectory tables. ENIAC could do in 1 day what a manual operation would require 300 days to perform; it could do 300 multiplications in one second while the fastest electromechanical devices of the day could perform only one multiplication per second.[4] Instructions to ENIAC were fed through externally located plug boards and switches.[5] In 1956, ENIAC was placed in the Smithsonian Institution.

---

[3] He was also something of a literary critic. In "The Vision of Sin," Tennyson wrote: "Every moment dies a man/Every moment one is born." Babbage wrote Tennyson and pointed out to the poet that since the population of the world was increasing, it would be more accurate to have the verse read: "Every moment dies a man, Every moment one and one-sixteenth is born." What he lacked in aesthetic taste he compensated for with mathematical precision!

[4] William Shanks, an Englishman, spent twenty years of his life computing π to 707 decimal places. In 1949, ENIAC computed π to 2,000 places in just over seventy hours and showed that Shanks had made an error in the 528th decimal place. Fortunately, Shanks was spared the knowledge that he had been both slow and inaccurate for he preceded ENIAC by 100 years.

[5] In one frustrating session in 1946, ENIAC blew out several hundred vacuum tubes in an attempt to divide by zero — no one had remembered to tell the machine that the task was impossible!

In 1945, Dr. John von Neumann, a Princeton mathematician, suggested in a paper (1) that *binary* numbering systems be used in building computers and (2) that computer *instructions* as well as the *data* being manipulated could be stored internally in the machine. These suggestions became a basic part of the philosophy of computer design. The binary numbering system is represented by only two digits (0 and 1) rather than the 10 digits (0 through 9) of the familiar decimal system. Since electronic components are typically in one of two conditions (on or off, conducting or not conducting, magnetized or not magnetized), the binary concept facilitated equipment design. A more thorough discussion of the binary concept will be left to a later chapter. In May, 1945, Dr. von Neumann demonstrated how computer instructions could be coded as numbers and thus stored internally in the machine along with the data.

With the aid of these new concepts, Mauchly, Eckert, and others at the University of Pennsylvania set out to construct a machine with a *stored program*, i.e., with the instructions for operation stored internally. Their next effort was EDVAC (Electronic Discrete Variable Automatic Computer). Design of the EDVAC had actually begun prior to the completion of ENIAC, but EDVAC was not completed until 1952. EDVAC was then the prototype stored program computer in the United States. It is still being used by the Army at the Aberdeen (Maryland) Proving Ground.

One reason for the delay in EDVAC was that Eckert and Mauchly founded their own company in 1946. From this firm came the first commercially available computer—the UNIVAC-I (UNIVersal Automatic Computer). In 1949, Remington Rand acquired the Eckert-Mauchly company, and in early 1951, the first UNIVAC became operational at the Bureau of the Census. This "medieval" relic was used until 1963 when it, too, went to the Smithsonian Institution. The first computer acquired for *business data processing* was a UNIVAC-I, which was installed at General Electric's Appliance Park in Louisville, Kentucky.

The Victorian period (1954-1960) The Victorian Period begins with this first business installation. There was initial reluctance on the part of IBM to enter the computer market, but the loss of Census Bureau business changed this attitude. IBM reacted rapidly to produce new commercial machines.[6] Other computer manufacturers were not idle.

---

[6] The IBM 650 first saw service in Boston in December, 1954. It was an all-purpose machine, was comparatively inexpensive, and was widely accepted. It gave IBM the leadership in computer production in 1955, and this leadership has never been challenged.

The six years of this period saw the adoption of computers by many firms. Business managers generally considered the computer to be an accounting tool; however, there was little attempt to modify existing accounting procedures. More than a few computers were obtained for their prestige value, rather than for the better satisfaction of managerial needs. Computer potential was underestimated.

A new breed of workers was required to instruct and operate the machines. Dissatisfaction developed because of the slowness with which jobs were prepared for the equipment. Improvements designed to speed up instruction coding were introduced.

Toward the end of this period, machines were made smaller, faster, and with greater computing capacity through improvements such as magnetic cores for internal storage of data and instructions. The vacuum tube, with its heat, bulkiness, and relatively short life, gave way to *solid state* components such as transistors and diodes. Introduction of these *second-generation* computers in 1960 marks the end of the Victorian Period. Unlike the early computers, the second-generation machines were designed from the beginning with business-processing requirements in mind.

Size and scope of computer market

Over a hundred different computer models have been built since 1954; thousands of machines have been installed. Yet in 1950 it was generally agreed by most businessmen (including the top executives of computer manufacturing firms) that 8 or 10 of the big "electronic brains" would satisfy the entire demand for such devices! This must go down in history as one of the worst market forecasts of all time.

In 1965, it was estimated that there were 30,800 computers of all sizes installed in the United States. The 1966 figure was estimated to be 35,200, while 85,000 computers is a projected number for 1975. These figures do not take into account the large number of foreign-produced machines being introduced in other countries. In dollar value, the 1966 domestic installations were estimated to be worth about $8 billion.[7] United States computer manufacturers produced equipment with a total estimated value exceeding $3 billion in 1966 alone.[8]

[7] All figures released by the American Federation of Information Processing Societies. See "85,000 Computers by 1975 . . . ," *Administrative Management*, vol. 27, June, 1966, pp. 52–54. The reader is cautioned that such figures are just estimates because manufacturers do not officially release installation data.

[8] See "Market Report," *Computers and Automation*, vol. 15, March, 1966, p. 11.

Computers, of course, come in various sizes, from the very large systems having monthly rentals up to $200,000 to the desk-sized systems renting for less than $1,000. Systems are usually classified as *large, medium,* or *small* in terms of computing capacity and cost. *Any* such classification, of course, tends to be arbitrary. Medium-scale systems rent for from $5,000 to $25,000 per month and sell for between $250,000 and $1 million. Large and small systems fall on either side of these ranges. The sale and rental price varies considerably for a specific computer model depending upon the selection of optional equipment (just as the price of a car varies with the selection of accessories).

In terms of *number* of installations (not value), large-scale systems represent about 3 percent of the total; medium-scale systems account for 14 percent; and small machines make up the remainder. Computers are rented in about three-fourths of all business installations.

A small-business note

For several years, computers were available only to the larger businesses for economic reasons. But developments of the past few years have brought computer capability to an ever expanding circle of smaller organizations.[9] Included in these developments are (1) the rapid increase in the number of commercial *computer centers,* (2) the development of efficient and low-cost small computers, (3) the establishment by small concerns of member-owned cooperative computer centers, and (4) the willingness (even eagerness) of larger firms to sell unused time on their machines.

A brief comment on computer centers (or *service bureaus* as they are sometimes called) is in order. These organizations may be subsidiaries of computer manufacturers, they may be independent (i.e., not affiliated with a manufacturer) national service chains, or they may be independent local firms. Some specialize in a particular industry's processing problems, while others offer a general service. They all perform a *service* to the small-business manager for a fee. They thus differ from firms which only sell excess computer time on a do-it-yourself basis. The computer center assumes the responsibility for performing a specific task by a certain time and for a certain fee.

---

[9] For a more comprehensive treatment of the subject of computers and small business, see Donald H. Sanders, *Introducing Computers to Small Business* (Park Ridge, Ill.: Data Processing Management Association, 1966).

SUMMARY

Data processing techniques have been undergoing evolutionary change since the beginning of mankind. This evolution has advanced through four stages from manual methods to the development of the computer. However, none of these stages should be considered obsolete for each has it place.

Mechanical tools were developed to extend man's capabilities in performing specific steps. Later mechanical and electromechanical devices enabled man to combine some steps in one operation. The computer, with its ability to store and act upon its own instructions, made possible automatic communication between processing steps.

There can be little doubt that the computer is responsible in large measure for the significant and sweeping change that is now taking place in the field of information processing. The next chapter examines some of the causes and effects of this revolution.

DISCUSSION QUESTIONS

1 Trace the evolution of manual methods of data processing.

2 (a) Who invented the first mechanical adding machine? (b) Why did he invent it? (c) How did it operate? (d) How many data processing steps did it perform?

3 (a) Why was Dr. Herman Hollerith hired by the U.S. Census Bureau? (b) What were the results of Dr. Hollerith's work?

4 Who was James Powers, and what were the results of his work?

5 Describe the punched card and the Hollerith code.

6 What is a field?

7 (a) How many business transactions are recorded on a punched card? (b) What is meant by unit record?

8 Explain the function of the following punched card machines:
(a) keypunch   (d) collator
(b) verifier   (e) accounting machine
(c) sorter   (f) interpreter

9 "Limited intercommunication is a disadvantage of punched card processing." Explain this sentence.

10 (a) What was the Analytical Engine ? (b) What features would it have had in common with modern computers? (c) Why wasn't it built?

11 (a) What was the Mark I? (b) Was it an electronic computer?

12 (a) What was the ENIAC? (b) How did it differ from the Mark I?

13 What important contributions to computer design were proposed by John von Neumann?

14 (a) What is a commercial computer center? (b) Give two examples of services they might perform for a small business.

SELECTED REFERENCES

"Accounting Machines and Punched-Card DP," *Dun's Review and Modern Industry*, September, 1966, pp. 138 - 139 ff.

Richard G. Canning, "The Changing Computer Market," *EDP Analyzer*, April, 1966.

An Introduction to IBM Punched Card Data Processing (IBM Corporation, Manual F 20-0074-0).

Donald H. Sanders, "Introducing Computers to Small Business," *Journal of Data Management*, June, 1966, pp. 72 - 75.

George Schussel, "IBM vs REMRAND," *Datamation*, May, 1965, pp. 54 - 57.

3. THE INFORMATION PROCESSING REVOLUTION: AN OVERVIEW

In Chapter 2 the evolution in the development of data processing methods was traced to the introduction of solid state computers in 1960. At that time there were probably less than 6,000 machines installed in the United States. Yet, in the next six years there was a sixfold increase in this figure. The value of computers installed increased proportionately from about $1.5 billion to over $9 billion.

As these figures imply, there are now revolutionary changes occurring in the age-old activity of processing data. The key elements in this information processing revolution are (1) the scope and magnitude of *environmental changes*, (2) the revolutionary changes in *computer technology*, and (3) the rapid advances in business information processing *systems*. In this chapter we shall examine each of these topics.

REVOLUTIONARY ENVIRONMENTAL CHANGES

In the operation of their businesses, managers must contend with the rapid scientific, social, and economic movements which are taking place in this country and in the world. Advances have been particularly rapid in the various *scientific* fields. As a result of scientific research, new products are constantly being developed, and new processes are rapidly appearing.

The rate of scientific change has undoubtedly been quickened by the world political situation. For example, the Russian Sputnik satellite brought about a public demand in this country for faster progress in missile and space technology and related areas. And, of course, computer technology has benefited from, and has contributed to, this expanded space effort. Consumer products are also frequently created or improved as a result of advances made in space research.

But scientific achievement is not limited to space. Technical information in many fields is expanding at an overwhelming rate. It is estimated that there is a 5 percent annual growth rate in the output of scientific information. Thus, in about fifteen years (because of compounding) the amount of such information will have again doubled.

Information retrieval has become a major problem in many scientific and business areas. Researchers sometimes spend considerable time and money on problems which have been solved and published elsewhere.[1] No one knows how much is spent each year in such duplication (what researcher wants to admit that his pet—and expensive—project was published in an obscure journal last year?), but the figure runs into the millions of dollars. Much work is currently being done in the area of computer-assisted information retrieval systems.

In addition to technical changes affecting products and production processes, the business manager must also cope with rapid *social* and *economic* change. The *population* of the United States is increasing at a staggering rate; it will expand by about 60 million in the next twenty years! These additional people must be fed, housed, clothed, educated, employed, and transported. Business activity obviously must expand (1) to meet the demands of additional population and (2) to meet the demands brought about by an increase in the overall standard of living (which is brought about, in part, by the increased productivity resulting from technological innovations).

Mass *education* contributes to social change. The number of college-age students and the proportion of such students actually attending classes have been increasing. College enrollment is expected to rise 45 percent between 1965 and 1970. The better educated citizen is more *mobile*, and mobility has created changes in distribution methods. Suburbs have grown, and new shopping centers have sprung up. Also, increased leisure time has business implications, e.g., markets for boats, camping equipment, etc., are improved.

Change has occurred in the *age composition* of the population. If you are over 27, you are in the older half. Products catering to a young market have been developed, while other products have been redesigned. Many firms have moved in the past few years from placing primary emphasis on production to a marketing orientation.

The implications of rapid scientific, social, and economic changes are clear—the business manager must be prepared to make continuous readjustments in his plans. He must make decisions about new products and existing products; he must make decisions about product prices, about new markets, and about the channels of distribution to use; and he must decide on matters of finance. To compete profitably in the future will require timely information of the highest possible

[1] In the September, 1960, issue of *Fortune*, Francis Bello wrote that a major electronics firm had paid $8 million for two patented inventions only to discover that they had no value — buried in the Patent Office files were documents which proved that both ideas had been anticipated earlier.

quality. The computer, which is undergoing rapid technological improvement, is the tool which can provide this information.

REVOLUTION IN COMPUTER TECHNOLOGY

An operating computer system is not a single black box; rather, it consists of a varying number of machines. There are devices for handling input, output, and computations. Many installations also have machines which store vast quantities of data. These storage devices are connected directly (or *online*) to the central processing machine and deliver and accept processed data without human intervention. All these machines make up the *hardware* of a computer installation.

In addition to hardware, computer manufacturers develop various types of programming aids or *software* to help customers make effective use of the equipment. Perhaps a brief example of one type of program preparation aid would be in order at this point. The program instructions required by a particular computer to do a task must be written in a special machine language code. Such instructions typically consist of combinations of numbers which have no meaning to a manager and which are quite tedious to code. In addition to remembering the various code numbers (42 might mean multiply), the employee performing the task of instructing the computer (a *programmer*) must decide and keep record of where in the machine he will store the instructions.

To aid the programmer, manufacturers have developed special coding *languages* which save time and are more convenient to use. The computer still has to receive instructions in its own built-in machine language, but the programmer can now write his instructions in a more convenient language form, perhaps using commonly understood symbols and/or English words.

But how does the machine execute instructions it cannot receive directly? It merely translates the programmer's instructions into machine-usable form by means of a separate translating program prepared by the manufacturer. (See Figure 3-1.) The translating program is in the form of punched cards or magnetic tape and is thus one example of computer software. There has been significant development in the technology of both hardware and software.

Development in hardware

Hardware technological development has been extremely rapid as may be seen by an examination of the factors of (1) size, (2) speed, (3) cost, and (4) information storage capacity.

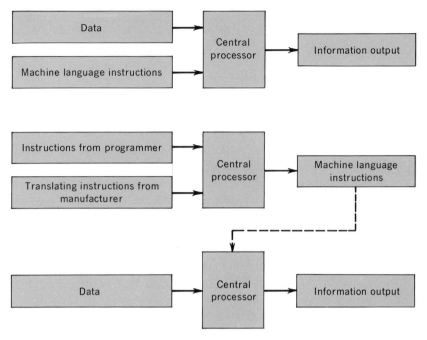

Figure 3-1

Size   The earliest computers were enormous machines (ENIAC, you will recall, weighed about 30 tons). The tubes used in this equipment produced considerable heat, which made it necessary to air condition the room where the machine was located. Using transistors instead of tubes, the second-generation computers were greatly reduced in size. For example, compact tube equipment contained an average of 6,000 components per cubic foot. The second-generation machines, however, could pack an average of 100,000 circuits into a similar space. Also, transistors were more reliable than tubes and generated little heat.

The *third-generation* computers,[2] which are now in operation, make use of microelectronic or *integrated circuits* on a large scale. Such circuits may be almost microscopic, but they contain the equivalent of many transistors. (Instead of 100,000 circuits per cubic foot, current technology makes it possible to pack 10 million circuits in the same space.) Figure 3-2 shows some of the integrated circuits used by the Burroughs Corporation. Dwarfed by an ordinary paper clip, each of these circuits contains the equivalent of over 150 separate electronic components.

---

[2] IBM's System/360 family of computers was the first to make use of integrated circuits. These machines were first announced on April 7, 1964. In 1966, System/360 machines estimated to have a value of $2.5 *billion* were shipped.

Such size reductions make it possible to produce, in a small package, a machine with the computing power of the earlier monsters. That many currently produced computers are also rather large merely gives an indication of the growth in computing capability.

Speed Component miniaturization has brought increased speed and improved performance to the latest computers. Current machines are nine hundred times faster than 1950 models. A job requiring 1 hour to complete in 1950 could now be finished in 3 or 4 seconds. Early computer speed was measured in *milliseconds* (thousandths of a second); second-generation machine speed was expressed in *microseconds* (millionths of a second); and third-generation devices have internal operating speeds measured in *nanoseconds* (billionths of a second).[3]

Cost We have seen the rapid growth in the number of computer installations. Linked with this rapid expansion—in fact, a significant cause of it—is the dramatic reduction in the cost of performing a specific number of operations. To illustrate, if automobile costs were reduced to the same degree that computation costs have been, you would not wash a dirty car—you would merely throw it away and buy another!

[3] Such speeds are difficult to comprehend. A space probe traveling toward the moon at 100,000 miles per hour would move less than 2 *inches* in one microsecond; it would only move the length of 10 fat germs in a nanosecond. More antiseptically speaking, there are as many nanoseconds in 1 second as there are seconds in thirty years.

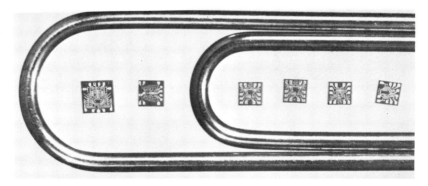

(a)

(b)

Figure 3-2. (a) Integrated Circuits (Enlarged) (Courtesy Burroughs Corporation); (b) Integrated Circuits (Actual Size) (Courtesy Burroughs Corporation)

Various analyses, using different machines, have been made in a comparison of costs to performance. One comparison showed that the cost of performing 1 million instructions had been reduced from $4.50 to 30 cents between 1955 and 1962. Another similar comparison of different hardware revealed a reduction from $5.20 to 13 cents between 1959 and 1965. It has been observed that "the cost of performing one million instructions has been reduced to between $\frac{1}{3}$ and $\frac{1}{5}$ its previous level every three years, for an average rate of decrease of 30% to 40% per year."[4]

Nor does it appear that the end is in sight in computational cost reduction. The cost of certain basic components will continue to decline. For example, in 1965 it cost about 20 cents to provide internal storage capacity for one binary number (down from 85 cents in 1960 and $2.61 in 1950). The comparable cost in 1970 is estimated to be from 5 cents to 10 cents, while the 1975 figure is set at $\frac{1}{2}$ cent![5]

Information storage capacity Information may be stored for use by a computer in a number of ways. The central processor of the computer, as we have seen, holds instructions and data internally in its *main storage* or *memory* unit. The internal storage capacity of early machines was quite small (2,000 to 4,000 "words"). With second-generation equipment, internal storage was available in excess of 30,000 words, while current machines can store hundreds of thousands of words internally.

Perhaps even more dramatic than the increase in central processor storage capacity has been the development of *external online* storage devices. These machines (which store data on magnetizable disks, drums, cards, and strips) are somewhat similar to reference libraries. They are connected directly to the central processor and may contain vast quantities of data, which are available as needed. Information which the computer may use is also stored externally in the form of punched cards and magnetic tape. This information, however, is *offline*, since the central processor does not have direct access to it (see Figure 3-3).

Maximum online external storage capacity in 1956 was about 10 million characters (letters or numbers). By 1961, this capacity had doubled, and by 1962 storage had increased to 100 million characters. But with the arrival of third-generation hardware also came the ability to store online over 100 billion characters—a growth factor of 10,000 in a decade![6] The time required for data to go from online storage to

---

[4] Richard G. Canning, *EDP Analyzer*, April, 1966, pp. 1-2.

[5] Figures released by American Federation of Information Processing Societies and appearing in *Administrative Management*, June, 1966, p. 53. Figures are averages.

[6] See Richard G. Canning, *EDP Analyzer*, November, 1966, p. 2.

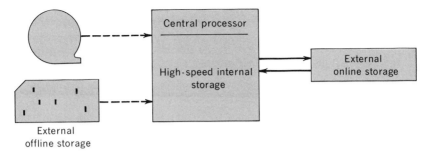

Figure 3-3. Computer Information Storage

use by central processor, although much slower than internal *access time*, is still measured in milliseconds.

Development in software

"Software" is the general term given to all program preparation aids.[7] Some software, e.g., the translating program described earlier, is prepared by the manufacturer for the customer as part of the product package. Much development work has gone into such translating programs in the past few years. Programming aids may also be obtained, on a custom-made basis and for a fee, from independent software consulting firms.

It should not be assumed, however, that software supplied by the manufacturer is free. Actually, the cost of the software may now represent 50 percent of the price paid by the user for the total product package. In the future, it is expected that software will become the *dominant* element in the cost of the product package (hardware production is automated; increasingly complex software must still be written on an artisan basis).

Generalized *application packages* (or *packaged programs*) have been developed by manufacturers since 1960 to take advantage of similiar informational needs of large numbers of businesses. Many retail stores, for example, sell on credit and thus must maintain credit records and billing operations. Since many such operations are essentially the same, a developed application package to perform these accounting tasks may be used by many retail stores with a minimum of modification. Application packages are equally feasible in other industries such as manufacturing, insurance, and transportation. Programming

---

[7] Some use the term "software" to include all services performed by the manufacturer for the customer. Others include in software the programs written by user employees for specific company jobs.

time can be greatly reduced in situations which fit the generalized package. As a means of selling their services, computer centers have been especially active since 1960 in promoting these packages for use by smaller firms.

One additional software development—*multiprogramming*—might be briefly mentioned at this point. "Multiprogramming" is the name given to the *simultaneous* execution of two or more different and independent programs by a single computer. Internal operating speeds are much faster than are the means of getting data in and out of the processing unit. With multiprogramming, it is thus possible for several user stations to share the time of the central processor. The computer can balance its workload by serving several programs. Without this *time sharing* feature, much of the capacity of the processing unit would remain unutilized. We shall take a closer look at the concept of time sharing later in the chapter.

Compatibility development

Compatibility is a term which may be associated with the software of a computer. If the programming aids, data, and instructions prepared for one machine can be used by another without conversion or program modification, the machines are said to be *compatible*. Many manufacturers of third-generation computers have designed "families" of machines to provide compatibility for the user.[8]

In addition to making machines which are compatible with their other products, some manufacturers are also making their machines compatible with the equipment produced by others. Thus, compatibility may exist both *within* a product line and *among* product lines.

The need for compatibility has been apparent for several years. Consider, for example, the plight of the expanding firm with an older machine which must process (as its longest program) a payroll requiring 7,000 characters in internal storage. The machine has an 8,000-character storage capacity, so all is well. But as the firm grows, new employees are added, and new pay scales are created. The payroll program eventually requires storage capacity of 9,000 characters. Several alternatives are open to the company's managers, but let us assume that they elect to acquire a new and larger machine.

All too often in the past, such a decision has required a costly rewriting of the programs developed for the old machine because of the lack of compatibility between it and its replacement. With compatible machines, however, a user may start with a small model geared to his requirements and convert to more powerful models as his workload ex-

[8] The IBM System/360 family of machines consists of a number of models differing in size and power. Yet several of these models are both hardware compatible and software compatible.

pands. The need to convert programs is substantially reduced. Also, greater exchange of programs, information, and data between users is possible.

The Federal government, as the largest single user of computers (10 percent of the market), has suffered because of past lack of compatibility. Various economic indicators, for example, are gathered by different agencies. Rapid consolidation of such data is desirable in economic planning. But data and program incompatibility have hindered the effort in the past. Thus, the Federal government has actively pushed the development of the compatibility concept.

The technological advances in computer hardware and software discussed in this section have both contributed to and been stimulated by the rapid environmental changes mentioned earlier. In the following section we shall examine the computer-oriented business information systems which have emerged (and are emerging) because of the desire by managers for *effective* information which will enable them to operate under conditions of rapid change.

COMPUTER-ORIENTED BUSINESS INFORMATION SYSTEMS

What are business information systems? Strangely enough, it is not easy to pin down these innocent-looking words. The difficulty does not lie in a lack of definitions. Rather, the difficulty lies in the difference in the scope and breadth of the existing definitions. For our purposes, *business information systems* are defined as the networks of data processing procedures developed in the organization, *and integrated as necessary*, for the purpose of providing managers with timely and effective information. A *procedure* is a related group of data processing steps or *methods* (usually involving a number of people in one or more departments) which have been established to perform a recurring processing operation. Figure 3-4 illustrates these definitions in the narrow context of information needed by personnel managers. Each line represents a procedure (consisting of a series of methods) which is directed toward achieving the objective of more effective personnel management. Each procedure produces needed information, and several procedures cut across departmental lines. The evaluation of performance procedure, for example, may require the cooperation of supervisors throughout the firm.

Our personnel information system is, of course, *only one* of several information producing activities in a business.[9] Among other such activ-

---

[9] Some writers treat the entire business as a single information system (singular), and the component parts of the business as subsystems. When such total integration is required, a single system would result from our definition. The reader is cautioned, however, that the degree to which systems (or subsystems) can and should be integrated is rather controversial at this time.

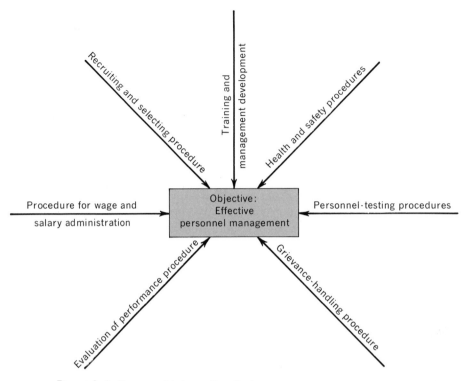

Figure 3-4. Personnel Information System

ities typically included are those in the areas of finance and accounting, production, and physical distribution. Thus, information is produced in a number of systems, and the success in consolidating this information may or may not satisfy the total needs of the business. In a number of companies the information needs have not been met, and efforts have been made, with varying degrees of success, (1) to provide better integration of the information processing activities by (2) making it possible to cut across application-processing and departmental boundaries. Some of these broader information systems concepts will be examined later in this chapter.

Difficulties with traditional systems

Traditional business systems have often been found wanting in the following respects:

1. Delays have occurred in receiving requested information. The desired information characteristic of timeliness has often been lacking.

2. Information has been expensive to produce. This is especially true when the information is wanted infrequently.

3. Information provided managers has failed to focus on areas of significance. The lack of selectivity in information produced has resulted in voluminous printouts. Too much unsifted data has made it difficult for managers to gain a deeper insight into their areas of responsibility. Richard Neuschel illustrates the problem:

> . . . the president of one company was found to be receiving 125 different reports: 5 daily, 18 weekly, 54 monthly, 26 quarterly, and 22 annually. Considering the frequency with which each of these reports was issued, he received, on the average, something over 250 separate issues of reports each month. This meant that, if he spent 15 minutes on each one, over one-third of his time would be absorbed in this activity alone.[10]

4. The several information-producing activities have not been sufficiently integrated. Improper emphasis has sometimes been given to the information produced for top managers — e.g., in a marketing-oriented business it might be better to present information in terms of products and customers rather than in terms of company departments and divisions.

To reduce difficulties experienced with traditional approaches, new systems concepts have been developed. These new concepts are classified into (1) *quick-response systems*, and (2) *broader systems*. They are manifestations of rapidly developing computer technology combined with the desire of managers to use this technology to meet increasingly demanding information requirements. It is possible, of course, for a specific business to make use of several of these concepts.

QUICK-RESPONSE SYSTEMS

Quick-response systems, as the name implies, have been developed to increase the timeliness and effectiveness of business information. More specifically, quick-response systems may:

1. Allow managers to *react more rapidly to changes in the external environment*. Information from field salesmen and suppliers can be more speedily assimilated. Managers may make direct inquiry of the system for infrequently needed information which is external to their usual needs, although the data may have been generated within the business.

2. *Reduce waste in the use of business resources*. For example, waiting time of customers, managers, and employees can be trimmed; more efficient control of valuable and perishable inventories such as seats on an airplane can be obtained.

3. *Allow more intricate applications to be processed within an acceptable waiting period*. For example, by having quick access to a machine, product research scientists may follow up on ideas which they might otherwise neglect if they had to wait for a long period of time to use the equipment.

[10] Richard F. Neuschel, *Management by System* (New York: McGraw-Hill Book Company, 1960), p. 207.

Quick-response systems may be described by a variety of Computerese terms. A glance through a few current business and computer magazines shows the subject is a veritable semantic jungle with many "experts" swinging from different definition vines. We shall attempt to cut through this jungle by examining the following concepts: (1) *online processing*, (2) *real time processing*, and (3) *time sharing*.

Online processing

The term "online" has several meanings. As we have seen, it refers to peripheral equipment connected directly to, and capable of unassisted communication with, the central processor. It is also used to describe the status of a person who is communicating directly with the central processor without the use of media such as punched cards and magnetic tape. Finally, it refers to a *method of processing* data.

Before looking at the meaning of the online processing concept, it is best to pause to describe a typical computer-processed activity. Let us look at an operation in the accounting office of a department store. A customer purchases a shotgun on credit (a sales *transaction*). The sales slip is routed to the accounting office, where it and others are collected for several days until a large batch accumulates. The data on the slips may then be recorded on some medium such as punched cards, which are sorted by customer name or charge-account number into the proper order for processing. Processing consists of adding the item and price of all the recent transactions to the customer's other purchases for the month. Thus, a customer accounts receivable master file, perhaps in the form of magnetic tape, must be updated to reflect the additional purchases. The order or sequence in which the additional transactions are sorted corresponds to the sequence on the master file. Figure 3-5 illustrates this *batch* (or *sequential*) *processing* proce-

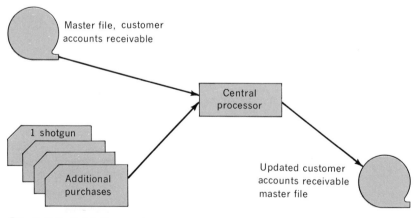

Master file, customer accounts receivable

1 shotgun

Additional purchases

Central processor

Updated customer accounts receivable master file

Figure 3-5. Batch Processing

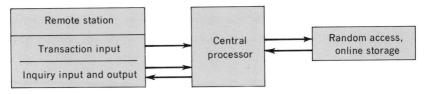

Figure 3-6. Online Processing

dure. At the end of the billing month the master file is used to prepare the customer statements.

Many other files may be updated periodically in similar fashion. A *file*, then, is a collection of related records and items treated as a unit. In our example the shotgun purchase would be one *item* on the customer's bill; the entire bill would represent one credit *record*; and the purchase records of all credit customers would be the accounts receivable *file*.

Batch processing has certain inherent disadvantages:

1. Input data and master files must be arranged in some common sequence prior to processing, and this sorting may be rather expensive in terms of time and money.
2. The time required to accumulate data into batches, in some instances, destroys much of the value of the data. The information that results from eventual processing is no longer timely.
3. To answer inquiries about the current status of the account of Mr. Zilch (who bought the shotgun) *between* processing periods is most difficult. If we assume that a magnetic tape master file and an alphabetic sequence are used, Zilch's record would be near the end of the file, and the entire file would have to be searched. Considering the trouble involved and the number of possible processing jobs waiting to be run on the computer, the inquiry would likely go unanswered until the next processing cycle — and by then, of course, some unwise credit decisions might have been made.

Online processing has been developed for certain applications as an answer to the deficiencies of batching. In contrast to batching, online (or random) processing permits transaction data to be fed directly into external online storage (or *random access* storage) from the point of origin without first being sorted. Appropriate records (which may be organized in the storage unit in either a sequential or random fashion) may therefore be more rapidly updated. Information contained in any record is accessible within a fraction of a second after inquiry. Thus, online processing systems may feature *random* and rapid input of transactions and immediate *access* to records as needed. (See Figure 3-6.)

The speed of processing *needed* by a business varies with the particular application. Online processing, although faster than traditional methods, may involve different degrees of quickness in the needed response. For example, a system may combine immediate access to records for inquiry purposes with *periodic* (perhaps, daily) transaction input and updating of records from a central collecting source. Such a system would be sufficient for many needs and would be simpler and less expensive than an online, real time system.

Real time processing

A *real time processing* operation is one in which the output is available quickly enough to be useful in controlling a current live activity. Thus, the words "real time" are generally used to describe an online processing system with severe time limitations. A real time system is online; an online processing system, however, *need not* be operating in real time.

Real time processing requires *immediate* (not periodic) transaction input from all input-originating stations. Many remote stations may be tied directly by high-speed communications equipment into the central processor. Records may be updated each minute, and inquiries may be answered by split-second access to these records.

An excellent example of a business real time processing installation is the SABRE system of American Airlines, which controls the inventory of airline seats available. A central computing center 30 miles north of New York City acts as a warehouse by receiving transaction data and inquiries directly (by over 31,000 miles of communications lines) from remote stations at over 1,000 reservation and ticket sales desks across the nation. In seconds, a customer may request and receive information about flights and available seats. If a reservation is made, the transaction is fed into the computer immediately, and the inventory of available seats is reduced. The reverse, of course, occurs in the event of a cancellation. What if a flight is fully booked? If the customer desires to be placed on a waiting list, data such as customer name and telephone number are maintained by the computer. If cancellations occur, waiting-list customers are notified by agents.

But there is yet another facet to the SABRE system. It is tied in with similar systems of 10 other airlines to provide an exchange of information on seat availability. Thus, an agent for any of the participating companies may sell space on *any* of the airlines if the system shows it is available.

Real time processing is required and cooperation is necessary among airlines because of the perishability of the product sold—when an airplane takes off, vacant seats have no value until the next landing. It would be a mistake, however, to assume that real time processing should be universally applied to all data processing applications. A quick-response system can be designed to fit the needs of the business.

Some applications can be handled with batch methods (e.g., payroll); some can be online (but not in real time); and some can utilize real time methods.

Time sharing

Managers cannot bear to see an idle computer—it is too expensive. For this reason time sharing has always existed in business installations in the sense that different user departments shared the total time of the computer by requesting and receiving processed output. Frequently, the users lined up at the machine according to some priority. In the quick-response context, however, there is a *much shorter* time scale involved, although the time restrictions may be less severe than those of real time systems described above.

Time sharing is a term used to describe a processing system with a number of relatively low-speed, online, *simultaneously usable* stations. The speed of the system and the use of multiprogramming allows the central processor to switch from one using station to another and to do a part of each job, until the work is completed. The speed may be such that the user has the illusion that he alone is using the computer. However, the available processing time at the central processor is being shared among the using stations.

Time sharing among units in a single organization is growing. Furthermore, a few time sharing installations have been established to service the needs of different businesses. In contrast to the typical arrangements made with a computer center (which assumes the responsibility for performing a task), the processing responsibility in a time sharing operation remains with the using business. Transactions are initiated from, and output is delivered to, the premises of the using firm at electronic speeds. The subscriber pays for the processing service in much the same way he pays for his telephone service: There is an initial installation charge; there are certain basic monthly charges; and, largest of all, there are per-transaction charges (like long-distance calls) which obviously vary according to usage.

Because of similarities with public utilities (such as telephone companies), such time sharing services have been called *information utilities* and *computing utilities*. The first commercial information utility was dedicated in November, 1965, in Cambridge, Massachusetts. Founded by Charles W. Adams, a former professor at M.I.T., Keydata Corporation was providing quick-response online service to 30 subscribers and 60 stations within a year. At least one subscriber replaced its computer with the service. Although such services are still rare, some writers are predicting that in the future regional and even national information utility networks will be created.

In addition to improving the quality and timeliness of information, many of these quick-response systems are taking a broader approach to the needs of the firm by attempting to provide better integration of information-producing activities. In the following section we shall briefly examine this development.

BROADER SYSTEMS

Why consolidate information? A most dramatic example of the consequences of failure to consolidate related pieces of information occurred at Pearl Harbor in 1941. Historians tell us that information available in bits and pieces and at scattered points, if integrated, would have signaled the danger of a Japanese attack.

Traditionally, business data processing has been organized by departments and by applications. Many computers were first installed for the purpose of processing a large-volume job such as payroll or customer billing. Other applications, treated independently, followed, but it soon became clear in many cases that the computer was not being effectively used. For example, data were being duplicated expensively; information from the payroll file and the personnel file could not be combined because of different methods of classifying employees.

Dissatisfied with such conditions, some businesses began studying how to consolidate activities. Various names are given to these efforts. Among the terms used are (1) *integrated systems*, (2) *single-flow systems*, and (3) *total systems*.

Integrated systems have as their objective the single recording of basic data into a *common* classifying code for the purpose of making maximum use of the data with a minimum number of human operations. A common example of this approach is found in the handling of sales orders. An order is received and confirmed on a special typewriter which produces a punched paper tape as a by-product. The sales data (customer name, address, items ordered, etc.) is punched on this tape, which may then be used as computer input to prepare shipping orders and the customer invoice. The same data are also used to update inventory, product sales, and accounts receivable files. Obviously, the same common classifying code must be used to represent the data in the several files.

Single-flow systems are designed around a *single* integrated information file. Transactions are posted to all records that they affect, on a one-time basis, to a total file located in a mass storage unit. The total file is not subdivided into applications.

Although the term "total systems" has been used in so many different ways that it is now too ambiguous to be of much value, it has been described as the ultimate result of the consolidation of integrated subsystems. Thus, the words have been used to describe a single information system—a "total" system which makes use of quick-response tools and techniques such as online mass storage, immediate updating of records from remote stations, and online inquiry.

"The present quest for 'total systems' should be recognized as a hazardous quest for the ideal."[11] It is not at all clear to what extent systems should be broadened. As a *philosophy*, however, the total systems concept has made a contribution. Computers *do* make certain consolidations possible; most of the older systems *were* too narrow. Many businesses are now working toward gradual integration of information-producing systems. The approach is generally somewhat conservative because (1) broad studies take a long time, are quite complex, require the efforts of highly paid employees, and often do not show any prospect for immediate tangible benefits; (2) substantial gains are still possible by placing new applications on the computer; (3) resistance is often encountered from managers who do not want to experiment with the familiar system; and (4) the planning and coordination of such a study is complicated, since in many cases no single individual can really understand the total system.

Before closing this section on broader systems, it should be pointed out that certain external developments may put pressure on businesses to commonly define and classify certain types of basic data which, in turn, may aid in development of better internal integration. As one example, we have already seen that airlines have integrated seat-reservation systems into an intercompany, data cooperative network. It is also expected that the sale of raw data will grow rapidly. These data are produced by the data supplier's computer in a form to be used as input by the customer's system. There must be agreement in data coding methods if effective use of the purchased data is to be obtained. Firms may have to decide whether to "make" their own data or "buy" it from these *data banks*, just as they have often had to make similar decisions about physical products. Examples of data for sale include: (1) marketing facts about product movement, volume of sales, and share of the market available from large grocery chains; and (2) financial facts about credit status and corporate financial outlook available from such information suppliers as credit bureaus, Dun & Bradstreet, and Standard & Poor's.

The above pages have shown some of the revolutionary developments in technology and the uses of this technology which have occurred since 1960. The rate of change in the future will be compounded by the changes made yesterday and today. The full potential of the computer has yet to be realized by businesses, but several are now in

---

[11] A. M. McDonough and L. J. Garrett, *Management Systems* (Homewood, Ill.: Richard D. Irwin, Inc., 1965), p. 7.

the process of moving out of a period of learning (though learning, of course, continues) into a period of innovation. To make such a transition will require highly qualified personnel; the demand for such people is tremendous. A quick glance at the help-wanted section of any city newspaper will verify this fact.

EMPLOYMENT OPPORTUNITIES

There is now, and there will continue to be, a shortage of qualified data processing personnel. To examine this employment picture more closely, let us use the following occupational categories: (1) data processing management, (2) systems design and analysis, (3) program preparation, and (4) computer operation.

Data processing management

According to the best estimates,[12] there were 30,000 qualified managers and supervisors in data processing installations in 1966. This figure fell about 10,000 *short* of the need at that time. The 1970 estimate is that 85,000 managers will be needed—an increase of 55,000 in a four-year time span! Keeping pace with demand, salaries have increased rapidly for good managers during the last few years. This trend will obviously continue. Qualified data processing managers can now expect to earn between $15,000 and $25,000 annually.

The data processing manager performs the administrative duties of all managers—i.e., he *plans* the activities of his department so that it will provide a quality product, a timely product, and an economical product; he *organizes* the human and physical resources of his department to achieve a smooth and efficient operation; and he *controls* these very expensive resources to achieve his planned objectives. He must possess technical competence in addition to managerial ability if he is to manage his department and maintain the respect of his subordinates. But too much emphasis on technical competence at the expense of managerial ability should be avoided. Too often in the past, the most skilled technician became the manager and quickly demonstrated a total lack of managerial ability.

Increasingly, people planning to seek a career in business computer management must first acquire a college degree. Courses in business administration, economics, data processing, and mathematics and statistics are desirable. Also, the importance of being able to work with people cannot be overemphasized.

[12]Dick H. Brandon, "Jobs and Careers in Data Processing," *Computers and Automation*, September, 1966, p. 25.

Systems design and analysis

There were approximately 60,000 qualified *systems analysts* available in 1966—a figure which fell 35,000 short of the need. The number needed in 1970 is set at 190,000. Thus, the employment opportunities in this area are apparent, with the shortage probably becoming more severe. (Is it likely that the number of qualified analysts will triple in just four years?)

What does an analyst do? There are often several grades of analysts (senior, junior, etc.), but basically the job consists (1) of examining the basic methods and procedures of current systems and (2) of modifying, redesigning, and integrating these existing procedures into new system specifications as required to provide the needed information. Typically, the analyst must know a great deal about the particular firm and the industry as well as about the uses and limitations of computers. Educational backgrounds vary, but many analysts have college degrees in business administration, economics, or the liberal arts. The analyst is often a prime candidate for promotion to more responsible management positions both in and out of data processing because of his broad knowledge of the business. The good analyst can expect to earn between $12,000 and $20,000 per year.

Program preparation

The job of the programmer is to take the systems designs of the analyst and transform these specifications into machine instructions or programs. In most cases the programmer will work very closely with the analyst during the systems design phase. In smaller organizations the systems analysis and program preparation functions are often combined. As with analysts, there are different job grades of programmers. In 1950 there were only a few hundred programmers, while in 1966 the number had grown to 120,000 (about 50,000 short of the need!).

There will be a demand for an additional 100,000 programmers by 1970. The good programmer earns between $10,000 and $15,000 annually. In scientific programming, a strong mathematics background is required; in business programming, the educational requirements depend on such factors as the system complexity, the industry, and the standards of the employer. Logical reasoning ability and attention to detail are required. A college education, however, is not necessarily a condition for employment although many businesses use a degree as a means of screening applicants.

Computer operation

The operation of a central processor and the related pieces of input and output equipment requires human attention. The *computer operator* must (1) set up the machine to run the different programs, (2) start the program run, (3) make checks to ensure proper operation, and (4) unload the computer. At the present time high school graduates qualify as operators; with future complex machines, however, additional educational levels may be required. In 1966 there was no shortage of employees in the operations group. Although their numbers are expected to show a 70,000-man increase by 1970, no problems are anticipated in meeting the need.

SUMMARY

An information processing revolution is quietly taking place. Rapid changes in scientific, social, and economic areas have stimulated and contributed to significant development in computer hardware and software (and vice versa) since 1960. Advances in hardware include (1) substantial reduction in the size, weight, and cost of equipment compared with the same features of earlier machines; and (2) significant increases in speed and storage capacity. Advances in software include (1) the improvement of translating programs designed to reduce tedious coding and (2) the development of application packages and multiprogramming. Computer users have benefited from the movement toward greater compatibility which allows them to exchange data and update equipment without having to rewrite programs.

Business managers have been required to plan better and to make swifter readjustments in their plans. As a result of difficulties experienced with traditional information systems, businesses have developed quicker-reacting and more-integrated systems as a means of meeting their informational needs. In some cases these systems have cut across company lines as well as departmental lines.

Critical shortages of qualified managers, systems analysts, and programmers exist now; they will become more severe in the next few years. For persons trained in these areas, employment opportunities appear to be unlimited.

DISCUSSION QUESTIONS

1 Why must business managers be concerned with the rapid scientific, social, and economic changes which are occurring?

2 (*a*) Give some examples of rapid technological change. (*b*) What social and economic changes are taking place?

3 (*a*) What is computer hardware? (*b*) Software?

4 Explain hardware technological developments in terms of the factors of size, speed, cost, and storage capacity.

5 Define the following terms:
- (a) millisecond
- (b) microsecond
- (c) nanosecond
- (d) external online storage
- (e) file
- (f) record
- (g) batch processing
- (h) online processing
- (i) multiprogramming
- (j) application packages
- (k) time sharing
- (l) compatibility
- (m) information utility
- (n) integrated systems
- (o) total systems

6 "If no extra charge is made for software by the computer vendor, then the software must be free." Discuss this statement.

7 (a) Why is compatibility needed? (b) Why is the Federal government interested in compatibility?

8 (a) What are business information systems? (b) What is a procedure? (c) A method?

9 What difficulties have managers experienced with traditional business information systems?

10 (a) Why have quick-response systems been developed? (b) What is the distinction between online processing and real time processing?

11 Identify and discuss the broader systems approaches which have been used to consolidate information processing activities.

12 Explain the job functions of the following data processing personnel:
- (a) data processing managers
- (b) systems analysts
- (c) programmers
- (d) computer operators

SELECTED REFERENCES

Dick H. Brandon, "Jobs and Careers in Data Processing," *Computers and Automation*, September, 1966, pp. 24-28.

Richard G. Canning, "Advances in Fast Response Systems," *EDP Analyzer*, February, 1967.

Kenneth O. Fisketjon, "Basic Considerations in Time-sharing," *Journal of Data Management*, April, 1966, pp. 14-18.

Walter J. Karplus (ed)., *On-line Computing* (New York: McGraw-Hill Book Company, 1967).

"Public Utility Data Services," *Dun's Review and Modern Industry*, September, 1966, pp. 155-156 ff.

Richard E. Sprague, "The Information Utilities," *Business Automation*, March, 1965, pp. 42-47.

Oliver W. Tuthill, "The Thrust of Information Technology on Management," *Financial Executive*, January, 1966, pp. 18-29.

4. INTRODUCTION TO COMPUTERS

Earlier pages have dealt with computers in general terms. In this chapter, however, we begin the closer examination of this exciting business tool. More specifically, in the next few pages we shall consider: (1) the *classes* of computers, (2) their *capabilities*, (3) their *limitations*, (4) their "learning" ability, and (5) their *functional organization*.

COMPUTER CLASSIFICATIONS

As you know, many firms offer tours of their facilities to interested parties. Let us assume that you are in a group visiting an insurance company. In the course of your visit, the tour guide asks you to identify the equipment located in a large room. Because you are an intelligent person, you respond that this is the firm's computer. The guide replies, "Yes, this is our medium-sized, third-generation, electronic, stored program, digital (a gasp for breath), general purpose, business computer."

You recognize what he meant by the "medium-sized," "third-generation," "electronic," and "stored program" terms. Computers are sometimes classified by size into large, medium, and small categories on the basis of computing power and cost. A medium-sized system might cost from $250,000 to $1 million. The third-generation age classification typically refers to equipment produced in the last half of the 1960s, while the electronic term distinguishes the equipment from mechanical and electromechanical processing machines which are much slower in their operation. The stored program concept is vital to the modern computer and refers to the ability of the machine to store internally a list of instructions which will guide it automatically through a series of operations leading to a completion of the task.

But what about the other classifying terms used by the guide—what exactly did he mean by "digital," "general purpose," and "business"? Let us look at each of these items.

Analog and digital computers

There are two broad classes of computing devices—the analog and the digital. The *analog* machine does not compute directly with numbers; rather, it measures continuous physical magnitudes (e.g., pressure, temperature, voltage, current, shaft rotations, length) which represent, or are *analogous* to, the numbers under consideration. The service station gasoline pump, for example, contains an analog computer which converts the flow of pumped fuel into two measurements— the price of the delivered gasoline to the nearest penny and the quantity of pumped fuel to the nearest tenth of a gallon. Other examples of analog computers are (1) the widely used slide rule, which permits computations by the movement of one length along another; and (2) the automobile speedometer, which converts drive-shaft rotational motion into a numerical indication by the speedometer pointer.

Analog computers are used for scientific, engineering, and process control purposes. Because they deal with quantities which are continuously variable, they give only approximate results. The speedometer pointer, for example, might give a reading of 45 miles per hour. But if the pointer were lengthened and sharpened, if the speedometer were calibrated more precisely, and if the cable were given closer attention, the reading might then be 44 miles per hour. Further refinements might give a reading of 44.5 miles per hour. A well-known soap product has claimed for years to be "99 and 44/100% pure." Under the best circumstances, an analog computer can achieve a somewhat higher degree of precision than this figure. But in a problem involving $1 million, an analog device might give answers only to the nearest hundred or thousand dollars.

The *digital* computer operates by *counting* numbers. It operates directly on numbers expressed as digits in the familiar decimal system or in some other numbering system. The ancient shepherd, it will be recalled, used stones to represent sheep, and these were counted one by one to determine the total number of sheep in the flock. Nothing was measured as an analogous representation of the number of sheep; they were counted directly, and their total was exact. Stones have been replaced by adding machines, desk calculators, and digital computers, but all employ the same counting rules we learned in grade school.

Digital computation results in greater accuracy. While analog computers may, under ideal conditions, be accurate to within .1 percent of the correct value, digital computers can obtain whatever degree of accuracy is required simply by adding "places" to the right of the reference or decimal point. Every youngster who has worked arithmetic problems dealing with circles knows that pi (π) has a value of 3.1416. Actually, however, the value is 3.14159.... In 1959, a digital computer worked the value of π out to 10,000 decimal places in a short period of time![1]

Digital computers, unlike analog machines, are used for both business data processing and scientific purposes.

Special purpose and general purpose computers

Digital computers may be produced for either special or general uses. A *special purpose* computer, as the name implies, is designed to perform one specific task. The program of instructions is built into the machine. Specialization results in the given task being performed economically, quickly, and efficiently. A disadvantage, however, is that the machine lacks versatility; it is inflexible and cannot be used to perform other operations. Special purpose computers designed for the sole purpose of solving complex navigational problems are installed aboard our atomic submarines, but they could not be used for other purposes unless their circuits were redesigned.

A *general purpose* computer is one which has the ability to store *different* programs of instructions and thus to perform a variety of operations. In short, the stored program concept makes the machine a general purpose device—one which has the versatility to make possible the processing of a payroll one minute and an inventory control application the next. New programs can be prepared, and old programs can be changed or dropped. Because it is designed to do a wide variety of jobs rather than perform a specific activity, the general purpose machine typically compromises certain aspects of speed and efficiency—a small enough price to pay in most cases for the advantage of flexibility.

Scientific and business applications

General purpose machines *may* be used for both scientific and business applications. The IBM 650 model, introduced late in 1954, was widely used for scientific and business jobs. But the earlier equipment was designed primarily to meet the needs of the scientific community, and it soon became apparent that the processing needs differed between the two types of applications. As a result, general purpose computers are now frequently oriented toward either scientific or business use. Of course, in many companies business computers are being used to solve engineering and scientific jobs, although (less frequently) the reverse may also be true.

[1] Alas, later more accurate work showed that this computer had made an error in the 7,480th decimal place.

Scientific and business machines typically differ in the design emphasis given to the following factors: (1) input/output volume and speed, (2) amount and speed of computations, and (3) storage capacity. Computer running time (an obvious expense) is determined by the *total* speed of input, processing, and output operations. High speed is desirable in the total processing job regardless of the type of application.

Scientific processing applications A research laboratory may wish to analyze and evaluate a product formula involving three variables and 15 terms (which results in 45 different values for each variable). The computer *input* would be the 15-term formula, the 135 values for the three variables, and the set of instructions to be followed in processing. The input is thus quite small. The *processing* involved, however, may well consist of hundreds of thousands of different computations—computations which may represent many months of labor if performed by other methods. The *output* necessary for a problem of this type may consist of a few typed lines giving a single evaluation or a few alternatives.

In short, the volume of input/output in scientific data processing is relatively small, and the speed with which these operations are performed is usually not too important. Computational speed, on the other hand, is a critical consideration since the bulk of the total processing job involves complex calculation. Storage capacity need only be sufficient to hold instructions, input data, and intermediate and final computational results.

Business processing applications In contrast to scientifically oriented computers, business machines feature faster input/output devices and greater storage capacity. An examination of a typical business application will usually show that the volume of data input and information output is quite large. For example, the billing operation associated with the credit card purchases of an oil company's products involves thousands of customers and hundreds of thousands of sales transactions each month. Each transaction represents input data, while each customer represents an output statement. The running time required by the computer to complete such a business application is determined by the input/output speeds obtainable.

Computational speed is less critical in business applications (1) because arithmetic operations performed on each input record represent a relatively small proportion of the total job and (2) because the internal arithmetic speed of the slowest computer is much greater than the speed of present input/output devices. As we have seen, time sharing is being used to prevent the computer from running idle while waiting for the arrival of more input data.

Processing characteristics	Scientific applications	Business applications
Input/output volume	Low	Very high
Input/output speed	Relatively unimportant	Very important
Ratio of computations to input	Very high	Low
Computation speed	Very important	Relatively unimportant
Storage requirements	Modest	High

Figure 4-1

Greater storage capacity is required for business applications. Internal storage must be available for instruction programs, which are often quite lengthy, as well as for the manipulation and maintenance of large masses of data. The relatively high cost of internal storage combined with increased business demand for economical storage capacity has resulted in the development of the online mass storage devices mentioned earlier.

Figure 4-1 outlines the differences between scientific and business applications.

The stored program, digital, general purpose, business computer (henceforth called "computer" for apparent reasons) possesses certain capabilities which are summarized in the next section.

COMPUTER CAPABILITIES

In the past, computers have been called "giant brains" by some and have been pictured as man's possible master by others. Although these views are exaggerated, it is clear that the computer is a powerful *tool* for extending man's brainpower. Peter Drucker has pointed out that man has developed two types of tools: (1) those which add to his capabilities and enable him to do something that he otherwise could *not* do (e.g., the airplane) and (2) those which multiply his capacity to do that which he is *already capable* of doing (e.g., the hammer).[2]

The computer falls into the latter category. It is an intelligence amplifier. It can enlarge brainpower because of the following properties:

1. *The ability to provide new time dimensions.* The machine works one step at a time; it adds and subtracts numbers; it multiplies and divides numbers (in most cases merely by a repetitive process of addition and subtraction); and it can be designed or programmed to perform other mathematical operations such as finding a square root. There is nothing profound in

[2] See Peter F. Drucker, "What the Computers Will Be Telling You," *Nation's Business*, August, 1966, pp. 84-90.

these operations — even the author can perform them! What is significant, as we know, is the speed with which the machine functions. Thus, man is freed from calculations to use his time more creatively. His time dimension has been broadened; he can obtain information now which could not have been produced at all a few years ago or which could not have been produced in time to be of any value. Karl Gauss, a German mathematician, at a young age had ideas which might have reshaped the study of mathematics in his time. Twenty years of his life were spent, however, in calculating the orbits of various heavenly objects. Were Gauss alive today, he could duplicate his calculations on a computer in a few hours and then be free to follow more creative pursuits.

2. *The ability to perform certain logic operations.* When two values, A and B, are *compared*, there are only three possible outcomes: (1) A is *equal* to B (A = B), (2) A is *greater than* B (A > B), or (3) A is *less than* B (A < B).[3] The computer is able to perform a simple comparison and then, depending on the result, follow one of three *predetermined branches* or courses of action in the completion of that portion of its work. (See Figure 4-2.) Thus, the computer has made a "decision" by choosing between alternate possible courses of action. Actually, however, it might be more appropriate to say that the computer has *followed* decisions made earlier by the programmer. But this simple ability to compare is an important computer property because more sophisticated questions can be answered by using combinations of comparison decisions.

3. *The ability to store and retrieve information.* We know that the computer places in internal storage both facts and instructions. The *access time* required for this information to be recalled from internal storage and be available for use is measured in microseconds or more precise units. Few machines used by man have this stored program ability — the instructions generally reside in man's mind and thus are outside the machine. Instructions and data are in a coded form which the machine has been designed to accept. The machine is also designed to perform automatically and in sequence certain operations on the data (add, write, move, store, halt) called for by the instructions. The number of operations which can be performed varies among computer models. The stored program may, as we have just seen, allow the computer to select a branch of instructions to follow from several alternate sequences. The program may also allow the computer to *repeat* or *modify* instructions as required. Computers communicate with human operators by using input and output devices, and they communicate with other machines.

4. *The ability to control error.* It is estimated that you or I would make one error in every 500 to 1,000 operations with a desk calculator. A computer, on the other hand, can perform hundreds of thousands of arithmetic operations every second and can run errorless for hours and days at a time. Computers also have the ability to check their own work. By a method known as *parity checking*, computers check on data when they enter storage, when they are moved internally, and when they leave in the form of output. Each character (e.g., number, letter) fed into the computer is represented in a coded form by several binary digits (0s and 1s) called *bits*,

---

[3] The possible outcomes form what logicians forebodingly call the *law of trichotomy*. Computers also compare numbers to see whether they are positive, negative, or equal to zero.

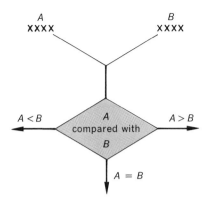

Figure 4-2

just as each number or letter in a punched card is usually represented by the Hollerith code. The parity check performed by the computer involves the examination of each character's code to determine whether bits have been added or lost by mistake. More will be said about parity checking in a later chapter.

It should not be assumed, however, that computers have unlimited capabilities or that they are free of error. They do have their limitations, and they have been involved in some classic mistakes.

COMPUTER LIMITATIONS

A publishing company customer recently received a computer-produced invoice requesting that he pay his bill in the amount of "W-2.C." The customer promptly forwarded his check for W-2.C as directed with a note saying, "Out here in the sticks, we dig this crazy new currency you folks have invented."[4] Billing operations have produced other computer goofs. For example, an insurance company kept sending a policy holder a bill for $0.00 and demanding payment, and in Fort Worth, Texas, a man was surprised a few months ago to receive a brief, rather cool, letter from an oil company telling him that his account was past due by $34.32. The man can be excused his surprise because he had never received a credit card from any oil company. Six weeks passed before the error was discovered, during which time the man kept protesting and the form letters (getting less and less cordial) kept coming in. Perhaps he felt as did another victim who said, "The computer is a complete revolution in the ways of doing business, . . . and as in any revolution some innocent people always get slaughtered."[5]

[4] Reported in *The Long Island Commercial Review*, May, 1966.

[5] Lee Berton, "Zip, Buzz, Whir, Clonk: Computers Botch Some of Their Jobs," *The Wall Street Journal*, July 6, 1966.

That such stories are carried in newspapers is indication enough that they occur only infrequently. Perhaps in most cases the errors may be traced to humans who failed to give proper attention to the following limitations:

1. *Application programs must always be prepared.* The machine does what it is programmed to do and *nothing else.* It can only operate on data — i.e., it can accept data, process it, and communicate results, but it cannot directly perform physical activities such as bending metal. (The processed information may be used, however, to control metal-bending machines.)

2. *Applications must be able to be quantified and dealt with logically.* The computer will not help the manager in areas where *qualitative* considerations are important. It will not, for example, signal a change in a trend until after the fact. It will not tell the manager whether or not a new product will be successful if marketed. The ultimate decision is of a qualitative nature because it is involved with future social, political, technological, and economic events; and sales volume levels are thus impossible to predict with certainty. The computer will *by simulation* let a manager know how a new product will fare under *assumed* price, cost, and sales volume conditions. The computer, in short, is limited to those applications which have precisely defined goals; furthermore, it must be possible to reach these goals by a logical series of instructions which consist of a specific number of steps. If the steps in the solution of the problem cannot be precisely written down, the application cannot be performed on today's commercial computers. And, as you know, each time the computer must make a choice all the alternate steps must have been foreseen and provided for by the programmer.

3. *Applications must weigh resources.* Merely because a computer *can* be programmed to do a job does not always mean that it *should.* Writing programs, although less tedious than in the past because of developments in software, is still a time-consuming and expensive human operation. Thus, nonrecurring tasks or jobs which are seldom processed are often not efficient areas for computer application at the present time. It is usually most economical to have programmers (a scarce resource) prepare programs for large volume, repetitive operations which will be used many times and which promise fast returns on the time invested in program preparation.[6]

EXPERIMENTS IN LEARNING

Much has been written in the past few years pro and con about the question of whether computers can be programmed to "think" and "learn." Part of the controversy probably stems from a lack of understanding about the processes involved in human thinking and learning. The computer can only do what it is instructed to do. But

[6] There are exceptions to this generalization, of course, where the importance of the nonrecurring task warrants the investment. An example might be the planning and scheduling by computer of a single multimillion-dollar office building.

research and experiments are being conducted in the use of computers to solve relatively ill-structured problems. For example, a machine has been programmed to play checkers and to modify its program on the basis of success and failure with moves used in the past against human opponents. The computer has continually improved its game to the point where it regularly defeats the author of the program. Thus, the machine has "learned" what not to do through trial and error.

Computers have also been programmed to play chess, prove mathematical theorems, and compose music, but thus far such research activities are limited and involve "thinking" on the part of the machine in a most limited sense.

Heuristic[7] is a word which means "serving to discover." It is used to describe the judgmental part of problem solving, e.g., that part dealing with the definition of the problem, the selection of strategies to follow, and the formulation of hypotheses and hunches. Man is *far superior* to the computer in the heuristic area of intellectual work. As man's learning and thinking processes become better understood, however, it may be possible to develop new programs and machines with improved heuristic abilities. Of course, the role of the computer will continue to be that of an intelligence amplifier; if it threatens to become the master, we can pull its plug!

COMPUTER ORGANIZATION

The computer solves problems and produces information in much the same way that you do. Let us illustrate this fact by first making a most disagreeable assumption: that in the near future you will have to take a written examination on the material covered in the first few chapters of an accounting book. For the past few days you have been reading the text, trying to catch up on your homework problems, and listening to your professor's lectures. You have written several pages of notes and have memorized various facts, concepts, and procedures. Finally, the examination period arrives, and you begin to work the test problems. Transactions are noted, and proper (?) accounts receive debits and credits. Procedures are followed, you hope, in the correct order. As time runs out, you turn your paper in to the professor and leave, resolving to pay somewhat closer attention to what he has to say in the future.

Five functions were performed in the above illustration (see Figure 4-3). These functions are:

1. *Input.* The input function involves the receipt of facts which can be used. You received data from your accounting text book and from your professor.

[7] This is pronounced hew-ris'tik.

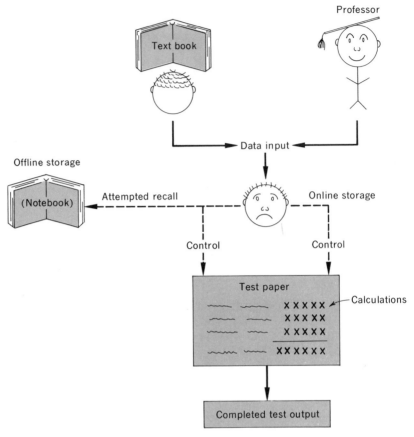

Figure 4-3

2. *Storage.* Facts received must be stored until they are needed. Your note-book (offline storage) and your brain (online storage) were used to store accounting information and the procedures to use for solving problems.

3. *Calculation.* On your test you performed the arithmetic operations of addition, subtraction, multiplication, and division, either manually or with the help of a desk calculator.

4. *Control.* On the exam it was necessary to follow certain procedures in the proper order or sequence — i.e., you could not total an account until all transactions had been recorded, and you did not record the last transaction of the month first because it might have been based on transactions occurring earlier in the month. Control, then, simply means doing things in the correct sequence.

5. *Output.* Your finished test was the output — the result of your data processing operations. It will provide your professor with part of the information needed to arrive at a decision about your final grade.

All computer installations perform these five functions. Figure 4-4 illustrates the functional organization of a computer. Let us briefly examine each part of this diagram.

Input

Computers, obviously, must also receive facts to solve problems. Data and instructions must be put into the computer system in a form which it can use. There are a number of devices which will perform this input function as we shall see in the following chapter. They may allow direct man-machine communication without the necessity of an input medium (e.g., the keyboard of a time sharing remote station), or they may present information which typically has been produced offline in batches on an input medium (e.g., punched cards). Regardless of the type of device used, they are all instruments of interpretation and communication between man and the machine.

Storage

The heart of any computer installation is the *central processing unit* (CPU). Within this unit are located the storage, control, and arithmetic-logic units. It is this central processor which makes comparisons, performs calculations, and selects, interprets, and controls the execution of instructions.

The storage section of the central processor is used for *four purposes*, three of which relate to the data being processed. First, data are fed into the storage area where they are held until ready to be processed.

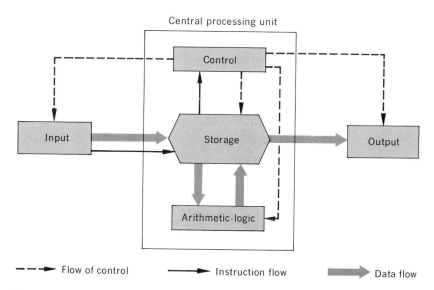

Figure 4-4. Computer Functional Organization

Second, additional storage space is used to hold data being processed and the intermediate results of such processing. Third, the storage unit holds the finished product of the processing operations until it can be released in the form of output information. Fourth, in addition to these data-related purposes, the storage unit also holds the program instructions until they are needed.

Arithmetic-logic

All calculations are performed and all comparisons (decisions) are made in the arithmetic-logic section of the central processor. Data flow between this section and the storage unit during processing operations—i.e., data are received from storage, manipulated, and returned to storage. No processing is performed in the storage section. The number of arithmetic and logic operations which can be performed is determined by the engineering design of the machine.

To briefly summarize, data are fed into the storage unit from the input devices. Once in storage, they are held and transferred as needed to the arithmetic-logic unit where processing takes place. Data may move from storage to the arithmetic-logic unit and back again to storage many times before the processing is finished. Once completed, the information is released from the central processor to the output device.

Control

How does the input unit know when to feed data into storage? How does the arithmetic-logic unit obtain the needed data from storage, and how does it know what should be done with them once they are received? And how is the output unit able to obtain finished information instead of raw data from storage? It is by selecting, interpreting, and executing the program instructions that the control unit of the central processor is able to maintain order and direct the operation of the entire installation. It thus acts as a central nervous system for the component parts of the computer. Instructions are *selected* and fed in sequence into the control unit from storage; there they are *interpreted*; and from there signals are sent to *other* machine units to *execute* program steps. The control unit itself does not perform actual processing operations on the data.

Output

Output devices, like input units, are instruments of interpretation and communication between man and machine. They take information in machine-coded form and convert it typically into a form (1) which can be used by humans (e.g., a printed report) or (2) which can be used as machine input in another processing operation (e.g., magnetic tape). In the following chapter we shall take a closer look at several output devices.

Extensive variety of configurations

As we have just seen, all computers are similar in terms of the functions performed. They may be vastly different from company to company, however, in the number and type of machines employed to perform these functions. Figure 4-5 illustrates the variety of possible machine combinations.

Let us briefly examine the modular unit box connected to the central processor in Figure 4-5. This concept of *modularity* (also called "open-ended design" and "upgrading") allows a computer installation to change and *grow*. To the original CPU can be attached additional units, e.g., more internal storage, as the need arises, just as additional freight cars can be hooked onto a freight train. Users can begin with small systems and build up the installation gradually; it is not necessary that final capacity be provided at the outset. In addition to "adding on," true modularity also makes it possible to replace smaller components with larger versions while other hardware remains unchanged.

How does the modularity concept differ, then, from compatibility? *Two different* machine systems are compatible if they can work together and accept the same input data and programs. A *single* system has modular capability if it can grow. Thus, a given installation may be both modular and compatible; it may possess only one feature; or it may have neither.

The input/output hardware and media shown in Figure 4-5 will be surveyed in the next chapters. We shall then take a closer look at the equipment composition and the operation of the central processing unit.

SUMMARY

Electronic computers may be classified in a number of ways. In this book we are interested in digital machines which count sequentially and very accurately; we are interested in general purpose equipment which can do a variety of jobs; and we are interested primarily in hardware which has been designed to process business-oriented tasks.

Computers extend man's brainpower; they are intelligence amplifiers which provide new dimensions in the time available for creative work. They are able to perform certain logic operations. Sophisticated questions can be answered by the combination of many simple machine "decisions." Computers can store and retrieve information rapidly and accurately.

But machines, like humans, are not infallible. They make errors, and they must be told exactly and precisely what to do. Although experiments are being conducted by extremely able researchers in the attempt to improve the

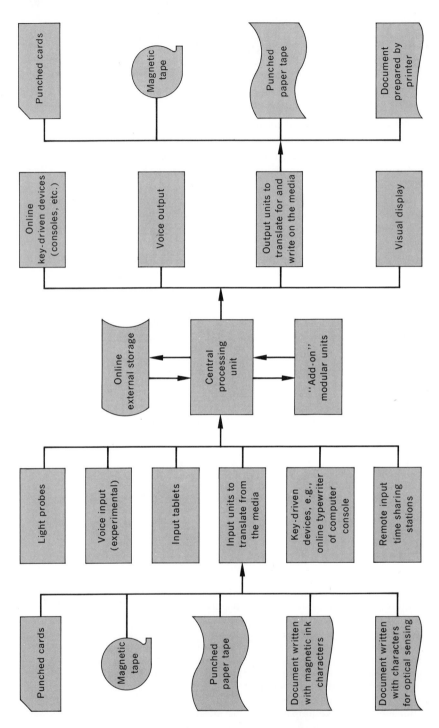

Figure 4-5. Input/Output Hardware and Media

68

machine's heuristic capabilities, they are restricted in practical use to applications which can be quantified and structured into a finite number of steps to achieve a specific goal. The writing of machine instructions is still an expensive and time-consuming operation, and it is for this reason that it is usually not feasible to process many nonrecurring jobs with a computer.

Computers are organized to perform the functional activities of input, storage, arithmetic-logic, control, and output. A great variety of machines and media is used in the performance of these functions.

DISCUSSION QUESTIONS

1 Discuss the various ways in which computers may be classified.

2 (*a*) What is an analog computer? (*b*) How does it differ from a digital computer?

3 How does a special purpose computer differ from a general purpose machine?

4 Compare and contrast the processing characteristics typically found in business and scientific applications.

5 Why is it possible to say that the computer is an intelligence amplifier?

6 Identify and discuss the limitations of computer usage.

7 What is meant by heuristic programming?

8 Identify and discuss the five functions which are performed by computers.

9 "The storage section of the central processor is used for four purposes." What are these four purposes?

10 (*a*) What functions are performed in the arithmetic-logic section of the central processor? (*b*) In the control section?

11 Explain the concept of modularity.

SELECTED REFERENCES

Thomas C. Bartee, *Digital Computer Fundamentals* (2d ed.; New York: McGraw-Hill Book Company, 1966), chap. 1.

James A. Campise and Max L. Wagoner, *The ABC's of ADP* (Park Ridge, Ill.: Data Processing Management Association, 1964).

"In EDP, Today's Word Is Modularity," *Administrative Management*, July, 1965, pp. 26 ff.

J. C. R. Licklider, "Computers: Thinking Machines or Thinking Aids?," *Management Review*, July, 1965, pp. 40–43.

5. INPUT/OUTPUT MEDIA AND DEVICES: I

Why have input/output (I/O) media and devices? The answer to this question, of course, is that they make it possible for data processing to occur—i.e., they make it possible for man to place data into and receive information out of the central processor. The computer installation can perform the necessary processing steps and communicate with man only through the I/O equipment. In this chapter we shall study some of the ways in which communication is accomplished. But before moving on to specific media and machines, let us look briefly at a few considerations which have an important bearing on the I/O activities.

SOME INPUT/OUTPUT OBSERVATIONS

It is important to understand that to perform efficiently and economically the data processing steps (classifying, sorting, calculating, etc.) mentioned in Chapter 1, data must first be grouped or organized in some logical arrangement. In business information systems, data have generally been organized into files of related records.[1] Obviously then, business data processing involves operations on records and files. Since our I/O activities will be concerned primarily with the maintenance of records and files, let us make sure we have a clear understanding of these data organization concepts.

A hypothetical accounts receivable application in a manual accounting system will be used to illustrate data organization. The accounts receivable file contains records for each customer showing such information as customer name, account number, address, amount owed, credit limit. Each record is filed alphabetically, by customer name, in the *transaction file* drawer as shown in Figure 5-1. Each record

---

[1] These data organization concepts were introduced in Chap. 3.

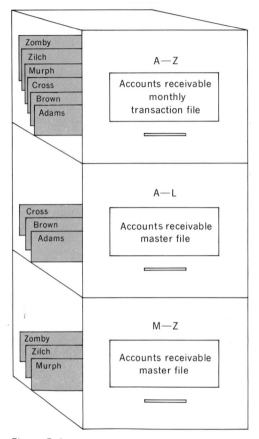

Figure 5-1

folder contains credit sales transaction tickets (items) which have been (1) *recorded* and *classified* by customer name, (2) *sorted* alphabetically, and (3) *stored* in the file drawer until the end of the month.

At the end of the month, the record folders are removed from the transaction file drawer, and the following processing steps are performed:

1. *Calculations* are made to determine the total amount puchased by each customer during the month.
2. The monthly transactions are used to revise and update the information contained in the *master file* in the bottom two drawers of the file cabinet.
3. The total amount owed is *communicated* to the customer in the form of a bill.
4. A report is prepared which *summarizes* for managers the pertinent information contained in the files, e.g., the total credit sales for the month, records which show slow payment, etc.

Processing is done sequentially (in alphabetical order) beginning with Adams and ending with Zomby. Thus, the data processing functions and the I/O activities take place within the organizational framework of the accounts receivable files. The master file has a degree of permanency, while transaction file data are emptied each month.

Computers replace manual methods, but files still must be maintained which continually receive and transmit information. These files may be sequentially organized and stored offline on such media as punched cards, punched paper tape, or magnetic tape. Or they may be randomly organized in online, mass storage units.

Records may be sequentially *processed* (batch processing), or they may be immediately accessed and updated by random access *processing*. Since it is quite easy to become confused about the meaning of the terms "sequential" and "random" when they are used with the words "processing" and "organization," let us pause to clarify this semantic entanglement.

When master files are stored offline, they are almost always sequentially *organized*. And when such files are updated, sequential *processing*, by means of appropriate I/O devices, is used. But when files are located in online storage, they may be organized sequentially *or* randomly. Thus, as Figure 5-2 shows, random access *processing* is possible with files organized *both* sequentially and/or randomly. Figure 5-2*a* shows conceptually the random selection and processing of records from a sequentially organized master file, while Figure 5-2*b* shows random file organization *and* random processing.

Because files vary in character, size, and location (online or offline), a wide variety of I/O media and devices has been developed. Managers thus must choose from a number of alternatives. A compromise is often necessary: Certain advantages are obtained only by the acceptance of certain drawbacks. There are a number of factors to consider in making the selection including:

1. *The volume of data to be processed.* In addition to considerations of equipment speed and capacity, the manager may also have to make provisions for processing peak volumes during certain periods of the year.
2. *The frequency of processing needed.* The total volume of data processing is, of course, affected by the frequency with which records must be updated. If records must be updated as transactions occur, then batch processing techniques must obviously give way to random processing techniques.
3. *The quality requirements.* To what extent can errors be tolerated in the information output? The higher the accuracy requirements, the greater the need may be to replace humans with machines which can "read" the source documents.

74

Online storage

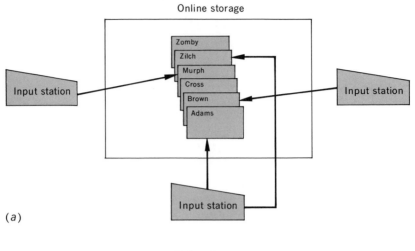

(*a*)

Online storage

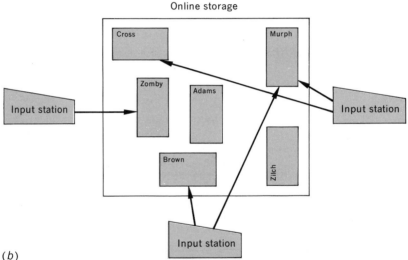

(*b*)

Figure 5-2. (*a*) Random Access Processing with Sequential File Organization; (*b*) Random Access Processing with Random File Organization

4. *The type and quality of output required.* Will the output be used by man, or will it be reused by the computer at a later time? How many reports will be needed? How frequently are they required? How many copies are needed? Answers to such questions have a direct bearing on the I/O selections.

5. *The nature of the source documents.* The methods for originating data, the types of source documents used, the message length, and the data form (alphabetic, numeric, or alphanumeric) must be considered.

The time required to complete a processing job is determined by the speed of input, processing, and output operations. The input and output of data have for several years been a bottleneck in a computerized system. In addition to slowing down the processing operation, input methods have often been costly and subject to errors. Duplication of effort has often been required to transfer data from source documents to a machine-acceptable form.

In the following pages of this chapter we shall examine media and related devices possessing most of the following characteristics:

1. Processing is accomplished with media which tangibly record data by the use of (*a*) holes in paper or (*b*) magnetized spots or patterns.
2. Batch processing methods are generally employed.
3. Input data preparation is offline relative to the central processor.
4. Data are frequently recorded in some humanly usable form before or at the same time the input media is prepared.
5. The media store the files (with proper care) for an indefinite period of time. The file storage is offline.
6. The volume of processing is often quite high.

PUNCHED CARDS

The punched card is the most familiar I/O medium. It performs a *dual purpose*: it is used to enter data into, and receive information out of, the central processor. Figure 5-3 shows a small punched card installation. Details were presented in Chapter 2 on some card characteristics and on the Hollerith code.

Figure 5-3. IBM System/360 Model 20 Computer (Courtesy IBM Corporation)

The typical card is 0.007 inch thick. This thickness is a compromise between processing speed (thicker cards can generally be processed faster) and storage space (but they take up more room). A small triangular piece is removed from a corner of each card. This corner cut is usually not made for any machine purpose. Rather, it merely helps the operator arrange the cards for processing. Cards from different file decks may also be colored or striped in some way for human identification. Also, the operator may make notes on the cards (e.g., "first card in file," "last card," "accounts receivable master file") since the machines will ignore the writing.

Although it is called a "unit record," the card does not necessarily contain all the data of a particular file record. It may merely contain data about one record item, and the complete record may thus consist of several cards. Files are organized sequentially in card trays. Batch processing methods are employed.

The cards must be properly stored when not in use. The humidity maintained in the storage room is important since cards lose moisture, shrink, and become brittle and buckled if the air is too dry. When the relative humidity is high, the cards gain moisture, swell, and warp. In either case, difficulties are likely to be encountered when the cards are processed. Cards are best stored standing on edge and under some pressure in compact trays designed for that purpose.

Punched card equipment

Manually operated keypunch machines, as we saw in Chapter 2, are the primary means of preparing punched cards. This is a tedious and expensive operation. Various approaches have been developed in an attempt to reduce the limitations of card preparation: (1) mark sensing can be used in some applications to eliminate manual keying; (2) prepunching into cards data used repeatedly (such as a customer's name and address) reduces key punching, improves accuracy, and speeds preparation time; (3) typing operations can be designed which will produce punched cards as a by-product, thus combining processing steps; and (4) data recording can be done directly on cards at the source (Figure 5-4).

Once the data are punched into the cards, they are fed into the central processor by means of a *card reader* (Figure 5-5). Cards are placed into a read hopper from where, on command from the program in the central processor, they are moved through the card feed unit past two brush-type reading stations (Figure 5-6). These stations sense the presence or absence of holes in each card column and convert this information into electrical impulses which the computer can accept. The

Figure 5-4. Source Record Punch (Courtesy Standard Register Company)

Figure 5-5. Card Reader (Courtesy Burroughs Corporation)

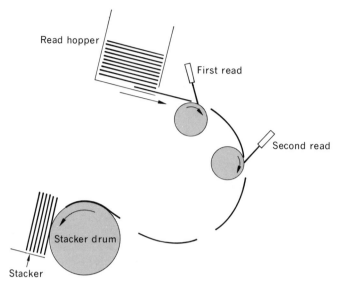

Figure 5-6. (Courtesy IBM Corporation)

reading brush rides on top of each card and makes contact with a roller beneath the card when a hole appears. This contact completes an electrical circuit.

The reading stations may use photoelectric cell readers in place of the brush-type devices. Photoelectric cells give off electrical energy when activated by light. Light shines on the card (and through the holes) as it passes the station. Photoelectric cells behind the cards are then activated by the bursts of passing light.

The card reader may compare the impulses received from each reading station as a check on the accuracy of the operation, or the impulses may be transmitted directly to the central processor where the check can be made.

After the cards have been read, they are fed into the stacker hopper. The maximum reading speed varies from 100 to 2,000 cards per minute depending on the machine used. When all 80 columns of the card are punched, a machine reading 2,000 cards per minute has a CPU input of 2,667 characters per second—a figure which is relatively slow for machine input although quite favorable when compared with a good typist's production of about five characters per second.

Cards may also serve as an output medium through the use of a *card punch* machine. Blank cards are placed in a punch hopper (Figure 5-7). Upon command from the program, they are moved, one at a time, to a punch station where processed information is received. After being punched, the holes in the card are compared at a second station with the punching instructions. If no error is detected, the card is then moved to a stacker. When errors are sensed in either reading or

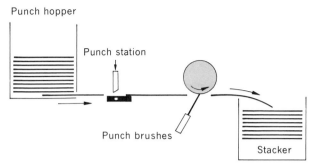

Figure 5-7. (Courtesy IBM Corporation)

punching operations, the device will stop until the error is corrected. The card-punching function is frequently housed with the card-reading activity in a machine called a *read punch* (Figure 5-8).

Output speeds are much slower than reading speeds owing to the slow electromechanical movement of the die punches. Cards are punched at the rate of 100 to 300 per minute. Because of this bottleneck in the processing operation, system analysts often try to keep the volume of punched card output to a minimum. Card punches have proven to be very useful, however, in producing documents which are later reentered into processing operations. An example of

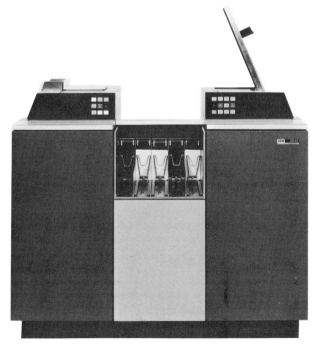

Figure 5-8. IBM 2540 Read Punch (Courtesy IBM Corporation)

such a *turnaround* application is the billing approach used by many public utilities. Bills sent to customers are in the form of cards prepared as computer output. Appropriate data are punched into this card. When a part or all of the card is returned by the customer with his payment, it may then be used as an input which requires no key punching.

Advantages and limitations of punched cards

Many businesses use punched cards as an I/O medium because they were used with the firm's unit record equipment prior to the introduction of the computer. But cards possess advantages other than merely being an old, reliable, and available medium. For one thing, they are complete records of transactions and are thus easily understood. Particular records can be sorted, deleted, and replaced without disturbing other cards. It may be possible to add more data to the cards if necessary. Magnetic and paper tapes lack these advantages. Also, as we have just seen, a card can be used as a humanly readable turnaround document as well as a processing medium. Tape media also lack this feature. Finally, cards are useful as an external storage medium for permanent records.

But cards have certain inherent disadvantages which may limit their use in or exclude them from use in a particular application. For example, the number of data characters (80) which can be punched per card is quite low—much less than the number of characters (2,000) which can be typed on the card with a typewriter. *Data density* is low because of the code used and the hole size required even when all 80 columns are punched. But in most business applications all the columns will *not* be punched, and data density is thus further reduced. For example, if the dollar amount of credit sales transactions in an exclusive retail store may reach or exceed $10,000.00, then the purchase amount field on each card must provide seven columns of space even though most purchases will be for much less (e.g., three columns would be unused if a purchase were made for $75.00).

Cards are fixed in length. If 85 characters are required, an additional card must be used. The size of the card deck is increased as is the time required to process it. Because tapes are continuous in length, they do not have this drawback.

The above paragraphs have implied that cards are bulky and slow to process—and they are. One-hundred cards, laid end to end, would extend more than 60 feet. But they could not store the data contained in less than a foot of magnetic tape. And while the *fastest* card reader can achieve a maximum input of 2,667 characters per second, an average input speed with magnetic tape might easily be 100,000 characters per second.

Cards may sometimes be misplaced or separated from their proper file deck. Also, as everyone knows, they cannot be folded, stapled, or mutilated. A bent corner or a warped card can jam equipment and further slow the processing. And obviously, the data in a card cannot be erased so that the card may be used again.

PUNCHED PAPER TAPE

Punched paper tape, like cards, is a dual-purpose medium which is suitable for computer input and output operations. It has long been used in wire communication systems where messages are punched on the tape offline at the sending station. The tape is then edited and corrected, and the data are sent to the receiving station at maximum transmitting speed.

Paper tape is often used with small scientific computers where the I/O volume is modest. It is used in business applications to record, reproduce, and communicate information. Perhaps its most popular business use is to capture data as by-products of some other processing activity. Time and labor are thus saved. (In Chapter 3 we saw punched tape used in this way in an integrated sales order application.) Small businesses frequently send tapes produced by special adding machines, accounting machines, and cash registers (Figure 5-9) to computer centers where they are used as inputs for computer-prepared reports and analyses. Similarly, many firms have regional offices which must supply data to the central headquarters computer. The expense of online remote stations is often not justified, and quite frequently paper tape is used for communication purposes. It may be sent through the mail since it is light, or wire communication facilities may be used. In the latter case, a machine at the receiving headquarters produces a duplicate of the tape being read at the sending station.

Data are recorded on the tape by punching round holes into it. The tape varies from about 0.75 to 1 inch wide and is generally from 300 to 1,000 feet in length. It is usually stored on reels, although unreeled strips may also be used. Tape, like the punched card, is laid out in rows and columns. The width of the tape depends on the number of parallel *channels* (or rows) along the length of the tape into which data can be punched. As is true with punched cards, a character of information is represented by a punch or combination of punches in a vertical column or *frame* across the width of the tape. Since there are 10 frames in each inch of tape, it is possible to record 10 characters in that space.

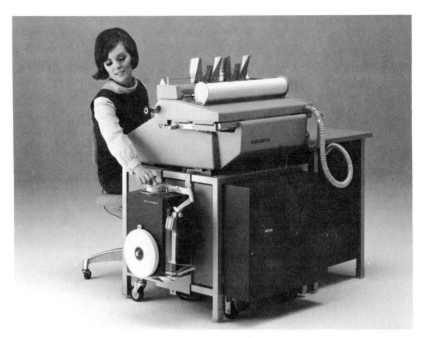

Figure 5-9. Paper Tape By-product of Electronic Accounting Machine Operations (Courtesy Burroughs Corporation)

The most commonly used sizes are five-channel tape used in teletype communications systems and eight-channel tape used by more recently developed equipment for business processing purposes. We shall consider only the eight-channel tape and its code.

Tape coding

Figure 5-10 illustrates the coding system employed with eight-channel tape. The bottom four channels are labeled to the left of the tape with the numerical values 1, 2, 4, and 8. (The series of holes between channels 4 and 8 are sprocket holes used to feed the tape through the machines and are not considered in the code.) Decimal digits 1 through 9 can be represented by a hole or a combination of holes in these bottom channels. For example, a single hole punched in channel 2 has a decimal value of 2, while holes punched in channels 4, 2, and 1 denote a decimal 7. The X and 0 channels serve the same purpose as zone punches in cards—i.e., they are used in combination with numerical punches to form alphabetic and special characters. Channel 0 used alone, of course, is the code for zero. The letter A is represented by zone punches in X and 0 plus numerical 1 hole. The letter

B has the same zone punches plus numerical 2, etc. The reader can examine the remainder of the letters to see the code pattern.

Thus far, the coding approaches of cards and tape have been similar. The check and end-of-the-line (EL) channels, however, perform special functions. You will notice that there is an odd number of holes punched in each frame. When the basic code requires an even number of holes, there will be an additional hole punched in the check channel. For example, the number 3 consists of punches in channels 1 and 2, thus giving an even number of holes. In this case there is also a punch in the check channel to raise the total to an odd number of holes. The reader can identify similar situations. Thus, all valid characters are formed with an odd number of holes, and this becomes the basis for checking the accuracy of the tape. This concept is known as *parity checking.* In this situation an *odd-parity* code is used, but even-parity checking is used in other data processing systems.

A punch in the EL channel occurs to signal the machine of a record on the tape—not required with the unit-record punched card, but a necessity with continuous length I/O media. Blank character positions (tape feed) are indicated by holes punched in all but the EL channel.

Input/output equipment

The data coded on punched tape are fed into the central processor by means of a *paper tape reader* (Figure 5-11). Tape readers, like card readers, sense the presence or absence of holes and deliver this information to the CPU. Sensing is accomplished at reading stations by the use of (1) electromechanical brushes or sensing pins or (2) photoelectric cells. The reading operation is similar to that of punched cards, so we need not dwell on it here. Electromechanical reading speed is quite slow—from less than 50 to only a few hundred characters per second. Photoelectric reading is faster, with speeds ranging from several hundred to almost two-thousand frames per second. About one-thousand characters per second are the rule, however, because of the mechanical problems associated with the movement of tape at speeds

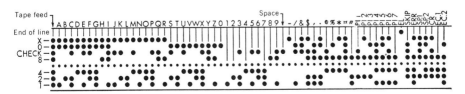

Figure 5-10. Eight-channel Paper Tape Code (Courtesy IBM Corporation)

Figure 5-11. Paper Tape Reader (Courtesy National Cash Register Company)

Figure 5-12. Paper Tape Punch (Courtesy National Cash Register Company)

exceeding 100 inches per second (10 characters per inch × 100 inches = reading of 1,000 characters per second).

Paper tape punches record information received from the CPU in the form of holes punched in blank tape (Figure 5-12). Punching is a mechanical operation and is thus quite slow. The speed of this operation ranges from about ten to three-hundred characters per second. Tape readers and punches are sometimes combined.

Advantages and limitations of punched tape

Punched paper tape provides certain advantages over punched cards. First, because it is a continuous length medium, there is no upper-limit restriction on the length of records, and no wasted space when records are short. Tape thus provides greater data density, which makes for easier handling and storage. Also, it is more economical than cards. The tape required to store 120,000 characters would cost only about one-third of the card figure if *all* columns were punched in the cards—an unlikely assumption in most cases. The equipment required for paper tape punching and reading is small, light, relatively simple in design (thus reducing maintenance costs), and less expensive than comparable card machines. As a result, tape machines can be combined with a variety of other business machines to produce by-product output. Because of this fact, tape has sometimes been referred to as the *common language* medium.

But punched tapes have their faults. It is more difficult to verify the accuracy of tape output than is the case with cards. Errors which are discovered cannot be corrected as easily as in the case of cards. An error in a card record requires repunching only one or a few cards, while an error in a tape means that the tape must be spliced or entirely repunched. Similarly, changes such as the addition to or deletion of records are more difficult with tape than with cards. These problems, of course, result from the continuous length of tape—a feature which may be an asset for some applications and a liability for others. Some firms use tape-to-card *converters* when necessary. Like cards, tape is easily torn and mutilated. Both media are far too slow to be used for online I/O operations in larger installations.[2]

MAGNETIC TAPE

Because of its relatively fast *transfer rate* (the speed at which data can be transferred from the input medium to CPU storage), magnetic

[2] Multiprogramming and time sharing, of course, will reduce the problem of severe mismatch of I/O and CPU speeds.

tape is the most popular I/O medium being used today for high-speed, large-volume applications. In addition to providing rapid input and output, it is the most widely used offline computer storage medium. The tape contained in a typical reel would be $\frac{1}{2}$ inch in width and 2,400 feet in length. Other sizes are available. One standard $10\frac{1}{2}$-inch reel (costing about \$25 and weighing about 4 pounds) is capable of storing over 20 million characters—the equivalent of more than 250,-000 fully punched cards! And while the *maximum* card-input transfer rate is 2,667 characters per second, magnetic tape can achieve transfer at the rate of over 300,000 characters in the same amount of time. The transfer rate for magnetic tape depends on such factors as (1) the data density of the magnetized marks (which varies) and (2) the speed with which the tape moves (usually about 100 inches per second).

The tape itself is quite similar to the kind used in a sound tape recorder. It is a plastic ribbon coated on one side with an iron-oxide material which can be magnetized. By electromagnetic pulses, business data are recorded in the form of tiny invisible spots on the iron-

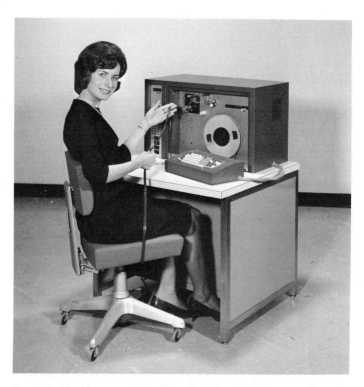

Figure 5-13. Magnetic Tape Encoder (Courtesy National Cash Register Company)

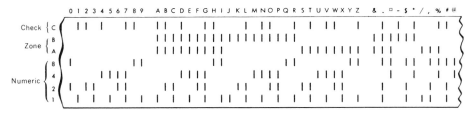

Figure 5-14. Seven-channel Magnetic Tape Code (Courtesy IBM Corporation)

oxide side of the tape, just as sound waves form magnetic patterns on the tape of a sound recorder. Both the data and the sound can be played back as many times as desired. And like the tape used on a recorder, computer tape can be erased and reused indefinitely (tape manufacturers claim that 20,000 to 50,000 passes are possible). Data contained in a tape are automatically erased as new data are being recorded. Thus, careful control and identification procedures are required to prevent important file tapes from being mistakenly used to accept computer output. Since people are unable to read information stored in the tape, it is difficult for a machine operator to distinguish between reels. *Tape librarians* are employed in large installations to maintain tape controls. When not in use, the tape reels are stored in protective, dust-resistant plastic cases.

Although it is possible to encode magnetic tape from source data manually (Figure 5-13), it may not always be practical. How, then, are new transactions placed on the tape? Frequently, new input data are captured in punched card or punched tape form and are then transcribed on magnetic tape by a special offline *data converter*. In very large installations, input and output data transcription may be performed by a smaller, general purpose computer system.

Magnetic tape coding

The coding philosophy of magnetic tape is similar to that of punched paper tape. Magnetic tape is divided horizontally into rows (called "channels" or "tracks") and vertically into columns or frames. Figure 5-14 illustrates a very commonly used seven-channel tape format. You will note that channel designations are quite similar to those used in eight-channel punched tape. Data are represented in a coded form.[3] The presence of a mark in Figure 5-14 indicates that the channel value is "on" while the absence of a magnetized spot signifies an "off" condition. Each vertical frame represents one data character. (Unlike punched cards and tape, the number of characters per inch *can vary*

[3] The code used here is called *binary-coded decimal* or BCD. In a later chapter we shall become better acquainted with BCD.

with magnetic tape. Tape density ranges from 200 to 1,500 frames per inch.)

The code is easily deciphered by one who understands the paper tape system. Let us ignore for a moment the parity check channel. The numerical values are determined by one or a combination of the bottom four channels, while the A and B zone tracks are used in conjunction with the numeric channels to represent letters and special characters. For example, the decimal 7 is represented by an on condition in channels 4, 2, and 1. You can test your understanding by observing the coding pattern used for the other alphanumeric characters. By now you may also have noticed the difference between this parity checking method and the one illustrated in the punched tape example. Here we have an *even-parity* check—i.e., all valid characters must have an even number of similarly magnetized spots. The parity check channel has a mark when necessary to achieve this condition. Odd-parity checking is also used with magnetic tape systems.

There is one other difference between this seven-channel code and the eight-channel code of punched tape. One of our channels is obviously missing! Magnetic tape, like paper tape, is a continuous-length, sequential file medium. How then can the computer distinguish between different records on the tape? Paper tape had an end-of-the-line channel for this purpose, but that track is missing here.

Figure 5-15 shows an accounts receivable file organized on magnetic tape. Customer records may be of varying length. They may also be combined into tape *blocks* of several records (Figure 5-16). For our purposes, however, it is convenient to think in terms of single-record blocks. The records are separated by blank spaces in the tape called *interrecord gaps*, which perform the end-of-line function. Interrecord gaps are automatically created by the computer system after the last character in a record (or block of records) has been recorded. These blank sections vary in width from about $\frac{1}{4}$ inch to 1 inch, with a $\frac{3}{4}$-inch gap being common. The first several feet of tape are unrecorded to allow for threading on the equipment. A reflective

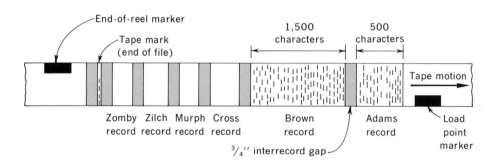

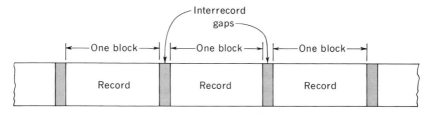

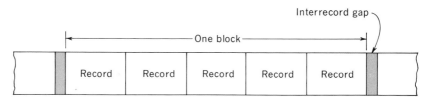

Figure 5-16. Fewer Interrecord Gaps Save Tape and Speed Data Input. This Is Important When Record Lengths Are Short. The Program of Instructions Separates the Records within a Block for Processing

marker known as the *load point* indicates to the equipment the beginning of usable tape, while a similar *end-of-reel* marker signals the end of usable tape. The markers are placed on opposite edges of the tape for machine identification purposes. The end of a file may be signaled by a special one-character record consisting of spots recorded in the 8, 4, 2, and 1 channels. This special character is called a *tape mark*. Some systems use other control means such as a $3\frac{3}{4}$-inch end-of-file gap to serve the same purpose.

Magnetic tape equipment

The magnetic tape units shown in Figure 5-17 are used for both data input (*reading*) and output (recording or *writing*). Called by such names as *tape drives* and *tape transports*, these machines read and write data on the tape by the use of *read-write heads* (Figure 5-18). There is one read-write head for each tape channel. Each head is a small electromagnet with minute gaps between the poles. In the writing operation, the tape moves over the gaps while electrical pulses from the CPU flow through the write coils of the appropriate heads causing the iron-oxide coating of the tape to be magnetized in the proper pattern. When the tape is being read, the magnetized patterns induce pulses of current in the read coils which feed the data into the CPU.

90

Figure 5-17. Magnetic Tape Units (Courtesy Honeywell Electronic Data Processing)

The tape is loaded onto the tape drive in much the same way that a movie projector is threaded (Figure 5-19). The tape movement during processing is from the file reel past the read-write heads to the machine reel. Tapes may move at speeds in excess of 100 inches per second, and they achieve this rate in a few milliseconds. Several methods are used to prevent tape damage from sudden bursts of speed. One such method is to use vacuum columns to hold slack tape, thus damping the inertial effect of the tape reels.

There are usually several tape drives used in an installation. In most applications, a tape is either read or written in a single pass.

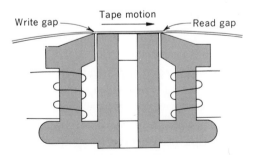

Figure 5-18. Read-Write Head (Courtesy IBM Corporation)

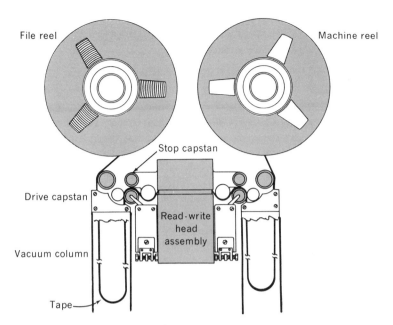

Figure 5-19. (Courtesy IBM Corporation)

Therefore, if we wish to update our master accounts receivable file, we may have one unit reading in the old master file, another feeding in recent transactions, a third introducing the processing instructions, and a fourth writing the updated master file. Small installations may have up to about six transports, while very large processors can handle over two hundred.

Advantages and limitations of magnetic tape

The *advantages* of magnetic tape can be summarized as follows:

1. *Unlimited length of records.* Unlike cards, any number of characters can be placed in a record. Files can be as long as necessary.
2. *Compact storage.* The data density, as we have seen, is far greater than that of cards and paper tape. Data handling is facilitated. Many firms keep their tapes in special air-conditioned vaults and thus provide safer storage for their records than is practicable with paper media and documents.
3. *Reduced cost.* A tape costs less than the hundreds of thousands of cards which it can replace. Storage space is reduced, and the tape can be re-used many times.
4. *Rapid transfer rate.* Neither cards nor punched tape can compare with magnetic tape in input/output speed.

5. *Protection against record loss.* In card systems, there is always the danger of losing or misplacing one or more cards from a file. Magnetic tape is a protection against this danger.

Magnetic tape, however, has several *disadvantages*. Included among these are:

1. *Need for machine interpretation.* Since the magnetized spots are invisible, they cannot, of course, be read by humans. A printing operation must be performed if it is necessary to check or verify tape data.
2. *Lack of random accessibility.* Because of the sequential nature of tape file processing, it is not generally suitable for jobs which require rapid and random access to particular records. Tape file processing is also not efficient when the job being processed calls for the use of only a small proportion of the total tape records. In either situation, too much time is wasted in reading records which will not be used.
3. *Environmental problems.* Specks of dust on a tape can be read as data characters or can cause an improper reading. Special dust-resistant cases must be used to store the tapes. The humidity of the storage area must be controlled. Care must be taken to keep the tape transports and the computer room as free of dust as possible. Careful control procedures must be followed to prevent an important file from being erased by mistake. (Instead of losing a card or two, the entire file might be lost — a revolting development!)

SUMMARY

Data are organized into files of related records and fed into computers for processing. The information needed by managers is the output obtained by processing files. These files may be organized in two ways — either sequentially or randomly. Batch processing is performed on sequentially organized files, while random access processing is possible with files organized in either way. A wide variety of I/O media and devices is available. The business manager must consider many factors in choosing the best approach for his firm.

Punched cards are the most familiar medium. They are easily understood, and they possess advantages because of their fixed length and unit record nature — e.g., some cards can be deleted, added to, sorted, etc., without disturbing the others. However, their data density is low, they are bulky, and they represent a slow means of input and output.

Punched paper tape is a popular means of capturing data as a by-product of another processing activity. Round holes are punched to represent data. Several coding systems are employed. Certain advantages accrue to paper tape because of its continuous length. There is no upper-limit restriction on the length of records and no wasted space when records are short. Paper tape is also more economical than cards. But error correction, additions, and deletions are more difficult than is the case with cards. And like cards, paper tape is a relatively slow I/O medium.

Magnetic tape is much faster. Its transfer rate is significantly improved by its high data density. It can be erased and reused many times and is thus very economical. Data are represented by a seven-channel code, and parity checking is used to reduce the chance of error. However, the coded magnetized spots are invisible, and thus a printing operation is required to check or verify tape data. Tape records lack random accessibility.

DISCUSSION QUESTIONS

1 Discuss the factors to be considered in selecting the alternate I/O media and devices.

2 A punched card is a dual-purpose medium. (*a*) What is the meaning of dual purpose? (*b*) What other media are dual purpose in nature?

3 Define the following terms:

(*a*) turnaround document (*f*) parity checking
(*b*) read punch (*g*) transfer rate
(*c*) data density (*h*) tape-recording density
(*d*) channels (*i*) interrecord gaps
(*e*) frame (*j*) load point marker

4 Discuss the advantages and limitations of punched cards.

5 Discuss the advantages and limitations of punched paper tape.

6 Explain how data are read from and written on magnetic tape.

7 Discuss the advantages and limitations of magnetic tape.

SELECTED REFERENCES

Thomas C. Bartee, *Digital Computer Fundamentals* (2d ed.; New York: McGraw-Hill Book Company, 1966), chap. 8.

J. A. Hodskins, "Paper Tape vs. Punched Card," *Journal of Data Management*, July, 1964, pp. 30-34.

Introduction to IBM Data Processing Systems (IBM Corporation, Manual F22-6517-2, 1964).

Norman Statland and John Hillegass, "A Survey of Input/Output Equipment," *Computers and Automation*, July, 1964, pp. 16-20 ff.

6. INPUT/OUTPUT MEDIA AND DEVICES: II

In spite of advances made in many areas of processing technology, input preparation in a majority of installations has not changed significantly in the past decade. Data are still taken from printed documents and recorded in machine-acceptable form by a manual keying operation. In many cases a further manual verification step is required to check the accuracy of the initial keying. Several devices, however, have been designed to eliminate manual keying by reading the characters printed on the source documents and converting the data *directly* into computer-usable input. In the first pages of this chapter we shall look at these *character readers*, which are generally used in high-volume, batch processing applications. *High-speed printers* are also considered.

The latter part of the chapter is devoted (1) to some I/O devices which are frequently found in online, random access processing situations; and (2) to complementary tools and concepts which facilitate I/O operations.

MAGNETIC INK CHARACTER RECOGNITION

Use and development

The magnetic ink character recognition (MICR) concept is widely used by banking and financial institutions as a means of processing the tremendous volume of checks being written.[1] Figure 6-1 shows a sample check coded with a special ink which contains tiny iron-oxide magnetizable particles. The code number of the bank to which the

---

[1] It has been estimated that 20 *billion* checks will be written each year by 1970! And the typical check may pass through two to four banks and be handled and read up to seven times before it is finally cleared.

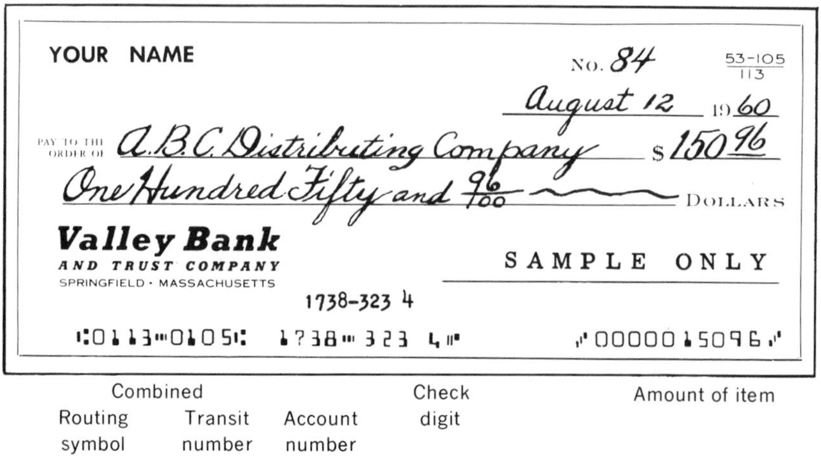

YOUR NAME No. 84 53-105 / 113

August 12 1960

PAY TO THE ORDER OF A. B. C. Distributing Company $150 96/100

One Hundred Fifty and 96/100 —————— DOLLARS

Valley Bank
AND TRUST COMPANY
SPRINGFIELD · MASSACHUSETTS

SAMPLE ONLY

1738-323 4

⑆0113⑈0105⑆ 1738⑈323 4⑆   ⑇00000150 96⑇

Combined   Check   Amount of item
Routing   Transit   Account   digit
symbol   number   number

Numbers at bottom of check are printed in approved E-13-B character shape

Figure 6-1. (Courtesy National Cash Register Company)

check will be written and the depositor's account number are precoded on the checks. The first bank to receive the check after it has been written encodes the amount in the lower right corner. The check at this point is a unit record and, like punched cards, may then be handled automatically through regular bank collection channels—e.g., from (1) the initial bank receiving the check to, perhaps, (2) the Federal Reserve bank to (3) the depositor's bank to (4) the depositor's account. The type font used (Figure 6-2) permits the reading equipment to distinguish between symbols.

Because of the nature of bank collection channels, any approach to automatic check processing must receive the support of the entire banking industry. In 1955, the American Bankers Association began to study the problem of how to improve check processing. The result of this study was the recommendation that magnetic ink characters be-

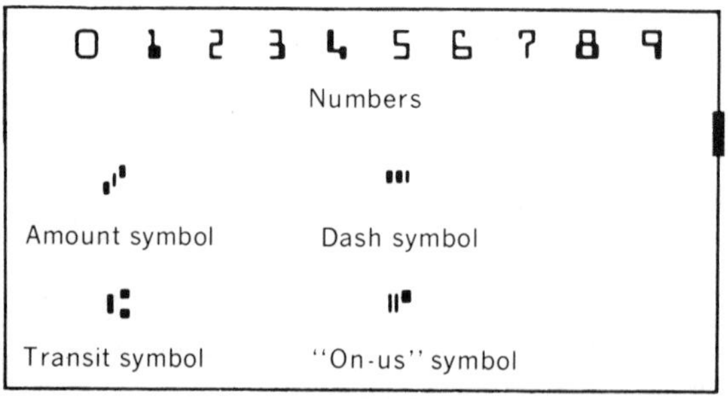

0 1 2 3 4 5 6 7 8 9

Numbers

Amount symbol   Dash symbol

Transit symbol   "On-us" symbol

Figure 6-2. (Courtesy IBM Corporation)

FEDERAL RESERVE BANKS WILL NOT HANDLE CHECKS
RECEIVED WITHOUT MAGNETIC INK NUMBERS
EFFECTIVE SEPTEMBER 1, 1967

Effective September 1, 1967, checks and drafts deposited with Federal Reserve banks will not be handled through regular bank collection channels if received without the magnetic ink (MICR) transit number. The new electronic processing demands such magnetic ink encoding.

To avoid the delays of special handling of your checks, please use only the printed checks which your bank furnishes. (If not convenient to carry your checkbook, keep a few blank checks with you.) **Do not use customer's draft forms or "changed" checks.**

You may be required to pay a service charge for collecting a check which cannot be processed electronically by the Federal Reserve banks.

TR-402   1-67

Figure 6-3

come the common language for checks. The development of MICR (although not painless) was possible only through the coordinated efforts of the American Bankers Association, check printers, equipment manufacturers, the Federal Reserve System, and the individual banks and their customers. The success of the MICR approach was illustrated when on September 1, 1967, Federal Reserve banks stopped handling, through the regular clearing channels, checks not encoded with magnetic ink (see Figure 6-3 for an announcement made earlier in 1967). The magnetic ink characters have also been accepted as a standard by the British Bank Association. Thus, the concept has now become international in scope.

Equipment

Magnetic ink character *reader-sorter* units (Figure 6-4) interpret the encoded data on checks (which vary in length, width, and thickness) and transfer this information to the CPU. They also sort the checks by account number, bank number, etc., into pockets. Input speed ranges from about 750 to 1,600 paper documents each minute.

As checks enter the reading unit, and immediately prior to the reading operation, they pass through a strong magnetic field which causes the iron-oxide particles to become magnetized. The read heads are then able to produce electrical signals as the magnetized characters pass beneath them. Each character pattern is divided into many segments and analyzed by built-in recognition circuits to determine which of the 14 characters has been sensed. Valid characters may then be fed directly into a general purpose computer, or they may be transferred to magnetic tape for later processing. The number of sorting pockets varies from 2 to 18.

Figure 6-4. Burroughs B116 Reader-Sorter (Courtesy Burroughs Corporation)

Advantages and limitations of MICR

There are several *advantages* associated with the use of MICR:

1. *High reading accuracy.* Checks may be roughly handled, folded, smeared, stamped, endorsed, and covered with extraneous markings. Yet, this does not prevent recognition with a high degree of accuracy. Portions of characters can be missing, and the characters may still be readable.

2. *Direct input with source document.* Processing is speeded because checks can be fed directly into the input device. In addition, the checks can vary in size and still be acceptable as input.

3. *Humanly readable data.* The type font used is easily recognized and read, if necessary, by clerical personnel.

4. *Reduction in bad check loses.* In the past merchants kept blank customer draft or courtesy check forms available for customers to fill in with the name of their bank, its location, etc., in addition to the amount of the check. Occasionally, honest people would make errors in filling in the information, their accounts could not be located, and the merchant might not have enough information to trace the customer. When people are required to use their own checks properly encoded, there is much less chance of this type of error. It is, of course, still possible for fraudulent checks to be written, but there is less likelihood that a merchant will find himself in the embarrassing position of having cashed a check drawn on an imaginary institution such as The East Bank of the Trinity River.

The primary *limitation* of MICR is that only a *small number of characters* are used. Since it was designed by and for the banking industry, MICR uses only the characters needed for bank processing. No alphabetic characters are available. Thus MICR has not been found suitable for general business applications. Also, clerical processing is still required to handle (1) damaged documents, (2) checks not encoded with the proper amount of ink, and (3) checks not encoded in the proper position. In spite of Federal Reserve policies, checks are written on uncoded forms and on forms where the writer has substituted the name of one bank for another—still a nuisance to the banking community.

OPTICAL CHARACTER RECOGNITION

Optical character recognition (OCR) may well become to businesses in general what MICR is to the banking community. The basic differences between MICR and OCR are: (1) The MICR process requires encoding with special ink, while OCR techniques make possible the reading of any printed character and (2) the magnetic ink reader is limited to 14 characters, while an optical reader may include alphabetic as well as numeric characters. Thus, the flexibility of OCR may make it possible for many businesses to eliminate or reduce the input keying bottleneck.

Uses of OCR

Although machines are available which will read handwritten numbers (Figure 6-5), the automatic reading of handwritten script is still some years in the future. (While your penmanship is undoubtedly beautiful, the author's presents a formidable challenge to the equipment designers.) Most OCR devices being used in business are designed to read *machine-printed* characters and simple handmade marks. For example, credit card systems use embossed plastic plates bearing the holder's account number in specially designed characters. When a credit sale is made at a gasoline station, the attendant uses an inexpensive imprinter (Figure 6-6) to record the data from the customer's card and the amount of the transaction onto a form which is then forwarded to a central processing point. There the document is read automatically by an optical instrument. The data may then be entered directly into the CPU, or they may be transferred to punched cards, punched tape, or magnetic tape for later processing.

Public utilities also use OCR in their billing activities. A water department, for example, may print the customer's name and account number on the meter-reading forms with characters which can be

Figure 6-5. IBM 1287 Optical Reader (Courtesy IBM Corporation)

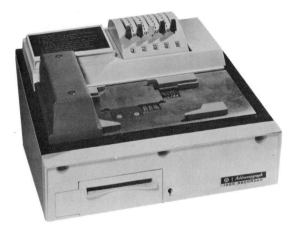

Figure 6-6. Addressograph 1455 Data Recorder (Courtesy Addressograph Multigraph Corporation)

optically interpreted. The meter reader then makes pencil marks in appropriate columns on the forms to designate the quantities used (an optical version, without special pencils, of the mark-sensing process used with punched cards). The completed forms are then optically processed, and the monthly bill is prepared by a high-speed printer connected to the CPU. The customer returns the bill with the payment; a clerk checks the amount of payment against the billed amount and notes partial payments by making the appropriate marks on the left side of the form; and the bill then becomes the machine input to update the customer's account record. Thus, the desirable turnaround character of utility billing is still maintained with OCR processing.

Other OCR uses include (1) the reading of school documents such as registration forms, attendance rosters, and grade reports to maintain student records in large metropolitan school systems; and (2) the reading of adding machine and cash register tapes for accounting and inventory control purposes. Also, the post offices in large cities use optical recognition equipment to read typed addresses and sort mail geographically. The use of Zip codes improves this sorting procedure.

Equipment

The ideal optical reader would be one which could read any character written in any form. It could accept documents of all sizes, and it would not be confused by smudges and other defects. Alas, the ideal machine is not yet available.

There are, however, several types of *optical readers* (Figure 6-7) which are available. Some are limited to mark reading; some are designed for reading turnaround documents and have alphanumeric capability, although the character locations, number of lines to be read, type font used, etc., permit only limited flexibility; and some are capable of reading entire pages of printed matter (upper- and lower-case letters, numbers, and punctuation marks). In all readers the printed marks and/or characters must be scanned by some type of photoelectric device which recognizes characters by the absorption or reflectance of light on the document (characters to be read are nonreflective).[2] Reflected light patterns are converted into electrical impulses which are transmitted to recognition logic circuits. There they are compared with the characters which the machine has been programmed to recognize and, if valid, are then recorded for input into

[2] Some machines break the scanned character down into distinguishable segments or spots for recognition purposes, while others scan the entire character without segmentation.

Figure 6-7. NCR 420 Optical Reader (Courtesy National Cash Register Company)

the CPU. If no suitable comparison is possible, the document may be rejected. Reading speed varies from about one-hundred to over two-thousand characters per second.

Advantages and limitations of OCR

The primary *advantage* of OCR is that it eliminates some of the duplication of human effort required to get data into the computer. This reduction in human effort can improve the quality (accuracy) of input data, and it can improve the timeliness of information processed. Also, OCR helps businesses cope with the paperwork explosion. If volume of processing is sufficiently high, OCR will result in cost savings. Input preparation at remote stations requires only the use of an imprinter or a typewriter—devices which are less expensive than other input preparation machines.

Among the *limitations* of OCR are:

1. There are specific (and rather inflexible) requirements for type font and size of characters to be used.

2. There is no standard type font such as is used with MICR.

3. The difficulty of controlling print quality causes reading problems in some applications — e.g., in typing there is the problem of uneven spacing, strikeovers, smudges, erasures.

4. Forms design, ink specifications, paper quality, etc., become more critical and must be more standardized than is the case when keypunch source documents are prepared.

5. The optical readers are not economically feasible unless the daily volume of transactions is relatively high (some multifont page readers are as expensive as medium-sized computers). Future development work on optical readers is expected to improve their technical capabilities and reduce their cost.

HIGH-SPEED PRINTERS

High-speed printers (Figure 6-8) provide information *output* from the CPU in the form of permanently printed characters which have meaning to humans. They are the primary ouput device when the information is to be used by man rather than by machine.

Significant improvements have been made in printers in the past few years. Because the earlier computers were scientifically oriented, the printed output was expected to be small. Therefore, many earlier printers were merely souped-up, one-character-at-a-time versions of electric typewriters. Such printed output facilities proved to be com-

Figure 6-8. High-speed Printer (Courtesy Burroughs Corporation)

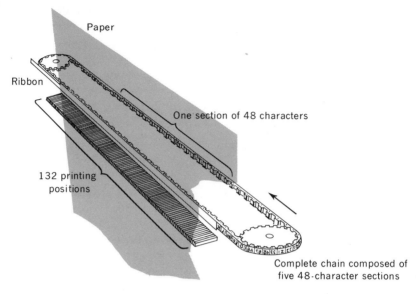

Paper

Ribbon

One section of 48 characters

132 printing positions

Complete chain composed of five 48-character sections

Figure 6-9. (Courtesy IBM Corporation)

pletely inadequate for business purposes. In fact, printing was a major bottleneck of the early business processing systems.

But with the introduction of second-generation equipment designed specifically for business use came greatly improved printing capability. Character-at-a-time printing gave way to *line-at-a-time* printing. Speed increased from about five 120-character lines per minute for typewriters to over 1,200 similar lines per minute for high-speed impact printers.[3] In other words, printing speed had gone from 600 characters per minute to over 140,000 characters per minute.[4]

High-speed line printers do not have movable carriages. Rather, they use rapidly moving *chains* (or trains) of printing slugs or some

[3] The two basic types of high-speed printers are *impact* and *nonimpact* devices. Impact printing is performed by the familiar method of pressing a typeface against paper and inked ribbon. Nonimpact (or electrostatic) printers generally form images by means of electrical and chemical processes. Nonimpact printing, while capable of producing over 5,000 lines per minute, produces only one copy, and the quality of that copy is not too good. Since the vast majority of printers used today are of the impact type, we shall limit our study to these machines. Future advances are expected in nonimpact methods.

[4] You will recall that some magnetic tape drives can write characters at a rate of over 300,000 *per second*. Thus, there is still a mismatch between output by printing and output by magnetic tape. Some very large computer systems write the CPU output on tapes, and the printing operation is then controlled offline from the large system by smaller computers. Small and medium-sized installations, however, perform the printing online.

form of a print *cylinder* to print lines of information on paper moving past the printing station. Figure 6-9 illustrates the *print chain* concept. The links in the chain are engraved character-printing slugs. The chain is capable of producing 48 different characters, and there are five sections of 48 characters each in the length of the chain. The chain moves at a constant and rapid speed past the printing positions. Magnetically controlled hammers behind the paper are timed to force the paper against the proper print slugs. The ribbon between the paper and the character leaves an imprint on the paper as a result of the impact. Obviously, careful timing is required to actuate the hammers in each printing position at the precise moment the desired character is passing. Printing speeds in excess of 1,200 lines per minute are possible with chain devices.

The *drum printer* uses a solid cylinder. Raised characters extend the length of the drum (Figure 6-10). There are as many circular *bands* of type as there are printing positions. Each band contains all the possible characters. The drum turns at a constant speed, with one revolution being required to print each line. A fast-acting hammer opposite each band picks out the proper character and strikes the paper against that character. Thus, in one rotation, hammers at *several* printing positions may "fire" when the A row appears; several others may strike to imprint D's, etc. At the end of the rotation, all necessary positions on the paper are printed. The paper then moves to the next line. This procedure may be repeated from 700 to over 1,500 times in a single minute.

Most of the tremendous volume of data and information which enters and leaves business computers each year is processed by the I/O media and machines which have now been introduced. However, other means of communication between man and machine are possible. In

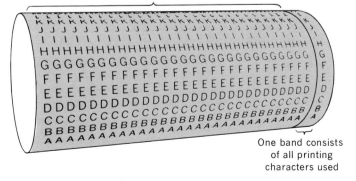

The number of bands corresponds to the number of printing positions

One band consists of all printing characters used

Figure 6-10. A Print Drum

the following pages we shall examine some I/O devices possessing one or more of the following characteristics:

1. Direct manual input/output of information may be possible without data-recording media being *required* – i.e., a direct man-machine *interface* is possible.
2. The relationship between user and machine is thus of an online nature.
3. Random access processing is common; file storage is online.
4. The volume of input data may be lower and/or more irregular than is the case with data processed by the means described in Chapter 5 and earlier in this chapter.

ONLINE TERMINALS

The most commonly encountered online terminal is the *console typewriter* (Figure 6-11), which enables the computer operator to enter data directly into, and receive information directly from, the storage unit of the central processor. When the keys of the typewriter are depressed, the code designation of the keyed characters is entered into storage. A visual record is also typed. In addition, the console type-

Figure 6-11. UNIVAC 1108 Computer Console (Courtesy Sperry Rand Corp., UNIVAC Division)

Figure 6-12. Honeywell Data Station (Courtesy Honeywell Electronic Data Processing)

writer may be used to (1) modify a portion of the program instructions, (2) test the program of instructions, (3) inquire about the contents of certain storage areas, (4) alter the data content of specific storage locations, (5) determine intermediate computing results, and (6) receive and type output information. Console typewriters, because of the slowness of their I/O operations, are seldom used if volume is significant.

Remote online *inquiry stations* (or desk sets) may be quite similar to console typewriters (Figure 6-12), but they are located away from the computer room. They may be in the next office, in a nearby building, or in the next state. And they may be connected to the CPU by a short cable or by a complex data communications system. There is quite a bit of variation among inquiry stations, because they are often designed to perform rather specific tasks. Since we have illustrated the use of such stations by airlines and others in Chapter 3 in the discussion of time sharing and real time processing, we need not dwell further here on the subject. Of course, remote stations, like main console type-

Figure 6-13. Input Terminal, RCA Spectra 70/630 Data Gathering System (Courtesy RCA Electronic Data Processing)

writers, produce input data and receive output information very slowly. But with many such time sharing stations online (and perhaps with batch processing jobs to perform) the CPU can be kept busy.

Online terminals functioning as *data collection* or *transaction-recording* stations have been developed in an effort to by-pass the preparation of punched cards, paper tapes, or magnetic tapes (Figure 6-13). Although data collection systems vary according to the application, they are all designed to perform a similar function—to get data from remote points into the computer as quickly as possible.

Transaction recorders are often found in factories to keep control of the inventory of parts and materials used in production. Let us assume, for example, that an employee needs a dozen hinges to complete a job. He gets the hinges and an identification card from a supply station. The card identifies the hinges by part number and contains any other *fixed* information (such as unit price) which is necessary. The worker inserts the card into a transaction recorder and then keys or moves levers to indicate the *variable* part of the transaction—the number of hinges taken, the job number, etc. He then pushes a transmit button to send the data to the computer where they are checked for accuracy and then accepted to update the proper record in the inventory file. If an error is detected, a signal is relayed back to the recording station. It is obvious, of course, that such a system requires random access processing.

Many savings institutions are also making use of online transaction-recording devices. Figure 6-14 shows an example of a teller's station in direct communication with the bank's central computer. Let us

Figure 6-14. Online Teller Console (Courtesy National Cash Register Company)

assume that a deposit is to be made by a customer. The customer presents his bankbook and the amount of his deposit to the teller, who inserts the book into a recorder and keys in the transaction data. The data are then sent to the computer which adjusts the customer's savings balance. The updated information is relayed back to the remote station where it is entered in the customer's bankbook. The entire transaction is accounted for in a matter of seconds.

VISUAL COMMUNICATION [5]

Preliminary sketches, design drawings, and engineering drawings are generally required in the design and development of new products and projects. When the designer first gets a new-product thought, he makes some preliminary sketches to get his idea down on paper so that it may be more thoroughly analyzed. As the design is modified, additional drawings may be required; when the idea is approved, further detailed production drawings are prepared. Thus, the preparation of drawings may occupy a substantial portion of the designer's time. Although it is possible to convert graphical material into numerical coordinates for purposes of computer analysis, this is a very time-consuming process if done manually.

Visual input

In recent years, *input* instruments have been developed which make it possible for the computer to receive human sketching directly.[6] One such instrument is an *input tablet*, which may be made of glass or plastic and is about the size of a sheet of paper. The tablet contains hundreds of copper lines which form a fine grid that is connected with the computer. Each copper line receives electrical impulses. A special pen or stylus attached to the tablet is sensitive to these impulses and is used to form the sketches. However, the pen does not mark directly on the tablet. To communicate with the machine, the designer merely draws on a piece of paper placed on the glass or plastic. The tablet grid then senses the exact position of the stylus as it is moved and transmits this information to the computer.

As the designer draws, the computer may display the developing

[5] The term "visual" is used here to refer to I/O techniques which enable man to communicate with machine through the use of a visual device resembling a television picture tube.

[6] For an excellent discussion of graphical devices, see Ivan E. Sutherland, "Computer Inputs and Outputs," *Scientific American*, vol. 215, September, 1966, pp. 86-96.

sketch on a _cathode ray tube_ (CRT), which is similar to a television screen (Figure 6-15). However, there is a difference between the drawing and the display. Poorly sketched lines are displayed as straight; poor lettering is replaced by neat printing; and poorly formed corners become mathematically precise. Changes and modifications in the drawing can be quickly made—e.g., a line can be "erased" from (or shifted on) the display unit with a movement of the stylus. Once the initial sketching is finished and displayed on the CRT to the satisfaction of the designer, he may then instruct the computer to analyze the design and report on certain characteristics. For example, the computer might be asked to work out the acoustical characteristics of a theater which the designer has sketched. The sketch may then be modified by the designer on the basis of the computer analysis, or the machine may be instructed to display a theater with more desirable acoustics. Such direct man-machine graphical communication enables the designer (1) to learn what effect certain changes have on the project and (2) to save valuable time for more creative work.

Figure 6-15. IBM 2250 Display Unit (Courtesy IBM Corporation)

Another graphical input instrument is the electronic *light pen*. This pen is a photocell placed in a small, easily handled tube (Figure 6-16). It may be used to "write" on the surface of the CRT. When the pen is moved by the user over the screen, it is able to detect the light coming from a limited field of view. The light from the CRT causes the photocell to respond when the pen is pointed directly at a lighted area. These electrical responses are transmitted to the computer, which is able to determine that part of the displayed drawing that is triggering the photocell response. Under program control, the pen can be used to modify a displayed image or add or delete lines.

Visual output

As we have just seen, computers use *display stations* to accept light-pen input and provide visual output. Businesses may also use many time sharing, online stations (Figure 6-17) to display information stored at a remote computer site. Data may be entered, revised, or updated from the stations through the use of a keyboard. A major difference between visual display stations and remote inquiry stations is that

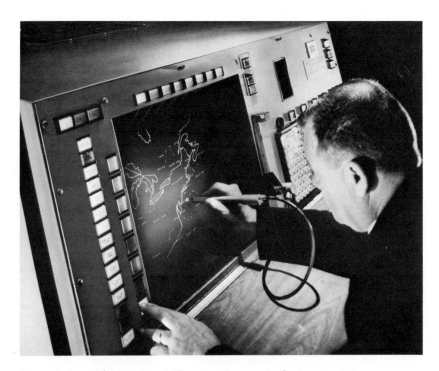

Figure 6-16. Light-pen Input (Courtesy Burroughs Corporation)

one uses a CRT and can receive information in graphical as well as printed form, while the other prints the received information on paper. Photographic equipment is sometimes used to make a permanent record of a display.

Although visual communication has proved to be extremely helpful in scientific and engineering fields, it has been less popular in business data processing areas up to now because of the high cost of equipment. But it is likely that this type of man-machine relationship will increase in the future as more applications are found and as systems become more sophisticated.

VOICE COMMUNICATION

Input units, basically, do nothing more than convert human language into machine language. Why, then, doesn't someone invent a machine which will enable a person to talk to the computer in English? As a matter of fact, a few manufacturers have done just that on an experimental basis. Although the vocabulary is quite small, sound waves have been converted into machine language. Speech recognition, however, will not become an economical input technique for some time.

Figure 6-17. IBM 2260 Display Station (Courtesy IBM Corporation)

When we look at the *output* side of verbal communication, however, we find that computers are now being used to give English responses to human inquiries. All the spoken words needed to process the possible inquiries are recorded on a magnetic drum or disk. Each word is given a code. When inquiries are received, the processor composes a reply message in a coded form. This coded message is then transmitted to an audio-response device which assembles the words in the proper sequence and transmits the audio message back to the station requesting the information.

Audio-response units are now being used by the Southwestern Bell Telephone Company and by the New York Stock Exchange. The telephone company uses audio response in the processing of intercepted calls, i.e., calls which are automatically given special handling because they are made to numbers which have been changed. The operator who receives the intercepted call asks for the number being dialed. She keys this number into the computer system, presses a start button, and is then free to handle the next intercepted call. The new number is automatically transmitted to the customer by the audio-response unit. The reply is so fast that the system is instructed to remain silent for an initial short period of time!

The New York Stock Exchange uses verbal output to direct inquiries from subscribers to the Exchange's quotation service. To receive up-to-the-minute information about a stock, the broker dials the code number of the stock over a private station phone. The dialed inquiry goes to the Exchange's computer, where it is processed. The broker immediately receives the latest information on stock prices and the volume of trading. About 400,000 inquiries a day can be handled by this system.

DATA TRANSMISSION

From time to time in the preceding pages we have referred to I/O stations which are connected to a central processor located at some distant point. One example of such a setup is airline reservation systems; another is inquiry stations used by manufacturing firms; and a third has just been mentioned—private telephone lines used to connect customers to a stock exchange computer. Let us take a closer look in this section at the data transmission techniques which facilitate I/O operations and which are available to businesses. *Data transmission*, of course, is simply the means by which data are transferred between processing locations.

There is, certainly, nothing new about data transmission. Human runners and messengers have been used since the beginning of recorded history. The Greek runner carrying the message of victory on the plains of Marathon has inspired a present-day athletic event. The

Pony Express won the admiration of a nation in the brief period of time before it was replaced by telegraph service. Railroads were using telegraph equipment for business data transmission in the early 1900s. And the U.S. Post Office transmits an enormous quantity of business data each week.

We have seen that there is a wide variety of I/O equipment from which the business manager can choose. Not surprisingly, there is also a wide range of data transmission services available from firms such as Western Union and American Telephone and Telegraph (the Bell Telephone System parent). Figure 6-18 shows some of the media and devices which can be used to achieve communication between remote and central points. The remote stations may be online or offline. Figure 6-18 also shows the most commonly used transmission *channels* or "highways" for carrying data from one location to another. These channels are wire lines, cables, or microwave radio circuits, which, like I/O techniques, vary in data handling speed.

The *teletype* channels transmit data at speeds of about five to twenty characters per second—speeds which may be quite adequate for input by means of manual keying or punched paper tape. If a business has a moderate data volume, it may prove economical to lease an exclusive teletype circuit. Such a circuit may be leased for night use only, for the entire day, etc.

Standard voice-grade *telephone* channels permit more rapid transmission. Data may be sent at speeds of over three-hundred characters per second. The actual maximum rate depends on the type of telephone service used—e.g., private (leased) lines may be somewhat faster than public lines. Telephone circuits are used to communicate large amounts of data originating in the form of punched cards, punched tape, and magnetic tape. A popular means of transmission is through the use of the Bell Telephone System's *Data-Phone* (Figure 6-19). The Data-Phone is connected to I/O equipment at the sending and receiving points and may be used for both voice and data transmission. Let us assume, for example, that a branch sales office is ready to transmit sales orders to the main plant. A clerk at the branch office dials the proper number at the main plant to notify it of a transmission. When the employee at the receiving station is ready to accept the message, both parties push a data button, at which point the voice communication cuts off and the data transmission begins.

If the data volume is sufficient between locations, it may be economical for the company to acquire leased lines which can be used for both voice and data purposes. If data volume will not support a private line, however, then the regular long-distance telephone network should be used. The Data-Phones are leased full-time, but the cost of data messages, like long-distance calls, is determined by time use.

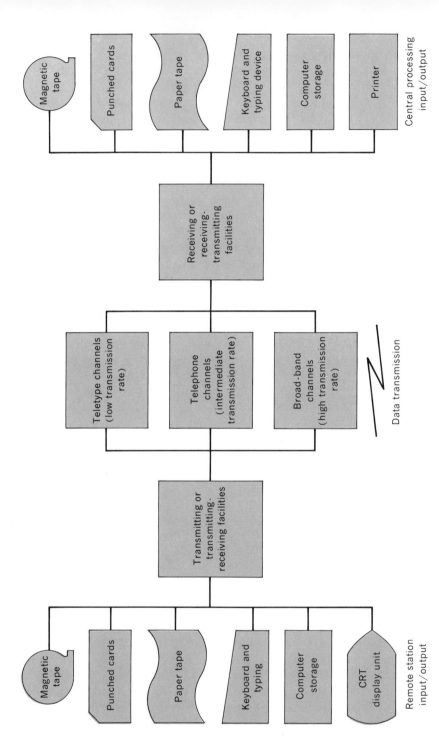

Magnetic tape

Punched cards

Paper tape

Keyboard and typing device

Computer storage

Printer

Central processing input/output

Receiving or receiving-transmitting facilities

Teletype channels (low transmission rate)

Telephone channels (intermediate transmission rate)

Broad-band channels (high transmission rate)

Data transmission

Transmitting or transmitting-receiving facilities

Magnetic tape

Punched cards

Paper tape

Keyboard and typing

Computer storage

CRT display unit

Remote station input/output

Figure 6-18

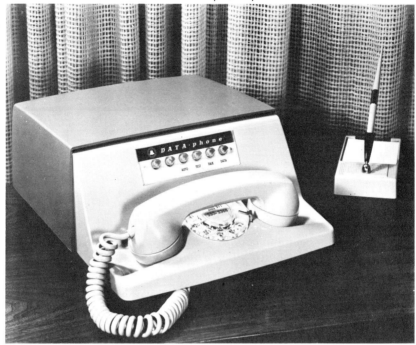

Figure 6-19. Data-Phone (Courtesy American Telephone and Telegraph)

Broad-band channels use very high-frequency electrical signals to carry the data message at maximum speeds of around 100,000 characters per second. These broad-band circuits may be groups of voice-grade wire channels, or they may be microwave radio circuits.

Such transmission facilities are expensive and are now required by only the largest companies. Broad-band facilities are used for transmitting data between magnetic tape units or from one computer storage unit to another. North American Aviation, Inc., for example, balances workloads among the computers in several divisions by transferring data from overloaded to "available-time" installations at the rate of 62,500 characters per second. And General Electric has broad-band circuits installed to connect computer centers at Schenectady and Syracuse, New York, and Valley Forge, Pennsylvania.[7]

With increased emphasis being placed on broader and faster-responding business information systems, the trend is definitely toward greater use of data transmission facilities. The American Telephone and Telegraph Company predicts that by 1970 its revenue from long-distance data transmission will *exceed* the revenue received from long-distance voice communication. And Western Union has predicted that 60 percent of the computers sold by 1975 will be linked in some way

[7] General Electric is using a Telpak service provided by the Bell Telephone System.

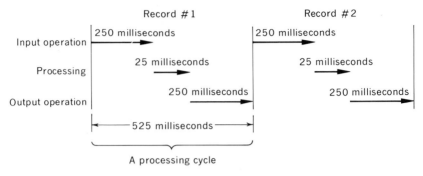

Figure 6-20. Serial (Unbuffered) Processing

to a data communications network. A considerable amount of research is being directed toward the improvement of data transmission—e.g., satellites, sometimes with laser beams, are being used to transmit data half-way round the world.

The wide range of data transmission services and the wide variety of I/O techniques present the business manager with an almost limitless number of alternatives. If he assumes that it is needed, what type of data communication would be best for his company? It is possible only to deal in generalities here, but the manager should consider the following factors in arriving at his decision:

1. *The number and location of I/O stations.* Is it necessary only to provide communication between two points, or is the scope of the data transmission operation broader? Do all stations transmit *and* receive data, or do some perform only one function?

2. *The accuracy requirements.* How accurate must the transmission be? Errors can occur. But various technical alternatives exist to achieve required degrees of reliability. A compromise between cost and accuracy is involved in the manager's decision.

3. *The volume of data to be communicated.* It is necessary to consider both the number of messages and the length of each message to arrive at the number of characters to be transmitted.

4. *The timing of messages.* Are messages transmitted at predictable intervals, or do they occur in a random manner? Are there peak load periods? If so, when? Are delays permissible — i.e., can the data load be scheduled to maintain a steady message flow and thus avoid peaks and valleys?

5. *The speed requirements.* Speed requirements are closely related to the above factors of volume and timing. Generally speaking, the greater the volume, the faster the data transmission facility must be, and the greater the cost. Of course, a faster transmission line can do more work, and thus the cost per character transmitted may well be reduced. It is obviously inefficient, however, to contract for fast facilities when the data volume and the needs of the firm could be satisfied at a slower (and less-expensive) level.

BUFFER STORAGE

We have seen that the total computer running time required to complete a task consists of input, processing, and output activities. Furthermore, processing is usually much faster than input or output. Figure 6-20 shows hypothetical time periods for each activity in the processing of a record. If the computer system performs the input-process-output cycle in a serial fashion, as shown in Figure 6-20, the system components, and especially the CPU, will be running idle much of the time. Since computer running time represents a substantial business expense, considerable attention has already been directed toward possible ways of using the system to full capacity. It was pointed out in Chapter 5, for example, that offline converters are frequently used to place data in punched card form on magnetic tape to allow faster online data input. Still, with serial processing there remains a mismatch between I/O speed and central processor capability.

Serial processing results in idle time. But why can't I/O operations be continued while computations are being made—i.e., why can't activities be performed simultaneously? The answer is that activities *can* be performed concurrently through the use of *buffer storage*. Buffer storage synchronizes the I/O devices with the processor and permits simultaneous and overlapping processing cycles.

How is this done? Let us look at Figure 6-21 for an explanation.

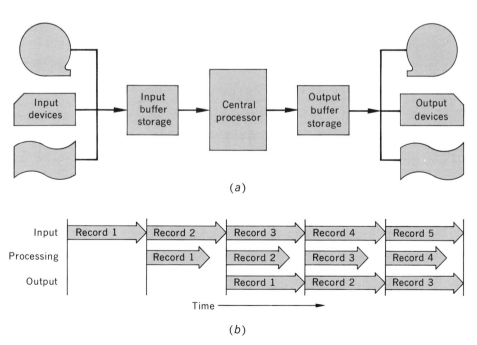

(a)

(b)

Figure 6-21. Data Buffering

Data from input equipment are fed into input buffer storage[8] as shown in Figure 6-21a. This input buffer has an important characteristic: It can accept data at slow input speeds and release them at electronic speeds. (The reverse is true of the output buffer.) The first input record is entered into the buffer and then, under program control, to the main storage unit where processing begins immediately. While the first record is being processed, the input unit is automatically reading data into buffer storage. The processed information for the first record is transferred under program control to the output buffer and then to an output device where the writing operation begins. As soon as the first record is released, the program instructs the buffer to transmit the second record for processing. Thus, at this point in time in a synchronized system,[9] record 3 is being fed into the input buffer, record 2 is being processed, and record 1 is being written by an output device (Figure 6-21b). The procedure continues until the task is finished.

Data may be fed simultaneously into buffers from a number of stations. Time sharing, of course, requires sophisticated buffering techniques. In addition to performing speed-changing and time sharing functions, buffers also help in translating the various human and machine codes into usable forms, i.e., one machine code into another, human language into machine code, or machine code into human language.

SUMMARY

Character readers offer businesses a way of reducing the manual effort involved in data input operations. Financial institutions have supported the development of MICR as a means of handling billions of transactions each year. The magnetic ink characters can be read even when they are smeared, stamped, or otherwise abused. The characters are humanly readable. Unfortunately for many firms outside the banking community, there are no alphabetic characters available in MICR. Optical character readers, however, have alphabetic as well as numeric capability and perform efficiently in a growing number of applications.

A high-speed printer is the primary output device when the information is to be used by man rather than by machine. Such printers have been improved significantly in the last decade. Character-at-a-time printers have been replaced by machines which print hundreds of lines each minute.

[8]Buffers are simply high-speed storage units. Thus, they may be found in some I/O devices; they may be obtained as separate small intermediate storage units; or they may consist of a section of the CPU main storage which has been reserved for buffering purposes.

[9]Although a *perfectly* synchronized system is rare, the use of buffering permits a much closer balance.

Console typewriters, remote inquiry stations, transaction recorders, input tablets and light pens, CRT-equipped display stations – all these online instruments – may enable man to communicate directly and randomly with any record stored in the computer. Console typewriters are used to modify and test programs and to enter and receive short messages. Inquiry stations may be similar to console typewriters but are remotely located and are commonly used in time sharing. Transaction recorders are designed to enter data directly from the point of origin, thus by-passing the need for media preparation. Visual communication devices have been used quite successfully for scientific and engineering purposes. There is an increase in the popularity of visual display stations for business purposes. Audio communication from computer to man has proven practical.

Data transmission facilities communicate information between remote points. A wide range of data transmission services is available. These services vary in data handling speed and in cost. The manager must plan carefully in choosing among the alternatives.

The use of buffer storage makes it possible for the processing system to work at or near full capacity. Buffers synchronize the I/O equipment with the CPU and permit simultaneous and overlapping processing cycles.

DISCUSSION QUESTIONS

1 Obtain a cancelled check, and explain the magnetic ink coding along the bottom of the check.

2 How do MICR reader-sorter units interpret the encoded data on checks?

3 Discuss the advantages and limitations of MICR.

4 Compare and contrast MICR and OCR.

5 Give some examples of how OCR might be used.

6 Discuss the advantages and limitations of OCR.

7 Define the following terms:
(*a*) character-at-a-time printing   (*f*) drum printer
(*b*) line-at-a-time printing   (*g*) man-machine interface
(*c*) print chain   (*h*) cathode ray tube
(*d*) impact printer   (*i*) light pen
(*e*) nonimpact printer   (*j*) data transmission

8 How may the console typewriter be used?

9 (*a*) What is the purpose of an inquiry station? (*b*) Of data collection stations? (*c*) Of display stations?

10 How may audio-response units be used? Give examples.

11 Identify and discuss the most commonly used transmission channels for carrying data from one location to another.

12 What factors should be considered by managers in determining the best means of data communication?

13 (*a*) What is buffer storage? (*b*) Explain how buffer storage permits activities to be performed simultaneously.

SELECTED REFERENCES

Richard G. Canning, "Significant Progress in Optical Scanning," *EDP Analyzer*, August, 1965.

John R. Pierce, "The Transmission of Computer Data," *Scientific American*, September, 1966, pp. 144-156.

Jacob Rabinow, "Optical Character Recognition Today," *Data Processing Magazine*, January, 1966, pp. 18-24.

F. H. Reagan, Jr., "Data Communications: What It's All About," *Data Processing Magazine*, April, 1966, pp. 20-26ff.

Norman Statland, "A Look at High-speed Printers," *Computers and Automation*, November, 1964, pp. 14-18.

Norman Statland and John Hillegass, "A Survey of Imput/Output Equipment," *Computers and Automation*, July, 1964, pp. 16-20ff.

Ivan E. Sutherland, "Computer Inputs and Outputs," *Scientific American*, September, 1966, pp. 86-96.

7. THE CENTRAL PROCESSING UNIT: I

It is now time to take a closer look at the central processor. As you will remember, the CPU contains the storage unit, the arithmetic-logic unit, and the control unit. In this chapter we shall be concerned primarily with the *storage unit and related topics*. More specifically, we shall examine (1) the *conceptual areas* of the storage unit, (2) the *locations* in the storage unit, (3) the *capacity* of storage locations, (4) the *numbering systems* associated with computers, and (5) the methods of *data representation* used. In the first part of the next chapter, we shall continue the examination of the storage unit; in the latter part we shall turn our attention to the arithmetic-logic and control units.

CONCEPTUAL STORAGE AREAS

We know that the storage unit contains the data to be processed and the program of instructions. Any storage location in the central processor has the ability to store *either* data or instructions—i.e., a specific physical space may be used to store data for one operation and instructions for another. The programmer (or the software prepared by the programmer) determines how the location will be used for each program (Figure 7-1).

For each program, there will be, typically, four areas assigned to group related types of information. These conceptual areas are shown in Figure 7-2. They are referred to as *conceptual areas* because it is important to remember that they are *not fixed* by built-in physical boundaries in storage. Rather, they vary (thus the broken lines in Figure 7-2) at the discretion of the programmer. Three of the four areas (input, working, and output) are used for *data* storage purposes. The *input storage* area, as the name indicates, receives the data coming from the input media and devices. The *working storage* space corre-

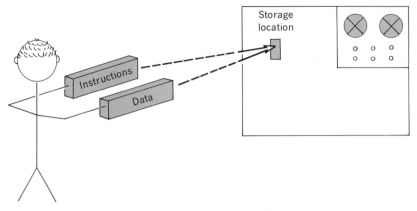

Figure 7-1. Either Data or Instructions May Be Placed in a Specific Storage Location

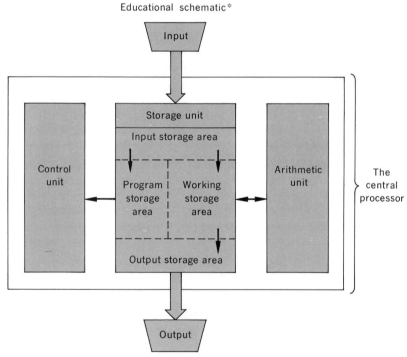

*The specific areas of storage used for a particular purpose (input storage, program storage, etc.) are not *fixed* but rather *vary* from program to program. The programmer defines the limits of these reserved areas for each of his programs. Therefore, broken lines (rather than solid ones) are used in the diagram to indicate this flexibility of area boundaries.

Figure 7-2. Conceptual Areas [Source: *Orientation to Electronic Data Processing* (Sperry Rand Corporation, UNIVAC Division, 1966), p. 64. Copyright material used through the courtesy of Sperry Rand Corporation, UNIVAC Division.]

sponds to a blackboard or a sheet of scratch paper: It is space used by the program to hold data being processed as well as the intermediate results of such processing. The *output storage* section contains processed information which is awaiting a writing (or *read-out*) operation. The *program storage* area, of course, contains the processing instructions.

A typical *data-flow* pattern is indicated in Figure 7-2. Data remain in the input area until needed. Since the actual processing occurs in the arithmetic-logic unit, data are delivered to this unit from input storage and processed, and the final results move through the output storage area to the user. Intermediate figures, generated in the arithmetic-logic unit, are temporarily placed in a designated working storage area until needed at a later time. Data may move back and forth between working storage and the arithmetic-logic unit a number of times before the processing is completed.

Instructions move from the program storage area to the control unit. The first program instruction is sent to the control unit to begin the step-by-step processing procedure. Other instructions move into the control unit at the proper time until the job is completed. Of course, the number of instructions and therefore the size of the program storage area depend on the length and complexity of the processing problem.

STORAGE LOCATIONS

The locations in the computer storage unit have been compared to such familiar things as post office boxes, hotel rooms, message boxes at hotel front desks, bins in a stock room, package deposit boxes in transportation stations, and the storage facilities of hat-check services. Figure 7-3 illustrates what each of the above things has in common— storage locations identified by a specific number and capable of holding many different items. The numbers may be post office box numbers, hotel room numbers, or part bin numbers. For example, a letter placed in a post office box yesterday may contain instructions on how to build a birdhouse; the card placed in the same box today may be an electric bill for $22.12. Instructions are stored one day and numerical quantities the next; contents change, but the box and the box number remain the same. The boxes differ only in their identification numbers.

In the computer there are also numbered storage locations for holding both data and instructions. These "boxes" or "cells" are referred to as *addresses*. Like a post office box number, the address number remains the same and is independent of the contents. But unlike a

00	01	02	03	04	05
06	07	08	09	10	11
12	13	14	15	16	17
18	19	20	21	22	23

Figure 7-3

post office box which can hold several different messages at the same time, an address stores only one unit of data at a time. The addresses in a storage unit containing 4,000 locations would be numbered from 0000 to 3999. Thus, one unique address will be designated 1776. It is necessary to emphasize that *there is an important distinction between the address number and the contents of the address.* Why is this distinction important? It is important because one of the basic principles of programming is that instructions deal directly with address numbers *rather* than with the contents of the address. For example, suppose that $155 is stored in address 1776. If the programmer wants that amount printed, he will not instruct the computer to print $155. Rather, he will order the machine to print 1776, and the computer will interpret this instruction to mean that it should *print the contents of address* 1776. Just as you can locate a friend in a strange city if you know that his home address is 4808 Hildring Drive, so too can the computer locate the desired information if it knows the location number. But it is the programmer's responsibility to keep track of the contents of each address.

Perhaps an example illustrating some of the concepts which have been introduced would be appropriate at this time. In our example let us consider a atlas aardvark. What is a atlas aardvark? Well, A. Atlas Aardvark is not a "what," he is a "who" — he is the Zoology Editor for Imprint Publishing Company. He is also the first person paid each week (Atlas has gone through life being first in line). Let's look at how his paycheck might be processed by Imprint's PAC (Peculiar Automatic Computer).

The payroll *data* are prepared on punched cards each week for each employee. Last week the following data were punched into Atlas's card: (1) he worked 40 hours; (2) he receives $5 an hour; (3) he has 20 percent of his total income taken out for taxes; and (4) he has hospitalization insurance which costs him $5 each week.

Instructions have been prepared by Imprint's programmer to direct the computer in the payroll operation. The following steps must be performed:

1. The machine must be started.

2. An employee's payroll data must be read into storage for processing.

3. Hours worked must be multiplied by the hourly rate to find the *total earnings*.

4. Total earnings must be multiplied by the withholding percentage figure to find the amount of tax deduction.

5. To the tax withheld must be added the hospitalization insurance deduction to arrive at the *total deduction* figure.

6. The total deduction must be subtracted from the total earnings to find the take-home earnings.

7. A check must be printed for the amount of the take-home earnings, and it must be made payable to the correct employee.

8. The machine must be stopped at the end of the processing operation.

Program instructions are also presented to the PAC in the form of punched cards.

Figure 7-4 shows the PAC storage locations. Although the programmer may assign the instructions to *any section* of the storage unit, he has chosen to read them into addresses 06 through 17. These locations thus become the *program storage* area. His first instruction (in address 06) identifies the locations for the payroll data (00, 01, 02, 03, and 04). The data could just as well have been placed in addresses 18 through 22; so this is also an arbitrary decision.[1]

Let us use Figure 7-5 to follow through the process which is required to prepare Atlas's paycheck. (The circled address numbers represent each step in the process.) After the programmer has loaded the instructions into storage, he places the payroll data cards into the card

---

[1] Obviously, the data could not go into addresses 06 through 17 since these locations are now occupied by instructions. If a payroll item were mistakenly entered into a program section location, it would "erase" the instruction properly located in the address. At some later time the item would enter the control unit where it would be interpreted as an instruction. If such an error should occur, the result would be quite unpredictable but invariably disastrous.

00	01	02	03	04	05
06 Read payroll data card into addresses 00, 01, 02, 03, and 04.	07 Write contents of address 01 into arithmetic unit.	08 Multiply contents of arithmetic unit by contents of address 02.	09 Duplicate preceding answer in address 05.	10 Multiply contents of address 03 by preceding answer in arithmetic unit.	11 Add contents of address 04 to preceding answer in arithmetic unit.
12 Subtract preceding answer in arithmetic unit from contents of address 05.	13 Move preceding answer to address 23.	14 Write check for amount in address 23.	15 Make check payable to contents of address 00.	16 If last card, stop processing.	17 Go to address 06.
18	19	20	21	22	23

Figure 7-4. PAC Storage

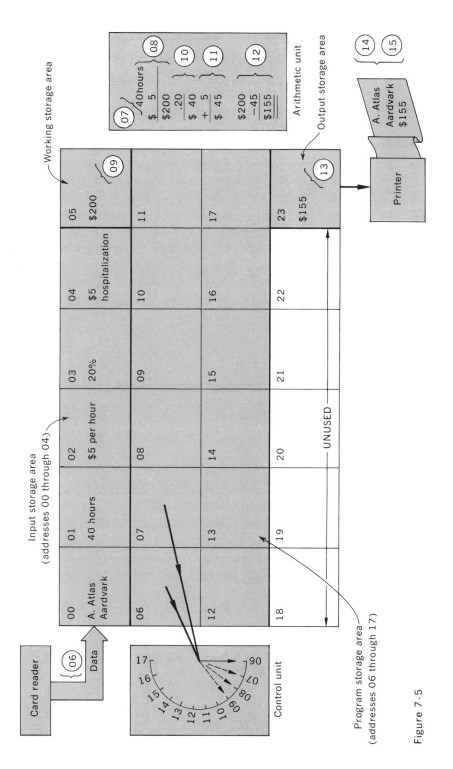

Figure 7-5

129

reader and sets the PAC controls to begin the processing at address 06, and the processing begins. This initial control setting feeds the first instruction into the control unit where it is interpreted. Signals are sent to the card reader, which carries out the command. Atlas's card is read, and the data are transferred to *input storage*. The control unit will execute the instructions automatically *in sequence* after the initial control setting until it is directed by a specific instruction to do otherwise. Therefore, as soon as the instruction in address 06 has been complied with, the control unit automatically begins interpreting the contents of address 07.

The next command instructs the control unit to copy the contents of address 01 into the arithmetic-logic unit. The control unit is not interested that the contents of 01 are 40 hours (the next employee's time may differ). It is merely concerned with carrying out orders; so 40 hours is placed in the arithmetic unit. And, in sequence, the processing continues: The 40-hour figure is multiplied by $5 per hour to find total earnings (instruction in address 08); this total earnings figure is duplicated (instruction, 09) in address 05, which is the *working storage* area; the tax deduction is found to be $40 (instruction, 10); the total deduction figure is $45 (instruction, 11); and Atlas's take-home pay is $155 (instruction, 12). The $155 is transferred to address 23 by the next order in the sequence. (It could just as easily have been placed in any of the unused locations.) From this *output storage* area, the information is sent to the printer, which, under program control, prints the paycheck. If Atlas's card had been the last one in the deck, the instruction in address 16 would have halted the process. Since other cards follow, however, the control unit receives the next order in the sequence. This instruction tells the control unit to reset itself to address 06. And so the process automatically begins again.

To summarize, several important concepts have been demonstrated in this example:

1. Input, working, output, and program storage areas are required, but they are not fixed in the PAC. Rather, they are determined by Imprint's programmer, and he had considerable freedom in the way in which he positioned the data and instructions.

2. The PAC is able to obey several *commands*, e.g., READ, WRITE, ADD, SUBTRACT, MULTIPLY, MOVE, GO TO. This ability to execute specific orders is *designed and built into* the machine. Every computer has a particular set or *repertoire* of commands which it is able to obey. Small computers may have only a few basic commands in their repertoires, while large machines have 100 or more.

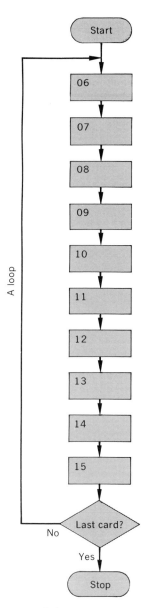

Figure 7-6

3. The output information desired by managers is produced by manipulating the facts and figures held in the storage locations. But the *instructions* which produce this output deal directly with the address numbers in the processing rather than with the contents of the addresses.

4. Computers execute one instruction at a time. They follow sequentially the series of directions until explicitly told to do otherwise. Figure 7-6 is a

diagram or *flowchart* of the payroll procedure. The computer moves through the instructions in sequence until it comes to a *branchpoint* and is required to answer a question: Have data from the last card been fed into storage? The answer to the question determines which path or branch the computer will follow. If the answer is no, then the procedure is automatically repeated by the use of the technique known as *looping*; if the answer is yes the processing stops.

CAPACITY OF STORAGE LOCATIONS

Up to this point we have not bothered to define the storage capacity of *each address*. All we have said is that an address holds a specific unit of data. Actually, the storage capacity of an address is *built into* the machine. In some machines each address may contain only a *single character* (9, A, $, *). These systems are said to be *character addressable*. Other machines are designed to store a *fixed number of characters* in each address (JONES, XY1234, GO TO 06). These characters are treated as a single entity or unit—i.e., the computer treats them as a single data *word* or instruction *word*. Thus, machines designed to store a specified number of characters in an address are said to be *word addressable*. Figure 7-7 shows character-addressable and word-addressable storage. Character-addressable machines, on the one hand, are said to have *variable word-length storage*. Word-addressable machines, on the other hand, are said to have *fixed word-length storage*.

Perhaps an example will help clarify the differences between fixed and variable word-length storage. Let us assume that we are again going to place payroll data into PAC storage. The following data concern Mr. Bill ("Crab") Grass, the Botany Editor at Imprint Publishing Company:

Employee	Hours worked	Hourly rate	Tax deduction	Hospitalization
Bill Grass	40	$4	15%	$5

Is PAC a fixed or a variable word-length machine? For illustration purposes only, we shall consider it to be both (after all, it is a Peculiar product).

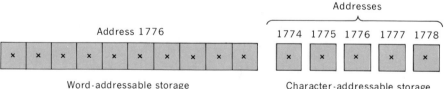

Word-addressable storage   Character-addressable storage

Figure 7-7

Address 00	B	I	L	L		G	R	A	S	S
Address 01									4	0
Address 02								4	0	0
Address 03									1	5
Address 04								5	0	0

(*a*)

	0	1	2	3	4	5	6	7	8	9
0	B	I	L	L		G	R	A	S	S
1	4	0	4	0	0	1	5	5	0	0
2										
3							Y			
4					X					

(*b*)

Figure 7-8. (*a*) Fixed Word-length Storage; (*b*) Variable Word-length Storage

Fixed word-length storage

We shall assume that each PAC address will store 10 characters.[2] Figure 7-8*a* shows how the payroll data might be organized in storage. Addresses 00 through 04 are used. Figure 7-8*a* also shows a disadvantage of fixed word-length storage. Each word must be 10 characters long, and these 10 characters must be moved and operated on as a unit. If, as in address 01, only two characters are needed, the other eight spaces in the word will be filled with zeroes or will be blank.[3]

Variable word-length storage

To realize more efficient use of storage space, variable word-length machines were developed for business purposes. Figure 7-8*b* shows how the payroll data might be stored if PAC were a variable word-length computer. Space to store 30 additional characters is now available. Each space has an address. The intersections of the numbers at the top and in the column to the left designate the address numbers.

[2] The number of characters which various machines can store depends on the machine design. Ten characters has been arbitrarily selected, although 10 is a common fixed word length.

[3] It is possible for a programmer to *pack* several data items into a single fixed-length word by using proper instructions. Of course, extra steps are required in the processing.

134

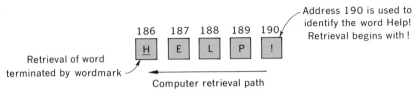

Figure 7-9

The name "Bill," for example, is stored in addresses 00, 01, 02, and 03. The letters X and Y have been placed in addresses 44 and 36 respectively to show the addressing approach.

The underlining marks in addresses 00, 10, 12, 15, and 17 represent *wordmarks* which have been placed there by the programmer. Although the marks may be viewed by us as the leftmost position or the beginning of each word, since we customarily read from left to right, to some popular business computers (e.g., the Honeywell 200 and the IBM 1401) the marks represent the end or *termination* of a word. Just as you move from right to left in adding columns of figures, so too do many computers move from right to left when processing a word.

How can a variable word-length computer *identify* the particular word it is seeking? With all fixed word-length computers this must be done by referring to an address number. But in a variable word-length machine a 10-character word (Bill Grass) has 10 addresses! The use of the wordmark resolves the dilemma. If the computer *stops* processing a word when the presence of a wordmark is sensed, what address number must be used to identify the beginning of that word? The answer obviously is the rightmost[4] address in the word or field.[5] Figure 7-9 shows how a *data word* is retrieved from storage for printing purposes. The command is the *instruction word* "PRINT 190." The machine automatically moves from address 190 serially to the left until a wordmark is encountered. The same command—PRINT 190— in a word-addressable machine would yield the same results (assuming that HELP! was located in that address) except that the machine would retrieve all the characters as a single unit.

---

[4] Other hardware will, of course, vary in design. For example, the IBM System/360 equipment uses the *leftmost* address in the word. And in place of a wordmark, an instruction to retrieve or transfer a particular data word would specify the *number* of addresses in that word.

[5] You will recall from Chap. 3 that punched cards are laid out in fields for business applications. These fields are established by the application designer and may vary in width from 1 column to 80. A variable word-length computer might just as easily have been termed a "variable field-length machine"—there is little or no distinction between the terms in this situation.

A comparison

To review our understanding of the above paragraphs, let us compare fixed and variable word-length storage systems:

1. *Storage efficiency.* Generally speaking, variable word-length equipment makes the most efficient use of available space for business purposes.

2. *Internal data transfer.* Depending upon the computer, data are transferred or retrieved a character at a time or a word at a time.

3. *Arithmetic speed.* Variable word-length machines perform arithmetic operations in a *serial* fashion, i.e., one position at a time. For example, when two 4-digit numbers are added, four steps are required. Fixed word-length computers, however, are classified as *parallel* calculators — i.e., they can add any two data words in a *single* step without regard to the number of digits in the words. Obviously, then, fixed word-length machines have faster calculating capability. But this faster speed must be paid for, since the necessary circuitry is more complex and thus more expensive.

4. *Size and usage.* The most popular small- and middle-sized business computers are generally variable word-length machines. This is not surprising if you remember that business applications place greater emphasis on I/O speed and storage capacity than on speed of computation. Variable word-length machines give managers what they want at the least possible cost. Large-scale computers use fixed word-length storage. These machines are typically used, at least part time and often exclusively, for scientific purposes, and such applications require the faster calculating and data transfer speeds provided.

It is apparent that each method of organizing the storage unit has advantages and drawbacks. It is interesting to note, however, that some third-generation compatible machines have been designed so that instructions may be used to obtain the advantages of both fixed and variable word-length storage.

Regardless of whether each address contains a single data character or a data or instruction word consisting of numbers, letters, special characters, or some combination, these facts must be in the coded form that the computer can use.

COMPUTER NUMBERING SYSTEMS

The business computer represents data in a code that is related to a *binary numbering system.* It is thus necessary to understand numbering systems. In the first part of this section we shall review the familiar decimal system in order to present certain basic concepts. We shall follow this presentation with a discussion (1) of binary numbers, (2) of binary arithmetic, (3) of octal numbers, and (4) of a binary coded decimal system.

DECIMAL TO BINARY CONVERSOM

$11_{10} = 1011_2$

Decimal numbers

We tend to take the decimal numbering system for granted because of the years of close association with it. Yet man existed on earth for centuries without it. The first systems were of an *additive* nature. That is, they consisted of symbols such as | for one, ‖ for two, ‖| for three, etc. Each symbol represented the *same value* regardless of the position it occupied in the number. Early Hebrew, Greek, and Egyptian numbers were additive. Roman numerals are also essentially additive. As you know, the symbol V represents the decimal 5 and does not change in value (even though its position changes) in the following numbers: V, VI, VII, and VIII(VI = V + I; VII = V + I + I; etc.). As Thomas Bartee writes:[6]

The only importance of position in Roman numerals lies in whether a symbol precedes or follows another symbol (IV = 4, while VI = 6). The clumsiness of this system can easily be seen if we try to multiply XII by XIV. Calculating with Roman numerals was so difficult that early mathematicians were forced to perform arithmetic operations almost entirely on abaci or counting boards, translating their results back into Roman-number form. Pencil and paper computations are unbelievably intricate and difficult in such systems. In fact, the ability to perform such operations as addition and multiplication was considered a great accomplishment in earlier civilizations.

Youngsters today can calculate answers to problems which would have baffled wise men of earlier centuries. A big factor in this advancement has been the development of *positional* numbering systems. In such systems there are only a limited number of symbols, and the symbols represent different values according to the position they occupy in the number (5 = V, but 51 does not equal VI because the meaning of 5 has changed with the change in its position). The number of symbols used depends on the *base* or *radix* of the particular system. The decimal system, of course, has a base of 10 and has 10 symbols (0 through 9). The *highest* numerical symbol will always have a value of 1 *less* than the base.

There is nothing particularly sacred about a base of 10. Probably the only reason it was originally developed and is now in widespread use is that man happens to have 10 fingers. Other systems have been created. For example, the Babylonians had a base of 60 (of course, they also did their writing on mud pies); the Mayas of Yucatán used a base of 20 (a warm climate and a group of barefooted mathematicians?); and a base of five is still used by natives in New Hebrides

[6] Thomas C. Bartee, *Digital Computer Fundamentals* (2d ed.; New York: McGraw-Hill Book Company, 1966), p. 40.

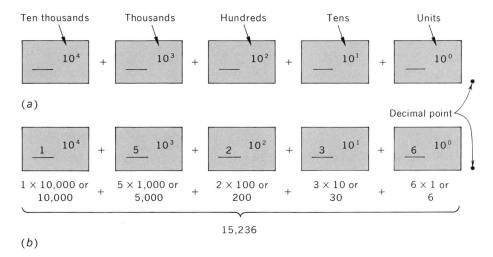

Figure 7-10

(one hand is wrapped around a spear and is thus not available for counting?). The Duodecimal Society of America advocates a change from base 10 to a radix of 12. It is pointed out in support of their position that not only would computations be easier since 12 is divisible by 2, 3, 4, and 6, but also such a base is compatible with inches in a foot, numbers in a dozen, etc.

By the arrangement of the numerical symbols[7] in various positions, any number may be represented. We know that in the decimal system each successive position to the left of the decimal point represents units, tens, hundreds, thousands, ten thousands, etc. We sometimes fail to remember, however, that what this means is that each position represents a particular *power* of the base. Figure 7-10*a* points out this characteristic. The digits of any number that might be placed in the blank spaces would be multiplied by an appropriate power of 10 to arrive at the total value. For example, the number 15,236 is shown in Figure 7-10*b* to represent the sum of

$$(\underline{1} \times 10^4) + (\underline{5} \times 10^3) + (\underline{2} \times 10^2) + (\underline{3} \times 10^1) + (\underline{6} \times 10^0).[8]$$

In *any* positional numbering system, *the value of each position represents a specific power of the base.* To test your understanding

[7] There is also nothing sacred about the shape of the symbols we use to represent quantities. We know that the symbol "2" has a certain meaning, but any number of other marks could be defined to serve the same purpose. A version of the Arabic numerals we use is thought to have originated in India around 200 B.C.

[8] Students occasionally forget their algebra and have to be reminded that n^0 is, by definition, 1; i.e., any number raised to the zero power equals 1.

of the concepts which have now been introduced, let us look at the following problems:

1. What is the decimal equivalent of 463_8? (The subscript 8 following the number 463 indicates that this is an *octal* base number.) Since the *base* is *now eight* rather than 10, the possible symbols are 0 through 7 (the symbols 8 and 9 do not exist in this case). Each position in the number 463_8 represents a power of its base. Therefore,

$$(\underline{4} \times 8^2) + (\underline{6} \times 8^1) + (\underline{3} \times 8^0). \longleftarrow \text{octal point}$$

   or $(4 \times 64) + (6 \times 8) + (3 \times 1).$

   or $(256) + (48) + (3). = 307_{10}$ the decimal equivalent

2. What is the decimal equivalent of 4221_5? (We have now shifted to a base-five numbering system.) The possible symbols in base five are 0 through 4. Each position in the number 4221_5 represents a power of its base. Therefore,

$$(\underline{4} \times 5^3) + (\underline{2} \times 5^2) + (\underline{2} \times 5^1) + (\underline{1} \times 5^0). \longleftarrow \text{quinary point}$$

   or $(4 \times 125) + (2 \times 25) + (2 \times 5) + (1 \times 1).$

   or $(500) + (50) + (10) + (1). = 561_{10}$ the decimal equivalent

3. What is the decimal equivalent of 1001_2? (We are now using a base of two.) With a base of two, the only possible symbols are 0 and 1. Again, each position in the number 1001_2 represents a power of its base. Therefore,

$$(\underline{1} \times 2^3) + (\underline{0} \times 2^2) + (\underline{0} \times 2^1) + (\underline{1} \times 2^0). \longleftarrow \text{binary point}$$

   or $(1 \times 8) + (0 \times 4) + (0 \times 2) + (1 \times 1).$

   or $(8) + (0) + (0) + (1). = 9_{10}$ the decimal equivalent

We now have progressed downward in this section from a numbering system using a base of 10 to one using a base of two. We might just as easily have moved in the other direction. What have these problems demonstrated? For one thing, we have seen that the lower the numbering base, the fewer the possible symbols which must be remembered. And with fewer symbols, there are smaller multiplication tables and fewer addition facts to memorize. But, as we have also seen, the smaller the base, the more positions there must be to represent a given quantity. Four digits (1001) are required in base two to equal a single decimal digit (9). You may also have observed that the decimal point becomes the "octal point" in a base-eight system, the "quinary point" in base five, and the "binary point" in base two.[9] It would thus appear that we have sneaked up on the *binary* or *base-two* numbering system used by digital computers.

---

[9]The point, of course, merely serves to separate the whole from the fractional part of a number. It may be called the "radix point" or the "real point" regardless of the numbering system being used.

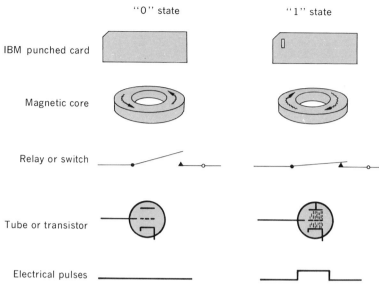

Figure 7-11. (Courtesy IBM Corporation)

Binary numbers

It was pointed out in Chapter 2 that Dr. John von Neumann suggested in a paper written in 1945 that binary numbering systems be incorporated in computers. Although the paper came too late to prevent the very first machines from using the decimal system, von Neumann's suggestions were quickly adopted in subsequent designs.[10]

Why the rush to binary? There are several very good reasons:

1. It is necessary that circuitry be designed only to handle two binary digits (bits) rather than 10. Design is simplified;[11] cost is reduced; performance is improved.

2. Electronic components, by their very nature, operate in a binary mode. As Figure 7-11 demonstrates, a switch is either open (0 state) or closed (1 state); a tube or transistor either is not conducting (0) or is (1); electrical pulses are either absent (0) or present (1); and small magnetizable rings are magnetized to represent either 0 or 1.

---

[10] The pioneering work in binary numbers was done by the German mathematician Gottfried Leibniz (1646 - 1716). Leibniz, in addition to being an inventor of the calculus, was also known to have suggested that binary rather than decimal arithmetic be taught in the schools. He would have approved of "new math" which does introduce public school children to binary numbers.

[11] The binary system is quite adaptable to the Boolean algebra concepts used in computer design.

140

Base 2	Base 5	Base 8	Base 10
0	0	0	0
1	1	1	1
10	2	2	2
11	3	3	3
100	4	4	4
101	10	5	5
110	11	6	6
111	12	7	7
1000	13	10	8
1001	14	11	9
1010	20	12	10
1011	21	13	11
1100	22	14	12
1101	23	15	13
—	—	—	14
—	—	—	15
—	—	—	16

Figure 7-12. Equivalent Numbers

3. Everything that can be done with a base of 10 can be done with the binary system.

Binary counting begins, just as with any number base, with 0 followed by 1. But now we have run out of symbols. How do we represent 2 when there is no such symbol? Just as we represent the next highest value in any base when we have used our highest number in the first position to the left of the real point, we use a zero place marker in the first position and put the next lowest symbol in the next position to the left. Thus, 2 in decimal is the same as 10 in binary. Or,

$$(\underline{1} \times 2^1) + (\underline{0} \times 2^0).$$
$$(2) + (0) = 2_{10}$$

Of course, 10_2 *is not pronounced ten*, for it is certainly not what we have been taught to associate with the word "ten." Names such as "toon" and "twin" have been given to 10_2, but they have not caught on. Perhaps "one zero" is as good a name as any.

Binary to decimal conversion The important thing to remember in counting in the binary system is that the place positions, instead of representing units, tens, hundreds, thousands, etc., now represent unit, 2, 4, 8, 16, 32, etc. Thus, the decimal value of 110011_2 is:

Power of base	2^7	2^6	2^5	2^4	2^3	2^2	2^1	2^0
Decimal equivalent	128	64	32	16	8	4	2	1
Binary number			1	1	0	0	1	1

Or $32 + 16 + 2 + 1 = 51_{10}$

To test your understanding of counting in various bases, see if you can fill in the blanks in Figure 7-12.

Decimal to binary conversion We have been converting binary numbers to their decimal equivalents. Let us now, by means of a *remainder method*, perform the reverse operation—i.e., let's convert a decimal number into binary form. For illustration purposes, the number 250_{10} is chosen. The conversion procedure simply consists of dividing the original decimal number by 2 and all successive answers by 2 until the process can continue no further. The binary value is read from the successive remainder values. For example,

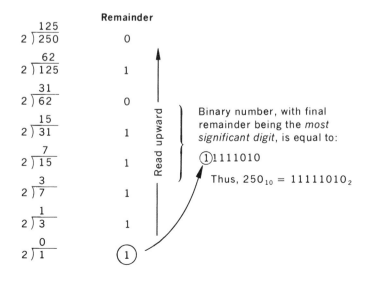

We may test the accuracy of this method by converting the binary number back to decimal form.

Power of the base	2^7	2^6	2^5	2^4	2^3	2^2	2^1	2^0
Decimal equivalent	128	64	32	16	8	4	2	1
Binary number	1	1	1	1	1	0	1	0

Or $128 + 64 + 32 + 16 + 8 + 2 = 250_{10}$

Binary arithmetic[12]

Addition   Binary arithmetic is simplicity itself. There are only four addition rules to remember:

$$0 + 0 = 0$$
$$1 + 0 = 1$$
$$0 + 1 = 1$$
$$1 + 1 = 0 \quad \text{and "carry" a 1}$$

We may demonstrate these rules by adding the binary equivalents of 15 and 10:

```
"carries" ──────▶  111
                  1111  = (15₁₀)
                  1010  = (10₁₀)
                 11001  = (25₁₀?)
```

In the first column, $1 + 0$ is 1, so we bring down that value and move to column two. There $1 + 1$ is 10, so we put down the 0 in the answer and carry the 1 to column three. In column three, the 1 carried plus the 1 in the column is again 10, so we repeat the previous step. In column four, the 1 carried plus the 1 in the top number is 10, necessitating a carry. The 1 in the bottom number plus the 0 is 1, which is put in the answer. A fifth column has the carried 1, so it is brought down to the answer. A check may be made by converting the binary value of the answer into decimal form. Does it equal 25?

Multiplication   Multiplication tables in base two are the answer to a third-grader's prayers:

$$0 \times 0 = 0$$
$$0 \times 1 = 0$$
$$1 \times 0 = 0$$
$$1 \times 1 = 1$$

[12] This discussion of binary arithmetic, and the treatment of octal numbers which follows, may be omitted without loss of continuity.

Let's multiply the following binary values:

$$
\begin{array}{r}
1101 = (13_{10}) \\
\times\,101 = (\ 5_{10}) \\
\hline
1101 \\
1101 \\
1111 \\
\hline
1000001 = (65_{10}?)
\end{array}
$$

"carries" $\longrightarrow$ 1111

As you can see, multiplication quickly becomes a problem in addition after you observe the customary procedure for arranging partial products. Does the answer equal 65_{10}?

Subtraction Subtraction is done by a method known as *complementation*. This approach may be used with *any* positional numbering system. To explain complementation, we shall follow a three-step procedure.

The *first step* in the procedure is to complement the subtrahend (the number being subtracted). This sounds grim, but it is really quite simple. The complement of a particular digit is found by subtracting that digit from another value which is *one less than the base*.[13] For example, the complement of the decimal 6 is 3 (6 is subtracted from 9 which is one less than the base of 10). The complement of the decimal number 3,540 is

```
  9999
- 3540
  6459
```

Once the subtrahend is complemented, the *second step* is to *add* the complemented number to the minuend. As a decimal example, let us subtract 3,540 (subtrahend) from 8,261 (minuend). As we have just seen, the complement of 3,540 is 6,459. Thus, we *add* this value to the minuend as follows:

```
  8,261
+ 6,459
 14,720
```

The *third step* is to perform the "*end-around carry*." Although this sounds like a football play, it merely means that the digit in the most significant position is moved and added to the value of the least significant digit. For example,

[13] A radix complement rather than the radix-minus-one complement may be used for subtraction purposes. The radix-minus-one approach is the more common.

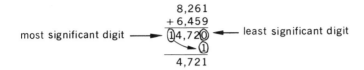

Thus, the answer to our problem (8,261 less 3,540) is 4,721 by the complementation method. (Does this check with traditional methods of subtraction?)

Now let us follow the same three steps to solve a binary problem. We shall subtract from 110101 (53_{10}) the value 101011 (43_{10}) as follows:

1. The first step is to complement the subtrahend. Since the base is now two, we shall subtract each value in the subtrahend from 1. That is,

        111111
      − 101011
        010100

   Notice, however, that all we have done is change the 1s in the subtrahend to 0s and the 0s to 1s. Thus, all the computer needs to do to the subtrahend is replace 1s with 0s and vice versa and then add. (If by now you have come to the conclusion that about all a computer basically does is add, you are correct.)

2. The second step is to add the complemented subtrahend to the minuend:

        110101
      + 010100
       1001001

3. The third step is to perform the end-around carry operation:

        110101
      + 010100
      ⓵001001   Is the problem answer of 1010 correct? Convert the
         ➛⓵   answer to a decimal figure to see.
        1010

It is as simple as that. Division basically involves repeated shifting and subtraction, and we need not be concerned with it here.

Octal numbers

Humans use decimal numbers; computers use the two binary digits. The octal (base-eight) numbering system possesses properties that make it a valuable shorthand or intermediate system. Programmers (and especially those programming on scientific machines) use it to help bridge the gap between decimal and binary. In fact, there are desk calculators for programmers which operate in the octal mode. The helpful properties of the octal system are:

1. Octal numbers (0 through 7) resemble decimal numbers more closely than do binary representations.

2. It is often quicker to convert a number from a decimal base to an octal base and then to binary (and vice versa) than it is to shift directly from decimal to binary.

3. It is much easier to convert numbers between binary and octal than it is to shift between binary and decimal.

We have seen earlier that to move from *octal to decimal* one need only convert the octal number into units, 8s, 64s, etc. The number 661_8 corresponds to 433_{10} ($\underline{6} \times 8^2 + \underline{6} \times 8^1 + \underline{1} \times 8^0$). But how do we move from *decimal to the octal* equivalent? We simply use the remainder method in the same way we did to convert decimal to binary, except that now we divide successively by 8 rather than by 2. To demonstrate, let's convert 433_{10} back to octal:

$$\begin{array}{r} 54 \\ \hline 8\,)\,433 \end{array} \qquad \text{Remainder} \quad 1$$

$$\begin{array}{r} 6 \\ \hline 8\,)\,54 \end{array} \qquad \qquad 6 \qquad \text{Again, the final remainder is the most significant digit.}$$

$$\begin{array}{r} 0 \\ \hline 8\,)\,6 \end{array} \qquad \qquad 6 \qquad \qquad 661_8 = 433_{10}$$

Obviously, there are fewer division steps required in moving from decimal to octal than there would be in converting directly to binary. But octal is also convenient because of its simple relationship to binary. (The base eight is a power of the base two—$8 = 2^3$—and one octal digit is always equal to three binary bits.) To convert from octal to binary (or vice versa), one need only determine the three-bit binary representation for each octal digit. These three-bit binary values are as follows:

Binary Octal

Binary		Octal
000	=	0
001	=	1
010	=	2
011	=	3
100	=	4
101	=	5
110	=	6
111	=	7

Decimal digit	Place value			
	8	4	2	1
0	0	0	0	0
1	0	0	0	1
2	0	0	1	0
3	0	0	1	1
4	0	1	0	0
5	0	1	0	1
6	0	1	1	0
7	0	1	1	1
8	1	0	0	0
9	1	0	0	1

Figure 7-13. Binary Coded Decimal
Numeric Bit Configurations

Therefore, to convert from *octal to binary* is as simple as this:[14]

$$\underbrace{7}_{111} \quad \underbrace{2}_{010} \quad \underbrace{5}_{101} \qquad \text{or} \qquad 725_8 = 111010101_2$$

And converting from *binary to octal* is equally simple. We merely divide the bits into groups of three, beginning at the binary point. For example, 1001100101, when properly divided, becomes 1/001/ 100/101, and this is quickly found to be 1145_8. In both cases the decimal equivalent is 613.

Binary coded decimal system

Up to this point we have been discussing "pure" binary numbers. Although computers designed for scientific purposes may use pure binary in their operations, business machines use some *coded or modified* version of pure binary to represent decimal numbers internally. Numerous data representation formats have been developed. The most

[14] You can verify the figures by converting both bases to decimal. The common decimal value is 469.

popular for business purposes, however, are the $\underline{binary}$ $\underline{coded}$ $\underline{decimal}$ or *BCD* codes.

With BCD it is possible to convert *each* decimal digit into its binary equivalent rather than to convert the entire decimal number into a pure binary form. The BCD equivalent of each possible decimal digit is shown in Figure 7-13. Because the digits 8 and 9 require four bits, *all* decimal digits are represented by four bits. Let us now see how much easier it is to work with BCD by converting 405_{10} into *both* BCD and straight binary:

405_{10} in BCD = 0100/0000/0101 or 010000000101

$$\underbrace{}_{4} \quad \underbrace{}_{0} \quad \underbrace{}_{5}$$

405_{10} in pure binary:

```
                        Remainder
          202
       2) 405              1   ⎞
          101                  ⎟
       2) 202              0   ⎟
           50                  ⎟
       2) 101              1   ⎟
           25                  ⎟
       2)  50              0   ⎟
           12                  ⎟
       2)  25              1   ⎬ = 110010101
            6                  ⎟
       2)  12              0   ⎟
            3                  ⎟
       2)   6              0   ⎟
            1                  ⎟
       2)   3              1   ⎟
            0                  ⎟
       2)   1              1   ⎠
```

With four bits there are 16 different possible configurations (2^4). The first 10 of these configurations are, of course, used to represent decimal digits. The other six arrangements (1010, 1011, 1100, 1101, 1110, and 1111) have decimal values from 10 to 15. These six arrangements are *not used* in BCD coding—i.e., 1111 *does not* represent 15_{10} in BCD. Rather, the proper BCD code for 15_{10} is 0001/0101. The "extra" six configurations are used by programmers for other purposes which we need not dwell on here.

We have seen that BCD is a convenient and fast way to convert numbers from decimal to binary. But it is hardly sufficient for busi-

Check bit	Zone bits		Numeric bits			
C	B	A	8	4	2	1

Figure 7-14. (Courtesy IBM Corporation)

ness purposes to have only 16 characters available. The following section explains how additional characters are represented in the central processor.

COMPUTER DATA REPRESENTATION

Instead of using four bits with only 16 possible characters, equipment designers commonly use *six bits* to represent characters in an *alphanumeric version of BCD*. Since the four BCD *numeric* place positions (1, 2, 4, and 8) are retained, this alphanumeric version is also frequently referred to as "BCD." To the four BCD positions are added two *zone* positions. With six bits it is thus possible to represent 64 different characters (2^6). A seventh parity-checking position is commonly added (Figure 7-14). We have already seen examples of alphanumeric BCD code being used to represent data in paper and magnetic tape. Now that the binary numbering system has been introduced it becomes clearer why the bottom rows of tape are labeled 8, 4, 2, and 1. These values merely represent positions to the left of the binary point. It was pointed out in the discussion of magnetic tape coding that the decimal 7 is represented by an on condition in the numeric channels marked 4, 2, and 1. It is now apparent that being "on" means that a 1 bit is represented in these positions, i.e., that $7 = 0111$ in BCD.

Data are generally stored internally by the use of tiny doughnut-shaped "cores" which may be magnetized in either of two directions.[15] These cores are thus capable of representing a 1 or a 0. Seven cores, stacked in a vertical column, may be used to represent a number, letter, or special character. Figure 7-15 shows how the decimal 7 is represented. An imaginary line passes through the cores. The shaded cores are magnetized in a direction which corresponds to a 1 bit. Like a switch, they may be considered in an on state. The unshaded cores are in an off state and represent a 0 bit. The A and B cores are the zone cores. A combination of zone (A, B) and numeric (8, 4, 2, and 1) cores may be used to represent alphabetic and special char-

[15] We shall have more to say about core storage in the next chapter.

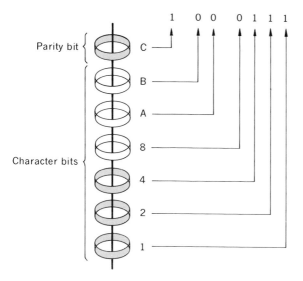

Figure 7-15. Alphanumeric BCD Character Location

acters just as they do in tape coding. The parity check core is also shown in the on state, indicating that even parity is used in this particular code. Figure 7-16 shows how, with the use of even parity, other selected characters may be represented in internal storage. Ignoring the parity check, you should be able to pick up the pattern and determine the codes for the letters D, E, F, M, N, and O.[16]

The six bits permit 64 different coding arrangements. This number is sufficient to code the decimal digits (10), capital letters (26), and a number of punctuation marks and machine control characters. Six bits are *not sufficient*, however, to provide lowercase letters, capital letters, and a greatly expanded number of special characters.

To permit greater flexibility in data representation, equipment designers have *extended* the six-bit alphanumeric BCD code to *eight bits*. With eight character bits it is possible to provide 256 different coding arrangements (2^8). Each eight-bit unit of information is called a *byte*. Bytes may be used to represent a single character, or the programmer may use the eight cores to "pack" two decimal digits into one byte.

Figure 7-17 shows the eight-bit Extended Binary Coded Decimal Interchange Code (EBCDIC) developed by IBM and used in that firm's

---

[16] These codes are: D = 11 0100; E = 11 0101; F = 11 0110; M = 10 0100; N = 10 0101; and O = 10 0110.

150

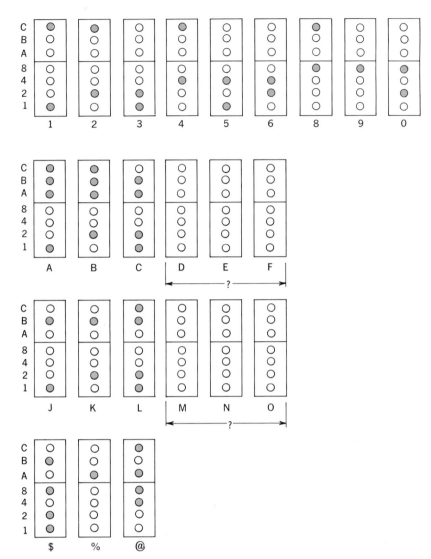

Figure 7-16. Alphanumeric BCD Internal Representation

System/360 family of computers.[17] The two leftmost bit positions in
the code are labeled "0" and "1" and are shown at the top of the
tables. The next two bit places in the code are also at the top of the
tables, while the last four bit positions are found in the vertical
columns to the left. Punctuation marks and control characters are
shown in the left table; alphanumeric characters are represented in

[17] Another expanded code is the American Standard Code for Information Interchange
(ASCII). Future data codes will most likely be either EBCDIC or ASCII (pronounced "askey").

the right. In the example box at the bottom of the figure we see how to use the code. An uppercase R is coded as:

$$\underbrace{11}_{01}\ \underbrace{01}_{23}\ \underbrace{1001}_{4567}$$

(Look up R in the right-hand table, and prove this representation.) Since all possible eight-bit combinations have not been assigned, EBCDIC provides room for future code expansion as needed.

SUMMARY

Storage locations may contain either data or instructions. For each program, data are typically stored in three conceptual areas — the input storage area, the working storage area, and the output storage area. Instructions are held in a program storage area. These areas are assigned by the programmer and vary in size and location depending upon the particular job being processed.

Locations in storage are identified by address numbers. The programmer (or software prepared by programmers) keeps track of address contents, because when instructions are written to manipulate these contents, they must indicate in some way the address locations. The programmer has a fixed number of instruction commands at his disposal. These commands are built into the particular machine being used. When running a program, the programmer sets the machine at the first instruction, and it then follows sequentially the series of directions until told to do otherwise.

Each address may contain either a single character or a word consisting of a fixed number of characters. Character-addressable machines also store words (fields), but instead of being fixed in length, these words are of variable length. Fixed word-length computers perform computations faster than variable word-length equipment and are therefore preferred in scientific installations. Most large-scale computers are organized with fixed word-length capability. Since calculations represent a lesser part of the business processing job, small- and medium-sized business computers are generally of variable word-length design for more efficient storage utilization.

Binary numbers are used to simplify computer design and to take advantage of the two states that electronic components may be in. Scientific computers may use a straight binary means of representing data. Business computers, on the other hand, use a binary-related code to designate numbers, letters, and special characters. Six-bit character codes are a popular means of representing alphanumeric data. Such codes are often alphanumeric versions of the four-bit binary coded decimal system. The six bits plus a parity check bit may be represented internally in the CPU by tiny magnetic cores stacked in a vertical column. The cores are magnetized in one of two possible ways and thus are capable of storing an electrical representation of 0 or 1.

Although 64 characters are represented with six bits, it may be desirable to have a larger number of bit configurations. Some third-generation computers are using eight bits (bytes) to code up to 256 different bit combinations.

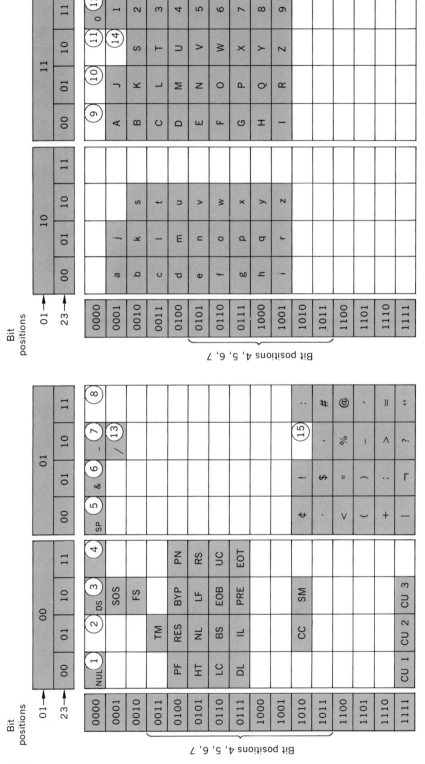

Special graphic characters

¢ Cent Sign
. Period, Decimal Point
< Less-than Sign
(Left Parenthesis
+ Plus Sign
| Vertical Bar, Logical OR
& Ampersand
! Exclamation Point
$ Dollar Sign

* Asterisk
) Right Parenthesis
; Semicolon
¬ Logical NOT
– Minus Sign, Hyphen
/ Slash
, Comma
% Percent
_ Underscore

> Greater-than Sign
? Question Mark
: Colon
Number Sign
@ At Sign
' Prime, Apostrophe
= Equal Sign
" Quotation Mark

Control characters

NUL Null
PF Punch Off
HT Horizontal Tab
LC Lower Case
DL Delete
CU1 Reserved for Customer Use
TM Tape Mark
RES Restore
NL New line

BS Backspace
IL Idle
CC Cursor Control
CU2 Reserved for Customer Use
DS Digit Select
SOS Start of Significance
FS Field Separator
BYP Bypass
LF Line Feed

EOB End of Block
PRE Prefix
SM Set Mode
CU3 Reserved for Customer Use
PN Punch On
RS Reader Stop
UC Upper Case
EOT End of Transmission
SP Space

Example	Type	Bit pattern bit positions 01 23 4567
PF	Control Character	00 00 0100
%	Special Graphic	01 10 1100
R	Upper Case	11 01 1001
a	Lower Case	10 00 0001
	Control Character, function not yet assigned	00 11 0000

Figure 7.17 (Courtesy IBM Corporation)

153

DISCUSSION QUESTIONS

1 (*a*) Identify and discuss the four conceptual storage areas. (*b*) What is the typical data-flow pattern in the storage unit?

2 Define the following terms:

(*a*) address   (*e*) wordmark
(*b*) command repertoire   (*f*) data word
(*c*) branchpoint   (*g*) instruction word
(*d*) looping

3 Explain the distinction between the address number and the contents of the address.

4 (*a*) Distinguish between word-addressable and character-addressable computers. (*b*) Compare fixed word-length and variable word-length storage systems.

5 (*a*) What is the difference between an additive and a positional numbering system? (*b*) Give examples of both types of numbering system.

6 "The highest numerical symbol will always have a value of one less than the base." Explain and give examples.

7 "In any positional numbering system, the value of each position represents a specific power of the base." Explain and give examples.

8 Why are computers designed to use the binary numbering system?

9 (*a*) What is the binary equivalent of 85_{10}? (*b*) What is the decimal equivalent of 1110011_2?

10 (*a*) What is 150_{10} in BCD? (*b*) What is the straight binary equivalent of 150_{10}? (*c*) Compare BCD and straight binary coding.

11 What would be the BCD code for the letter G? Refer to Figure 7-16.

12 Why has the six-bit alphanumeric BCD been extended to eight bits (EBCDIC)?

SELECTED REFERENCES

Thomas C. Bartee, *Digital Computer Fundamentals* (2d ed.; New York: McGraw-Hill Book Company, 1966), chap. 3.

Introduction to Electronic Data Processing (Wellesley Hills, Mass.: Honeywell Electronic Data Processing, 1966), pp. 20–38.

Introduction to IBM Data Processing Systems (IBM Corporation, Manual F22-6517-2, 1964).

Orientation to Electronic Data Processing (UNIVAC Division, Sperry Rand Corporation, 1966), pp. 59–74.

8. THE CENTRAL PROCESSING UNIT: II

We continue our survey of the CPU in this chapter with an examination of storage devices in terms of the *properties* which they possess. We shall then be in a position to study the *types of storage devices* which are available. In the final pages of the chapter we shall turn our attention to the CPU's *arithmetic-logic* and *control units*.

PROPERTIES OF STORAGE DEVICES

A storage device, of course, is any instrument which can accept entering data, hold them as long as necessary, and produce them when necessary. Storage capability may be *classified* as either internal or external (Figure 8-1). *Internal storage* is nothing more than the built-

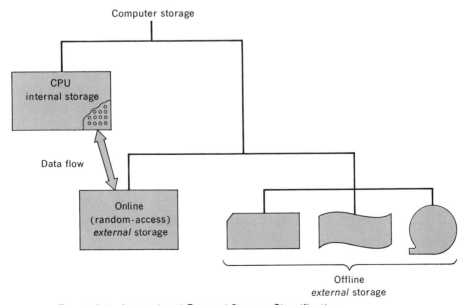

Figure 8-1. Internal and External Storage Classification

in storage section of the CPU. It is referred to by a number of other terms including *high-speed storage, main memory,* and *primary storage.* An internal storage section is basic to all computers.

External storage is a catch-all classification. If data are not stored internally in the CPU, then they must be contained in some external form. External storage may be by means of *online* devices, or it may be *offline* in the form of cards, paper tape, or magnetic tape. It is often called *high-capacity storage, auxiliary memory,* and *secondary storage.* Online equipment provides random access to records; records in offline storage are sequentially organized.

Business data processing managers are generally faced (sooner or later) with difficult decisions in determining the internal and external storage requirements of their companies. In making their decisions, managers should consider data storage facilities in terms of *their measurable properties* of *speed, capacity, safety,* and *record accessibility.* Another consideration should be that of making an *economical* choice. In short, the following questions should be considered:

1. *What processing speeds are required?* Processing speed is affected by many factors including *access time.* Access time is defined (1) as the time interval between the instant when data are called for from a storage device and the instant the data are available for processing (i.e., the read time) and (2) as the time interval between the instant when data are ready to be stored and the instant when storage is effectively completed (i.e., the write time). The *fastest* access time is available from internal (high-speed) storage. Speeds vary, of course, but some processors may retrieve or store a character in less than a microsecond. External random access storage units are slower, with access speeds measured in milliseconds. The unattainable ideal would be an access time of zero. To the human mind, however, the nanosecond speed of some internal storage units is virtually zero. If processing speed is the paramount consideration and cost is secondary, then the manager may choose a CPU with sufficient internal storage to hold all the necessary data. The amount of "necessary data" brings us to the subject of storage capacity.

2. *What storage capacity is needed?* The amount of data to be stored now and in the future must be considered by the data processing manager. He also has to determine the storage capacity properties of various pieces of hardware, and this is not always as easy as it sounds. For example, a manufacturer's literature may advertise a machine with 16,000 addressable storage locations. (This figure is usually abbreviated 16K where K — or kilo — represents thousands.) But is the machine word- or character- addressable? If word-addressable, how many characters are there in the fixed word? And if character-addressable, what is the number of bits in the character? (An eight-bit byte provides greater storage than a six-bit character because two decimal digits may be packed in a byte.) A fixed word-length storage of 16K may be considerably larger than a variable

word-length storage of 24K. And, converting storage capacity of word- and character-addressable machines to the number of characters which each may hold is not altogether reliable because fixed word-length storage may result in some unused capacity. The largest third-generation computers can store over two-million bytes of data internally. Online external devices have much greater storage capability and may store hundreds of millions of characters. Also, the amount of data which can be stored on magnetic tape is limited only by the space available to store the tape reels.

3. *How safe are the data?* Most businesses consider it highly desirable not to lose data stored internally or in random access devices in the event of a power failure in the equipment room. Commercial storage equipment is able to hold data permanently in the absence of power and is therefore said to be *nonvolatile*. However, some CPU's used for military purposes have been designed with volatile storage for reasons of security. Data recorded in punched cards are as permanent as the cards themselves. But it usually is more economical if storage space can be *erased* and reused when the need for the original data no longer exists. We have already seen how old data are erased on magnetic tape when new data are being written. Similarly, old data held in internal and online external storage are erased as new data are read into the location. This is sometimes referred to as *destructive read-in*. But it is generally best for stored data *not* to be erased from their original address when they are being recorded in another storage location. Such *destructive read-out* would occur in magnetic core storage were it not for built-in circuitry which automatically restores the data in the original location. The data processing manager should be interested in storage facilities which are not only safe, but which are as durable and as compact as possible.

4. *What type of record accessibility is required?* If all the needs of the business can be satisfied by batch processing methods performed on sequentially organized files, then the data processing manager should not be interested in online storage devices. On the other hand, should random access capability be indicated, then the data processing manager must determine which of the several alternatives best meets his needs.

5. *What is the most economical choice?* The business manager is frequently faced with the need to accept reduced performance in one area to reduce cost. Compromises between the storage properties of speed, capacity, and record accessibility are required in the interest of economy. For example, internal storage provides the fastest access time and random access capability, but the cost is highest per character stored; the use of magnetic tape provides the least expensive means of storage, but because of serial record accessibility the time required to process a particular record may be measured in minutes.

When random access is needed, the manager must ask himself the question: Can I substitute in place of high-speed storage slower but less-expensive online equipment which will meet my needs? For business purposes the answer to this question is usually yes. Random access units store data on magnetic drums, magnetic disks, or magnetic cards or strips.

Although these units will be studied later in the chapter, it should be mentioned here that selection among these auxiliary storage units also involves compromise. Magnetic drums have fast access times, but they generally do not have the storage capacity of disks and cards or strips. In fact, with auxiliary units there is frequently an inverse relationship between speed and cost per character stored, on the one hand, and storage capacity, on the other. That is, as storage capacity increases, the access time becomes slower, but the cost per character stored is reduced.

We have seen that internal and external storage units vary with respect to such properties as speed, capacity, permanence, record accessibility, and cost. Managers often find that it is desirable to *combine* different means of storage to get the best package. In the following sections we shall examine more closely the types of internal and external storage devices.

TYPES OF INTERNAL STORAGE DEVICES

Figure 8-2 shows the more common means of computer storage and the way or ways in which these storage facilities have been and are being used. In the following pages we shall consider each of these approaches.

Early internal storage

The ENIAC used vacuum tube storage. Each tube was able to hold a single bit. Storage capacity was tiny by present standards, and ENIAC was huge and therefore quite slow in operation. The most popular computer in the mid-1950s (the IBM 650) used a magnetic drum as the internal storage instrument. The drum is a metal cylinder which is coated with a magnetizable material such as iron oxide or a nickel-cobalt alloy. Although drums may still be used for internal storage in small processors, their relatively slow access times (when compared with magnetic cores and thin films) prevent them from being used in this manner in most cases. But when compared with other auxiliary storage units, they are quite fast. They are thus used extensively when fast auxiliary storage of modest capacity is needed. We shall postpone further discussion of drums to the section on external storage units.

During the mid-1950s magnetic core storage appeared in large-scale vacuum tube computers such as the IBM 704. Since that time internal core storage has been improved, and production techniques have been refined to the point where magnetic cores are used in most current commercial computers.

	Uses of storage devices		
Types of storage	*Internal*	*Online External*	*Offline External*
Magnetic drum	x	x	
Magnetic cores	x	x	
Thin films	x		
Memory rods	x		
Magnetic tape			x
Punched cards			x
Punched paper tape			x
Magnetic disks		x	x
Magnetic cards and strips		x	x

Figure 8-2. Uses of Storage Devices

Magnetic core storage

In the last chapter we saw that magnetic cores are tiny doughnut-shaped rings which can be magnetized in either of two directions. These rings are pressed from a ferromagnetic and ceramic mixture and are then baked in an oven. Early cores had an outside diameter of about a twelfth of an inch. Access time was in the 10- to 20-microsecond range. But pressure to improve the properties of speed, capacity, and cost resulted in the development of highly automatic production techniques for pressing, baking, testing, and assembling the cores. The core size has been reduced, access time has been improved, storage capacity has increased to over a million bytes (with each byte represented by eight data cores and a parity check core), and the cost per bit of storage has been reduced. A typical core now measures about a twentieth of an inch in diameter, but some of the fastest cores have diameters of less than a fiftieth of an inch.[1] Access speeds now range from less than 500 nanoseconds to 2 microseconds.

In 1820, Hans Christian Oersted, a Danish scientist, noticed that when a small compass was placed near a current-carrying wire, there was a deflection of the compass needle. Furthermore, Oersted found

[1] To get some idea of core size, locate a recently minted dime, and look at the words "ONE DIME" on the tail side. The "O" in the word "ONE" would be about the size of a typical core. The fastest cores would be about the size of the period at the end of this sentence.

Current is applied   Current is removed;
                            core remains magnetized

Figure 8-3. (Courtesy IBM Corporation)

that the needle was responding to a magnetic field which was produced by the current flow, and when the direction of current flow
changed, so did the direction of the magnetic field. It was later discovered that a changing (expanding or collapsing) magnetic field
would induce a current flow in a wire. These principles, discovered
years ago, are employed in the internal core storage of computers.

Figure 8-3 shows that if a wire carrying a sufficiently strong electrical current passes through a core, the core will be magnetized by the
magnetic field created around the wire. Perhaps you have wrapped a
wire around a nail and connected the ends of the wire to a battery to
make an electromagnet. You might have been surprised when you dis-
connected the battery to find that the nail still had the ability to act
as a magnet. As Figure 8-3 shows, the core, like the nail, remains
magnetized after the current stops.

In Figure 8-4, the current flow from left to right has magnetized the
core in a counter-clockwise (0 bit) direction. But when the current
flows in the opposite direction, the core becomes magnetized in a
clockwise (1 bit) fashion. A core can be quickly changed from an off
or 0 bit condition to an on or 1 bit state simply by reversing the current flow passing through the core (Figure 8-5).

A large number of cores is strung on a screen of wires to form a core
plane. These planes, resembling square tennis rackets, are then stacked
vertically to represent data. As we saw in the last chapter, seven cores
are needed to code six-bit characters in internal storage and to provide for a parity check. Some storage planes are 128 cores wide and
128 cores long, thus giving a total of 16,384 cores per plane. *Seven*
such planes are needed to store 16,384 characters. The imaginary line

Figure 8-4. (Courtesy IBM Corporation)

Current is applied   Core is magnetized   Current is reversed;
                                              the core reverses
                                              its magnetic state

Figure 8-5. (Courtesy IBM Corporation)

drawn through the cores in seven planes in Figure 8-6 shows the physical location of a letter as it might be temporarily stored.

A question frequently asked by students is how, among the thousands of cores, is it possible to select and properly magnetize just seven in such a way that the desired character is *read into* storage? Let's use an imaginary plane with only 81 cores to see how *one* bit in a character is selected (Figure 8-7). The other six bits making up the character are similarly chosen in the other planes. To make selection possible, two wires must pass through each core at right angles. If the *total* current needed to magnetize a core were sent along a single wire, every core through which the wire passed in getting to and from the selected core would also be magnetized—a most undesirable situation. But by sending only *half* the necessary current through each of two wires, only the core at the intersection of the wires is affected.

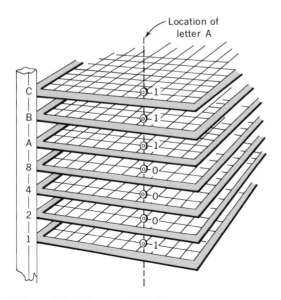

Figure 8-6. (Courtesy IBM Corporation)

1/2 current

1/2 current

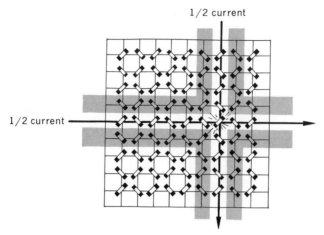

Figure 8-7. (Courtesy IBM Corporation)

All other cores in the plane either receive no current effects at all or receive only half the amount needed to magnetize. Figure 8-8 shows a closeup of a selected core magnetized to represent a 0 bit.

With a character now read into core storage, how does the computer *retrieve* it? For retrieval a third *sense* wire must be threaded diagonally through each core in a plane. The computer tests or reads-out the magnetic state of a core by again sending electrical current pulses through the two wires used in the read-in operation. The direction of this current is such that it causes a 0 to be written at that core position. If the core is magnetized in an on or 1 state, the writing of a 0 will abruptly *flip* the magnetic condition of the core, and the changing magnetic field will induce a current into the sense wire. The reaction picked up by the sense wire tells the computer that the core contained a 1 bit. If *no reaction* is sensed, the computer will know that the core is already magnetized in the 0 state. Since only one core is being read at any given instant in a plane, only a *single* sense wire need be threaded through all the cores.

But wait a minute! If all cores storing a character have been changed from a 1 state to a 0 state as a result of the reading, haven't we destroyed the character in its original location? The answer to this is usually yes—but only momentarily. Fortunately, by means of a fourth *inhibit* wire[2] the cores containing 1 bits are restored to their original state following destructive read-out. Simply stated, the processor now tries to write back 1s in every core read an instant earlier. If the core

[2] This wire, like the sense wire, runs through every core in a plane because only one core at a time in a plane is being restored.

in the plane was originally a 1, it will be restored; if it was originally a 0, it will remain that way, and a pulse of current will be sent through the inhibit wire in the plane to cancel out the attempt to write a 1.

Today magnetic cores dominate the internal storage picture for several reasons: (1) they are durable; (2) they provide safe, nonvolatile storage; (3) they provide access time measured in nanoseconds; (4) they are inexpensive in their operation, and they are erasable; (5) they provide fast random accessibility to records; and (6) they are compact in size—millions can be packed into a single cabinet. Figure 8-9 shows a core storage unit capable of holding up to 2 million bytes of data (or up to 18 million magnetic cores). Magnetic core *external storage* is available but is expensive when compared with other slower, online alternatives.

In the future, however, the cost of the circuitry necessarily associated with magnetic cores may make them less desirable.

Thin films

Internal storage units made from *thin films* may replace core storage in popularity in the future. In the early 1950s, it was found that a tiny rectangle or circle of magnetic material could be deposited on an insulating glass or plastic base so that it could be magnetized in either of two stable preferred directions. Such film spots possess *po-*

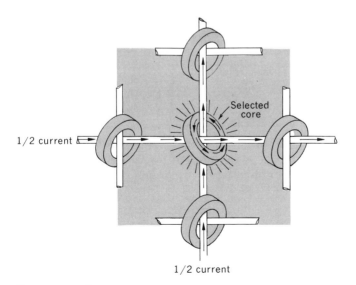

Figure 8-8. (Courtesy IBM Corporation)

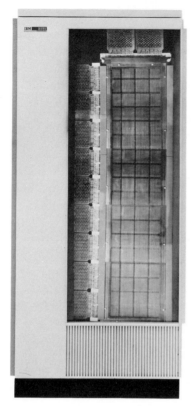

Figure 8-9. IBM 2361 Core Storage (Courtesy IBM Corporation)

tential[3] cost advantages over cores. They are made directly from bulk materials rather than from individual components which must be stamped, baked, and tested.

The film itself is only a few millionths of an inch thick and may be made of alloys containing nickel and iron. The circuitry required for moving data to and from the storage spots usually consists of strips of conductive material etched on a nonconductor. The thin film storage plane may then be sandwiched between circuit-carrying overlays—an operation requiring careful attention. Nondestructive read-out is possible when thin film storage is used, and access time is faster. Figure 8-10 shows a thin film storage frame now being used in the Burroughs B6500 computer. Tiny rectangular storage locations are used. Access time is about 300 nanoseconds. The frame shown provides the computer with 245,000 bits of storage.

---

[3]At this time, cores still are generally less expensive per bit of storage provided.

Memory rods

Thin film storage cells do not have to be in the form of flat spots or rectangles. Instead, they may be in a plated-wire form. The National Cash Register Company has adopted this storage approach in its NCR 315 Rod Memory Computer. Figure 8-11 shows an enlargement of one such wire—or *rod*—which is capable of storing 40 bits. This rod is plated with a thin film of nickel-iron alloy. The actual size of a large number of storage rods is shown in Figure 8-12. The rods are assem-

Figure 8-10. Thin-film Storage Frame (Courtesy Burroughs Company)

Figure 8-11. Rod Memory Element (Courtesy National Cash Register Company)

bled into a rod stack or storage module similar to the one shown on top of the cabinet in Figure 8-12. A number of these rod stacks may then be used in processors, such as the one shown in Figure 8-13, to provide storage for 40,000 to 160,000 characters. Access time for a group of four bits is about 200 nanoseconds.

Figure 8-12. (Courtesy National Cash Register Company)

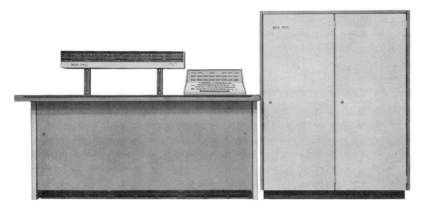

Figure 8-13. NCR 315 Rod Memory Processor (Courtesy National Cash Register Company)

TYPES OF EXTERNAL STORAGE DEVICES

Offline external storage[4]

We have already dealt elsewhere with the means of providing offline external storage through the use of punched cards, punched paper tape, and magnetic tape, so we need not dwell long on these media here. It should be remembered, however, that many firms find that their *total* data processing needs are being met quite satisfactorily through the use of offline storage media. In spite of the pronouncements to the contrary by a few of the more enthusiastic boosters of broader and faster-responding business systems, sequentially organized files will be stored on tapes and cards in the foreseeable future. This is true because:

1. An unlimited amount of data may be safely retained in this way.

2. Batch processing is acceptable — perhaps even preferable — for some jobs.

3. Offline media often provide the least-expensive means of data storage.

4. Magnetic tape processing, in situations where sequentially organized files are feasible, is frequently less expensive than random access processing.

In the remainder of this section we shall look at different types of popular random access storage units. It is interesting to note that

[4]Offline external storage may be referred to as *nonaddressable bulk storage.* The term "nonaddressable" refers to the fact that records are not randomly addressable. In other words, random access processing is not economically feasible with these media. Online external storage is, as might be expected, sometimes called *addressable bulk storage.*

168

some of these devices are *flexible* in the sense that the storage instruments associated with their use may be either online or offline. Magnetic disks, for example, resemble large phonograph records, have mass storage capability, and can be used indefinitely for online purposes. But the disks (and the data contained) can be removed and stored offline just like tapes or cards.

Magnetic drums

Magnetic drums were an early means of internal storage. Now, however, they are used primarily as auxiliary storage when fast response is of greater importance than large capacity. For example, they may be used to store mathematical tables, data, or program modifications that are frequently referred to during processing operations.

A magnetic drum is a cylinder which has an outer surface plated with a metallic magnetizable film. (Figure 8-14 shows three large UNIVAC Fastrand drums being tested prior to final assembly.) A motor rotates the drum on its axis at a constant and rapid rate.

Data are *recorded on* the rotating drum and *read from* the drum by

Figure 8-14. UNIVAC Fastrand Drums (Courtesy Sperry Rand Corporation, UNIVAC Division)

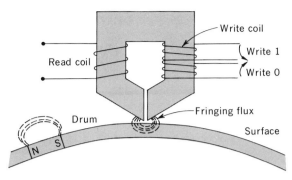

Figure 8-15. (Courtesy IBM Corporation)

read-write heads which are positioned a fraction of an inch from the drum surface (Figure 8-15). As is the case with magnetic tape, data are recorded on the drum surface when pulses of current flow through the tiny wires of the write coils and set up magnetic fields. Current flow in one write coil produces a 1 bit; current in the other produces a 0-bit magnetic field. The writing of new data on the drum erases data previously stored at the location. The magnetic spots written on the drum surface remain indefinitely until they too are erased at a future time. Reading of data recorded on the drum is accomplished as the magnetized spots pass under the read heads and induce electrical pulses in the read coils. Because millisecond time is desired in the reading and writing operations, the drum rotates several thousand times each minute.

The binary coded data spots are arranged in *bands* or *tracks* around the circumference of the drum. A *fixed* read-write head is often employed for *each* band. Bands vary in width depending upon whether a character or fixed-length word is being stored. Some drums (e.g., the Fastrand drum shown in Figure 8-14) may have thousands of bands. To reduce the circuitry costs associated with a large number of read-write heads, some drum units have a *single* horizontally movable head to serve *all* bands (Figure 8-16a), while other drum

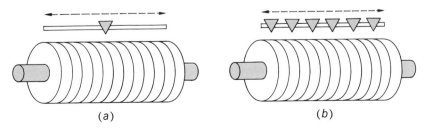

Figure 8-16. (a) Single Read-Write Head; (b) Multiple Read-Write Heads

devices (including Fastrand) have multiple heads, each of which serves a number of adjacent bands (Figure 8-16b). [5]

The computer is able to access stored records directly because each drum has a specific number of addressable locations. A band may be divided into sections, and each section may be given an identifying number as shown in Figure 8-17. The width and number of bands, the number of characters which may be stored in a section, and the number of addressable sections varies among hardware lines.

Random access time is basically determined by the delay time required for an addressed location to be positioned under a read-write head.[6] Although several factors are involved, let us consider only two:

1. *Number of read-write heads.* The most rapid access is achieved when there is a head for *each* band on the drum. The *rotational delay* of the drum then determines the access time. If the address containing the data to be read has just passed the head when the CPU sends a reading signal, there will be a delay while the drum makes a complete revolution. The measured time in this case is the *maximum* access time. If the address to be read were just passing under the head when the signal arrived, the *minimum* access time would be achieved. The *average* access speed is equal to about half the time required for the drum to make a revolution. If a single head is used to serve *all* bands, costs will be reduced, but access time will be slower. Not only will rotational delay continue, but a new factor — *positional delay* — will be introduced. Time will now be required to locate and position the head over the proper band. Multiple head units which allocate one head to serve several adjacent bands are a compromise between speed and cost. Although they are not as fast as units with heads for each band, they are less expensive. Yet they have less positional delay than single head units.

2. *Speed of drum rotation.* A drum moving at 2,000 revolutions per minute takes 30 milliseconds to complete a single revolution. Any increase in rotational speed serves to decrease the rotational delay.

   Average drum access times range from below 20 milliseconds for high-speed, limited-capacity units to about 100 milliseconds for the larger-capacity hardware. The faster drums are small in circumference (and there-

[5]The Fastrand drum, for example, uses 32 read-write heads; each head serves 96 adjacent bands; and all heads move horizontally together.

[6]Technically speaking, magnetic cores and thin films have random access storage capability, while most online external devices including drums have *direct*, but not *random*, access to records. "Random access" refers to a storage device in which the access time is independent of the physical location of the data. Since the drum access time varies with the physical location of stored data, it is more technically correct to say that drums provide direct access. The distinction is usually not observed, however, and the online units presented here are generally described as being random access equipment.

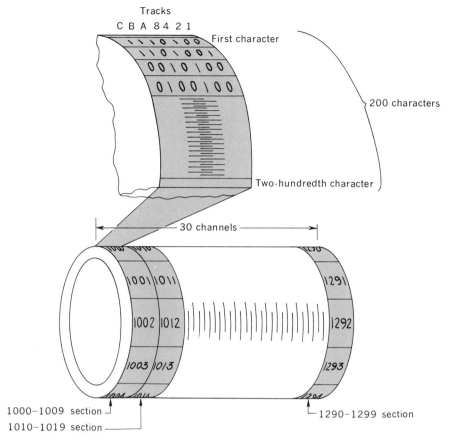

Tracks
C B A 8 4 2 1

First character

200 characters

Two-hundredth character

30 channels

1000-1009 section
1010-1019 section

1290-1299 section

Figure 8-17. (Courtesy IBM Corporation)

fore have limited space for storage), have high rotational speeds, and are the most expensive per volume of storage. The larger drums have more surface area for storage but slower access time. Drum units typically store 130,000 to 8 million characters, although the UNIVAC Fastrand equipment has a minimum capacity in excess of 60 million characters.

Magnetic disks

Magnetic disks resemble oversized phonograph records. Unlike plastic phonograph records, however, disks are made of thin metal plates which will not warp and which are coated on both sides with a magnetizable recording material. Several disks (the number varies) are permanently mounted on a vertical shaft which rotates at a high, constant speed (usually over one thousand revolutions per minute). A space is left between the spinning disks to allow small read-write

172

heads to move to any storage location. Data are organized into a number of concentric circles or *tracks*, each of which has a designated location number.

Reading and writing operations are similar to those of drums. Data are recorded in specific locations as magnetized spots. Read-in is destructive; read-out is nondestructive. Figure 8-18 shows one type of read-write head arrangement. Arms, resembling teeth in a comb, move horizontally among the individual disks. The two heads mounted on each arm service two disk surfaces. On command from the CPU the proper head moves to the specified track and the desired data are read as soon as they spin under the head. Figure 8-19 is a double-exposure photograph showing another head arrangement. The heads are shown in various positions over the whirling disk. Only two disks (four surfaces) are used in this Burroughs high-speed disk file, but they are capable of storing almost 5 million characters.

Some of the older units contain stacks of 25 or 50 disks mounted on a single shaft and served by a *single access arm*. To locate data, the arm must move vertically to the proper disk and then horizontally to the proper track. Access times are, of course, quite slow. Multiple read-write heads eliminate the vertical movement. The disks in the first units were supposed to remain permanently in their cabinets. Since that time, however, smaller disks have been developed which

Head services
bottom surface of
upper disk

Head services
top surface
of lower disk

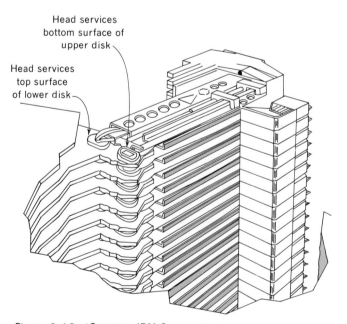

Figure 8-18. (Courtesy IBM Corporation)

Figure 8-19. (Courtesy Burroughs Corporation)

can be removed and stored much like magnetic tape. (They are, however, much more expensive than a reel of tape.)

Two sizes of interchangeable *disk packs* are shown in Figure 8-20. The larger pack of 11 disks to the left can store nearly 26 million bytes (or 52 million digits). There are 200 tracks on each surface. Such a disk pack is housed with seven others (Figure 8-21) to provide 88 disks and about 207 million bytes of storage. It takes only a minute to replace this pack and thus replace 26 million characters. The ninth disk drive shown in Figure 8-21 is a spare which can be put into operation in the event one of the other drives is being serviced. The smaller pack of six disks shown in Figure 8-20 holds over 7 million bytes of data. It may be removed from its disk drive (Figure 8-22) in a few seconds. The disk drive shown in the background of Figure

Figure 8-20. IBM Disk Packs (Courtesy IBM Corporation)

8-20 has 50 larger disks which remain in the cabinet. Its storage capacity is over 200 million bytes.

The average access time of representative disk hardware ranges from 20 to 600 milliseconds; storage capacity varies from 500,000 to over 200 million characters online (there is no limit to the number of disk packs which can be stored offline). Generally speaking, disk units have greater storage capability than drums but are not as fast. One can, of course, find exceptions to this generalization.

Magnetic cards and strips

Wouldn't it be nice to combine the magnetic tape advantages of low-cost, high-storage capacity with the advantages of rapid and direct

Figure 8-21. IBM 2314 Direct Access Storage Facility (Courtesy IBM Corporation)

Figure 8-22. IBM 2311 Disk Drive (Courtesy IBM Corporation)

record accessibility? This is essentially the objective of magnetic cards and strips. A magnetic card or strip may be considered to be a length of flexible plastic material upon which short pieces of magnetic tape have been mounted in a side-by-side arrangement. A number of cards is placed in a cartridge. Like disk packs, these cartridges are removable in a minute or less. Card and strip equipment generally has high-storage capability, and the cost per character stored is low. Data are erasable, but access speed is relatively slow when compared with drums and disks. This type of storage approach is used with such equipment as the National Cash Register CRAM (Card Random Access Memory) and the IBM Data Cell.

The CRAM unit (Figure 8-23) contains a cartridge which holds 256 cards. Each card is 14 inches long but is much wider than a strip of magnetic tape. The cards in a cartridge, and a number of tracks on each card, are addressable by the CRAM unit. The cards are suspended from rods in the cartridge (Figure 8-24). When data are to be written on, or read from, a particular card, the CPU sends a signal to drop the proper card into a vacuum handling device. It then is wrapped

Figure 8-23. NCR CRAM Unit (Courtesy National Cash Register Company)

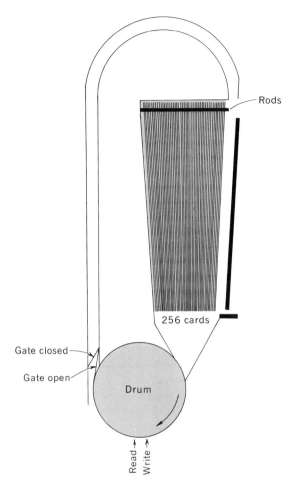

Rods

256 cards

Gate closed

Gate open

Drum

Read →
Write →

Figure 8-24. (Courtesy National Cash Register
Company)

around a rapidly rotating drum which moves it past read-write heads.
After the read-write operation, the card is returned to the cartridge
and the other 255 cards. The average access time is 235 milliseconds;
storage capacity of a *single* cartridge is 16 million alphanumeric characters. A number of CRAM units may be connected to a single CPU
to provide online storage for additional millions of characters.

The IBM Data Cell Drive (Figure 8-25) provides virtually unlimited
large-bulk storage and direct access to records. *Each* Data Cell unit
has a storage capacity of 400 million bytes; *eight* such Data Cell units
may be attached to a single control unit to provide 3.2 *billion* bytes of
storage; and up to 48 control units may be attached to a large Sys-
tem/360 computer.

Figure 8-25. IBM 2321 Data Cell Drive (Courtesy IBM Corporation)

You will notice in Figure 8-25 that the Data Cell cartridge is a cylinder which resembles a snare drum. There are 10 replaceable *cells* in this cylinder (four are visible in the picture). Each of the 10 cells contains 200 magnetizable strips; each strip is 13 inches long and $2^{1}/_{4}$ inches wide. On one side of the strip is an iron-oxide magnetizable coating, while on the other side there is an antistatic carbon coating. The strip is divided into 100 data tracks and has an identifying coding tab.

Let's assume that the CPU is instructed to retrieve data from a specific strip. A signal is sent to the Data Cell Drive, which rotates the storage cartridge until the proper cell is positioned beneath the Drive's access station. At the station the particular strip is withdrawn, is pulled upward by a revolving drum past the read-write heads, and is then returned to its original position. The time for this procedure averages about 450 milliseconds. A writing operation is similarly

07	08	09	10	11
Write contents of address 01 into arithmetic unit	Multiply contents of arithmetic unit by contents of address 02	Duplicate preceding answer in address 05	Multiply contents of address 03 by preceding answer in arithmetic unit	Add contents of address 04 to preceding answer in arithmetic unit

Figure 8-26. (Source: Figure 7-4)

performed. The read-write drum housing can be seen in Figure 8-25 directly above the cartridge.

All the bulk storage units introduced in this chapter have been magnetic devices. New high-resolution *photographic* media, however, are being developed to store trillions of bits of data. Data density is many times greater with photographic material,[7] and although film is generally not erasable, it may play a more important role in future storage techniques.

In addition to the storage function, every CPU must have components to perform the arithmetic-logic and control functions. In the remainder of the chapter we shall study these units.

THE ARITHMETIC-LOGIC UNIT

In the preceding pages we noted that the arithmetic-logic unit is where the actual data processing occurs. All calculations are performed and all logical comparisons are made in this unit. In Chapter 7 we traced through a simplified program to process Editor Aardvark's weekly paycheck. Some of the program instructions used then are reproduced in Figure 8-26.

The instruction in address 07 calls for the computer to write the contents of address 01 into the arithmetic unit. Implicit in this instruction is the requirement that the arithmetic-logic unit have storage capability. It must be able to store temporarily the data contained in address 01. Such a special purpose storage location is called a *register*. Several registers will be discussed in the following paragraphs because they are basic to the functioning of the arithmetic-logic and control units.[8] The number of registers varies among computers as does the data-flow pattern. Let us trace the instructions in Figure 8-26 through the PAC computer.

---

[7] A piece of film $1\frac{3}{8}$ by $2\frac{3}{4}$ inches has been developed which can store several million bits.

[8] The computer operator is able to determine the contents of the several registers in the CPU by observing small console display lights designed for the purpose.

07	08	09	10	11
CLA 01	MUL 02	STO 05	MUL 03	ADD 04

Figure 8-27

Up to this point we have written out the instructions in addresses 07 through 11 so we would understand them. Figure 8-27 shows how these same instructions may be coded and stored for PAC's convenience. The first processing instruction, CLA 01, tells PAC to CLear the contents of the arithmetic-logic unit of all data and to Add (store) the contents of address 01 to a register known as the *accumulator*. Thus, 40 hours—the contents of address 01—is now held in both address 01 and the accumulator (Figure 8-28*a*).

The second instruction in address 08 is MUL 02. The computer interprets this instruction to mean that the contents of address 02 ($5) are to be MULtiplied by the contents in the accumulator (40 hours) to get Aardvark's gross pay. Execution of this instruction may take the following form (Figure 8-28*b*):

1. The contents of address 02 are read into a storage register[9] in the arithmetic-logic unit.

2. The contents of the accumulator and the contents of the storage register are given to the *adder*. The *adder* (and its associated circuits) is the primary arithmetic element because it also performs subtraction, multiplication, and division on binary digits. We need not dwell on the technical points of adder operation, although you may recall that we saw earlier that computations (by adders) in variable word-length machines are two digits at a time (serial), while computations with fixed word-length processors are two words at a time (parallel).

3. The product of the multiplication *is stored in the accumulator*. The 40 hours previously there has been erased by the arithmetic operation.

The third instruction in the processing sequence is STO 05. The contents in the accumulator are STOred in address 05. The read-in to address 05 is destructive to any information which might be there. The read-out from the accumulator is nondestructive (Figure 8-28*c*). The fourth instruction, MUL 03, is handled exactly like the second instruction, so we need not repeat the execution.

---

[9] This register is sometimes called a *distributor*. Some machines move data directly from storage to the adder.

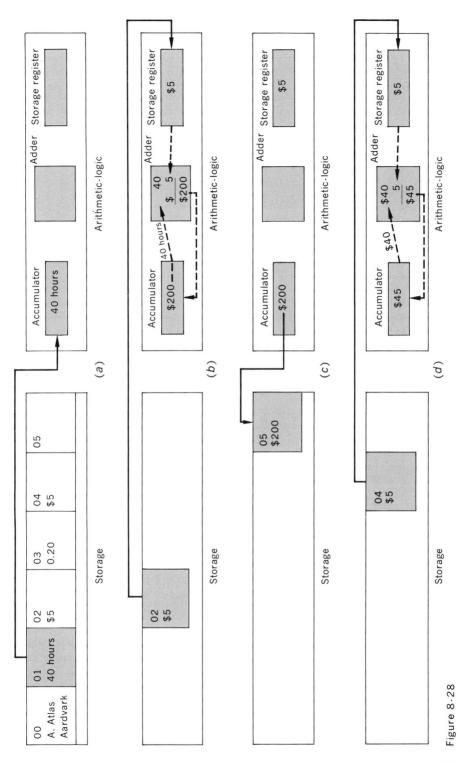

Figure 8-28

181

The fifth instruction in the sequence, ADD 04, simply tells the computer to <u>ADD</u> the contents of address 04 to the contents of the accumulator. The hospitalization insurance deduction of $5 is the contents of 04; the tax deduction of $40 is now the contents of the accumulator. Why? Because when the fourth instruction is carried out, the $200 in the accumulator is multiplied by 20 percent (the contents of 03) to get a product which is then stored in the accumulator. As Figure 8-28 d shows, the contents of 04 are read into the storage register (thus erasing the previous contents); the adder totals the contents of the accumulator and the storage register; and the sum is stored in the accumulator.

It is apparent that every arithmetic operation requires two numbers and some result. Subtraction, for example, requires a minuend and a subtrahend to find a difference; multiplication uses a multiplicand and a multiplier to find a product. From a functional standpoint there should thus be three registers for computational purposes—two to store the numbers temporarily and one to store the result of the calculations. As we have just seen, however, the accumulator may perform two functions—the storage of first a number and then the result. Of course, in a later processing step the result in the accumulator becomes one of the digits to be manipulated. The number of registers in the arithmetic-logic unit varies, but some approach is required to handle the two numbers and the result.

Logic operations generally consist of comparisons. The arithmetic-logic unit may compare two numbers by subtracting one from the other. The sign (negative or positive) and the value of the difference tell the processor that the first number is equal to, less than, or greater than the second number. Three branches may be provided in the program for the computer to follow depending on the result of such a comparison. Many processors are designed with a *comparer* in the arithmetic-logic unit. Data from the accumulator and the storage register are examined by the comparer to yield the logic decision. Alphabetic data may also be compared according to an order sequence.

THE CONTROL UNIT

The control unit of the processor *selects*, *interprets*, and *executes* the program instructions. The arithmetic-logic unit responds to commands coming from the control unit. There are at least two parts to any instruction: the *command* which is to be followed (e.g., ADD, SUB, MUL, GO TO) and the *address* which locates the data or instructions to be manipulated. The basic components contained in the PAC control unit are the *instruction register*, the *sequence register*,[10] the *address register*, and the *decoder*.

Let us trace an instruction through the PAC control unit to see how it is handled. We shall again use Aardvark's pay data along with the payroll program shown in Figure 8-27. Let us assume that the instruction in address 07 has just been executed and that 40 hours is the contents of the accumulator. The following steps are performed in the next *operating cycle* (the circled numbers in Figure 8-29 correspond to these steps):

1. The instruction in address 08 (MUL 02) is *selected* by the *sequence register* and read into the *instruction register* in the control unit. (The sequence register does not store the instruction. We shall have more to say about the sequence register in step 5 below.)

2. The command part of the instruction (MUL) and the address part (02) are *separated*. The command is sent to the decoder where it is *interpreted*. The computer is built to respond to a limited number of commands, and it now knows that it is to multiply.

3. The address part of the instruction is sent to the *address register*.

4. The signal to move the contents of address 02 into the arithmetic-logic unit is sent; the command to multiply goes to the arithmetic-logic unit where the instruction is *executed*.

5. As the multiplication is being executed, the sequence register in the control unit is increased by 1 to indicate the location of the next instruction address. When the program was started, the sequence register was set to the address of the first instruction by the programmer. By the time the first program instruction was finished, the contents of the sequence register had automatically been advanced to the next instruction address number. In other words, the first address in the payroll program was 06 (read data in), and the sequence register was set to 06. As that instruction was being executed, the sequence register automatically moved to 07 and then to 08, and now it is again automatically moved to 09. It keeps this up until instructed to do otherwise. From the last chapter you will recall that when the sequence register gets to address 17, it encounters an instruction that reads GO TO 06. This command alters the normal stepping of the sequence register and resets it at address 06.

6. The instruction at address 09 moves into the instruction register, and the above steps are repeated.

We may identify separate processor phases or cycles in the above procedure. Step 4 is the *execution cycle*. The other steps comprise the *instruction cycle*. Thus, there are two phases in the performance of

[10]The instruction register is also called the "operation register" and the "control register," while the sequence register is sometimes referred to as the "control counter."

184

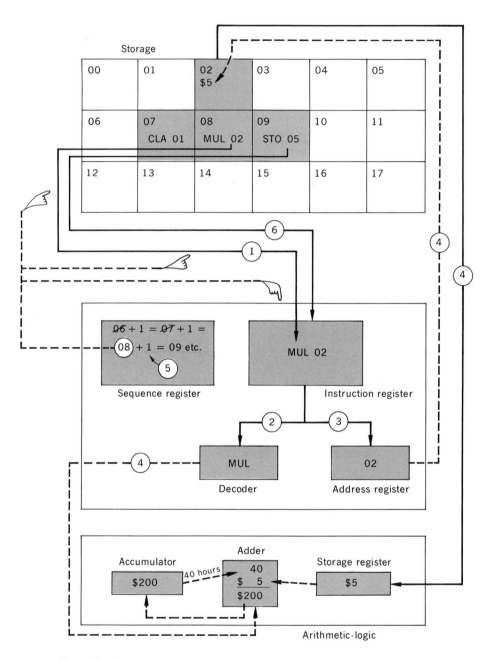

Storage

00	01	02 $5	03	04	05
06	07 CLA 01	08 MUL 02	09 STO 05	10	11
12	13	14	15	16	17

6

1

4

4

06 + 1 = 07 + 1 =
08 + 1 = 09 etc.
5

Sequence register

MUL 02

Instruction register

2   3

4

MUL

Decoder

02

Address register

Adder

Accumulator

$200

40 hours

40
$ 5
$200

Storage register

$5

Arithmetic-logic

Figure 8-29

each instruction. Computers are generally *synchronous*—i.e., the various operations are synchronized by an electronic clock which emits millions of regularly spaced electronic pulses each second. Commands are interpreted and executed at proper intervals, and the intervals are timed by a specified number of these pulses.

SUMMARY

Internal and external storage devices may be measured and evaluated in terms of their speed, storage capacity, safety, record accessibility, and cost. Business managers often find it desirable to combine several approaches to get a package which suits the needs of their company.

The fastest storage units are typically found internally in the CPU. Generally, internal storage is provided by planes of magnetic cores, although thin films are also available in high-speed computers. In the future, thin films may replace cores in popularity. Internal storage is the most expensive per character stored.

External storage units may be online or offline. Speed is generally sacrificed and cost per character stored is frequently reduced as mass storage capacity is increased. Offline external storage is usually preferred by business managers when serial or batch processing methods are suitable. When direct, rapid accessibility to any file record is most desirable, online external storage is chosen. A manager may choose among the magnetic drums, disks, and cards or strips equipment which offers the best characteristics of speed, capacity, and cost for his particular needs.

The arithmetic-logic unit does the actual processing under program control. During the execution cycle, data are moved into one or more registers located in the arithmetic-logic unit. There they are manipulated by adder circuits to yield a result which may be stored in a register (e.g., the accumulator) in the arithmetic-logic unit, or the result may be transferred to some other storage location.

The control unit selects, interprets, and sees to the execution of instructions in their proper sequence. Several basic registers are required to perform the control function.

DISCUSSION QUESTIONS

1   Distinguish between online and offline external storage.

2   Define the following terms:
   (a) access time
   (b) nonvolatile storage
   (c) destructive read-in
   (d) sense wire
   (e) inhibit wire
   (f) addressable bulk storage
   (g) random access time
   (h) disk pack
   (i) register
   (j) synchronous computer

3 What factors should be considered in determining the data storage facilities that are needed?

4 "With auxiliary storage units there is frequently an inverse relationship between speed and cost per character stored, on the one hand, and storage capacity, on the other." Explain and give examples.

5 (a) How is information stored in ferromagnetic cores? (b) Once stored, how is it retrieved?

6 Why may thin films replace core storage in popularity in the future?

7 What factors determine random access time of magnetic drums?

8 Compare magnetic cards or strips with magnetic tape.

9 (a) What is the accumulator? (b) What is the adder?

10 Define and explain the function of (a) the instruction register, (b) the sequence register, (c) the address register, and (d) the decoder.

SELECTED REFERENCES

Thomas C. Bartee, *Digital Computer Fundamentals* (2d ed.; New York: McGraw-Hill Book Company, 1966), chap. 7.

David C. Evans, "Computer Logic and Memory," *Scientific American,* September, 1966, pp. 75-85.

Introduction to IBM Data Processing Systems (IBM Corporation, Manual F22-6517-2, 1964).

9. PROGRAMMING ANALYSIS

In the past four chapters, attention has been focused primarily on computer hardware. But hardware alone does not solve a single business problem. Until the processor is given a detailed set of problem-solving instructions, it is merely an expensive and space-consuming curiosity.

The procedure to be followed in using computers to process business problems involves a number of steps:

1. *Definition of the problem and the objectives.* The particular problem to be solved, or the tasks to be accomplished, must be clearly identified; the objectives of managers in having the tasks performed must be known. Identifying the problem and the objectives seems to be an obvious step, but it is sometimes overlooked with unfortunate results.

2. *Problem analysis.* Data pertaining to the problem must be gathered, organized, and interpreted. Tasks currently being performed by noncomputer methods should be examined. From this analysis may come a recognition of computer potential, i.e., a recognition that the problem could justifiably be processed with a computer.

3. *System review and design.* The present procedures should be reviewed to determine what improvements are possible. These procedures should be redesigned to meet the current needs of the business. Broad system specifications should outline the scope of the problem, the form and type of input data to be used, and the form and type of output required.

4. *Programming analysis.* The broadly defined system specifications must be broken down into the specific arithmetic and logic operations required to solve the problem.

5. *Program preparation.* The specific steps must next be translated or coded into a language and form acceptable to the processor.

6. *Program operation and maintenance.* The coded program must be tested prior to being used on a routine basis; conversion to the new approach must be made; the program must be properly stored when not in use; and it must be revised and maintained as company needs change.

The purpose of this chapter and the one which follows is to survey the process of programming briefly. As used in this text, *programming* is defined as the *process* of converting broad system specifications into usable machine programs of instruction. In short, programming consists of the final three steps in the above procedure.[1] In this chapter we shall look at *programming analysis*; in Chapter 10 *program preparation* and *maintenance* will be examined. It is assumed that the first three steps of the above procedure—the *system analysis* phase—have been completed. We shall look more closely at these three very important steps in a later chapter.

INTRODUCTION TO COMMON TOOLS OF ANALYSIS

Two common tools used for analysis purposes are the *flowchart* and the *decision table*.

Flowcharts

Flowcharts have existed for a number of years and have been used for a variety of purposes. For example, Figure 9-1 shows in graphical form the logic which might be involved in getting a haircut. As used in business data processing, however, a flowchart is a graphic tool or model which provides a means of recording, analyzing, and communicating problem information. For example, appropriate symbols may be used by an analyst to *record* quickly the flow of data in a current business procedure from the originating source, through a number of processing operations and machines, to the output report. The flowchart "picture" or schematic may assist the analyst in acquiring a better understanding of the procedure than would otherwise be possible. It may also aid in procedure *analysis* and then in improvement—e.g., it may point out bottlenecks which may be eliminated in the flow of data. Flowcharts are frequently used to *communicate* the essential facts of a business problem to others whose skills are needed in the solution.

Here we shall be interested in two basic kinds of flowcharts. The *system flowchart* provides a broad overview of the processing operations which are to be accomplished. Primary emphasis is placed on data flow among machines, i.e., on input documents and output

[1] Sometimes the term "programming" is used to refer only to program preparation or *coding* (step 5 above). In large companies the early steps are usually performed by system analysts although the later steps are generally handled by programmers and computer operators. Close cooperation is, of course, required.

reports. The amount of detail furnished about *how* a machine is to convert the data on input documents into the desired output is limited. A *program flowchart*, on the other hand, does present a detailed graphical representation of how steps are to be performed *within* the machine to produce the needed output. Thus, the program flowchart evolves from the system chart. In a following section we shall take a closer look at these two types of charts.

Decision tables

A table that presents all the conditions or contingencies which are to be considered in the solution of a problem together with all the actions or decisions which may be taken is known as a *decision table*. Simply stated, a decision table is used to present the logic of a program. And because it does present program logic, it may be used as a substitute for, or as a supplement to, a *program* flowchart. Decision tables are especially useful when the program logic is such that a number of alternate paths or branches must be considered before the ultimate action can be taken. We shall return to the subject of decision tables later in the chapter.

FLOW CHARTING

System flowcharts

In the design of all flowcharts it is necessary that standard *symbols* be used to record and communicate problem information clearly. In the past (and even today) a variety of shapes were used to represent the same concept, while users sometimes attached different meanings to the same symbol. In June, 1966, the United States of America Standards Institute, as a means of reducing confusion, approved a set of symbols which could be used for systems and program flowcharts. These are the symbols which will be used in the remainder of the text.

Since system flowcharts emphasize inputs and outputs and are primarily designed to show the flow of data through the entire data processing system, symbols representing input, output, and general processing (Figure 9-2a) are frequently used in them. The same basic I/0 symbol may be used to show *any* type of media or data. The arrows connecting the shapes indicate the direction of data flow. The main flow is generally charted from top to bottom and from left to right. The *shape* of the symbol, and *not its size*, identifies the meaning. For example, the rectangular processing box may vary in size, but the

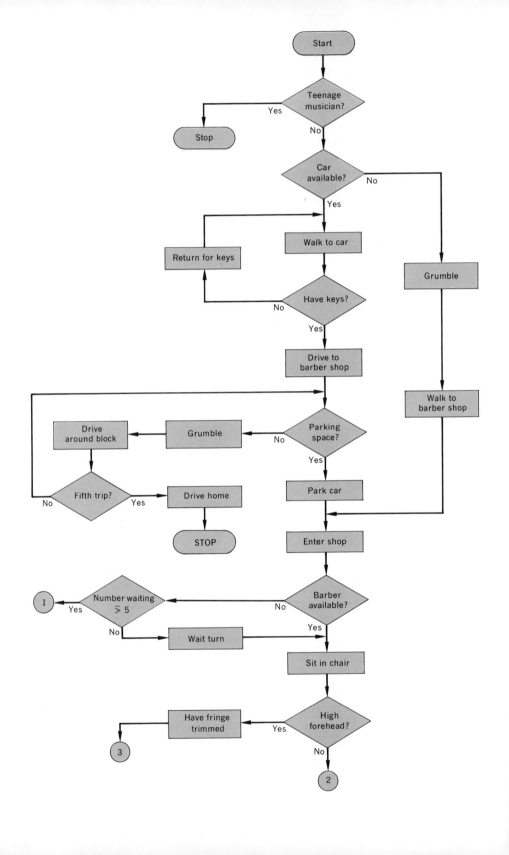

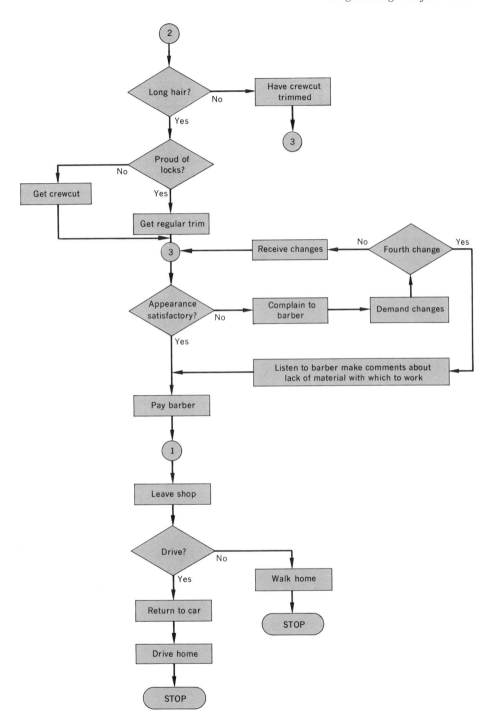

Figure 9-1. How to Get a Haircut

192

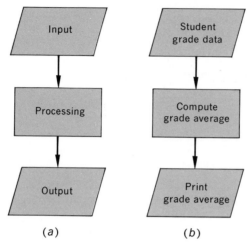

(a)   (b)

Figure 9-2. Basic System Charting Symbols

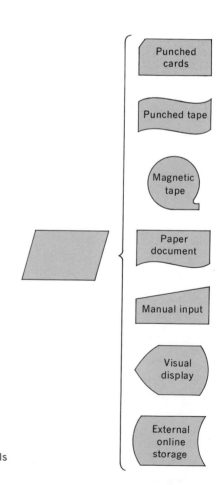

Figure 9-3. I/O Substitution Symbols

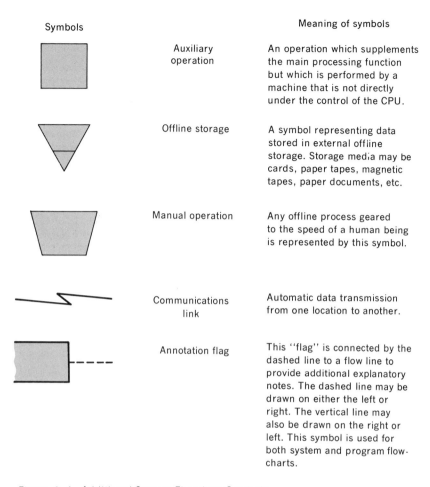

Symbols		Meaning of symbols
	Auxiliary operation	An operation which supplements the main processing function but which is performed by a machine that is not directly under the control of the CPU.
	Offline storage	A symbol representing data stored in external offline storage. Storage media may be cards, paper tapes, magnetic tapes, paper documents, etc.
	Manual operation	Any offline process geared to the speed of a human being is represented by this symbol.
	Communications link	Automatic data transmission from one location to another.
	Annotation flag	This "flag" is connected by the dashed line to a flow line to provide additional explanatory notes. The dashed line may be drawn on either the left or right. The vertical line may also be drawn on the right or left. This symbol is used for both system and program flowcharts.

Figure 9-4. Additional System Flowchart Symbols

shape still designates that processing is being performed. Notation within the charting symbol further explains what is being done (Figure 9-2b).

Frequently, the basic I/0 symbol is *replaced* in system flowcharts by other I/0 symbols whose shape suggests the type of media or device being employed (Figure 9-3). These symbols are familiar to us since they have been used in earlier chapters. Additional commonly used system flowchart symbols are shown and described in Figure 9-4.

With these additional shapes, we may define in greater detail the chart shown in Figure 9-2b. The problem involved is a simple one:[2]

---

[2]We shall trace this problem through the programming process. A simple problem has been deliberately chosen so that problem details will not confuse the issue while basic introductory file processing and coding concepts are presented.

Professor Balford Sheet, an accounting professor, wishes to compute an average (arithmetic mean) grade for a beginning accounting student based on the 30 tests he has given during the semester. (Professor Sheet teaches a rigorous course!) In Figure 9-5 we see that the system followed by Bal Sheet is one in which the grade data for the student are punched into cards which are then fed into a computer for processing. The computed average is printed, and Professor Sheet manually updates his grade book and then prepares his final grade report on the student. We shall be concerned with only one student, but, of course, any number of student grade averages could easily be automatically processed by the computer.

Program flow charting

As we noted earlier, program flowcharts evolve from system flowcharts. In Bal Sheet's grade preparation diagram, a single processing box is labeled "compute grade average." Unfortunately, such an instruction is not sufficient for the computer. Thus, as a part of the programming process the programmer must specify each step needed to compute the average grade. In short, the *single* processing box labeled "compute grade average" becomes the basis for a detailed *program* flowchart.

Only a few symbols, when properly arranged, are needed in program charting to define the necessary steps. These symbols are illustrated in Figure 9-6 and are described below.

Input/Output   The basic I/0 symbol is also used in program flow charting to represent any I/0 function. The specific symbols designating cards, tapes, etc., are generally not used with program diagrams. Figure 9-7 presents a portion of a program chart (the total chart shows the steps required to compute the average grade by Professor Sheet). The I/0 symbol designates that a punched card containing a student grade is to be read into the computer. The same symbol, of course, could be used to represent any output form.

Processing   Again, the rectangle represents processing operations. But now the processing described is a *small segment* of the major processing step called for in the system chart. Arithmetic and data movement instructions are generally placed in these boxes. Two processing symbols are shown in Figure 9-7. The upper box provides for the accumulation of the total number of points in the CPU arithmetic-logic unit. Thus, when the last grade card has been read, the total of all the test scores will be stored in the accumulator. To get an average grade, as every-

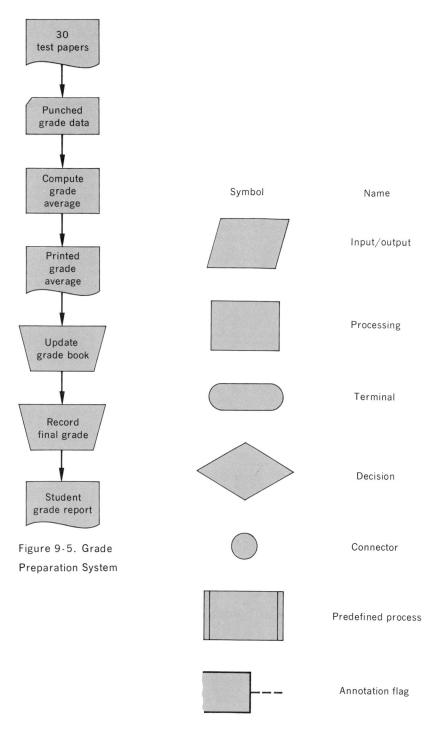

Figure 9-5. Grade
Preparation System

Figure 9-6. Program Flowchart Symbols

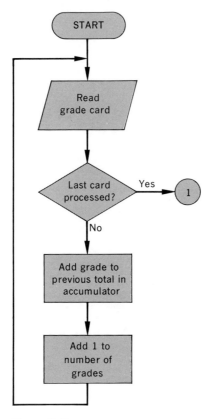

Figure 9-7

one knows, the total number of points must be divided by the number of tests taken. The lower processing box in Figure 9-7 gives the denominator; the upper box, the numerator.

Termination The terminal symbol, as the name suggests, represents the beginning and the end of a program. It may also be used to signal a program interruption point when information may enter or leave. For example, to detect certain errors in input data the programmer may provide a special program branch ending in a terminal symbol labeled "HALT."

Decision The I/0 and processing symbols, typically, have two flow lines (one entry and one exit), while the terminal has a single entrance or exit line. The diamond-shaped decision symbol, on the other hand, has one entrance line and *at least* two exit paths or branches. As Figure 9-7 shows, exit paths may be determined by a yes or no answer to some stated condition—in this case the condition to be determined is whether or not the last grade card has been processed. If the answer is yes, then the total of all test scores is contained in the accumulator, and the program can branch away from the *loop* which it has been following by reading cards and totaling scores successively. If the answer is no, the program continues to process the grade cards until they are all accounted for. Decision boxes are also used to show the result of a *test* or a *comparison* (Figure 9-8).

Connector   The *circular connector* symbol is used when additional flow lines might cause confusion and reduce understanding. Two connectors with identical labels serve the same function as a long flow line—i.e., they show an entry from another part of the chart, or they indicate an exit to some other chart section. How is it possible to determine if a connector is used as an entry point or an exit point? It is very simple: If an arrow *enters but does not leave a connector*, it is an exit point, and program flow is transferred to that identically labeled connector which *does* have an outlet. Two connector symbols labeled "3" were used in the haircut example chart earlier in the chapter to represent a junction point and to eliminate confusing lengthy flow lines.

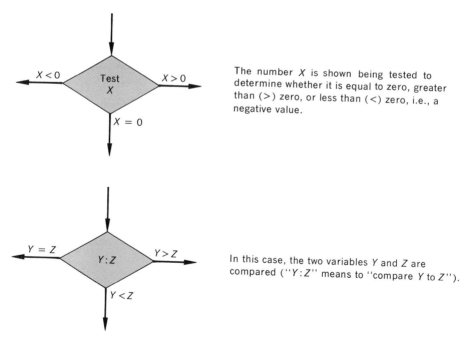

The number X is shown being tested to determine whether it is equal to zero, greater than (>) zero, or less than (<) zero, i.e., a negative value.

In this case, the two variables Y and Z are compared ("$Y:Z$" means to "compare Y to Z").

Figure 9-8. Decision Symbol Examples

198

Figure 9-9 completes the chart begun in Figure 9-7 and shows the program steps which must be performed by Professor Bal Sheet to compute the average grade. This chart also illustrates the use of connector symbols. As we have seen, when the last card is processed, the computer is ready to figure the average grade. This step is performed by the first processing instruction below the upper connector labeled "1." The remaining steps in the chart are self-explanatory.

Predefined process Programmers frequently find that certain kinds of processing operations are repeated in one or more of the programs used by their company. For example, a department store programmer may find that the steps needed to compute cash discounts are being repeated

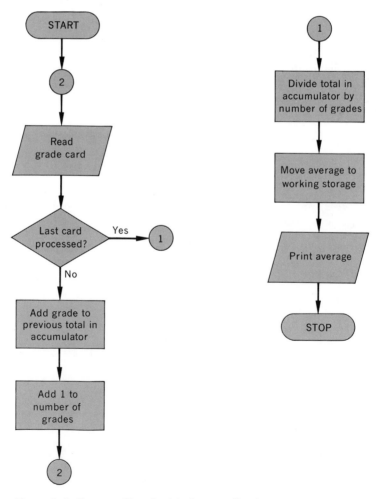

Figure 9-9. Program Flowchart to Average Grades

several times in some programs and are being used in a number of different programs. Instead of rewriting this small subordinate routine each time it is needed, the programmer can prepare it once and then integrate it into the program or programs as required. "Libraries" of these predefined processes or *subroutines* are often maintained to reduce the cost and time of programming. Thus, a single predefined process symbol replaces a number of operations which are not detailed at that particular point in the chart. In short, the subroutine receives input from the primary program, performs its limited task, and then returns the output to the primary program.

Annotation flag The comments made in Figure 9-4 also apply to program flowcharts.

Benefits and limitations of flowcharts

The following *benefits* may be obtained through the use of flowcharts:

1. *Quicker grasp of relationships.* Before any problem can be solved, it must be understood. The relationships which exist among problem elements must be identified. Current and proposed procedures may be understood more rapidly through the use of charts. It is usually quicker and easier for an analyst or programmer to chart a lengthy procedure than it is for him to describe it by means of pages of written notes. Thus, more time may be devoted to acquiring understanding.

2. *Effective analysis.* The flowchart becomes a model of a program or system which can be broken down into detailed parts for study. Problems may be identified; new approaches may be suggested.

3. *Effective synthesis.* Synthesis is the opposite of analysis — it is the combination of the various parts into a whole entity. Flowcharts may be used as working models in the design of new programs and systems. Elements of old approaches may be combined with new design ideas to give an effective processing plan.

4. *Communication.* Flowcharts aid in communicating the facts of a business problem to those whose skills are needed in the solution. The old adage that "a picture is worth a thousand words" contains an element of truth when the pictures happen to be flowchart symbols.

5. *Proper program documentation.* Program *documentation* involves collecting, organizing, storing, and otherwise maintaining a complete historical record of programs and the other business documents associated with the firm's data processing systems. Proper program documentation is needed for the following reasons:

   a. If projects are postponed, proper documentation which indicates the problem definition, the task objective, the extent of prior work, etc., will not have to be duplicated.

b. If programs are modified in the future (and modification occurs in many cases), proper documentation will brief the programmer on what was originally done and will thus help him to understand the problem better.

c. If a new computer system is installed, proper documentation will aid greatly in program conversion.

d. If staff changes occur, proper documentation will help new employees understand the existing programs.

From what we have seen of the nature of flowcharts, it is obvious that they provide valuable documentation support for any program.

6. *Efficient coding.* The program flowchart acts as a guide or blueprint during the program preparation phase. Instructions coded in a programming language may be checked against the flowchart to make sure that no steps are omitted.

7. *Orderly testing and debugging of programs.* If errors are discovered in the program when it is given a test run, the flowchart helps in the *debugging* process — i.e., it helps in detecting, locating, and removing mistakes. The programmer can refer to the chart as he rechecks the steps and logic of the written instructions.

8. *Efficient program maintenance.* The maintenance (through necessary modification) of operating programs is facilitated by flowcharts. The chart helps the programmer concentrate his attention on that part of the information flow which is to be modified.

In spite of their many obvious advantages, flowcharts have a few *limitations.* The first is that complex and detailed charts are sometimes laborious to plan and draw—especially when a large number of decision paths are involved. A second limitation in such a situation is that although branches from a *single* decision symbol are easy to follow, the actions to be taken given certain specified conditions would be difficult to follow if there were *several* paths.

The flowchart in Figure 9-10 shows how a department store handles the billing of *overdue* accounts. A late payment penalty is charged to accounts thirty or more days overdue.[3] The amount of the penalty is based on the unpaid balance in the account: If the balance is over $200—i.e., if the balance is *not* equal to or less than ($\leq$) $200—the penalty is 3 percent; otherwise a 2 percent charge is levied. The amount of the penalty must be added to the next bill sent to the customer. If the account is sixty days or more overdue (≥ 60), a warning message is printed on the bill. Accounts which are *less than* thirty days overdue (< 30) are not included in this procedure. But in the

[3] In Fig. 9-10, the symbol $\geq$ means "equal to or greater than." Therefore $\geq$ 30 refers to accounts equal to or greater than thirty days overdue. Similarly, $\leq$ means "equal to or less than."

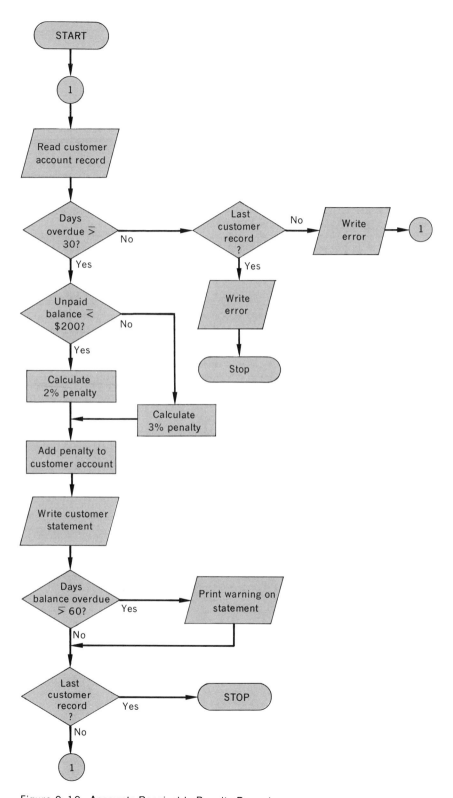

Figure 9-10. Accounts Receivable Penalty Procedure

event that such an account is entered by mistake, provision is made to prevent it from being processed. The store's credit manager handles, on an individual basis, those accounts which remain unpaid after a certain time.

Although the procedure in Figure 9-10 is relatively simple, it is not immediately obvious, for example, what actions would be taken if a particular account with a balance of $300 were sixty days or more overdue. (What actions *would* be taken?) Of course, with more complex problems the appropriate actions become much more obscure when flowcharts are used. Under such circumstances, flowcharts may be replaced or supplemented by decision tables.

DECISION TABLES

A decision table can be a powerful tool for defining complex program logic. Figure 9-11 shows the basic table format. The table is divided by the bottom horizontal heavy line into two main parts: the upper part, which contains the *conditions and questions* that are to be considered in reaching a decision, and the lower part, which contains the prescribed *action* to be taken when a given set of conditions is present. The conditions and questions are written in the *condition stub* to the left of the vertical heavy line. The contents of the condition stub correspond to the statements and questions contained in the decision symbols of the flowchart; the *condition entries* to the right of the heavy vertical line in the figure correspond to the branches or paths going out from decision symbols in a flowchart. Thus a condition entry may be a simple yes (Y) or no (N); it may be a symbol which shows relationship between variables ($>$, $<$, $=$, $\geq$, etc.); or it may be the outcome of certain tests (code 1, code 2, etc.). The

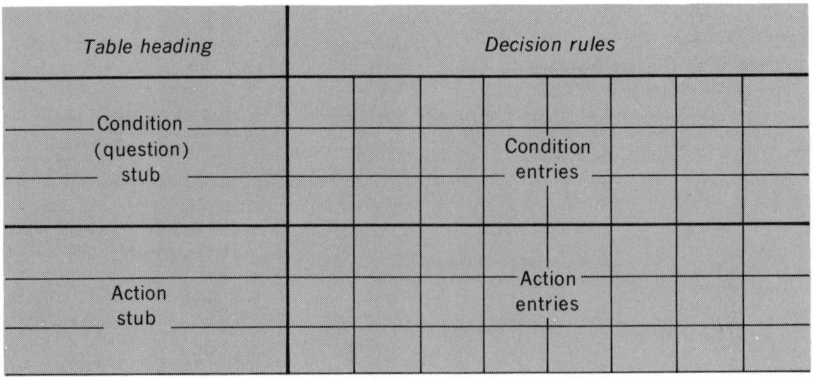

Figure 9-11. Decision Table Format

action statements—which correspond to the action statements located in nondecision symbols of a flowchart—are written in the *action stub*. The conditions may be listed in any convenient order; the actions are listed in the order in which they are normally executed. Decision rule columns are present in the *body* of the table to the right of the condition and action stubs.

A maze of possible flow paths may exist between START and STOP in a program. *Each* of the columns in the table body is the equivalent of *one* path through the flowchart and is called a *rule*. When a table is completed, each rule column which is used contains one or more condition entries. An example should help clarify matters.

Figure 9-12 shows the decision table for the accounts receivable penalty procedure charted in Figure 9-10. You will notice that the statements in the condition stub correspond to the questions being asked in the flowchart decision symbols. You will also note that the action statements correspond to the directions given or implied by the other flowchart symbols. A few paragraphs earlier this question was asked: What actions would be taken if an account with a balance of $300 were sixty days or more overdue? Let us now look at column 4 (which follows that particular path through the flowchart) to check

Accounts receivable penalty procedure	Rule number						
	1	2	3	4	5	6	7
Condition Number days balance overdue	$\geq$ 30	$\geq$ 30	$\geq$ 60	$\geq$ 60	< 30	< 30	
Number days balance overdue	< 60	< 60					
Unpaid balance $\leq$ $200?	Y	N	Y	N			
Last customer account record?	N	N	N	N	N	Y	Y
Action Calculate 2% penalty	x		x				
Calculate 3% penalty		x		x			
Add penalty to customer account	x	x	x	x			
Write customer statement	x	x	x	x			
Print warning on statement			x	x			
Write error					x	x	
Go to next account record	x	x	x	x	x		
Stop						x	x

Figure 9-12. Decision Table for Accounts Receivable Penalty Procedure (Source: Figure 9-10)

the answer. The first entry in the column shows that the account is sixty days or more overdue. The second condition is irrelevant in this case, so the space in rule 4 is left blank. The second entry tells us that the unpaid balance is not equal to or less than $200, so therefore it must be greater than that figure. The third entry merely shows that the last record has not yet been processed. Thus, the set of conditions in rule 4 has defined our problem! (The other condition sets have defined all the other feasible paths or situations.)

Now what about the *answer* to the problem? An x has been placed in column 4 opposite each appropriate action which helps satisfy the given set of conditions. You can compare your answer with the one indicated in Figure 9-12. You may also want to trace through the table and the flowchart to see what actions are taken when other possible conditions occur.

In our simple example we have compared a decision table with the flowchart of the problem. But in actual practice, tables are not necessarily compared with charts. Why? Simply because there may be no flowchart. As noted earlier, tables may be used as chart substitutes. A number of small interconnected tables may be quickly constructed to express the logic required to solve complex problems.

Benefits of decision tables

The following benefits may be obtained through the use of decision tables:

1. *Less danger of omitting a logical possibility.* Tables force the analyst to think the problem through. For example, if there are three conditions to be considered, each of which can be answered yes or no, then there are 2^3 or 8 possible paths or rules.[4] Some of these conceivable paths may not, of course, be pertinent to the problem. But by knowing the total number of paths, the analyst lessens the danger of forgetting one.

2. *Better communication between interested parties.* Tables can perform a valuable communication function. An analyst may design a new system and present it in the form of a table or tables to other analysts, to programmers, and to managers and executives. The table format is easily followed by others. Flowchart symbols, on the other hand, are not always standardized, and this factor may hinder their communication value. Tables appear to be easier for many managers to follow than flowcharts. An operating

[4] These rules contain the following entries:

(1)	(2)	(3)	(4)	(5)	(6)	(7)	(8)
Y	Y	Y	N	Y	N	N	N
Y	Y	N	Y	N	Y	N	N
Y	N	Y	Y	N	N	Y	N

manager can quickly trace and verify those paths in the procedure which are of greatest interest to him.

3. *Easier construction and adaptability.* Tables are easier to draw up than comparable flowcharts. They are also easier to change, since it is a relatively simple matter to add conditions, rules, and actions to a table.

4. *More compact program documentation.* Several pages of flow charting may be condensed into one small table. And, of course, it is easier to follow a particular flow path down one column than it is to follow the same path through several flowchart pages.

5. *Direct conversion into computer programs.* It is possible for the contents of a decision table to be coded directly into a language which the computer understands. For example, DETAB/65 (DETAB stands for DEcision TABle, while 65 refers to 1965) is a software aid which converts table contents directly into programs written in the COBOL language.[5]

Decision tables appear to have an edge over flowcharts in expressing complex decision logic. However, they are not as widely used as flowcharts because (1) many problems are simple, have few branches, and lend themselves to charting; (2) charts are able to express the *total sequence* of events better; and (3) charts are familiar to, and preferred by, many programmers who resist changing to the use of tables.[6]

SUMMARY

Before a computer can be used to solve a business problem, the problem itself must be defined. Problem data must be gathered, organized, and analyzed. From problem analysis may come ideas for improvement of old methods. New approaches to problem solving may be designed. Once broad system specifications have been determined, the programming process may begin. The first step in programming is to break the broad specifications down into specific arithmetic and logic operations. The remaining steps are (1) to prepare these operations in a form which the processor can accept and (2) to test and convert to the new programs and to revise and maintain them as needed. These remaining steps will be considered in the next chapter.

The basic tools of programming analysis are flowcharts and decision tables. System flowcharts provide the broad overview required for programming analysis to begin. Program flowcharts evolve from the system charts. A set of standardized charting symbols is presented in Figures 9-2 to 9-4. When com-

[5] COBOL stands for COmmon Business Oriented Language, and will be described in the next chapter.

[6] There are a number of reasons for such resistance. One is that if tables were used, new techniques and habits would have to be acquired, and programmers, like the rest of us, prefer to stay with familiar methods. Also, it is easy to see that some programmers, familiar with such software aids as DETAB/65, might feel that tables were a threat to their position.

pared with pages of written notes, flowcharts help the programmer obtain a quicker grasp of relationships. Charts also aid in communication, provide valuable documentation support, and contribute to more efficient coding and program maintenance.

A decision table is an excellent means of defining complex program logic. In this respect it has an edge over flowcharts. A table is easy to construct and change. It is more compact, provides excellent program documentation, and is an aid in communication.

DISCUSSION QUESTIONS

1 Identify and discuss the steps which must be followed to use computers to process business data.

2 (a) What is a system flowchart? (b) How is it used?

3 (a) What symbols are used in system flowcharts to represent input and output? (b) To represent a manual operation?

4 (a) What is the purpose of a program flowchart? (b) How does it differ from a systems flowchart?

5 (a) What symbols are used in a program flowchart to represent input and output, processing, decision, terminal, connector? (b) Construct a flowchart on a problem of your choice using these symbols.

6 What is a subroutine?

7 Discuss the benefits and limitations of flowcharts.

8 Why is proper documentation required?

9 (a) What is a decision table? (b) Explain the basic parts of the decision table. (c) What is a rule?

10 What benefits may be obtained from the use of decision tables?

SELECTED REFERENCES

Richard G. Canning, "How to Use Decision Tables," *EDP Analyzer*, May, 1966, 11 pages.

W. W. Martin, "Flow Charting: Shorthand, Analysis & Model," *Systems & Procedures Journal*, March-April, 1966, pp. 14-22.

James I. Morgan, "Decision Tables," *Management Services*, January-February, 1965, pp. 13-18.

Harley H. Rudolph, Jr., "Flow Charting: A Systems and Control Technique," *Management Services*, September-October, 1966, pp. 24-30.

10. PROGRAM PREPARATION

The purpose of this chapter is not, of course, to make a programmer of the reader; entire books have been written which have this as their objective. Rather, the purpose here is to give the reader an idea of what a programming language is and of what is involved in expressing simple problems in a language which is acceptable to a computer. Therefore, in the following pages we shall look at (1) *the computer instruction*, (2) *computer languages*, (3) *program coding*, and (4) *programming aids*.

THE COMPUTER INSTRUCTION

A program, we know, is a complete set of written instructions which enables the computer to process a particular application. Thus, the instruction is the basic component in program preparation. Like a sentence, an instruction consists of a subject and a predicate. The subject, however, is usually *not* specifically mentioned; it is, instead, some *implied* part of the computer system which is directed to execute the command that is given. For example, if a teacher tells a student to "read the book," the student will interpret this instruction correctly even though the subject "you" is omitted. Similarly, if the machine is told to "ADD 0184," the control unit will interpret this correctly to mean that the arithmetic-logic unit is to add the contents of address 0184 to the contents of the accumulator.

In addition to an implied subject, every computer instruction has an explicit predicate consisting of at least two parts. The *first* part is referred to as the *command* or the *operation code*; it answers the question: What?—i.e., it tells the computer what operation it is to perform. Each machine has a limited number of built-in commands which it is capable of executing. The *second* explicit part of the instruction, known as the *operand*, names the object of the operation.

In general terms, the operand answers the question: Where?—i.e., it tells the computer where to find or store the data or other instructions which are to be manipulated. Thus, an operand may indicate:

1. The location where data to be processed are to be found.
2. The location where the result of processing is to be stored.
3. The location where the next instruction to be executed is to be found. (When this type of operand is not specified, the instructions are taken in sequence.)

The *number* of operands, and therefore the structure or format of the instruction, *varies* from one computer to another. Up to this point we have dealt only with instructions having a *single* operand. But in addition to the *single-address* format there are also *two-address* and *three-address* command structures.

In earlier chapters we have seen that several instructions may be required to complete an arithmetic operation when a single-address format is used. For example, Figure 10-1a shows the procedure which may be required to add two numbers and store the result. Figure 10-1b shows how an addition may be handled in a two-address machine, while Figure 10-1c demonstrates a three-address instruction format. The three-address design is well suited to arithmetic operations which, by their nature, normally require two values to yield a third. Yet for nonarithmetic operations, three operands may not be needed, and thus the design may waste storage space. However, variable word-length computers frequently have the ability to vary the number of operands in the instruction word. Of course, the programmer must prepare his instructions according to the format required by the machine with which he is working.

The *execution* of program instructions was traced through the arithmetic-logic and control units in Chapter 8 so we need not repeat that topic here. It is worth noting, however, that the number of registers in the arithmetic-logic and control units varies with the design of the instruction format.

Command repertoire

The number of commands in a machine's repertoire may range from less than 30 to more than 100. These commands may be classified into arithmetic, logic, data movement, and control categories. The *arithmetic* commands to permit addition, subtraction, multiplication, and division are, of course, common in business computers. *Logic* com-

Command	Operand	Explanation
(1) CLA	0184	Three steps are used to perform an addition and a storage operation. The accumulator is cleared of previous data, and the number in address 0184 is then put in that register (1). The number in address 8672 is added to the first number. The result is now in the accumulator (2). The result in the accumulator is stored in address 1273 (3).
(2) ADD	8672	
(3) STO	1273	

(a)

Command	First operand	Second operand	Explanation
(1) ADD	0184	8672	The number in address 8672 is added to the number in location 0184. The result may automatically be stored in address 0184 by the computer circuitry. Of course, this erases the original number contained in 0184, so if that number is to be saved, it must be duplicated elsewhere *prior* to the add instruction. Instructions (2) and (3) show how this could be done. Instruction (2) duplicates the contents of 0184 in 0185 prior to the addition order (3).
(2) MOVE	0184	0185	
(3) ADD	0184	8672	

(b)

Command	First operand	Second operand	Third operand	Explanation
(1) ADD	0184	8672	1273	The number in address 8672 is added to the number in 0184, and the result is stored in address 1273.

(c)

Figure 10-1. Command Structures (a) Single-address Structure; (b) Two-address Structure; and (c) Three-address Structure

mands are available to permit comparison between two values. They are also provided to alter the sequence of program instructions. For example, a command to BRANCH ON CONDITION TEST might tell the computer to branch to an instruction located at a specified address *if* value A were greater than value B. Otherwise, the program would continue in sequence. *Data movement* commands provide for the transfer of data within the CPU. An example of a situation which calls for such a command is shown in Figure 10-1*b*. If the programmer of the two-address processor wishes to preserve the number in address 0184 for future use, he must copy the number in another location prior to the add instruction. *Control* commands are required (1) to transfer data from input devices into the CPU storage unit, (2) to define computer words in variable word-length processors, (3) to interrupt and/or halt the processing operation, and (4) to transfer information from working storage to output devices.

Figure 10-2 presents the command repertoire of a popular business computer. Instruction lists for several other business processors are similar. A symbolic code used to represent each command is also shown in Figure 10-2.

COMPUTER LANGUAGES

In writing his program instructions, the programmer must use a language which can be understood by the computer. There are several approaches which can achieve man-machine communication. To illustrate these approaches, let us assume that the computer only understands Russian, while the programmer's language is English. How can communication occur? One approach is for the programmer to code laboriously, with the help of a translating dictionary, each of his instructions into Russian prior to giving them to the processor. This approach is fine from the machine's standpoint, but the programmer finds it awkward.

Another approach is a compromise between man and machine. The programmer first writes his instructions in a code which is easier for him to relate to English. Unfortunately, this code is not the machine's language (Russian), so it does not understand the orders. However, the programmer has an answer to the dilemma. When he gives the computer the coded instructions, he also gives it another program—one which enables it to translate the instruction code into its own language. In other words, the translating program corresponds in our example to an English-to-Russian dictionary, and the translating job is turned over to the machine. The programmer finds this approach much more to his liking; the machine—being a machine—has no objection. The compromise approach between man and machine is the one which is followed in business programming.

A third approach, and a most desirable one from man's point of view, is for the machine to accept and interpret instructions written (without constraints) in everyday English terms.[1] The semantic problems involved in this approach, however, are formidable. John Pfeiffer points out that while the sentence "time flies like an arrow" may seem clear to man, it is subject to several machine interpretations. One

[1] As we shall soon see, the COBOL language uses English words, but there are a number of constraints imposed on the way these words are employed.

Command code	Command name
	ARITHMETIC COMMANDS
A	Decimal add
S	Decimal subtract
M	Decimal multiply
D	Decimal divide
BA	Binary add
BS	Binary subtract
ZA	Zero and add
ZS	Zero and subtract

	LOGIC COMMANDS
EXT	Extract
HA	Half add
SST	Substitute
C	Compare
B	Branch (unconditional)
BCT	Branch on condition test
BCC	Branch on character condition
BCE	Branch if character equal
BBE	Branch on bit equal

	DATA MOVE COMMANDS
MCW	Move characters to wordmark
LCA	Load characters to A-field wordmark
EXM	Extended move
MAT	Move and translate
MIT	Move item and translate
MCE	Move characters and edit

	CONTROL COMMANDS
SW	Set wordmark
SI	Set item mark
CW	Clear wordmark
CI	Clear item mark
H	Halt
NOP	No operation
CAM	Change addressing mode
CSM	Change sequencing mode
SCR	Store control registers
LCR	Load control registers
MC	Monitor call
SVI	Store variant and indicators
RVI	Restore variant and indicators
RNM	Restore normal mode
PDT	Peripheral data transfer
PCB	Peripheral control and branch

Figure 10-2. Command Repertoire, Honeywell Model 200 Computer

incorrect translation, for example, might be: "Time the speed of flies as quickly as you can." ("Time" is considered a verb.) Another false interpretation might be that "certain flies enjoy an arrow." ("Time" is now considered an adjective, while "like" is interpreted as a verb.)[2]

In this section we shall consider the following three language categories: *machine language, symbolic language*, and *procedure oriented language*. We shall deal primarily with categories here rather than with specific languages used with specific machines for very simple reasons: There are probably more than 1,000 programming languages, and some of these languages have dozens of dialects![3] Some languages can be used only with a single machine; some can be used with several models of the same manufacturer but cannot be used with other makes; and some can be used with more than one make and model.

Machine language

Early computers were quite intolerant—the programmer had to translate his instructions into the machine language form which the computers understood. Of course, this language was not Russian. Rather, it was a string of numbers which represented the command code and the operand address. To compound the difficulty for the programmer, the string of numbers was often not even in decimal form. For example, the instruction to ADD 0184 looks like this in the IBM 7040 machine language:[4]

0001000000000000000000000010111000

In addition to remembering the dozens of code numbers for the commands in the machine's repertoire, the programmer was also forced to keep track of the storage locations of data and instructions. The initial coding often took months, was therefore quite expensive, and often resulted in error. Checking instructions to locate errors was about as tedious as writing them initially, because their code numbers became as meaningless to the programmer within minutes after he had prepared them as they appear to us. And if a written program had to be modified at a later date, the work involved could take weeks to finish.

[2] See John Pfeiffer, "Machines That Men Can Talk With," *Fortune*, vol. 69, May, 1964, pp. 153–156 ff.

[3] COBOL is a business-oriented language which is somewhat standardized. Yet there can be a number of different COBOL dialects depending on the make and model of the processor being used.

[4] In this case, the last eight bits represent 0184.

Symbolic language

To ease the programmer's burden, *mnemonic* command codes and *symbolic* addresses were developed in the early 1950s. The word "mnemonic" (pronounced ne-mon-ik) refers to a memory aid. One of the first steps to improve the program preparation process was to substitute letter symbols for basic machine language command codes. Figure 10-2 shows the mnemonic coding used in the Honeywell model 200 computer. Each business computer now has a mnemonic code although, of course, the actual symbols vary among makes and models.[5] For example, erasing old data in the accumulator and then adding the contents of an address to it is a common command. The mnemonic code used in the Honeywell 200 is ZA (Zero and Add). In other machines the symbol for the same operation may be CLA (CLear accumulator and Add) or RAD (Reset accumulator and ADd). Machine language is *still used* by the computer in the actual processing of the data, but it first translates the specified command code symbol into its machine language equivalent.

The improvement in the writing of command codes set the stage for further advances. It was reasoned that if the computer could be used to translate convenient symbols into basic commands, why couldn't it also be used to perform other clerical coding functions such as assigning storage addresses to data? This question led to *symbolic addressing*—i.e., it led to the practice of expressing an address, not in terms of its absolute numerical location, but rather in terms of symbols convenient to the programmer.

In the early stages of symbolic addressing, the programmer initially assigned a symbolic name and an actual address to a data item. For example, the total value of merchandise purchased during a month by a department store customer might be assigned to address 0063 by the programmer and given the symbolic name of TOTAL. Also, the value of merchandise returned unused during the month might be assigned to address 2047 and given the symbolic name of CREDIT. Then, for the remainder of the program, the programmer would refer to the *symbolic names rather than to the addresses* when such items were to be processed. Thus, an instruction might be written "S CREDIT, TOTAL" to subtract the value of returned goods from the total amount purchased to find the amount of the customer's monthly bill. The computer might then translate this symbolic instruction into the following machine language string of bits:[6]

[5] Some examples of symbolic programming languages are IBM's Autocoder and Honeywell's Easycoder.

[6] This example uses a format and the machine language of the Honeywell 200.

011111	011111111111	000000111111
Command code	2047	0063
(S)	(CREDIT)	(TOTAL)

Another improvement was that the programmer turned the task of assigning and keeping track of instruction addresses over to the computer. The programmer merely told the machine the storage address number of the *first* program instruction, and then all others were automatically stored in sequence from that point by the processor. If another instruction were to be added later to the program, it was not then necessary to modify the addresses of all instructions which followed the point of insertion (as would have to be done in the case of programs written in machine language). In such a case, the processor automatically adjusted storage locations the next time the program was used.

The programmer no longer assigns actual address numbers to symbolic data items as he did initially. "In fact, all the coder has to do is specify where he wants the first location in his program. The assembly program will take it from there, allocating a location for each instruction and each word of data."[7]

The *assembly program* is the software aid which translates the symbolic language *source program* into a machine language *object program*. Figure 10-3 may help to clear up any confusion about the three different programs. The following steps (numbered in Figure 10-3) take place during the *assembly* and *production* runs:[8]

1. The *assembly program* is read into the computer where it has complete control over the translating procedure. This program is generally supplied by the manufacturer of the machine as part of the total hardware-software package.

2. The *source program* written by the programmer in the symbolic language of the machine is recorded on an input medium such as punched cards.

3. During the assembly the source program is treated as data and is read into the CPU an instruction at a time under the control of the assembly program.

4. The assembly program translates the source program into a machine language *object program,* which is recorded on tapes or cards as the output of the assembly run. It is important to remember that during the *assembly run* no problem data are processed. That is, the source program is *not be-*

[7] Herbert D. Leeds and Gerald M. Weinberg, *Computer Programming Fundamentals* (2d ed.; New York: McGraw-Hill Book Company, 1966), p. 64.

[8] This general procedure was briefly mentioned in Chap. 3.

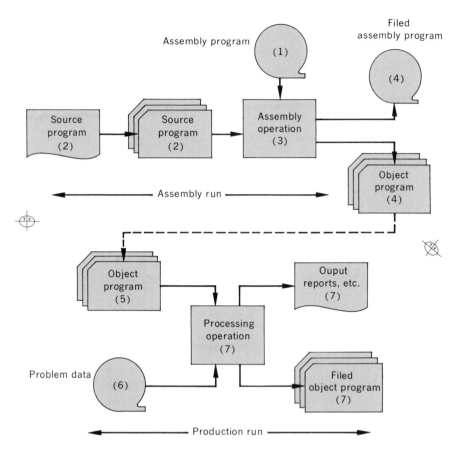

Figure 10-3. Converting Symbolic Language to Machine Language

ing executed; it is merely being converted into a form so that it *can* be executed. After the assembly run, the assembly program is filed for future use.

5. The object program is read into the CPU as the first step in the *production run.*

6. Problem data, recorded on a suitable input medium, are read into the CPU under object program control.

7. The application is processed, the information output is properly received, and the object program is filed for future repetitive use.

To summarize, symbolic languages possess many advantages over machine language coding. Much time is saved (in some cases coding time has been reduced by 60 percent); detail is reduced; fewer errors are made (and those which are made are easier to find); and programs are much easier to modify.

Procedure oriented language

Coding in symbolic language is still time consuming. Also, symbolic languages are *machine oriented*—i.e., they are designed for the specific make and model of processor being used. Programs would have to be recoded if the company acquired a different machine. Furthermore, the programmer writing instructions in a machine's symbolic language must have an intimate knowledge of the workings of that processor. Finally, the earlier assembly programs produced *one* machine instruction for each source program instruction.

To speed-up coding, later assembly programs were developed which could produce a *variable* amount of machine language code for *each* source program instruction. In other words, a single *macro instruction* might produce *several* lines of machine language code. However, these more-advanced assembly programs were still machine oriented; they were still written to meet the requirements of a specific equipment line.

The development of mnemonic techniques and macro instructions led to the development of *procedure oriented* languages.[9] As the name implies, languages have been created which are oriented toward a specific class of processing problems. In other words, a class of similar problems is isolated, and a language is developed to process these types of applications. A number of languages have been designed to process problems of a scientific-mathematic nature. Other languages have appeared which emphasize the processing of business applications.

Unlike symbolic programs, procedure oriented programs may be used with a number of different hardware makes and models with little or no modification. Thus, reprogramming expense is greatly reduced when new equipment is acquired. Other advantages of procedure oriented languages are (1) they are easier to learn than symbolic languages, (2) they require less time to write, (3) they provide better documentation, and (4) they are easier to maintain. Also, a programmer skilled in writing programs in such a language is not restricted to using a single machine.[10]

Naturally, a source program written in a procedural language must also be translated into a machine-usable code. The translating pro-

[9] These are also called "high-level languages" and "problem oriented languages."
[10] Sometimes these advantages must be traded off against some loss of efficiency in the compiler object program. Certainly, a programmer *skilled* in the machine oriented language of a particular processor should be able to produce a more efficient object program, i.e., one which takes less storage space, runs faster, etc., than the average programmer working with a procedural language. Whether it would be economical for him to do so, however, is another matter.

gram which performs this operation is called a *compiler*. Compilers, like advanced assembly programs, may generate many lines of machine code for each source program instruction. A *compiling run* is required before problem data can be processed. With the exception that a compiler program is substituted for an assembly program, the procedures are the same as those shown in Figure 10-3. The production run follows the compiling run.

Common procedural languages

The first compiler had the name A-2 and was developed in 1952 by UNIVAC's Dr. Grace M. Hopper. Since that time, many procedural languages have been produced—generally by equipment manufacturers and/or by committees of interested parties. In 1956, UNIVAC also produced a language to solve mathematical problems (MATH-MAT-IC) and one to process commercial problems (FLOW-MATIC). Most procedural languages have emphasized one of these two paths. Slightly later, the IT (Internal Translator) was developed, which could be used by both the IBM 650 and the Burroughs 205 Datatron. This marked the first time that a compiler was used with equipment produced by different manufacturers.

FORTRAN   In 1954, an IBM-sponsored committee began work on a scientific-mathematic language. The result of this effort was FORTRAN (FORmula TRANslation), which was introduced in 1957 for the IBM 704 computer. Since its introduction, FORTRAN has been widely accepted and has been revised a number of times.[11] All IBM computers designed since 1957 have had a FORTRAN compiler. In fact, the overwhelming majority of *all* makes and models now in use have FORTRAN capability. Because of this widespread acceptance, the American Standards Association in 1962 began work on a FORTRAN standard language. This standard has now been accepted.[12]

---

[11] FORTRAN II is the most commonly used version. There is also a FORTRAN IV, which has some additional features.

[12] In statistical sampling procedures, a commonly used measure is the standard deviation which has the following formula:

$$\sqrt{\frac{\Sigma X^2 - (\Sigma X)^2/N}{N-1}}$$

where Σ represents "the sum of" a value; X represents the variable being sampled; and N represents the size of the sample. A single FORTRAN statement to instruct the processor to compute a standard deviation may then look like this:

```
STDEV = SQRT [(SUMSQ - SUM**2/SIZE)/(SIZE - 1.0)]
```

ALGOL   In 1957, a group of international mathematicians met to begin the design of a language suited to their needs. ALGOL (<u>ALGO</u>rithmic <u>L</u>anguage) was the eventual result of this effort. Like FORTRAN, ALGOL has been revised several times in the past few years. While it is used extensively in Europe, its "competitor," FORTRAN, is the dominant scientific language in the United States.

COBOL   The COBOL (<u>CO</u>mmon <u>B</u>usiness <u>O</u>riented <u>L</u>anguage) language, written by a committee, was designed to serve two purposes. The first was that COBOL was specifically to be a tool of the business data processing community. The second purpose was that COBOL was to help users achieve program compatibility. The design group gathered at the Pentagon in Washington, D.C., in May, 1959, with the official sanction of the U.S. Department of Defense—the world's largest single user of computers. Members of the <u>CO</u>nference of <u>DA</u>ta <u>SY</u>stems <u>L</u>anguages (CODASYL) represented computer manufacturers, government agencies, user organizations, and universities. The CO-DASYL Short-Range Committee which prepared the COBOL framework consisted of representatives from Federal government agencies (the Air Material Command, the Bureau of Ships, and the Bureau of Standards) and from computer manufacturers (IBM, Honeywell, Burroughs, RCA, UNIVAC Division of Sperry-Rand, and Sylvania). From June to December, 1959, this committee worked on the language specifications. Their final report was approved in January, 1960, and the language specifications were published a few months later by the Government Printing Office.

     Also in 1960, the Department of Defense announced that it would not purchase or lease any computer which did not have an available COBOL compiler unless the manufacturer could prove that such software would not enhance machine performance. Early in 1961, Westinghouse Electric Corporation followed this lead by stating that all new equipment which they installed would have to have COBOL capability. Other large corporations followed with similar policies. With such backing, it is not surprising that since 1961 COBOL compilers have been prepared for all but the smallest commercial processors. Other CODASYL committees have continued to maintain, revise, and extend the initial specifications. COBOL has been used extensively for the past few years. We shall look at a simple COBOL example in the next section.

PL/I   Developed by IBM and a committee of users for the IBM System/360 family of computers, in the mid-1960s, PL/I (<u>P</u>rogramming <u>L</u>anguage I) is being promoted as a universal language—i.e., it is reputed to be a single high-level language which can be used to solve all types of business and scientific problems efficiently. As a scientific language, PL/I appears to be an extension of FORTRAN; however, COBOL-type data description is also used. Because there is the possibility that PL/I could replace both FORTRAN and COBOL, it has caused a great deal of controversy. Computer users are naturally anxious to protect the gigantic investment they have in FORTRAN and COBOL programs, and some fear the PL/I development will come at the expense of continued improvement in both of these languages. The measure of success of a language, of course, is determined by its use. How successful PL/I will be remains to be seen. It is definitely a language to watch.

Language selection

The large number of programming languages, the differences in compiler performance, the vast range of types of computing problems, the needs and hardware of the particular user, and the abilities of different programmers—all these factors combine to make language selection unbelievably complex. Yet the data processing manager must often evaluate and choose among the language alternatives available. Obtaining answers to the following questions may help in this evaluation:

1. *Are company programmers familiar with the language?* In many cases, the language used is simply the one which is best known to the programmers. If a language is not familiar, can it be learned quickly? Is it easy to use?

2. *What is the nature of the application?* Does the language perform well in applications of this type? Was it designed for such applications?

3. *Is a satisfactory compiler available?* There is an important distinction between a language and a compiler. A procedural language is a humanly convenient set of rules, conventions, and representations used to convey information from man to machine, while a compiler is a translator written by one or more programmers. It is entirely possible that a good language, when used with an inefficient compiler, will yield unsatisfactory results.

4. *How frequently will the application be processed?* If an application is processed repeatedly, attention must be given to operating speed, i.e., the time required to complete a production run. A symbolic language program usually has a shorter operating time than does a program of the same application written in a higher-level language. If the job is run frequently enough, the value of the operating time saved may be more than enough to offset the cost of additional time spent in program preparation. For limited-life

220

jobs, however, the faster the possible programming time is (with procedural languages), the more economical the approach.

5. *Is a hardware change anticipated during the life of the application?* Conversion of procedure oriented programs is easier and faster; machine oriented programs may have to be completely rewritten.

6. *Is the language being periodically improved and updated?* Will new machines continue to accept the language source programs?

PROGRAM CODING

In Chapter 5 we saw that business data processing often involves manipulating files of related records. These files, of course, vary in character, size, complexity, and location. A typical computer file processing job may consist of the following steps: (1) each input record is read into the computer; (2) there it is processed; (3) each updated record is then read out into an output file; and (4) when all records have been processed, they may be used as the bases for reports and summary measures. An example in Chapter 5 showed the processing of an accounts receivable file. Other common business file processing examples include the company payroll and the preparation of sales analyses by salesman, by region, or by product.

Because of his propensity to test and his willingness to incur low ratings in student opinion polls, Professor Balford Sheet, of Chapter 9 fame, has presented us with a problem which contains the *basics* of file processing. This problem is to determine the average (arithmetic mean) grade of Mr. A. Valiant Student—the sole survivor in Professor Sheet's accounting course. Each of the 30 grades recorded for Mr. Student represents a *single record*. Each grade score (or record) is punched into a card and read into a computer for processing. The processing operation involves adding together the individual grade scores. After each grade record is processed, it is then written on an output report by a high-speed printer. This written report is the output file on Val Student. When all records are processed, the machine then computes and prints a summary measure—the average score—which becomes the basis for Val's course grade.

Professor Sheet has written his program instructions in the COBOL language. In the remainder of this section we shall trace through the coding required for this example problem.[13]

Figure 10-4 shows the written source program prepared on a special

[13] For a more-thorough treatment of the COBOL language, see the list of publications cited at the end of this chapter.

IBM
COBOL PROGRAM SHEET
Form No. X28-1464-1 U/M 050
Printed in U.S.A.
Sheet _1_ of _4_
Identification AVERAGES (73-80)

System

Program AVERAGE GRADE

Programmer BAL SHEET   Date 10/13/99

Graphic / Punch

Punching Instructions   Card Form# *

```
SEQUENCE
(PAGE)(SERIAL)  A   B
 3   4 6 7  8   12      16      20      24      28      32      36      40      44      48      52      56      60      64      68      72
001010  IDENTIFICATION DIVISION.
   020  PROGRAM-ID.  'AVERAGES'.
   030  AUTHOR.  BAL SHEET.
   040  DATE-WRITTEN.  OCTOBER 13, 1999.
   050  DATE-COMPILED.  OCTOBER 13, 1999.

   060  ENVIRONMENT DIVISION.
   070  CONFIGURATION SECTION.
   080  SOURCE-COMPUTER.  IBM-360 F30.
   090  OBJECT-COMPUTER.  IBM-360 F30.
   100  INPUT-OUTPUT SECTION.
   110  FILE-CONTROL.
   120      SELECT GRADE-CARDS ASSIGN TO UNIT-RECORD 2540R.
   130      SELECT REPORT ASSIGN TO UNIT-RECORD 1403.

   140  DATA DIVISION.
   150  FILE SECTION.
   160  FD GRADE-CARDS, DATA RECORD IS GRADE-RECORD
   170      LABEL RECORDS ARE OMITTED.
   180  01 GRADE-RECORD.
   190      02 INITIALS-1  PICTURE IS A.
   200      02 INITIALS-2  PICTURE IS A.
   210      02 LAST-NAME   PICTURE IS A(12).
   220      02 SCORE       PICTURE IS 999.
   230      02 FILLER      PICTURE IS X(63).
```

* A standard card form, IBM electro C61897, is available for punching source statements from this form.

Figure 10-4

221

COBOL PROGRAM SHEET

Form No. X28-1464-1 U/M 050
Printed in U.S.A.

IBM

System ___
Program ___
Programmer ___   Date ___

Punching Instructions — Graphic ___ Punch ___ — Card Form# ___ — *

Sheet 2 of 4   Identification AVERAGES (73-80)

```
SEQUENCE
(PAGE) (SERIAL)  A  B
 3  4  6 7  8  12

002 010  FD  REPORT, DATA RECORD IS PRINT-LINE
    020      LABEL RECORDS ARE OMITTED.
    030  01  PRINT-LINE        PICTURE IS X(132).
    040      WORKING-STORAGE SECTION.
    050  77  ONE       PICTURE IS 9  USAGE IS COMPUTATIONAL-3  VALUE IS 1.
    060  77  ACCUMULATOR    PICTURE IS S99999  USAGE IS COMPUTATIONAL-3
    061      VALUE IS ZERO.
    070  77  NO-GRADES    PICTURE IS 99  USAGE IS COMPUTATIONAL-3
    071      VALUE IS ZERO.
    080  77  AVERAGE    PICTURE IS 999  USAGE IS COMPUTATIONAL-3
    081      VALUE IS ZERO.
    090  01  HEADING-LINE.
    100      02  FILLER     PICTURE IS X(10)  VALUE IS SPACES.
    110      02  FILLER     PICTURE IS X(6)   VALUE IS 'NAME'.
    120      02  INITIAL-P1   PICTURE IS A.
    130      02  FILLER     PICTURE IS X   VALUE IS '.'.
    140      02  INITIAL-P2   PICTURE IS A.
    150      02  FILLER     PICTURE IS XX  VALUE IS '.'.
    160      02  LAST-NAME-P   PICTURE IS A(12).
    170      02  FILLER     PICTURE IS X(99)  VALUE IS SPACES.
    180  01  HEAD-LINE-2.
    190      02  FILLER     PICTURE IS X(21)  VALUE IS SPACES.
    200      02  FILLER     PICTURE IS X(12)  VALUE IS 'TEST RESULTS'.
    210      02  FILLER     PICTURE IS X(99)  VALUE IS SPACES.
```

* A standard card form, IBM electro C61897, is available for punching source statements from this form.

Figure 10-4. (continued)

COBOL PROGRAM SHEET

Form No. X28-1464-1 1/UW 050
Printed in U.S.A.

System

Program

Programmer

Date

Punching Instructions

Graphic

Punch

Card Form #

Sheet 3 of 4

Identification AVERAGES

SEQUENCE (PAGE) (SERIAL)	CONT	A	B		
003010		01	DATA-LINE.		
020			02 FILLER	PICTURE IS X(5)	VALUE IS SPACES.
030			02 LABEL	PICTURE IS X(7)	VALUE IS SPACES.
040			02 FILLER	PICTURE IS X(9)	VALUE IS SPACES.
050			02 SCORE	PICTURE IS ZZ,ZZ9.	
060			02 FILLER	PICTURE IS X(105)	VALUE IS SPACES.
070			PROCEDURE DIVISION.		
080			OPEN-PARA.		
090			OPEN INPUT GRADE-CARDS OUTPUT REPORT.		
100			INITILIZ-PARA.		
110			PERFORM HEADING-ROUTINE.		
120			PROCESS-PARA.		
130			READ GRADE-CARDS AT END GO TO TOTAL-PARA.		
140			ADD SCORE OF GRADE-RECORD TO ACCUMULATOR.		
150			ADD ONE TO NO-GRADES.		
160			MOVE SCORE OF GRADE-RECORD TO SCORE OF DATA-LINE.		
170			WRITE REPORT FROM DATA-LINE AFTER ADVANCING 1 LINES.		
180			GO TO PROCESS-PARA.		
190			TOTAL-PARA.		
200			MOVE ACCUMULATOR TO SCORE OF DATA-LINE.		
210			WRITE REPORT FROM DATA-LINE AFTER ADVANCING 2 LINES.		
220			DIVIDE NO-GRADES INTO ACCUMULATOR GIVING AVERAGE ROUNDED.		
230			MOVE AVERAGE TO SCORE OF DATA-LINE.		
240			MOVE 'AVERAGE' TO LABEL.		

* A standard card form, IBM electro C61897, is available for punching source statements from this form.

Figure 10-4. (continued)

IBM COBOL PROGRAM SHEET

Form No. X28-1464-1 U/M 050
Printed in U.S.A.
Sheet 4 of 4
Identification
AVERAGES
73] [80

System

Program

Programmer

Date

Punching Instructions

Graphic

Punch

Card Form#

*

SEQUENCE				
(PAGE)	(SERIAL)	A	CONT. B	

```
004010    WRITE REPORT FROM DATA-LINE AFTER ADVANCING 2 LINES.
   020    CLOSE GRADE-CARDS REPORT, STOP RUN.
   030    HEADING-ROUTINE.
   040    MOVE INITIALS-1 TO INITIAL-P1.
   050    MOVE INITIALS-2 TO INITIAL-P2.
   060    MOVE LAST-NAME TO LAST-NAME-P.
   070    WRITE REPORT FROM HEADING-LINE AFTER ADVANCING 0 LINES.
   080    WRITE REPORT FROM HEAD-LINE-2 AFTER ADVANCING 2 LINES.
```

* A standard card form, IBM electro C61897, is available for punching source statements from this form.

Figure 10-4. (continued)

224

COBOL coding sheet. The heading information is self-explanatory. Each page has 25 lines and is designed to facilitate key punching (the numbers at the top of the sheet correspond to columns in an 80-column card). Each line is numbered by the programmer to indicate proper card sequences after the punching is completed. The first three spaces in a line indicate the *page number* (001, 002, etc.), while the next three spaces give the *line number* (010, 020, 030, etc.). It is customary to number lines by increments of 10 so that insertions may be made later in the program if needed—e.g., so that a line labeled 160 may be followed later by 161, 162, 163, etc. A dash (-) is written in column 7 if a *word* is continued from the previous line. The letters A and B directly over columns 8 and 12 indicate *margins* which are used in COBOL "punctuation."

There are two types of COBOL words—*reserved words* and *supplied words* (or *names*). Reserved words such as SELECT, ASSIGN, READ, USAGE, COMPUTATIØNAL, and PICTURE have special meaning to the compiler and *must* be used according to COBOL language rules. Supplied words or names such as GRADE-CARDS, GRADE-RECØRD, NØ-GRADES, REPØRT, and HEADING-RØUTINE, are assigned by the programmer.[14] In other words, a supplied word may be anything which has meaning to the programmer and which does not violate any of the language rules.[15]

Identification division

In Figure 10-4, the first entry (page 001, line 010) is IDENTIFICA-TION DIVISIØN. This is the *first* of *four* basic *divisions* in a COBOL source program. This division consists of one required *paragraph* which identifies the program (line 020). Additional optional paragraphs (with reserved names) may be included to identify the program author (line 030), to show the dates when the program is written and compiled (lines 040 and 050), and to furnish other desirable information. Like this sentence, division and paragraph headings must end with a period.

---

[14] Because the letters O, I, and Z resemble the numbers 0, 1, and 2, it is customary that they be written Ø, I, and Ƶ.

[15] Supplied words may be made up of combinations of characters taken from the 26 letters of the alphabet, the numerals 0 through 9, and the dash or hyphen (-). No blank spaces are permissible within a word. INVENTØRY-ØN-HAND is a valid supplied word because the dashes replace blank spaces. No more than 30 characters may be used in a word, nor may a word *begin* or *end* with a dash.

Environment division

The second COBOL division is the *environment division* (line 001060). This division describes the specific hardware being used and is therefore machine oriented. Since Professor Sheet has access to an IBM System/360 model 30 computer (Figure 10-5), the required *configuration section* of the environment division must reflect this fact. Lines 080 and 090 tell us that the program is compiled and run on this particular machine. The "F30" refers to the internal storage capacity (F) and the model number (30). The required *input/output section* describes the online I/O devices which are used in the processing. Lines 120 and 130 tell us that the input data cards (containing Val Student's individual test grades) are read by an IBM model 2540 card read-punch (Figure 5-8). The output report is printed by an IBM model 1403 printer. The environment division of a COBOL program must be rewritten any time the program is to be processed on different equipment. This rewriting, however, usually presents no problem.

Figure 10-5. IBM System/360 Model 30 (Courtesy IBM Corporation)

```
DATA DIVISION
File section

    FD   File name.........................
         01   Record name.......................
              02   Description of record item...........
              02   Description of record item............ .
              02   Description of record item...........
         01   Record name.......................

              .
              .
              .

    FD   File name.........................
         01   Record name.......................
              02   Description of record item...........
              02   Etc.

              .
              .
              .
```

Figure 10-6. File Section Organization

Data division

The *data division* (line 001140) is the third of the four COBOL divisions. In our example, there are two sections—the *file section* and the *working storage section.* The function of the file section (line 150) is to describe all data which enter or leave the CPU storage unit. Since business data are organized into files of records which consist of items, the file section entries are also grouped into these organizational levels, as shown in Figure 10-6. Every file to be processed is identified by a file description (and the letters FD) on the COBOL coding sheet.

In our example we have only two simple files—an input GRADE-CARD file and an output REPØRT file. The description of the GRADE-CARD file begins on line 001160 of Figure 10-4. There is only a single *type* of record in the input file, and this type of record is given the name of GRADE-RECØRD in line 160. The description of the items included in this type of record (an 80-column card) begins on line 190. In lines 190 through 220 we see that provision is made on the input cards for two initials, a last name, and a grade score. The COBOL words "INITIALS-1," "INITIALS-2," "LAST-NAME," and "SCØRE" are names which have been coined by Programmer Bal Sheet; they will be referred to again in the last division of the program.[16]

---

[16] *Every* supplied name mentioned in the procedure division must be described in the data division.

Example	Meaning
Picture is 999999.	The data item consists of six numeric characters.
Picture is 9(6).	Another way of expressing the preceding example.
Picture is 99V99.	The data item has four numeric characters with a decimal point between the second and third characters.
Picture is AAAAA.	There are five alphabetic characters in the data item.
Picture is XXXX.	Four alphanumeric characters are reserved for this data item.

Figure 10-7

The word "PICTURE," used in lines 190 through 230, is a reserved word which describes the data items. (Figure 10-7 shows the form and meaning of representative PICTURE clauses.) For example, the PICTURE IS A description tells the CPU the *size and class* of the words "INITIALS-1" and "INITIALS-2"—i.e., a *single* character tells the CPU that the size is one, and the character A also tells it that the class is *alphabetic*. The contents of the word "LAST-NAME" occupy 12 alphabetic character spaces. On line 220, the PICTURE IS 999 description indicates to the CPU that SCØRE occupies three spaces and that the data class is *numeric*. Line 230 is used to absorb unused space in the input records. The symbol X, when used in a PICTURE clause, specifies to the CPU that the character may be anything available in the machine's character set. On line 230, X(63) refers to 63 blank spaces. You will note that a total of 80 character spaces have been accounted for in lines 190 through 230. These 80 characters, of course, correspond to the 80 columns in the input record cards.

The output REPØRT file is described in Figure 10-4 (page 222) by lines 002010 through 002030. The output record is named "PRINT-

LINE," and a printer with 132 characters per line is being used. The detailed description of the printed output format is left to the working storage section.

The second major component of the data division is the working storage section. In Chapter 7 we saw that the working storage area of the CPU is a portion of internal storage set aside temporarily to hold data being processed and also to hold intermediate results of that processing. As might be expected, entries in the working storage section of the data division specify the memory locations which are needed during processing to hold (1) intermediate results, (2) exact record descriptions, and (3) other frequently used independent items.

The intermediate results and other items which are independent of any record are assigned a special level number (77) and must appear first in the working storage section. Following these entries come record descriptions (with a level code of 01). In our example, there are four independent items which are assigned specific working storage locations by the compiler program. The names and descriptions of these items are as follows:

1. ∅NE (line 002050). The word "∅NE" is used in the final COBOL division and is therefore defined and assigned to working storage. The number 1 occupies the *location named* "∅NE." This word is used for computational purposes.

2. ACCUMULAT∅R (lines 060 and 061). The word "ACCUMULAT∅R" identifies the location which stores Val Student's total test points during the processing — i.e., as the score on each test is read into the computer, it is added to the previous points, and the total is kept in ACCUMULAT∅R storage. The initial value of ACCUMULAT∅R is 0. Provision is made to store five numeric characters.

3. N∅-GRADES (lines 070 and 071). The word "N∅-GRADES" has been created by Programmer Sheet to represent the number of test grades processed. The initial value of this word is set at 0, but when the processing is completed, the number 30 is stored in the N∅-GRADES location. When Val's average grade is computed, the amount stored in ACCUMULAT∅R is divided by the number stored in N∅-GRADES.

4. AVERAGE (lines 080 and 081). The *result* of dividing N∅-GRADES into ACCUMULAT∅R is stored in the working storage location named "AVERAGE." Space is provided for three numeric characters. (Unfortunately, no student has ever come close to an average grade of 100 in Professor Sheet's course, but it *is* possible.)

The remainder of the working storage section describes the format of the printed output report shown in Figure 10-8. Program lines 100 to 170 describe the top line of print in Figure 10-8, while program lines 190 to 210 define the contents and location of the second printed

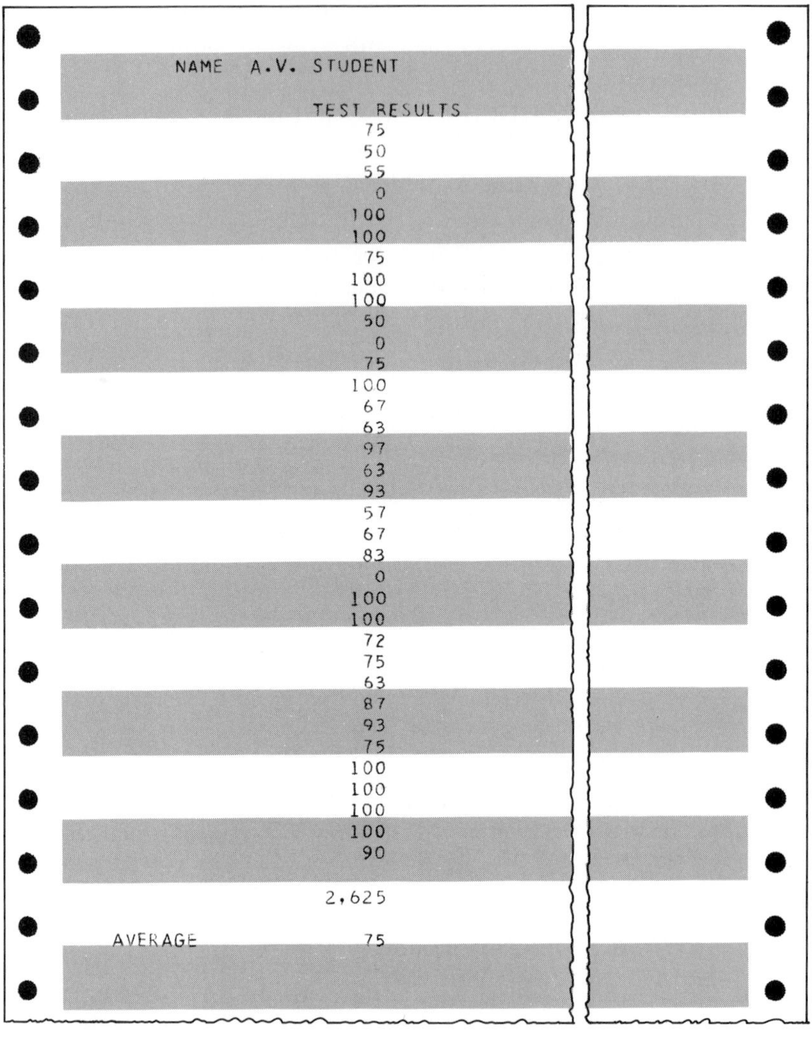

Figure 10-8

line. In this second printed line (HEAD-LINE-2), for example, the first 21 spaces are blank. Then, beginning with space number 22, the 12 fixed characters (TEST RESULTS) between the quotation marks[17] in program line 200 are printed. The remaining 99 spaces across the output report page are blank. The first six lines of the COBOL program sheet (Figure 10-4, page 223) describe the format of the last two printed lines on the output report.

[17] A COBOL word bounded by quotation marks is known as a *literal constant*.

Procedure division

The remaining lines of the COBOL example (Figure 10-4, pages 223 and 224) specify the steps which the computer follows in processing the application. The steps in this final *procedure division* make use of the names of records and independent items which are so precisely defined in the data division. The flowchart in Figure 10-9 may help us trace through the necessary steps. The numbers beside each flowchart symbol correspond to the line numbers of the COBOL example (Figure 10-4, pages 223 and 224).

The first paragraph in the procedure division (ØPEN-PARA) is used to open the input and output files. The second paragraph (INITILIZ-PARA) instructs the printer to PERFØRM the HEADING-RØUTINE, which results in the first two lines being printed on the output report Instructions in the HEADING-RØUTINE paragraph tell the computer to move two initials and a last name from the CPU input storage area to specifically named locations (INITIAL-P1, INITIAL-P2, and LAST-NAME-P) in the working storage area. The printer then follows the format prescribed in line 002090 through 002210 of the program to print the two heading lines on the output report.

Processing steps are given in the third paragraph (PRØCESS-PARA):

1. The *first* test grade (a 75) is added to the contents of ACCUMULATØR, and the total value (initially 75) is stored in ACCUMULATØR.

2. The contents of working storage location ØNE are added to the contents of working storage location NØ-GRADES — i.e., 1 is initially added to 0.

3. The grade of 75 is moved to working storage location SCØRE in the DATA-LINE record (see line 003050).

4. The contents of the DATA-LINE record — containing at this time only the grade of 75 — are printed on the output report. The program then loops back, another card is read, and the procedure is repeated.

When the last grade record is processed, the program branches from PRØCESS-PARA to TØTAL-PARA to compute the summary grade average. In 30 tests, Val Student scored 2,625 points.[18] When the last card is processed, this total is stored in the ACCUMULATØR location. To write this figure on the output report, the figure is first read into the SCØRE location in the DATA-LINE record and from there it is moved to the printer. The total still remains in ACCUMU-LATØR, however, because read-out is nondestructive. To compute

[18] The breakdown of the test scores is shown in Fig. 10-8. Val finished strong.

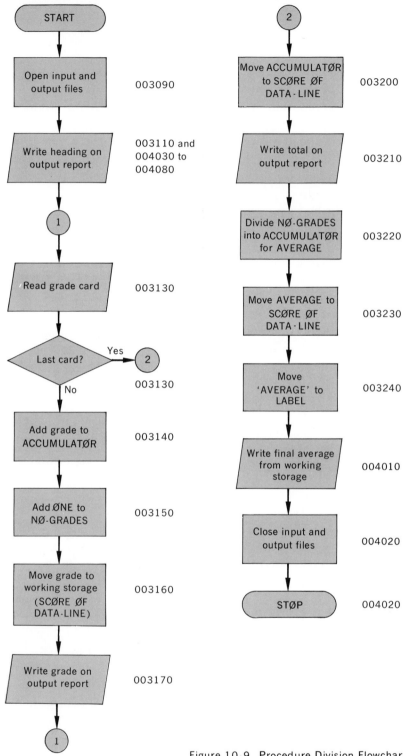

Figure 10-9. Procedure Division Flowchart

the average grade, the contents of NØ-GRADES (30) are divided into the ACCUMULATØR contents (2,625). The resulting average of 75 is stored in location AVERAGE. From there it also is moved to the SCØRE location in the working storage area. The instruction on line 003240 replaces the seven blank spaces in location LABEL in the DATA-LINE record with the seven characters between the quotation marks, i.e., with 'AVERAGE.'[19] The contents of the DATA-LINE record are then printed as the last line of the output report by the instruction on line 004010. The job is now completed, so the files are closed and the run is stopped.

Program debugging and maintenance

Because of its simplicity, our example program did not require debugging. However, when a complex program is prepared, it is *unusual* for it to run correctly and produce the expected results the first time it is tested. Several test runs (using hypothetical test data which yield a known result) are often required before all errors can be found and removed. In fact, time spent in debugging often equals or exceeds the time spent in program coding. Many errors are due to faulty program *logic* and mistakes of a *clerical* nature. The failure to provide for a possible program branch may be included in the former category; key punching errors and mistakes in coding punctuation may be included in the latter.

After the program appears to be correct, there is frequently a transitionary cutover period during which the job application is processed both by the old method and by the new program. The purpose of this period, of course, is to verify processing accuracy.

Production-run programs are continuously being modified and improved. Sometimes the object program can be patched to include small modifications so that a compiling run is not necessary. Program maintenance is an important duty of the programmer and may involve all steps from problem definition through analysis, design, and program preparation. It is not unusual to find a programmer spending 25 percent of his time on this activity.

PROGRAMMING AIDS

Although it is still a time-consuming and expensive process, considerable improvement has been made in programming since the early days

[19] Data location AVERAGE should not be confused with the literal constant 'AVERAGE.'

234

of computers. A listing of factors which have improved programming performance includes the following:

1. *Assembly and compiler programs.* We have already seen how these aids improve program preparation time while reducing error.

2. *Subroutine libraries.* A subroutine, you will remember, is a well-defined set of instructions which performs a specific arithmetic or logic operation. Subroutines are classified as open or closed (Figure 10-10). An *open subroutine* is inserted or spliced directly into the main program at any point where it may be needed. The *closed subroutine*, on the other hand, remains a separate program which is typically used several times during the processing. An instruction in the main program branches program control to the subroutine location. When the subroutine operation is completed, another branch instruction transfers control back to the main program. It is obvious that a good library of tested subroutines (which are prepared by equipment manufacturers and furnished to their customers) can often speed the writing of new programs.

3. *Application programs.* Application or packaged programs were introduced in Chapter 3. In addition to subroutines, manufacturers have prepared entire programs for applications which are of a general nature and which are common to the needs of many firms in an industry. For example, IBM

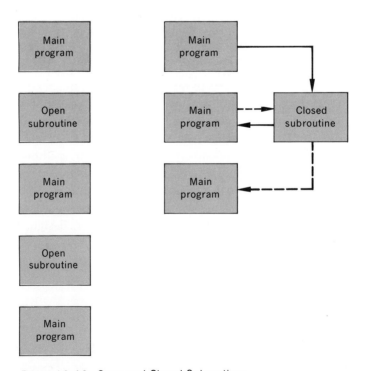

Figure 10-10. Open and Closed Subroutines

and Honeywell have prepared programs to suit the needs of a number of businesses in the areas of banking, insurance, distribution, and manufacturing. Other manufacturers have similar packages available. These "canned" programs can reduce programming time and expense since they are readily available and have been debugged. They must, of necessity however, be broad enough to cover a number of contingencies. Thus, they may not be as efficient as a specially prepared program in terms of storage space used and running time required.

4. *User groups.* Users of similar machines have formed associations to share experiences and to exchange information and programs. In 1955, for example, a number of organizations using large-scale IBM machines met to form a user group known as "SHARE" — an acronym said to mean the "Society to _H_elp _A_lleviate _R_edundant _E_ffort."[20] Meetings are held biannually, with IBM paying part of the expenses. Members of the group have access to a library of contributed programs. Other manufacturers help sponsor groups which use their equipment – e.g., USE is a UNIVAC organization, and SWAP is a Control Data Corporation group.

5. *Software consultants.* A number of independent software consulting companies have been formed to help businesses with their programming problems. The better of these consulting firms can often provide specialized software to their clients that is not available from the manufacturer or that is more efficient than the software provided by the manufacturer. Consultants can, for a fee, supplement a firm's own programming staff during overload periods created by conversion to a new machine or by preparation of complex new system programs.

SUMMARY

Although computers vary with respect to the number of commands which they can execute, they are all similar in that they must ultimately receive their instructions in a machine language form. Early programmers had to code instructions laboriously into this machine language.

To ease the programmer's burden, mnemonic command codes and symbolic addresses were developed in the early 1950s. The development of machine oriented symbolic languages led to further programming improvement first in the form of macro instructions and then in the form of procedure oriented languages. The procedure oriented languages tend to be directed toward either scientific or commercial problems. The selection of a language, like the selection of hardware, is a complex task.

Many businesses use COBOL. This procedure oriented language consists of identification, environment, data, and procedure divisions.

A program must, generally, be debugged before it can be used. Debugging often takes as much time as is required to perform the initial coding; sometimes it can take much longer. Maintenance of production run programs is

[20] Other groups known as GUIDE and COMMON are also partially sponsored by IBM.

an important part of a programmer's job. To aid the programmer, equipment manufacturers provide assembly and compiler programs, application programs, and subroutines.

DISCUSSION QUESTIONS

1 "Every computer instruction has an explicit predicate consisting of at least two parts." Identify and explain these two parts.

2 Compare the command structures of single-address, two-address, and three-address machines.

3 What types of commands are found in a computer's repertoire?

4 What are the differences among machine languages, symbolic languages, and procedure oriented languages?

5 (a) What is an assembly program? (b) What is a source program? (c) An object program? (d) Explain the relationship among these three programs.

6 Define the following terms:
(a) macro instruction   (e) data division
(b) machine oriented language   (f) debugging
(c) compiler   (g) open and closed subroutines
(d) COBOL reserved words

7 (a) What is FORTRAN? (b) For what type of problems was FORTRAN designed?

8 (a) What is COBOL? (b) How did it originate? (c) For what purposes was COBOL designed?

9 (a) What is PL/I? (b) How did it originate? (c) How may PL/I represent a threat to FORTRAN and COBOL?

10 Discuss the factors to consider in language selection.

11 What are the main divisions of COBOL?

12 Discuss the programming aids which have been developed.

SELECTED REFERENCES

Wayne S. Boutell, "Problem-oriented Languages: FORTRAN vs. COBOL," *Management Services*, May-June, 1966, pp. 41-48.

COBOL (UNIVAC Division, Sperry Rand Corporation, Manual UT 2470).

Gordon B. Davis, *An Introduction to Electronic Computers* (New York: McGraw-Hill Book Company, 1965), chaps. 11-15.

Herbert D. Leeds and Gerald M. Weinberg, *Computer Programming Fundamentals* (2d ed.; New York: McGraw-Hill Book Company, 1966).

Fritz A. McCameron, *COBOL Logic and Programming* (Homewood, Ill.: Richard D. Irwin, Inc., 1966).

Stanley M. Naftaly, "How to Pick a Programming Language," *Data Processing Digest*, November, 1966, pp. 1-14.

James A. Saxon, *COBOL* (Englewood Cliffs, N.J.: Prentice-Hall, Inc., 1963).

Gerald M. Weinberg, *PL/1 Programming Primer* (New York: McGraw-Hill Book Company, 1966).

11. MANAGEMENT AND COMPUTERS: AN ORIENTATION

In Chapter 1 it was pointed out that the first objective of this text was to provide a general orientation to the computer for students of business. This orientation has now been completed. In earlier chapters we have seen what a computer is, what it can and cannot do, and how it operates.

The second text objective is to focus attention on the impact which computers have had (and are having) on business managers and on the environment in which managers work. In the remaining pages of this book we shall concentrate attention on this second objective by examining managerial problems associated with the introduction and use of computers. The purpose of *this* chapter is (1) to define and explain a number of basic *management concepts* which are used, (2) to point out certain *managerial implications* arising from computer usage, and (3) to present an overview of the managerial problems associated with the *introduction and use of computers*.

MANAGEMENT CONCEPTS

What is management? For our purposes, we shall define *management* as the process of achieving organizational objectives through the efforts of other people. From this definition we shall emphasize three important points. The first point is that management is a *process*—i.e., *management consists of a number of interrelated steps or functions* which, when satisfactorily performed, lead to the achievement of goals. The *second* point is that without specific objectives being established, the effective practice of management is most difficult, if not impossible. The *third* point is that the successful practice of management involves people working together in harmony to achieve desired results.

The business manager is a practitioner of the art and science of management. It is his job to carry out the basic management functions necessary to attain company goals. Of course, the objectives pursued vary according to the manager's mission. The goal of a production manager may be to produce a specified number of units in a certain time period; the goal of a marketing manager may be to meet a sales quota; and the goal of the company president may be to see that the firm earns a satisfactory profit on the capital invested. But although objectives sought by managers vary, the managerial functions or activities which they perform in the course of their work are common to all. In other words, the activities of *planning, organizing, staffing,* and *controlling* are performed by all managers.[1]

Planning

The planning function involves (1) the selection of both short-run and long-run business objectives and strategies; (2) the development of business policies and procedures which help achieve objectives; (3) the establishment of operating standards which serve as the basis for control; and (4) the revision of existing plans in the light of changing conditions. To plan is to *decide in advance* a future course of action. Thus, planning involves decision making. In fact, the following *planning steps* might also be considered the *steps in rational decision making*:

1. *Identify the problem or opportunity.* Planning may begin when a manager understands and has defined the problem or opportunity which he faces.

2. *Gather and analyze pertinent facts.* To plan and make decisions, managers must be supported by *information* which is timely and accurate.

3. *Determine suitable alternatives.* The manager must seek out the most attractive courses of action among those possible.

4. *Evaluate and select most-appropriate alternative.* The task facing the manager here is to weigh the alternatives in light of established objectives and then to select that plan which best meets the needs of the company.

5. *Follow-up on decision.* A broad plan may require supporting supplementary plans. For example, if the result of the above steps is a decision to acquire a computer, then additional plans must be made to select and train the necessary operating personnel.

---

[1]This is not necessarily an exhaustive list of *all* the functions performed by managers. It is, rather, those functions which we shall be referring to in this text.

Organizing – Staffing

If goals are to be realized and if plans are to be carried out, it is necessary that people work together in harmony. The organizing function involves the grouping of work teams into logical and efficient units. For example, workers in a manufacturing company may be formally grouped into production, sales, and finance divisions. Workers in each of these divisions, in turn, may be organized into smaller units or departments. Thus, the sales division might include advertising, sales promotion, direct selling, and marketing research departments. Salesmen engaged in the direct selling activity might be further grouped or organized by sales territory, by product line sold, and by type of customer contacted.

Managers at each organizational level receive the delegated authority to assign tasks to employees so that goals may be achieved. Managers at all levels also have the task of coordinating the efforts of individual employees so that all members of the work group are working together efficiently. To sum up, *organizing* is "the grouping of activities necessary to accomplish goals and plans, the assignment of these activities to appropriate departments, and the provision for authority delegation and coordination."[2]

One aspect of the *staffing* function consists of selecting people to fill the positions which exist in the organizational structure of the business. Other aspects of the staffing activity include (1) the training of employees to meet their job requirements, (2) the preparation of employees for promotion to positions of greater responsibility, and (3) the reassignment or removal of employees when such action is required.

In his work of organizing and staffing, the manager is constantly making decisions. For example, plans to acquire a computer will call for serious thought about where in the organization the computing facility should be located. Such plans will also require staffing decisions.

Controlling

The control activity is a follow-up to planning; it is the check on current performance to determine whether planned goals are being achieved. The control process involves several steps:

[2] Harold Koontz and Cyril O'Donnell, *Principles of Management* (3d ed.; New York: McGraw-Hill Book Company, 1964), p. 205.

1. *Predetermined goals or standards must be established.* If the controlling function is to be performed properly, goals or standards must be established by business planners. These standards may be expressed in *physical* terms (the goal of the production manager may be to produce 100,000 units each month; the goal of the sales manager may be to sell this amount monthly; and the goal of a production foreman may be to produce units meeting specified machined tolerances). Standards may also be expressed in *monetary* terms in the form of operating cost budgets, capital investment budgets, and sales revenue quotas.

2. *Performance must be measured.* The actual performance must be measured promptly and accurately. Computers may help managers control by furnishing them with timely performance information.

3. *Actual performance must be compared with standards.* Variations are noted at this point. Computers can be used to make this comparison, and managers may be furnished with information *only* when variations are outside certain specified limits.

4. *Appropriate control decision must be made.* If performance is "under control," the manager's decision may be to do nothing. If the standards now appear to be unrealistic, they may have to be revised (replanning now becomes necessary). Deviations may be corrected by reorganizing work groups or by adding additional employees. Thus, decisions may be made at this point which will require *further* planning, organizing, and staffing activities. If outstanding performance is noted, the appropriate action may be to reward the individuals or groups responsible.

The process of management is a continuing one. The *order* of the managerial functions presented here (planning, organizing, staffing, and controlling) is a logical one, but in practice managers carry out these functions simultaneously. "Plans beget subordinate plans, old plans require modifications, and new plans develop while old ones are in effect. Thus it is impractical to insist on a special time sequence for the various functions."[3]

MANAGERIAL IMPLICATIONS IN THE INTRODUCTION AND USE OF COMPUTERS

In the preceding section, we saw that all managers perform a number of interrelated activities to achieve business goals. The success of any business, of course, is determined by how well managers perform these functions. And how well these activities are carried out is dependent upon how well the information needs of managers are being met. Why? Because each function involves decision making, and decision making must be supported by information which is timely and accurate. It is

---

[3] *Ibid.*, p. 39.

not surprising, therefore, that the acquisition and use of a computer (or any tool which promises to improve the quality and timeliness of information) have important managerial implications.

Perhaps the most important single factor determining success or failure of a computer installation is the extent to which the top managers of the company support the effort to improve management information systems. After all, the information output of the computer installation should be designed to serve the needs of these operating executives. It might be expected, therefore, that they would seek to participate actively in all phases of the design and installation of the new data processing system. Alas, such leadership has often been lacking! For example, in 1963 the management consulting firm of McKinsey & Company, Inc., surveyed 27 of the nation's largest computer users and reported in their findings that 18 of the 27 companies obtained results from their use of computer systems which could only be described as marginal at best. One of the conclusions of this study is that "computer-systems success is more heavily dependent on executive leadership than on any other factor. No company achieved above-average results without the active participation of top management."[4]

Many executives, apparently feeling that the introduction of a computer is strictly a technical problem, have been content to define vaguely the goals of the new system and then to turn the entire program over to the data processing specialists. Without precisely defined information needs and without the backing at the top which is often required to secure cooperation and to overcome resistance to change, the data processing group may be excused if its effort has produced applications which fail to use the computer efficiently. As we shall see in the following paragraphs, the introduction and use of computers are *more than a technical problem*; the attention and involvement of top executives are required.

Planning and control implications

The information output produced by the data processing system supports the planning and control decisions of managers. Company goals and policies are established on the basis of reports received from the data processing system; plans are made on the basis of trends and opportunities which are revealed; alternatives are chosen on the basis of

[4] John T. Garrity, *Getting the Most out of Your Computer* (New York: McKinsey & Company, Inc., 1963), p. 13.

facts received; and control decisions are triggered by reports indicating that action is required.[5] Inadequate information, of course, will lead to missed trends and opportunities, to errors in the selection of alternatives, and to costly delays in taking corrective action in out-of-control situations.

The acronym GIGO (Garbage In, Garbage Out) is sometimes used in data processing circles. This inelegant acronym points out the obvious fact that the value of the output of a data processing system depends on the quality of the input data. If a manager does not want to run the risk of basing his decisions on "garbage," he must participate in the design of the computer system. For as McGill has noted:[6]

The moment management loses control over the planning, it abrogates a basic prerogative: determining the kind of information it requires for the effective control and planning of the business.

Organizational implications

The organizational structure of any company is determined, in part, by the work which is done and by the employees who do this work. But when a computer is introduced into a business, the work of many employees (and managers) *may be altered*; work groups may be realigned; data processing jobs which were formerly handled in a number of departments may be consolidated into a single unit; and activities in some departments may be sharply curtailed.

When the work of organizational units has changed because of the introduction of computers, it is often desirable to restructure the organization in the interests of greater efficiency. For example, a new department may be created to accommodate expanded electronic data processing activities, while other organizational units may need to be consolidated or eliminated. Such decisions require the attention of the top executives in the company.

[5] In Chapter 18 of Exodus, Jethro gives good advice when he tells Moses to delegate some of his routine leadership duties to subordinates and to concentrate his attention on the more important exceptions which the subordinates are unable to handle. This idea is called the *principle of exception* in management literature. Control reports based on this exception principle may be triggered only when actual performance varies from planned standards. Managers are thus relieved of much routine paper shuffling and are freed to concentrate attention on more important matters.

[6] D. A. C. McGill, *Punched Cards: Data Processing for Profit Improvement* (New York: McGraw-Hill Book Company, 1962), p. 142.

Staffing implications

From the organizational implications just related, it is obvious that the introduction of a computer also requires personnel adjustments. Staffing decisions are required (1) to select and train workers for new jobs and (2) to deal with employees whose jobs have been eliminated or reduced in content. Resistance may be expected from employees and managers because of significant changes occurring in the alignment of work groups, in the content of individual jobs, and in the methods of performing data processing tasks. Proper planning and leadership may reduce this resistance, but such leadership should come from a high level.

Economic implications

Computers are expensive. It is the duty of top company officials to determine whether or not a computer can be economically justified. As we saw in Chapter 1, a computer *may* improve profits (1) by helping to reduce expenses while revenue remains stable or (2) by helping to increase revenue without a corresponding increase in expenses. But there is no guarantee that profits *will* be improved merely because a computer is installed. In fact, many firms have invested large sums in computer installations and have received returns of *less* than a dollar for each dollar spent. For example, two out of three of the 27 large companies surveyed in the McKinsey & Company study did not recover their original investment after four years of operations.

Of course, merely to recover the original investment is hardly sufficient, for the money invested in a computer could otherwise be put to use in an alternate manner which might be quite profitable. Computer acquisition is a difficult capital investment decision; it must be recognized as such by the top officers in the company. They must also be aware that the level of expenditures initially required is frequently *underestimated* and that this level may continue to increase in the years after acquisition. For example, in a study of 33 leading manufacturing concerns, the management consulting firm of Booz, Allen & Hamilton found that expenditures for computer-based activities are $185 million a year. It was also found that "after the computer is introduced in a company, it tends to pervade more and more functions and operations, becoming an increasingly important cost factor in company operations."[7]

[7] James W. Taylor and Neal J. Dean, "Managing to Manage the Computer," *Harvard Business Review*, vol. 44, no. 5, September–October, 1966, p. 102.

Implications for decision-making techniques

Several decision-making tools or techniques have been developed in recent years and have been classified under the general headings of *operations research* (OR) or *management science*. Operations research involves the study of overall company operations by means of mathematical models. Computers have supported the growth of OR, and this growth promises to have an expanding impact on the way managers perform their managerial functions.[8] In particular, the computer-based OR techniques of *PERT—CPM*, *linear programming*, and *simulation*—have managerial implications.

PERT and CPM Both PERT (Program Evaluation and Review Technique) and CPM (Critical Path Method) are network models which are used to plan, schedule, and control complex projects. The basic concepts of both PERT and CPM are virtually the same. The following procedure must be used to set up one of these models:

1. *All* the individual *activities* to be performed in the project must be identified.

2. The *sequence* of *each* activity must be determined — i.e., it must be known what elements have to be completed prior to the start of, and what tasks cannot commence until after the finish of, a particular activity.

3. The *time* required to complete each activity must be estimated.

4. The *longest sequence* of activities in the project must be identified. The sum of the individual activity times in this sequence becomes the total project time, and this sequence of activities is known as the *critical path*.

Network models have gained wide-spread acceptance. The Department of Defense requires that they be used on all major defense contracts, and most major construction projects employ them. The use of PERT and CPM improves the *planning* function because it forces managers to identify all the activities which must be performed. *Control* is also improved because attention can be focused on the sequence of activities in the critical path. Also, a manager often has the option to trade project cost against project time. That is, he may be able to reduce the time required to complete certain activities in the critical path and thus reduce total project time, if he is willing to accept a higher job cost figure. Computations for small network models can be

---

[8] It has been said that today many businessmen use mathematics and statistics the way a drunk uses a lamppost — for support rather than for illumination. If this is true today, will it be true tomorrow?

produced manually, but a computer is needed with networks of any significant size. Most computer manufacturers have packaged PERT and CPM programs available.

Linear programming   Not be be confused with computer programming, linear programming models are used to find the *best combination* of limited resources to achieve a specified objective (which is, typically, to maximize profit or minimize cost).[9] One important class of linear programming applications is in blending operations where the objective is often to minimize the cost to produce a given amount of a blended product. For example, cattle feed may be a mixture of minerals, grains, and fish and meat products. The prices of these ingredients are subject to change, so the least-expensive blend to achieve specified nutritional requirements is subject to variation. Linear programming can help managers quickly determine the correct blend to use to minimize cost while meeting product specifications. Linear programming is also used in the blending of gasoline, sausage, metals, and ice cream.

In addition to blending, linear programming is being used for such diverse purposes as scheduling manpower, selecting media for advertising purposes, determining minimum transportation costs from given supply points to specified points of delivery, and determining the most profitable product mix to produce with a given plant and equipment. Practically all linear programming applications require the use of a computer. As a powerful *planning* tool, linear programming enables a manager to select the most appropriate alternative among those available. It is also a technique which may aid the manager in carrying out his other functions. Its use in scheduling manpower, for example, has definite staffing implications.

Simulation   In the physical sciences, experimental tests may be performed in a laboratory using small models of a process or an operation. Many complex variations may be possible in these experiments, and the results merely show the scientist what happens under certain controlled conditions. Simulation is similar to scientific experimentation, in that managers may evaluate proposed strategies by constructing business models and then by determining what happens to these models when certain conditions are given. A simulation model is thus a trial-and-error problem-solving *approach*; it is also a *planning* aid which may be of considerable importance to top executives.

Simulation models have been used to help managers decide whether

---

[9] In linear programming, the relationship between the resource variables is linear; i.e., a change in one variable results in a proportionate change in another.

or not to expand company operations by acquiring a new plant and equipment. Among the dozens of factors which affect such a decision are present and potential size of the total market, present and potential company share of the total market, product selling prices, and the investment required. In determining the investment needed, simulation has been used to aid managers in deciding the plant layout and the number and types of machines which must be provided.

Simulation models are also used to improve inventory management. The problem of managing inventories is complicated because there are conflicting desires among organizational units and what is best for one department may not be best for the entire business. To illustrate, the purchasing department prefers to buy inventories of supplies and raw materials in large quantities to have a low unit price; the production department also likes to have large inventories on hand to eliminate shortages and to make possible long—and efficient—production runs; and the sales department is in favor of large inventories of finished goods to prevent lost sales caused by out-of-stock conditions. But the finance department views with concern larger inventory levels since storage expense is increased, risk of spoilage and deterioration is increased, and money is tied up for longer periods of time. Through the use of simulated inventory amounts and simulated assumptions about such factors as inventory reorder lead times and cost of being out of stock, managers can experiment with various approaches to determine better or more profitable inventory levels.

Of course, in many respects there is nothing new about simulation. As Franklin Lindsay points out:[10]

A corporate planner who sets forth half a dozen alternative investment schemes, together with the costs and expected return from each, is simulating each alternative so that his board of directors can judge their relative merits. But the new mathematical tools, together with high-speed computers, extend tremendously the capabilities of simulation processes.

Systems implications

In introducing a computer to a business, top-level managers are called on to make many important decisions. Perhaps none is more important than the philosophy which the top executives decide to follow in the determination of new data processing systems. As we saw in Chapter 3, emphasis in many companies is being placed on designing broader information systems. The computer makes consolidations possible, and many older business information systems need to be stream-

[10]Franklin A. Lindsay, *New Techniques for Management Decision Making* (New York: McGraw-Hill Book Company, 1963), p. 60.

lined. But the feasibility (or even desirability) of a single "total" information system is a controversial subject. At the present time a total system is more a philosophy than a fact. For example, the approach being followed by the 33 manufacturing firms surveyed in the Booz, Allen & Hamilton study is to integrate applications gradually into broader systems. Some of the reasons for a conservative approach are listed in Chapter 3.

But there is usually some movement toward consolidation, and a decision should be made on the extent to which information processing systems should be integrated when a computer is introduced. Related to this decision is another which has an important, direct bearing on the organizational structure of the firm. The issue to be decided is to what extent the new systems should concentrate or *centralize* control in the hands of the top-level managers. With a computer a greater degree of centralized control *can* be supported in a business because top managers can be furnished with information from outlying divisions in time to decide on appropriate action. Without computers, such action must be determined by a lower-level manager because of time, distance, and familiarity factors. But although greater centralized control *can be supported* with a computer, it is not *a requirement.* The degree of centralized control which should exist in the new system is determined by managerial judgment and not by computer usage.

In addition to such important matters as the degree of systems integration and the degree of centralized control, there are other system decisions which may be called for. For example, to what extent and in what areas (if any) should real time systems be employed?[11] The impact of systems decisions is usually felt throughout the business; such decisions are too important to be left to lower-level managers. A guiding philosophy from the top can help avoid a number of problems.

INTRODUCING AND USING COMPUTERS

The managerial functions of planning, organizing, staffing, and controlling must be performed in preparing for, introducing, and using a computer. In this section (which is also an outline of the following chapters) we shall look at some of the management problems which are usually associated with such a project. All too often in the past the possible magnitude of these problems has not been appreciated by managers, with the result that cost and time factors have been underestimated.

[11] For one writer's views on the limitations of real time systems, see John Dearden, "Myth of Real-time Management Information," *Harvard Business Review*, vol. 44, no. 3, May–June, 1966, pp. 123–132.

For the most part, the firms which have been successful in making computers pay off have been thorough in the initial planning stages. A careful *feasibility study* is required to answer the following questions:

1. What data processing improvements are desired – i.e., what are the data processing objectives of the firm?

2. Has proper attention been given to systems review and redesign?

3. Is computer usage the *best* way to achieve the objectives? Have noncomputer alternatives been evaluated?

4. Have *all* computer alternatives been considered? (A firm *need not* have an *in-house* installation – i.e., it need not acquire its own machine – to have access to computer capability. The use of computer centers or time sharing stations is a possible alternative.)

5. If an in-house installation is justified, have all feasible machines and vendors been considered?

6. Have different acquisition methods (rental, lease, or purchase) been evaluated?

7. Have personnel and organizational aspects been reviewed? The subject of the feasibility study will be considered more carefully in Chapter 12.

If, as a result of careful study and planning, a decision is made to order a computer, then the following additional plans must be developed:

1. *Technical preparation plans.* Prior to the delivery of the equipment, the computer site must be laid out and prepared; initial programs must be written and debugged. Technical preparation is considered in Chapter 13.

2. *Personnel preparation plans.* Resistance to change is to be expected, and plans should be made at an early stage to reduce this resistance. Staffing plans should be made to fill the new jobs which will be created. For example, selecting and training programmers should take place early so that they may begin preparing the initial programs. If jobs will be eliminated – and this is often the case – plans should be made to alleviate the possible hardships caused by displacement and reassignment. These personnel topics are developed further in Chapters 13 and 14.

3. *Organizing plans.* The acquisition of a computer will usually have an impact on the firm's organizational structure. The effects of other changes are often reflected in organizational stress. It is important that adequate attention be given to the composition and location of the computer department. In Chapter 15, the subject of organization and the computer is examined.

4. *Control plans.* Output information produced by the data processing system is, of course, used by managers to control the business. But if this output

information is to be of value, its quality must also be controlled. Therefore, effective system control procedures should be established. The quality of input data should be considered, and internal controls to minimize error and disclose fraud when, and if, it occurs should be created. The subject of computer controls is considered in Chapter 16.

Successful computer users spend much time in planning their original installations. And when they begin to consider the feasibility of converting to other machine models later, they spend as much (if not more) time on this planning effort. *Many of the plans indicated above will be required in a later conversion.*

SUMMARY

Managers achieve organizational objectives through the efforts of other people. To do this they are required to perform the managerial activities of planning, organizing, staffing, and controlling. These activities are interrelated; in practice, a manager may be carrying out several functions simultaneously.

The top-level managers of a business should support and actively participate in the design and installation of new management information systems. In many cases they will, of course, have to rely on the advice of data processing specialists. But the decision to introduce computers in an organization has managerial *implications which go far beyond* the mere acquisition of a piece of technical equipment. Information vital to the support of planning and control decisions is affected by the computer system which develops; the entire organizational structure may undergo stress and alteration; the nature and number of jobs is affected; the economic consequences are often hard to predict; and the decision-making techniques which have been used by managers in the past may have to be changed.

In the chapters that follow, we shall examine some of the managerial problems associated with the introduction and use of computers. In so doing we shall also focus attention on the impact which computers have had (and are having) on managers and on the environment in which they work.

DISCUSSION QUESTIONS

1 (*a*) What is management? (*b*) What activities or functions must be performed by all managers?

2 (*a*) What is involved in the planning function? (*b*) What steps must be followed in planning?

3 Explain the managerial functions of organizing and staffing.

4 Identify and discuss the steps in the control process.

5 (*a*) What planning and control implications are there in the introduction and use of computers? (*b*) Organizational implications? (*c*) Staffing implications? (*d*) Economic implications? (*e*) Decision-making implications? (*f*) Systems implications?

6 (*a*) What are PERT and CPM? (*b*) What is linear programming? (*c*) What is simulation?

SELECTED REFERENCES

E. Leonard Arnoff and M. J. Netzorg, "Operations Research: The Basics," *Management Services*, January-February, 1965, pp. 42-51.

Ernest Dale, *Management: Theory and Practice* (New York: McGraw-Hill Book Company, 1965).

Norman J. Driebeek, "What is Operations Research?," *Systems & Procedures Journal*, November-December, 1965, pp. 15-18.

Harold Koontz and Cyril O'Donnell, *Principles of Management* (3d ed.; New York: McGraw-Hill Book Company, 1964).

James W. Taylor and Neal J. Dean, "Managing to Manage the Computer," *Harvard Business Review*, September-October, 1966, pp. 98-110.

Roger C. Vergin and Andrew J. Grimes, "Management Myths and EDP," *California Management Review*, Fall, 1964, pp. 59-70.

12. THE FEASIBILITY STUDY

A *feasibility study* is the investigation made by an organization to determine the desirability of using a computer to achieve *specific* objectives. When the use of a computer appears to be justified, the feasibility study team may also frequently recommend the hardware specifications which seem to meet the needs of the company best. Feasibility studies are also used by firms with computer capability to investigate the suitability of converting to another machine model.[1] In this chapter we shall examine (1) the *essential nature* of feasibility studies, (2) the *prerequisites* to a successful study, and (3) the *steps* in the feasibility study approach.

ESSENTIAL NATURE OF FEASIBILITY STUDIES

There are at least three reasons why it is important for a business to conduct a feasibility study: (1) Substantial investment may be involved in the computer decision, and a proper study *reduces the risk of loss*; (2) common *pitfalls may be avoided*; and (3) changes and improvement in old data processing methods signaled by a *study may point the way to substantial benefits.*

Reducing economic risk

There are numerous examples, to be found in data processing books and magazines, of businesses which have *not* achieved any economic benefits from their computers. For example, four years after it had acquired a computer installation, one New York company was paying

---

[1] In this chapter we shall emphasize the approach followed by businesses considering their *first* computer. Much of what follows, of course, is equally applicable in a conversion feasibility study.

computer operating costs of over $2 million each year (some $300,000 more than had been expected) and "was still more than 2 million dollars short of recovering its original investment."[2] Nor is this just an isolated example. It has been estimated (1) that about 40 percent of all computer-using organizations have *not* received economic benefits equal to their investments; and (2) that this 40 percent "failure" rate may be expected to continue in the next five years.[3] "It has further been estimated that some 90% of all new data processing installations exceeded their initial budget and failed to meet their installation schedule."[4]

The figures in the preceding paragraph illustrate that acquiring a computer is a difficult capital investment decision which may carry an element of economic risk. Under the best conditions, and with the benefit of a thorough feasibility study, the data processing costs associated with introducing and using a computer are difficult to estimate. This difficulty is not caused by hardware rental or purchase costs, for such costs are predictable. Rather, the difficulty is caused by the unpredictability of software and operating costs (which may be much greater than hardware costs). And, of course, when expenses are hard to pin down, tangible savings resulting from computer usage become equally difficult to predict. Although a properly conducted feasibility study does not eliminate the economic risk involved, it may substantially reduce it. Few managers would think of investing in a new building or production line without first giving the matter considerable thought and study. The same sound management practices which are used to evaluate other important investment opportunities must also be applied to evaluate the feasibility of acquiring a computer.

Avoiding common pitfalls

We have just seen that financial loss may be the possible *end result* of failure to conduct an appropriate feasibility study. In the past, numerous mistakes which have been made by managers have contributed to this undesirable end. These same snares or pitfalls will undoubtedly serve in the future as the *means* by which unwary man-

[2]John T. Garrity and V. Lee Barnes, "The Payout on Computers: What Management Has Learned about Planning and Control," *Management Review*, vol. 53, December, 1964, p. 6.

[3]See Dick H. Brandon, "The Need for Management Standards in Data Processing," *Data and Control Systems*, September, 1966, p. 27.

[4]*Ibid.*

agers (through their failure to conduct a proper study) will bring about financial losses for their firms. Some of the more common mistakes to be avoided are presented below:

1. *The crash program pitfall.* Most well-managed initial computer conversions currently require from fifteen to thirty months to complete.[5] Yet it is not uncommon for managers to attempt a crash program conversion in much less time because (1) they do not appreciate the magnitude of the job; (2) they have ignored the current data processing system until it is badly strained, and a computer is seen as an urgent solution; (3) they wish to achieve immediately the benefits which the computer is supposed to provide; and (4) they can get delivery of the hardware in, perhaps, six months, so the delivery date arbitrarily dictates the conversion time available. All too often, the data processing system produced in a crash program fails to meet the needs of the business, requires that a disproportionate amount of time be taken to correct errors and oversights after it has been designed, encounters considerable resistance from company personnel who have not been properly prepared for the change, and is much more costly to operate than had been expected.

2. *Lack of top management support.* As we saw in Chapter 11, converting to a computer is more than a technical problem. Because of the managerial implications involved, top company managers should actively support the study, and lower-level managers should participate in the design of any new systems which are developed. In past studies, such leadership has often been absent.

3. *Failure to specify problem areas and objectives.* A feasibility study should be directed toward *specified problem areas.* In other words, it should investigate the alternate ways of improving specific operations. In examining problem areas, the study team should be directing its efforts toward achieving *specified objectives,* e.g., designing a system to reduce administrative operating costs. It is the job of top officers to specify what they want done. Primary emphasis in a feasibility study should be placed on the quality of the management information produced by present and proposed systems. A computer should be considered *only* when the study indicates that problems can best be solved, and objectives can best be reached, by electronic means. Failure to specify problems and objectives is a planning blunder which occurs more often than might be expected.

4. *The hardware approach pitfall.* In the above paragraph we have emphasized that a feasibility study should follow what might be termed a "systems approach." All too frequently, however, executives have acted as though their primary objective was to get a computer first (often for pres-

[5]The exact time will depend, of course, on the complexity of the change. The fifteen- to thirty-month range is typical when the conversion is to a computer system utilizing magnetic tapes.

tige purposes) and *then* to decide on its use. If a study (it is no longer a feasibility study) is made at all when such a climate exists, it is made in large part to determine what applications can be placed on the machine when it arrives. Sometimes the study team is expected to prepare a report in support of the predetermined decision. The hardware approach usually ignores the effects of change on personnel.

5. *The piecemeal approach pitfall.* The study team should give careful attention to *redesigning* systems for greater efficiency and better integration. Although a step-by-step approach[6] to a total system is followed by most firms, the study team should be encouraged to seek integration wherever possible; new systems should not be designed which will impede future integration efforts. Installations seldom, if ever, achieve excellent results when manual records are simply converted and processed on a computer. Yet failure to redesign computer applications has been a common pitfall in the past.

6. *Inadequate staffing pitfall.* The study team should consist of members who are capable and creative. They should have an intimate knowledge of the business, and/or they should be competent in the technical areas of data processing. Unfortunately, the people needed for the survey are often the ones whose talents are in demand elsewhere in the organization. Yet these people should be released from their other duties for lengthy periods of time to complete the study properly. Entrusting the study effort to an "average" group yields only average results at best.

7. *Excessive reliance on computer vendors.* Some business managers have turned the job of making a feasibility study over to an equipment manufacturer. Of course, computer vendors do provide many services. But objectivity is bound to suffer if a vendor representative plays a significant part in making the study. His job is to sell machines, and his recommendation will be to install his equipment.

8. *Estimation errors.* Company managers may avoid serious mistakes if they are aware of the following error patterns which have appeared in past estimates: (1) initial program preparation and debugging times have been underestimated; (2) the difficulty of training programmers has been understated; (3) the degree of employee resistance to change has been underestimated; (4) program running times have been unexpectedly high (this error often contributes to improper hardware selection); (5) the organizational impact has not been considered or has been underestimated; (6) savings have been overstated; and (7) costs have been underestimated. In short, problems and costs have often been underestimated while savings have been overstated.

---

[6]The *step-by-step approach* is defined here as the strategy of converting specific applications to the computer while moving gradually toward more integrated systems. Although integration is generally desirable, some companies have experienced unsatisfactory results by attempting a study which was *too large* in view of their personnel and financial resources.

Pointing the way to benefits

A primary benefit of the feasibility study is that a company is able to steer clear of many of the pitfalls described above and is thus able to reduce the possibility of financial loss. An additional benefit is that the time and money invested in a feasibility study often yield tangible benefits for a business in the form of systems savings. Many data processing systems have evolved over long periods of time, with the result that procedures continue to be used even though they have become outdated, similar reports are duplicated in different departments, and obsolete reports continue to be prepared after they are no longer useful. The feasibility study, by uncovering such waste, duplication, and inefficiency, can lead to significant cost reductions *regardless* of whether or not a computer is installed. In fact, it is likely that the cost reductions attributed to many computers are more properly the result of systems improvement. For example, after careful study one company found that its inventory control procedures could be substantially improved, so it ordered a computer. However, since the machine would not be delivered for a year, the company decided to go ahead with whatever improvements were possible in the interim period. It found that 80 percent of the total savings could be obtained without the computer and that the cost of the machine was not justified by the remaining savings. The computer order was cancelled.[7]

STUDY PREREQUISITES

A well-managed survey is conducted only after several prerequisite planning steps have been accomplished. Included in these prerequisites are (1) the definition of the *scope and objectives* of the study and (2) the *appointment of the study group.*

Scope and objectives

We saw in the preceding section that a feasibility study should be directed toward improving specific operations. It is the job of one or more high-level executives to determine which areas should receive attention. The nature and scope of the operation(s) which is (are) to be investigated should be clearly defined; the organizational units in the company which are to be included and excluded should be iden-

---

[7]See John Dearden and F. Warren McFarlan, *Management Information Systems* (Homewood, Ill.: Richard D. Irwin, Inc., 1966), p. 29.

tified; and the degree to which efforts should be made to consolidate data processing procedures should be clarified. You will remember from Chapter 1 that if the operations which are to receive study attention have one or more of the following properties, they may well prove to be suitable applications for computer processing:

1. A large data volume is required to produce *needed* information.

2. Rapid processing speed is both desired and necessary.

3. The task is of a repetitive data handling nature.

4. A high degree of accuracy is both desired and necessary.

5. Processing complexities make noncomputer alternatives impractical.

Once the general scope and direction of the investigation have been determined, it is next necessary to specify the objectives which are to be pursued. Since these objectives will shape the character of the end product of the feasibility study, it is important that careful attention be given to their formulation. Figure 12-1 summarizes some goals which are commonly sought.[8] These objectives reflect the tangible and intangible benefits which are frequently attributed to computer usage.

The selection of goals, of course, should be based upon the work that *needs to be done* and not upon the work that a computer is capable of doing.[9] For example, a computer may be able to give up-to-the-minute information in many processing areas. But if shorter processing time is *not needed* by the business, it is foolish to pay extra for this "benefit." In many companies multiple objectives are pursued. In this case, the top managers may have to assign *priorities* to guide the study team. Important and profitable short-range improvements which are consistent with long-range management information objectives may be given first priority.

Appointment of study group

A group must usually be appointed to perform the actual study. The purpose and scope of the investigation and the time available should determine the group composition. In a small business, the "group" may be a single analyst, but in larger organizations two or more team members are usually chosen. Regardless of the group's size, team

[8] See Chap. 1 for a review of computer benefits and objectives.

[9] After all, at this point in a feasibility study it is by no means certain that a computer is the answer to the problem.

Expense reduction objectives
(Benefits of a tangible nature)

1. Reduce clerical labor expense
2. Reduce supervisory and other nonclerical labor expense
3. Reduce equipment expense
4. Reduce space and overhead expense
5. Reduce supplies expense
6. Reduce inventory carrying expense

Revenue raising objectives
(Benefits which are usually intangible)

1. Shorten processing time
2. Increase processing capacity to expand marketing efforts
3. Acquire more accurate information
4. Acquire more comprehensive information
5. Improve operating control
6. Improve customer service
7. Acquire new information (sales analyses, cost analyses, etc.)
8. Achieve better planning through the use of operations research techniques

Other objectives

1. Attain prestige and a progressive image
2. Meet clerical labor shortages
3. Prepare required government reports

Figure 12-1. Common Feasibility Study Objectives

members are usually selected by top executives for the offsetting talents they can bring to the job. Although the requirements for specialized knowledge may vary, it is common to find at least one team member who possesses a knowledge of the information needs of the business and another who is familiar with systems and the technical side of data processing. In most cases, team members should be appointed to participate in the study on a full-time basis. The team leader should be chosen on the basis of proven managerial ability. He is required to plan, organize, and control the entire project. It is his job (1) to understand the scope, purpose, and objectives of the study; (2) to schedule and coordinate the team effort and keep interested parties informed of the team's progress; (3) to secure the cooperation of company employees who can contribute to the study; and (4) to achieve the end objectives.

It is usually desirable for the selected team members to hold *design sessions* with the departmental managers of all organizational units which are affected by the study. These design sessions enable the department managers to participate in setting or revising specific study goals. It is only logical that such managers should have an important voice in determining preliminary systems objectives. After all, they should be able to make significant suggestions to guide the team since they should be the most familiar with the existing methods and procedures. Furthermore, they are the ones whose performance is affected by any changes, and they are the ones whose cooperation is needed if the study is to yield the most satisfactory results.

When it appears that all interested groups (top-level managers, managers of affected operating departments, and the study team) have agreed on objectives, the study leader should put these goals *in writing* and send them to all concerned for approval. If differences about scope or objectives remain, they should be resolved in additional preliminary design sessions. Although such meetings may appear to be unproductive to those who are impatient to get on with the job, their costs "most often end up being small relative to later costs caused by incomplete, and possibly erroneous, definition and directions."[10]

It is appropriate to point out here that a repeating or *iterative process* may be followed before the study prerequisite phase is considered complete. In other words, there is no definite number of steps to be followed before the detailed study approach can begin. A top-level company officer may be convinced that a problem exists which calls for a feasibility study; he may prepare a general statement of objectives; and he may appoint a manager to conduct the investigation. There then may be a number of design sessions called to translate general objectives into more specific goals. During these sessions the interested groups may enlarge or reduce the scope of the study; objectives may be similarly changed. It is also quite possible that the study leader will not select some of the team members until after the preliminary design sessions have been completed, because the extent of the study may not be definite until that time.

Before the detailed investigation begins, the team leader should prepare a written *charter* for approval by the top-level executive or the steering committee in charge of the overall data processing program. Such a charter, when approved, should include:

1. A detailed statement of the scope of the study and of the objectives which will be pursued.

2. A grant of authority to permit the team to cross departmental lines and receive top priority on the working time of specified individuals. (People to be contacted should be informed of this authority grant by a top company executive.)

[10] Marvin W. Ehlers, "Management's Blunder Buffer," *Business Automation*, March, 1966, p. 40.

3. A target date for completion of the survey recommendations and interim dates for the presentation of progress reports to the executive or steering committee in charge.

FEASIBILITY STUDY APPROACH

A feasibility study is conducted to provide information for decision-making purposes. You will remember from Chapter 11 that the questions to be decided include the following three. (1) Is it desirable to use a computer to achieve specific objectives? (2) If so, is an in-house installation preferable? (3) If an in-house installation is needed, what hardware should be selected? Answers to these and other questions should be included in the recommendations presented by the study team to interested top executives. In arriving at their decisions, the team should follow an approach which is nothing more than the rational decision-making process outlined in Chapter 11. In other words, the steps in the feasibility study approach are to (1) *identify the problem*, (2) *gather data on current operations*, (3) *analyze current operations and determine suitable alternatives*, (4) *decide on most appropriate alternative*, and (5) *follow up on decision*.

Identification of the problem

We have chosen to classify problem definition as a prerequisite. But in a broader sense it is, of course, the first step in the overall study approach. We need not belabor this step further here, but it should be emphasized that a basic problem in any feasibility study is that of determining computer justification. A dictionary tells us that *to justify* is to vindicate or show sufficient grounds for an action. Computer usage seems to be justified only when one or more of the following conditions is present:

1. Greater processing speed is both desired *and necessary.*
2. Complexities of data processing require electronic help.
3. Computer investment is offset by monetary or intangible benefits.

The last of these three conditions is of paramount importance to a business organization, for as Richard H. Hill, Vice-President of Informatics, Inc., notes: "*A computer installation in an economic enterprise can never be justified except in economic terms.*"[11]

[11] Richard H. Hill, "Computer Economics," *Data Processing Digest*, vol. 12, May, 1966, p. 3. (This is the second in a series of articles entitled "Data Processing . . . Practically Speaking.")

Gathering data on current operations

In the prerequisite stage it is likely that some preliminary data gathering will have been done. A more detailed examination, however, is needed before specific alternate courses of action can be proposed. Thus, the main purpose of this fact-finding step is to acquire a thorough understanding of present methods and to detect the strengths and weaknesses of these methods. Perhaps as a result of information brought to light during this step, the team may seek permission from top executives to revise the scope and goals of the investigation.

Since this fact-finding step becomes the basis for later analysis and recommendations, the data gathered must be accurate and complete. Although the information to be collected may vary from one study to another, in most cases the team needs to answer the following questions about the operations being surveyed. (1) What source information is used? (2) What work is done? (3) What business resources are being used? (4) What results are achieved? Figure 12-2 lists some of the more specific questions which are frequently asked.

Business computer installations should be justified in economic terms; therefore, it is important that alternate systems be evaluated on the basis of expected contribution to the economic well-being of the company. Many well-managed firms may base their ultimate decision to acquire a computer on a *return-on-investment* analysis. Such an analysis is based on a monetary savings figure arrived at by *comparing the costs* of the present system with those of an alternate. The team should therefore be sure that *current costs* are accurately and completely identified. It is equally important that data processing *volume* figures be known. Why? Because the volume of data processing required must be known to determine the complexity and cost of *alternate* systems which may be proposed. The following cost figures related to the operations under study should be collected:

1. Charges for payroll and associated fringe benefits
2. Costs of equipment used in the processing (equipment costs may be in the form of rental or depreciation charges)
3. Charges for office materials, supplies, forms, etc.
4. Overhead charges (cost of office space used, insurance, utilities, etc.)

There are several useful tools and techniques which the team may use to gather data. One such tool is the *systems flowchart*, introduced in Chapter 9. Beginning with the source document inputs, each step in the operation is charted using the proper symbols. Files and equip-

What source information is used?

What source documents are received?
What source documents are used?
Where do they originate?
What is the frequency of input—daily, weekly, or monthly?
What is the maximum volume received? The minimum? The average?

What work is done?

What records and files are being kept to support the operation?
How frequently—daily, weekly, or monthly—is the operation being performed?
What is the volume or magnitude of work in each phase of the operation? What
volume fluctuations occur in the operation? What is the cause of these fluctuations?
What is the flow of work, i.e., what sequence of steps is followed to perform the
operation?

What business resources are used?

What departments are involved in the operation? What place in the organization
do they occupy? What is the primary function of these departments?
How many people are involved? What are their skill levels?
How many man-hours are needed?
How much time is required to complete each step?
What equipment is being used? For how long?
What materials and supplies are being used?
How much does it cost to perform the operation?

What results are achieved?

What output reports are prepared?
What is their purpose?
Who uses the reports?
What use is actually being made of the reports?
How accurate are they?
How timely are they?

Figure 12-2. Data-gathering Questions

ment which are used are identified; the sequence of steps in the processing procedures is shown; the different departments involved are
located; and the output results are presented. Although the chart
may also indicate processing frequencies, input and output volumes,
workers performing each step, time required to complete each step,
and the materials and supplies used, such information is frequently
noted on separate *questionnaire forms* which may be keyed to steps
in the flowchart.[12]

[12] One of the best guides to gathering data about present methods is the IBM booklet
entitled *Documentation Techniques* (IBM Corporation, Manual C20-8075). This
booklet gives examples of forms which are useful in the fact-finding process.

Manuals of procedures (if they exist) and previous studies in related areas (if well documented) are valuable sources of information for the team. But probably the most important data-gathering technique is the *personal interview*. Interviews with operating supervisors and employees are needed to verify existing documentation. (The procedure in a manual may not be the procedure described by the supervisor, and the supervisor's version may differ from the one actually being used!) Interviews are also needed to gather the procedural information required to prepare the flowchart and fill in the questionnaire forms. To verify interview accuracy, a study analyst may take an input document and "walk it through" the processing procedure. A walk-through is a good time for the analyst to obtain opinions from employees on how the procedure might be improved.

It is important that the analyst conduct the interviews with skill and tact. He should plan his questions prior to the interview, make an appointment in advance with the person being interviewed, and explain the purpose of the interview and how the information obtained will be used. He should avoid being openly critical of current methods. In short, the analyst should remember that preoccupation with other matters at the expense of proper human relations will quickly ruin any chance for real achievement.

When the interviews are completed and the study team feels that it has gathered all the necessary facts, it should, as a final check on accuracy and completeness, present these data to the interested department managers for their review and approval.

Data analysis and determination of alternatives

Once the data-gathering phase has been completed, the next step is to analyze current operations and determine suitable processing alternatives. During the fact-finding stage the primary emphasis is placed on *what* is being done; in this step in the approach the interest is in *why* things are being done as they are and *how* they can be improved.

Perhaps the first alternative to the present procedures which should be considered is an *improved and modified version* of these procedures.[13] Earlier in the chapter we saw that one of the benefits of a feasibility study is that significant savings are sometimes achieved through systems improvement alone. Once opportunities for improvement in present methods have been identified, it is *then* possible to compare the more efficient procedures with the other possible alterna-

---

[13] This alternative might include acquiring new equipment other than a computer. Often, however, considerable savings can be achieved with little or no additional equipment investment.

tives, e.g., an in-house computer installation or the use of a computer center. In other words, other alternatives should *not* be compared with obsolete and outdated procedures. It is quite possible, as we saw in the inventory control example earlier in the chapter, that an alternative which is attractive when compared with obsolete methods might not be the best choice when compared with redesigned procedures. Another reason for improving present procedures is to prevent useless forms, reports, and records from being preserved in a conversion to an alternative.

Data gathered in the fact-finding stage are analyzed to detect weaknesses and to determine the real needs of the business. The information, in turn, makes it possible for the study team to develop an efficient set of data processing specifications for each area of study. Figure 12-3 lists some of the possible questions which should be answered during this review and design stage.

The variety of different business systems, the difficulty of describing these systems, the wide range of equipment (mechanical, electromechanical, and electronic) which can be used, the speed with which equipment is changing, the lack of static testing conditions caused by a rapidly changing business environment—all these factors prevent the formulation of exact rules to follow in analyzing existing systems and designing new alternatives. Questions such as those in Figure 12-3 may be presented as a *guide*. But the success of the entire project is determined by the ingenuity of the team in arriving at those answers which satisfy company needs.

Several tools may be helpful in analyzing current procedures and in designing alternatives. Personal *interviews* should again be used. It was noted earlier in the chapter that it is important for operating managers (i.e., department heads) to have a strong voice in the preliminary design sessions. It is equally important that these managers be closely associated with the development of new system specifications. *Additional* design sessions supplemented by individual interviews may be desirable at this point in the study.

Analysis of systems *flowcharts* also proves helpful. Bottlenecks may be disclosed; unnecessary files may be discovered (e.g., the charts may show a file where information is stored, but from which little or nothing is being removed); and duplications may be identified.

Another useful analytical tool is the *grid* or *input/output* chart. Figure 12-4 shows an example of such a chart. The purpose of this tool is to show the relationship which exists between system inputs and outputs. The time factor is ignored. In Figure 12-4 the system source documents are listed in the rows to the left of the chart, while the output reports produced by the system are identified in the col-

Procedural considerations

1. Are documents being produced relevant to the needs of the business? When were they originated? Who originated them? For what purpose?

2. Is faster reporting desired? Is faster reporting necessary? Can the processing sequence be improved? What would happen if the document were delayed? If it were eliminated?

3. Is greater accuracy needed? Could less accuracy be tolerated, i.e., is the expense involved in error checking greater than the cost of committing the error? Is adequate control maintained over document preparation? Does excessive control add to expense?

4. What monetary value would the user place on the document? Would he be willing to have his department charged with part of the cost of preparation?

5. Is the document in a useful form? Has writing been minimized? When were forms designed? Who designed them? For what purpose?

6. Does an output document cause action when it is sent to a manager? If not, why is it sent? If it does, what decisions are made?

7. Is the document filed? If so, for how long? How often is it referred to? Does the filing cost exceed the value of having the document available?

8. Can documents be combined? Is the same information duplicated on other reports? In other departments? If so, can procedures be integrated?

9. Is there any part of the document which is ignored? Are unnecessary facts recorded? Are additional facts needed? Are the correct number of copies prepared?

10. Is exception reporting feasible? Do current reports clearly point out exceptions?

11. Are additional documents needed? What additional documents? Is computer processing required? Are packaged programs available which will meet the needs of the business?

12. Is system capacity adequate? Do bottlenecks exist? Is overtime required? What can be done to eliminate peak loads?

13. Is customer service adequate? What improvements can be made?

Personnel and organizational considerations

14. Are documents being prepared in the proper departments? By the right people? Could departments be combined? Could any work units be eliminated? What effects would organizational change have on personnel?

15. What effect will procedural change have on personnel? Are personnel agreeable to such change? What has been done to reduce resistance to change? What will be done with workers whose jobs are eliminated or changed? If new jobs are created, has proper consideration been given to selecting and training workers to staff these vacancies?

Economic considerations

16. What will be the cost of processing data with revised current procedures? What will it cost to satisfy company needs by other alternatives? If the cost of using the computer is greater, are intangible benefits available which are worth the extra expense?

Figure 12-3. Questions for Analysis and Design

Input source documents	Output reports							
	1	2	3	4	5	6	7	8
Form A	x			x				
Form B		x		x				
Form C			x					
Form D						x		
Form E		x		x				
Form F			x					x
Form G					x		x	

Figure 12-4. Input/Output Chart

umns. An x is placed at the intersection of a row and column when a particular source document is used in the preparation of a specific report. For example, form A is needed in the preparation of reports 1 and 4.

The grid chart enables the analyst to identify and isolate *independent subsystems* quickly for further study. This is done (1) by drawing a vertical line down any *single* report column and *then* (2) by drawing a horizontal line across any row with a covered x, etc., until further vertical and horizontal lines are impossible. For example, if we draw a line down column 1, we cover only one x—the one indicating that form A is used in preparing report 1. If we then draw a horizontal line along the form A row, we cover the x in column 4. We then draw a vertical line down column 4 and a horizontal line along any row with a covered x. The result of this procedure is that forms A, B, and E and reports 1, 2, and 4 combine to form an independent subsystem.

It is assumed at this point that the study team has analyzed the current operations, has prepared a detailed set of written (documented) systems specifications with the study objectives in mind, and has settled on the alternatives which it feels will best achieve the desired goals. The prepared specifications should include:[14]

1. *The input requirements.* Included in the input specifications should be the source documents to be used, the means of preparing and transmitting these documents, the frequency of preparation, and the volume figures expected.

2. *The processing specifications.* The new procedures must be defined. It should be clearly indicated how the inputs will be used to prepare the

[14] See Joseph I. Barnett, "How to Install a Management Information and Control System," *Systems & Procedures Journal*, vol. 17, September–October, 1966, p. 13.

desired outputs. All files and records to be used and maintained should be identified; frequency of file usage must be known; and processing volumes (both current and expected) associated with the files should be specified.

3. *The output requirements.* Included in the output specifications should be the form, content, and frequency of reports. Volume figures are also needed.

4. *Control needs.* The controls required to provide the necessary input/output accuracy and timeliness should be specified.

Decision making: study team

A computer installation is justified when the economic benefits (both tangible and intangible) are greater than comparable benefits received from other alternatives. The alternatives to be evaluated vary, of course, from one company to another. In many situations noncomputer choices may be preferable; for smaller organizations, the use of a computer center or a time sharing station may be the best approach.[15] But for purposes of this text we shall assume that the study team believes that an in-house installation is justified.

Before such a decision is reached, however, the team should compare the expected benefits to be received from using the computer with the benefits to be expected from streamlined current procedures. The costs to be considered in such a comparison include those of the present procedures *which will be changed* by using the computer as well as those *new* cost items which will be incurred if the change is made. *Recurring* operating expenses which are affected by a change include the charges for labor, equipment, materials, and overhead. *Nonrecurring* or one-time costs of making the change can be substantial. Included in the nonrecurring expense category are the costs of initial programmer training, the costs of preparing the physical facilities, and the cost of initial program preparation, debugging, and conversion.

Once the decision has been made (with the approval of top company executives) to concentrate study attention on an in-house installation, there are a number of other questions which confront the team members before they can prepare their final recommendations. These questions include:

1. Which computers should be considered? What equipment best meets the needs of the company? Can outside consultants make a contribution in equipment selection? Is the delivery date acceptable?

2. Which machines offer the greatest return on investment? Can the com-

[15] For a discussion of the computer center alternative, see Donald H. Sanders, *Introducing Computers to Small Business* (Park Ridge, Ill.: Data Processing Management Association, 1966), pp. 79–83.

pany afford the investment at this time? Do other investment opportunities available to the firm yield a greater return? What return do top managers consider to be satisfactory on their investment in plant and production equipment? Does a computer yield such a return? If not, should one be acquired?

3. Have all possible acquisition approaches (rental, lease, purchase) been evaluated?

4. Have organizational and personnel aspects received proper consideration? (These aspects will not be considered here but will be discussed in Chapters 13 and 15.)

Equipment evaluation and selection   Equipment selection in the earlier days of computers was a relatively simple task. Today, however, because of the growth in the number of possible machine configurations, evaluation and selection are difficult. Whole families of machines are available from several manufacturers, and we have seen that the variety of I/O equipment which can be selected is large. *To select* is to choose from a number of more or less suitable alternatives. Thus, the team should not, normally, limit its evaluation to the equipment produced by one manufacturer. Instead, evaluation should be based on the ability of a number of machines to process the detailed set of written systems specifications which the team has prepared.

One selection approach which has been widely used[16] is to submit the systems specifications to computer manufacturers (who seem *most likely* to be able to meet the company needs) with the request that they prepare bids.[17] The vendors interested in competing select the equipment in their lines which they feel best satisfies the system specifications. Formal proposals are prepared by the manufacturers, and it is then up to the team to evaluate these proposals and make a decision. Some of the evaluation factors to be considered are shown in Figure 12-5.

On the surface it would appear that the bidding procedure would yield excellent results—and sometimes this is the case. But all too often the manufacturers do not spend the time and money required to prepare the proposals they are capable of making. This is especially true if the computer representative feels that his chances of receiving

---

[16] Another approach which has frequently been used with unfortunate results is to turn the entire feasibility study over to one or more manufacturers and request that they submit proposals based on their investigations. This is a pitfall which the study team has avoided.

[17] It is often a good idea for the study group to invite manufacturers' representatives to a preliminary meeting. The purposes of such a meeting are (1) to explain briefly the objectives of the business in acquiring a computer and (2) to determine those vendors who are interested in submitting a proposal.

A. *Economic factors*

   1. Cost comparisons
   2. Return on investment
   3. Acquisition methods

B. *Hardware factors*

   1. Hardware performance, capacity, and price
   2. Presence or absence of modularity
   3. Number and accessibility of back-up facilities
   4. Firmness of delivery date
   5. Effective remaining life of proposed hardware

C. *Software factors*

   1. Programming languages available (not promised)
   2. Efficiency of available software
   3. Availability of useful packaged programs, program libraries, and user groups
   4. Firmness of delivery date on promised software

D. *Service factors*

   1. Facilities provided by manufacturer for checking new programs
   2. Training facilities offered and the quality of training provided
   3. Programming assistance and conversion assistance offered
   4. Maintenance terms and quality

E. *Reputation of manufacturer*

   1. Financial stability
   2. Record of keeping promises

Figure 12-5. Factors in Equipment Selection

the order are none too good or if the order itself is not apt to be very substantial. Sometimes the system specifications are altered to improve the procedures or, perhaps, to place the vendor's equipment in the best possible light. The study team is then forced to compare bids based on different specifications—a very difficult comparison indeed! Frequently the program running times are underestimated in the bids. For example, the times required to load the machines, rewind tapes, and rerun jobs that do not check out are underestimated or ignored. Errors of this type may affect the equipment configurations recommended by the manufacturer and may result in the acquisition of hardware with inadequate capability to meet expanding needs. (When a machine of the wrong size is obtained, it usually proves to have inadequate capacity rather than excessive capacity. Thus, modular capability—the ability to add on components of greater capacity—can be an important machine characteristic.)

If the bidding approach has these shortcomings, how can a business obtain more meaningful and objective comparison data? One way may be to rely on qualified data processing consultants for advice. Another approach, and one which is growing in popularity, is to use *simulation programs* to project how different equipment models perform and respond to given systems specifications. In other words, *a computer is used to make decisions about computers.* For example, COMRESS, Inc., a Washington, D.C., consulting organization, has a series of simulation programs known as SCERT (Systems and Computers Evaluation and Review Technique). The SCERT programs are capable of comparing the input, output, and computing times required to process specific applications on all available commercial computers made in this country. The General Services Administration, a housekeeping agency of the Federal government, has employed SCERT to help in the selection of 10 large-scale computer systems for its regional offices.

Regardless of the approach used, once equipment facts are obtained, the study team must compare the quantitative factors (costs, capacity, speed, etc.) and the qualitative factors (service, reputation of the manufacturer, etc.) listed in Figure 12-5 to reduce the number of alternatives further. To determine if there is economic justification for acquiring computing equipment, a return-on-investment analysis should be made.

Estimated return on investment[18] The costs associated with the equipment remaining should be compared with the cost of the improved current methods of performing the work. Let us assume that as a result of one cost comparison it is expected that there will be negative effects on the company's after-tax earnings for the first three years, but that after this initial period substantial positive returns will be forthcoming. The study team feels that a computer should yield a satisfactory return over a six-year period or it should not be acquired. Top executives of the company are accustomed to receiving a 10 percent return on investments made in production equipment. It is their feeling that unless the computer investment yields a similar return, it should be postponed.

---

[18] Although capital investment analysis is generally beyond the scope of this text, the concept of the time-adjusted return on investment may be briefly introduced to show its importance in the computer acquisition decision. For further information on the subject, see Chap. 19 of Robert N. Anthony, *Management Accounting* (3d ed.; Homewood, Ill.: Richard D. Irwin, Inc., 1964).

Armed with the above information, the study team makes the following analysis:

Year	(1) Effects on cash flow of acquisition	(2) 10% discount factors*	(3) Present value of cash flow
1	$ − 100,000	0.9091	$ − 90,910
2	− 75,000	0.8264	− 61,980
3	− 25,000	0.7513	− 18,782
4	+ 50,000	0.6830	+ 34,150
5	+ 100,000	0.6209	+ 62,090
6	+ 150,000	0.5645	+ 85,675
		Total	$ + 10,243

*From Billy E. Goetz, *Quantitative Methods: A Survey and Guide for Managers* (New York: McGraw-Hill Book Company, 1965), Table 8a, p. 526.

Column (1), the effects on cash flow, represents the economic effects expected by the team if improved current procedures are replaced by a selected computer system. In other words, this column shows the expected effects of the acquisition on net income plus depreciation. Column (2), the column labeled "10% discount factors," shows the *present value* of $1 received in years 1, 2, 3, etc., when the required rate of return is 10 percent. In other words, 10 percent interest on $0.9091 is $0.0909 at the end of one year. Thus, the present value ($0.9091) plus the interest ($0.0909) gives $1 at the end of a year. Column (3), the present value column, is the product of column (1) multiplied by column (2). The *time-adjusted* return on investment is exactly 10 percent if the total of the present value column is zero. A negative total means that the 10 percent return cannot be expected. In our example, the estimated return is found to *exceed* the required rate.

Before leaving the subject of return on investment, it might be well to point out that 20 of 33 "outstandingly successful" manufacturing companies studied in a survey conducted by the management consulting firm of Booz, Allen & Hamilton make use of formal return-on-investment analyses in their computer decisions. Furthermore, "the companies evaluating potential applications on the basis of return on investment tend to be the same ones rated highest in applying the computer to their most important needs."[19]

[19] James W. Taylor and Neal J. Dean, "Managing to Manage the Computer," *Harvard Business Review*, vol. 44, September–October, 1966, p. 107.

Acquisition methods[20]   Computers may be acquired through *rental* agreements with the manufacturer, through long-term *leasing* arrangements with someone other than the manufacturer, or through *purchase*. It is the job of the team to evaluate these acquisition methods and recommend the one best suited to the company.

Rental is the most popular acquisition method—about three-fourths of the computer installations are acquired in this way. The rental method is popular, of course, because no large purchase amount is required. It is the most flexible method in the sense that the agreement may be cancelled without penalty after a rather brief usage period. Thus, a company does not run the risk of owning a data processing system which no longer is adequate. But the rental method is the most expensive *if* the equipment meets the company needs for a long period of time—perhaps four or five years or longer. Rental charges generally remain the same throughout the life of the rental agreement; however, additional charges may be added to the user's bill when the equipment is used beyond a specified number of hours each month. Maintenance of the equipment is performed by the manufacturer, and the cost is included in the rental price. If a firm decides to purchase the machine later, it may be able to apply some small part of the rental charges to this purchase.

Although the rental method is the most popular, there is evidence of a trend toward greater equipment *purchasing*. This is especially true of the Federal government. In 1962, 83 percent of government equipment was rented; by 1965, this figure had been reduced to about 50 percent. There are several reasons for the somewhat greater interest in purchasing. The first reason is that it is the least expensive of methods when hardware is kept over a long period of time—again, four or five years or longer. Another reason is that third-generation computers are expected to be a basic product in manufacturers' lines for a number of years. When compared with earlier models, these new machines are more reliable and are expected to have a longer physical life and a greater residual or salvage value in a developing used-computer market. In short, some managers consider the risk of *functional obsolescence* (wearing out) and *technological obsolescence* (becoming outdated) to be less than was once the case. Finally, some companies with experience in computer usage now feel that they can do a better job of long-range system planning, and are therefore less reluctant to become "locked in" to a particular hardware configuration.

---

[20] As in the case of capital investment analysis, the economics of the rental, lease, or purchase decision is generally beyond the scope of this book. For further treatment of the subject, see Irving I. Solomon and Laurence O. Weingart, *Management Uses of the Computer* (New York: Harper & Row, Publishers, Incorporated, 1966), pp. 187–198.

Under a typical *leasing* arrangement, the user tells the leasing company what equipment it wants. The leasing organization then purchases this equipment and leases it to the user for a long-term period (usually three to five years). This method combines some of the advantages of both renting and purchasing. Like purchasing, leasing is more economical over the lifetime of the lease than renting; and there are usually no additional charges when hardware is used beyond a specified number of hours each month, e.g., when equipment is used on a two-shift basis. And like renting, leasing requires no large purchase amount. Maintenance costs are included in the lease charges, which, unlike rental payments, decline after a specified period. The user is often given the opportunity to apply part of the lease charges toward purchase of the equipment. The main drawback to leasing is that the user usually contracts for the equipment over a long period of time and there is the possibility that the system will become inadequate prior to the end of the lease.

Figure 12-6 summarizes the advantages and disadvantages of each acquisition method. The study team should carefully weigh these merits and faults before making its choice. The following topics should be considered in the evaluation: (1) rental and lease charges, (2) purchase price, (3) the system life of the equipment, (4) maintenance costs, (5) the salvage or residual value of the equipment at the time of disposal, (6) the required rate of return on investment or the interest rate on borrowed funds, (7) the future value of current dollars, and (8) the tax considerations for each alternative.

Presentation of recommendations

Working from a detailed statement of the scope of the study and of the objectives which were to be pursued, the team has gathered data on the processing procedures under examination. These facts have been analyzed, and from this analysis has come a detailed set of improved system specifications designed to achieve the study goals. After careful consideration of the possible alternatives, the team has decided that a computer installation is justified. In addition, they have also decided that a particular computer model is best, that acquiring this model yields a satisfactory return on the investment required, and that one method of acquisition is most desirable. These decisions have been made by the team. But the *final* decisions are made by top-level managers in the organization. It is the job of the study team to recommend; it is the responsibility of top executives to decide.

Rental

Advantages

1. No large purchase price required.
2. Risk of technological obsolescence reduced.
3. Maintenance included in rental charges.
4. Agreement may be cancelled without penalty after brief period.
5. Greater flexibility in changing equipment configurations.
6. Possibility of applying some part of rental charges to later purchase.

Disadvantages

1. Most expensive if equipment is used for long period of time.
2. Rental charges remain same throughout life of agreement.
3. Rental charges may increase when monthly usage exceeds a specified number of hours.

Lease

Advantages

1. Less expensive than rental over life of the lease.
2. No large purchase price required.
3. Maintenance is included in the lease charges.
4. No additional charges when equipment is used beyond a specified number of hours monthly.
5. Lease charges decline after specified period.
6. Possibility of applying part of lease charges toward later purchase.

Disadvantages

1. User contracts for equipment over long time period.
2. Reduced flexibility—user is obligated to pay a contracted charge if lease is terminated prior to end of lease period.

Purchase

Advantages

1. Generally least expensive if machine is kept over long time period.
2. No additional charges when equipment is used beyond specified number of hours monthly.
3. Certain tax advantages accrue to the purchaser.

Disadvantages

1. Equipment maintenance not included in the purchase price.
2. Risk of technological obsolescence—of being "locked-in" to a system which does not continue to meet changing company needs.
3. A large initial capital outlay is required.

Figure 12-6. Factors to Consider in Equipment Acquisition

The final report of the study team should cover the following points:

1. A restatement of study scope and objectives

2. The procedures and operations which will be changed

3. The anticipated effects of such changes on organizational structure, on physical facilities, and on company information

4. The effects on personnel and the personnel resources available to implement the change

5. The equipment chosen, the reasons for the choice, and the alternatives considered

6. The economic effects of the change, including cost comparisons, adequacy of return on investment, and analysis of acquisition methods

7. A summary of the problems anticipated in the changeover

8. A summary of the benefits to be obtained from the change

Final decision making: top managers

Because of the managerial implications involved, the final decisions must be made at the top. It is the responsibility of top managers to evaluate the recommendations of the study team, to detect any evidence of bias[21] which may be present in these recommendations, and to decide whether or not the benefits outweigh the disadvantages.

Suspicion of bias or of an inadequate study may be justified if the points outlined above are not included in the recommendation report. For example, suspicion is probably warranted if little or no mention is made of the personnel or organizational aspects of the change, if the problems associated with the change appear to be insignificant, if the alternatives considered are really just "straw men" which are obviously inadequate, or if feasibility depends on vaguely defined intangible benefits.

Follow up on decision

If the decision is to accept the recommendations of the team, the top executives should follow up this decision by establishing project performance controls. Personnel must be selected to do the work; an implementation schedule should be drawn up;[22] and periodic reports on installation progress should be required. Efforts should be made to meet the anticipated problems—e.g., steps should be taken to reduce

[21] After all, if the change is made, the members of the study team may move into positions of greater influence.

[22] PERT and CPM techniques have been used with good results in scheduling installation activities.

employee resistance to the change. In the following two chapters we shall consider some of the technical and personnel preparations which have to be made.

Once the computer has been installed and is in operation, a thorough appraisal should be made[23] to answer the following questions:[24]

1. Are procedures being followed? Are all new procedures being processed on the computer? Have old procedures been eliminated? If not, why not?

2. Are any modifications or refinements indicated as a result of operating experience?

3. How do operating results compare with original objectives and predictions? Are economic benefits being obtained? If there is deviation, what is the cause? What can be done to achieve expected results?

Additional audits should be conducted from time to time to make sure that efficient use is being made of the computer. The subject of computer control will be discussed further in Chapter 16.

If the decision is *not* to acquire a computer, a follow-up on this decision may also be needed. Rising labor costs, reduced computing costs, and other factors may make the use of a computer more attractive in the future. To the "no" decision perhaps should be added "not yet."

SUMMARY

A feasibility study is made by an organization to determine the desirability of using a computer to achieve specific objectives. Failure to conduct such a study subjects the firm to probable financial loss; a proper investigation, on the other hand, usually yields positive benefits and helps the firm avoid making common mistakes.

The steps in the feasibility study approach are to (1) identify the scope of the problem and the objectives to be gained, (2) gather the facts on current operations, (3) analyze these facts and determine suitable alternate procedures, (4) choose the most appropriate alternative, and (5) follow up on the decision.

In a broad sense, the end result of a computer feasibility study is a single decision — to use or not to use a computer. But as we have seen in this chapter, there are an uncountable number of decisions which must be made by the study team during the course of its work. The success of the information processing system produced depends on the quality of these decisions.

[23] Data processing personnel should know in advance that such a follow-up will be made.

[24] See Richard F. Neuschel, *Management by System* (2d ed.; New York: McGraw-Hill Book Company, 1960), pp. 319–320.

278

DISCUSSION QUESTIONS

1 (*a*) What is a feasibility study? (*b*) Why are feasibility studies essential?

2 What are some of the common mistakes which have been made in the past because of improperly conducted feasibility studies?

3 What benefits may be obtained from feasibility studies?

4 What are the prerequisite planning steps to a well-managed feasibility study?

5 What objectives are commonly sought through computer usage?

6 Define the following terms:
(*a*) design sessions (*c*) charter
(*b*) iterative process (*d*) input/output chart

7 Identify and explain the steps to be followed in conducting a feasibility study.

8 (*a*) What questions should be answered during the fact-finding stage of the feasibility study? (*b*) During the analysis and design stage?

9 (*a*) Discuss the equipment selection approaches which may be used. (*b*) What factors should be considered in equipment selection?

10 Why should return on investment in computer equipment be considered during the feasibility study?

11 Discuss the possible computer acquisition methods.

SELECTED REFERENCES

Joseph I. Barnett, "How to Install a Management Information and Control System," *Systems & Procedures Journal*, September–October, 1966, pp. 10–14.

Richard G. Canning, "Equipment Selection," *Data Processing Digest*, June, 1966, pp. 1-8.

Kenneth C. Cole, "Evaluating Proposals from Computer Manufacturers," *Management Services*, November–December, 1965, pp. 28-34.

Documentation Techniques (IBM Corporation, Manual C20-8075).

George H. Heilborn, "The Art of Leasing Computers," *Computers and Automation*, January, 1967, pp. 42–46.

Richard H. Hill, "Computer Economics," *Data Processing Digest*, May, 1966, pp. 1-11.

13. PREPARING FOR CHANGE: I

There are a bewildering number of tasks—involving both technical and personnel considerations—which must be performed in the many months between the time the computer is ordered and the time the conversion to electronic data processing is completed. From the *technical* standpoint, a site must be prepared to house the equipment, programs must be prepared and debugged, conversion must be made to new procedures, and operating controls must be established. From the *personnel* standpoint, plans should be made to prepare employees for the change, to select and train workers for new jobs which will be created, and to alleviate hardships caused by the elimination of existing jobs.

Once the top administrators of a company decide to order a computer, their next step is to see that a strong manager is appointed and given the authority to plan, organize, staff, and control the installation effort. One of the first jobs of this data processing manager is to see that competent programmers are selected and given initial, formal training to carry out the conversion. From this point on, the manager will be involved in planning and scheduling the many jobs which must be completed. A number of preparation tasks will go on *simultaneously*—additional workers may be selected; programmers must be given further training; detailed systems analysis must be performed; programs must be prepared, debugged, and made ready for conversion; and the physical computer site must be readied.

Because of the difficulty of knowing how long each preparation phase will take, it is usually necessary for the data processing manager to revise plans and schedules frequently. You may remember in the preceding chapter that one authority estimated that installation schedules are not met 90 percent of the time. Difficulties with technical tasks such as program preparation and debugging are almost always the cause of failure to meet installation schedules. Because the difficulties encountered in technical preparations are obvious and measurable and need immediate correction, attention in the past has too often been focused on the technical aspects of the change at the expense of proper personnel preparation. Yet personnel considerations are of critical importance to the overall success of the project.

Technical preparation matters are examined in the first part of this chapter. Included in this treatment is a discussion of (1) *site preparation*, (2) *program preparation and conversion*, and (3) *vendor assistance*. Since many of these activities will go on simultaneously, there is no chronological order to the presentation. In the remaining pages of the chapter, attention is shifted to the subject of *personnel preparation* and to the problem of *resistance to change*. The subject of personnel preparation is continued in the following chapter, where the topics of personnel selection and training and the effect of electronic data processing on employment are studied.

TECHNICAL PREPARATIONS

Site preparation

Obviously, a location to house the computer must be prepared prior to delivery. Preferably, this location should be chosen for its accessibility to those departments in the business which will be closely associated with the computer operations. The computer vendor is able to offer valuable assistance in site planning. Vendors have, naturally, had considerable experience in such matters, and in this case their interests and the interests of the customer are usually the same. Both want the computer housed in an environment which is as safe and as trouble-free as possible; both want a site which, when trouble occurs, provides easy service access to the equipment; both are interested in the efficient use of space and in an adequate amount of space to allow for future expansion if necessary; and both are interested in housing the computer in attractive surroundings.

Space, layout, and location   The physical dimensions of the equipment to be housed; the location and length of power and connecting cables; the space needed to allow service access to this hardware; the data movement patterns; the storage room needed for input/output media, supplies, spare parts, and maintenance equipment; and the number and size of work areas, offices, and conference rooms—all these factors must be considered in determining the *space* requirements and the *layout* of the computer site. Future expansion needs should always be considered. The *location* of this site, from an *economic* standpoint, should probably be chosen to minimize the length of lines of communication between the computer site and the departments closely associated with electronic data processing. But factors *other* than economics are often given top priority. For example, the company president may want a showcase installation enclosed in glass, expensively furnished, and located where it can be seen by large numbers of people.

Physical arrangements The physical matters which are usually considered in site preparation include the requirements for *air conditioning and power, raised flooring,* and *fire protection.*

Earlier computers needed large amounts of *air conditioning* to dissipate the heat generated by the vacuum tubes. Comparatively little heat is generated by current solid state models, but air conditioning is still needed for reasons of employee productivity, and dust, temperature, and humidity control. We saw in an earlier chapter that dust particles on magnetic tapes (or magnetic disks) could cause reading errors during processing. The filtering action of air conditioning reduces the amount of dust in the air and thus helps to improve reading performance. We have also seen that punched cards and magnetic tapes function best when stored in areas of controlled temperature and humidity.

Provision must be made at the site to meet the electrical *power requirements* of the computer. Vendors furnish information on equipment power needs. If rewiring is called for (and some rewiring is usually needed), the job should be done by company electricians or by a qualified electrical contractor in accordance with building codes and fire insurance rules.

The pieces of equipment in a computer installation are connected together by a number of cables. Each piece of equipment must also, of course, be connected in some way to a power outlet. Yet in attractive computer sites (Figure 13-1) there are no unsightly cables lying around on the floor to trip employees or become frayed and dangerous. A usual practice is to install a *raised* or *false floor* and then run the cables beneath this floor. If not run beneath the flooring surface, the cables should at least be protected from damage with metal or wooden coverings.

Consideration must be given to *fire protection.* Since much of the data stored on cards and tapes may be irreplaceable, fireproof materials should be used wherever possible in the site preparation. A fireproof vault to store vital records, programs, etc., might be a wise investment. Adequate fire alarm facilities should be provided, but a

Figure 13-1. (Courtesy Sperry Rand Corporation, UNIVAC Division)

sprinkler system should probably not be used in the computer room because of the water damage to media and equipment which might result from its use.

The cost of site preparation can range from a very modest figure to hundreds of thousands of dollars depending on the extent of remodeling or construction required. Some separate showcase buildings have been constructed for the sole purpose of housing the computer. Furnishings may range from the austere to the luxurious depending on the wishes of top executives.

Program preparation and conversion

The purpose of this technical preparation phase is to perform the following activities:[1]

1. *Program analysis.* The systems specifications defined during the feasibility study should be broken down into the specific arithmetic and logic operations required to solve the problems. *Program flowcharts* and/or *decision tables* are tools commonly used for this purpose.

---

[1]Since these activities have been dealt with at some length elsewhere in this book, we need only summarize them at this time. See Chaps. 9 and 10 for additional information.

2. *Program preparation.* When the arithmetic and logic operations have been identified, they must be translated or coded into a language and form acceptable to the processor which has been ordered.

3. *Testing and debugging.* The coded programs must then be tested and (generally) debugged before they can be considered ready for use.

4. *Parallel running.* When the computer arrives, there should be a shakedown or parallel running period during which applications are processed by both currently used and new methods as a final check before the cutover to the new system occurs. The same input data should be used, and the results of the parallel processing compared. If significant differences appear, both current and new procedures must be examined to determine the cause.[2] Final conversion to computer production runs comes from satisfactory performance during this shakedown period.

The activities associated with the program preparation and conversion phase may represent 50 percent or more of the total human effort required from feasibility study inception to conversion completion. John D. MacLean, a consultant with the firm of Peat, Marwick, Mitchell and Co., notes in this connection that "experience has indicated that the ratio of systems research and design effort to computer program writing, testing, documenting and system debugging is about 40 percent-60 percent."[3] Because of the time and complexities involved, this phase must begin as soon as possible. The efficient use of applications programs and other software aids may help to speed up the program preparation activity. It is during this activity, too, that many firms have made valuable use of the knowledge and experience of software consulting organizations.

Careful documentation (for the reasons explained in Chapter 9) is required during the performance of all the activities associated with program preparation and conversion. Yet when schedules begin to slip, documentation should not be slighted. Time made up at the expense of proper documentation is likely to be a very temporary gain, only to be lost at high cost in a later period when the programs must be tested and program corrections and changes made.

[2] Sometimes a better approach is the *pilot testing* operation where the input data for a *previous* month's operations are processed by the computer and the results are compared with the results obtained from current processing methods. Pilot tests are helpful in debugging as well as in final testing. It is often not necessary to incur the costs of two different systems, since the pilot tests can be run on the vendor's equipment prior to delivery of the user's hardware. Also, in many cases parallel runs are impractical: the two systems to be compared are really not very comparable because of system redesign.

[3] John D. MacLean, "Caution: Crash Computer Conversion," *Systems & Procedures Journal,* January–February, 1967, p. 9.

Before conversion can be achieved, current files must be changed into a form acceptable to the processor. This can be a tremendous task, and it is one which is often underestimated. Files should be consolidated, and duplicate records eliminated; errors in current files must be detected and removed; and transcribing errors must be found *before* the changeover rather than later when they cause system malfunctions. Manual procedures which are to be developed or changed must also receive attention. And new forms must frequently be designed both for new manual procedures and for support of the computerized operations.

The conversion time is almost always a period of personnel and organizational strain. Data processing personnel may work long hours and be subjected to pressure to complete the conversion. Unforeseen problems, last-minute changes, and the disruption of data processing services to using departments, customers, suppliers, etc., may contribute to these pressures.[4] It is at this time that cooperation between the data processing specialists and the managers and employees of affected departments is badly needed. Yet it is precisely at this time that cooperation frequently breaks down because of improper personnel preparations.

Vendor assistance

The computer manufacturer stands ready to provide a number of services of a technical nature to help the customer make the transition to computer usage. The following kinds of assistance are commonly offered:

1. *Training.* The vendor provides introductory training for the programmer candidates selected by the user. Included in this training are details about the specific processor model ordered and about the programming language which will be employed. Brief executive seminars may also be held to acquaint managers with a few of the basic computer concepts. The subject of training will be considered further in the next chapter.

2. *Program preparation.* The vendor may assign a full-time site representative to help with program preparation. This representative knows the computer; he knows how to program it; and he can furnish on-the-job training to the user's programmers. If the customer is important enough, larger amounts of programming help may be obtained. But it is risky to place too much reliance on the site representative because company personnel may then not be adequately prepared to take over program preparation and program maintenance when the representative leaves. Of course, the

---

[4]Consultants have been used to advantage to shorten the disrupting conversion period.

competency of site representatives varies. And even the best ones may not know much about the user's business.

3. *Programming aids.* Program preparation is aided by the software which the vendor can furnish. The availability and efficiency of assembly languages, compilers, etc., are an important consideration, as is the availability of subroutines and packaged programs which can be used to advantage.

4. *Testing and debugging.* Most vendors make free testing and debugging time available (the amount varies) on equipment similar to the user's hardware prior to its arrival. The site representative, of course, is also available to help with the predelivery testing and debugging of prepared programs. A larger amount of free machine time may be furnished for these purposes after the hardware is installed.

5. *Site preparation and installation.* We have already seen that the vendor can be of considerable help in site preparation. Vendor engineers, of course, install the hardware and make the necessary tests to be sure it is operating properly before it is turned over to the user.

PERSONNEL PREPARATIONS

As the preceding section suggests, there are many technical aspects to consider in installing a computer system. Furthermore, there are many unexpected problems of a technical nature which can appear to harass the data processing manager and other executives during the preparation period. In view of these difficulties, it is perhaps understandable that executives and data processing specialists have been so preoccupied with technical matters that they have frequently fallen into the trap of ignoring the personnel and psychological aspects of the transition. In short, the emphasis has too often been placed on work rather than on workers.

Personnel preparations should receive considerable attention during the feasibility study period and at the same time that technical preparations are being made, so that employees will accept changes with a minimum of resistance. That such resistance can endanger the entire project is vividly shown by the following statement made to the author by a data processing manager whose company was dropping the use of electronic data processing (EDP):[5]

Office supervisory personnel failed to comply with the detailed new procedures due to disinterest, and this is why EDP has not worked. We couldn't

[5] See Donald H. Sanders, "Personnel Management Approaches of Small Firms to the Change to EDP," *Advanced Management Journal,* vol. 31, October, 1966, p. 56. See also Donald H. Sanders, *Introducing Computers to Small Business* (Park Ridge, Ill.: Data Processing Management Association, 1966), p. 96.

get these lamebrains to do what they were told to do and we didn't have necessary direct communication with top management.

There were two basic reasons for the complete failure of this installation. One reason was that the data processing manager did a poor job of personnel preparation; the other reason was that when almost inevitable resistance to the change then occurred, the top management support vital to overcoming this opposition was lacking.

In the remaining pages of this chapter we shall look at the subject of *employee resistance* to change. More specifically, we shall examine the following topics: (1) *resistance is the rule*, (2) *forms of resistance*, (3) *reasons for resistance*, (4) *employees who resist*, and (5) *suggestions for reducing resistance*.

Resistance is the rule

The first punched card machine was built by a French weaver by the name of Jacquard. The cards contained punched instructions which enabled the machine to weave designs into cloth. In the early 1800s the Frenchman was physically attacked, and his equipment wrecked in Lyons, France, by workers who feared that the machine was a threat to their job security. Earlier, in the mid-1700s, a mob of English spinners smashed the first workable multispindle frames for the same reason. Although it is certainly true that the *rate* of change today is unprecedented, it is clear from these examples that there is nothing new about either change or resistance to change.

Although generally appearing in a less violent form, resistance to the change to electronic data processing is the rule rather than the exception. George S. McIsaac, a management consultant, sums up the situation when he writes:[6]

Resistance to change is a normal part of the process of change. Dealing with this resistance, therefore, must be a necessary component of the planning involved in any successful innovation.

Forms of resistance

Resistance to change may appear in many ways. The extreme forms are explained by Heckmann and Huneryager in these words:[7]

[6] George S. McIsaac, "How to Practice What We Preach in Making Business Changes," *Business Horizons*, vol. 6, Summer, 1963, pp. 29–30.

[7] I. L. Heckmann, Jr., and S. C. Huneryager, *Human Relations in Management* (Cincinnati: South-Western Publishing Company, 1960), p. 425.

At one extreme people suffer a temporary disequilibrium in need satisfaction, ask a few questions about the change, quickly adjust to it, and resume their previous behavior. At the other extreme, reaction can take the form of open opposition, rebellion, and even destruction.

Between these extremes may be found a number of other symptoms including the following:

1. *Withholding data and information.* A rather common form of resistance is for employees to withhold information about current operations. Even after the computer is installed, input data may be withheld or turned in late.

2. *Providing inaccurate information.* Input data containing known inaccuracies are submitted to sabotage processing results.

3. *Distrusting computer output.* Some supervisors continue to maintain their old methods after the conversion is made. In one case it was found that "the payroll supervisor was insisting that his clerks recalculate the pay of the company's 1,000 hourly workers after each payroll had been completed by the IBM 1401."[8]

4. *Showing lowered morale.* A general lowering of employee morale may result in lack of cooperation, sloppy effort, an attitude of indifference, increased absenteeism and tardiness, an increased number of grievances, sullen hostility, jealousy, etc., etc., etc.

Employee reaction to change depends, of course, on the individual. It also depends, in part, on the answers to such questions as: (1) What are the nature and magnitude of the change? (2) Why is it being made? (3) Who is backing it? (4) Who will administer it? (5) When will it take place? (6) Where in the organizational structure will the change be felt? (7) What has been the extent of personnel preparation? (8) Does the firm have a history of good personnel relations? (9) Does the firm have a reputation for innovation and change?

Reasons for resistance

It is not too difficult to compile a list of the motivating forces which may stimulate one or more individuals to seek business changes. Included in such a list are (1) dissatisfaction with the *status quo* together with a desire for greater knowledge and understanding; (2) the desire to create, to excel, and to be a leader in the use of new techniques and in the development of new products and services; and (3) the pursuit of economic benefits.

[8] George Berkwitt, "Middle Managers vs. the Computer," *Dun's Review and Modern Industry,* vol. 88, November, 1966, p. 42.

But changes sought by some may appear to others to be a *threat*—
a threat which prevents them from satisfying certain basic needs, or
one which decreases the level of their need satisfaction. That a proposed change does *not* actually affect an employee's need satisfaction
may be irrelevant from a resistance standpoint. What *is* relevant in
this situation is that if the employee *believes* that he is threatened
when he learns of the proposed change, he will no longer feel secure.
"Only when he recognizes that the change will not affect his need
satisfaction, or when he adapts himself to a change that in fact does
decrease or prevent the satisfaction of a need, will equilibrium return
and resistance disappear."[9]

What are these needs which motivate behavior? What needs do
people attempt to satisfy? Psychologists tell us that human needs may
be classified into a series of ranks or levels as follows:[10]

1. *Physiological needs.* These needs are at the lowest level and are the most
   primitive. Included in this category are the need for food, clothing, shelter,
   sleep. They are necessary for survival and thus receive first priority. When
   these needs are thwarted, they override in importance all others in motivating behavior; but when they are regularly satisfied, they cease to direct
   human behavior.

2. *Safety needs.* The needs for protection against danger, threat, or depriva-
   tion begin to dominate man's behavior when the physiological needs are
   satisfied. The change to a computer may appear to threaten the security of
   employees, and thus they may be motivated to resist.

3. *Social needs.* When physical needs are satisfied and security is not threatened, social needs, i.e., the need to belong to a group, to associate, to be
   accepted by others, become important motivators. Any change which
   threatens to break up or reorganize an existing department or group may
   motivate resistance for both social and safety reasons.

4. *Ego needs.* When the first three need levels are all reasonably satisfied,
   the ego needs become important motivators of behavior. There are two
   kinds of egoistic needs: (1) those that relate to the *self-esteem* of an individual, e.g., the needs for self-confidence, for achievement, for independ-
   ence and (2) those that relate to the *reputation* of an individual, e.g., the
   needs for status, for recognition, for respect. "Unlike the lower needs,
   these are rarely satisfied; man seeks indefinitely for more satisfaction of
   these needs once they have become important to him."[11]

[9] Heckmann and Huneryager, *op. cit.*, p. 421.

[10] See Douglas McGregor, *The Human Side of Enterprise* (New York: McGraw-Hill
Book Company, 1960), pp. 36–39.

[11] *Ibid.*, p. 38.

5. *Self-fulfillment needs.* The final level in the need hierarchy reflects the desire of an individual to realize his own potential, to continue to develop, and to be creative.[12]

Against the above background of needs which man seeks to satisfy, we may identify some of the reasons why people are motivated to resist the change to electronic data processing:

1. *The threat to safety need satisfaction.* The fear of loss of economic security is a basic reason for resistance to change. Computers have a reputation for replacing people; therefore, there is the understandable fear of loss of employment and/or of reduction in salary.

2. *The reduction in social need satisfaction.* The introduction of a computer often calls for a reorganization of departments and work groups. When change causes a breaking up of compatible human relationships and a realigning of personnel, it also causes a reduction in social need satisfaction. Resistance to such a proposed change may be anticipated; it diminishes to the extent that the individual forms new friendships, associates with, and is accepted by, the new group.

3. *The reduction in ego need satisfaction.* The satisfaction of egoistic needs is threatened or thwarted in a number of ways by the change to computer usage. The individual needs to be self-confident; but self-confidence may be shaken by the lack of knowledge about, and experience with, computers. The equipment is strange to him, and he may fear that he will be unable to acquire the new skills necessary to work with it. He may also believe that his lack of knowledge is a weakness which will be exposed if he attempts to learn more from knowledgeable people in the company. In short, the individual's *self-esteem* may suffer as a result of the change; therefore, the change is to be resisted. Egoistic needs relating to the *reputation* of the individual are also threatened by change. Fear of loss of status and/or prestige is an important reason for resistance by both managers and employees. For example, if the change promises to reduce the number of employees in, and the importance of, a department — and this often happens — then the department manager may oppose the change because his own status is threatened. He may also resist because to admit that the change is needed is to admit that he has tolerated inefficiency — an admission which can hardly be expected to enhance his reputation. An experienced employee who has the respect of his fellow workers because of his knowledge of old procedures may also suffer a loss of prestige. When the old procedures were used, workers came to the experienced employee for information and advice; when the new procedures are installed, however, the experienced employee is no longer looked to for information,

---

[12] We may now rephrase an earlier statement in this way: the attempt to satisfy ego and self-fulfillment needs by one individual through the sponsorship of innovation and change may appear to others to threaten the satisfaction of their safety, social, and ego needs.

because his knowledge of the new procedures may not be any greater than that of other workers.

Employees who resist

Nonsupervisory employees resist change for a number of reasons— because they fear that they will lose their jobs, because they fear that they will be transferred away from their friends and into a strange department, because they fear that they will be unable to acquire the new skills which will be required, and because they feel that they will be downgraded and will lose status and prestige. "Everyone acknowledges that employees resist change. That fact has been well documented. . . . In contrast, managers like to think of themselves as alert, forward-looking individuals who are always seeking ways to improve company operations."[13] Unfortunately, from the standpoint of computer installation success, this self-evaluation of managers is more a fiction than a fact. "The cold fact is that many of today's managers are decidely unreceptive to the idea of change, and they are the ones who create the greatest obstacles to a successful change in organizational structure and methods."[14]

Although a manager may suffer economic loss because of the change to computer processing, the more usual motivating force behind his resistance, as we saw above, is the threat of a reduction in ego need satisfaction. Many managers feel that their positions are being threatened (and indeed this may be the case). In a very real sense those who may be most affected by the change are being asked to help plan and implement it. But it is unrealistic to expect a manager to be enthusiastic about changes which threaten his own position. Proper personnel preparation must include managers as well as nonsupervisory employees. For as Professor Thomas L. Whisler of the University of Chicago writes, ". . .this resistance is characteristic of all men, or at least of that portion of mankind which includes both executives and professors."[15]

[13] Ben Miller, "The Manager: Roadblock to Change?," *Management Review*, vol. 50, April, 1961, p.4.

[14] *Ibid.*, p. 5.

[15] Thomas L. Whisler, "The Manager and the Computer," *The Journal of Accountancy*, vol. 119, January, 1965, p. 30. Whisler also notes (in a lighter vein) that college professors of business react to the business changes being made because of the computer in much the same way as managers. There are the "reluctant ones" who are afraid of obsolescence; there are the "impatient ones" who are eager to innovate and to sweep aside outdated approaches; and there are the "economists" who

Suggestions for reducing resistance

What steps can be taken to prepare personnel for the computer transition? Unfortunately, there is no simple formula which prevents resistance and insures a successful transition. But there are some guidelines and suggestions which have been developed as a result of practical experience and social research which may, when used with care, help to reduce the level of employee opposition. Included in these suggestions are the steps to:

1. *Keep employees informed.* Personnel at all levels should be kept informed, at regular intervals, of planned changes. Information relating to the effects of the change on employees and their jobs should be presented. Topics to be discussed should include loss of jobs, employee transfers, the extent of necessary retraining, the reasons for the change, the benefits of the change, how the change affects various departments, what is being done to alleviate employee hardship. When it is possible to do so, employees should be assured that the change does not interfere with the satisfaction of their personal needs. Basic company objectives should be reviewed; the motives behind these objectives should be identified; and the contribution which the change makes to goal achievement should be explained. It should be emphasized that the change is not due to a hasty or arbitrary personal decision on the part of some top executive.

2. *Seek employee participation.* Employees are more likely to support and accept changes which they have a hand in creating. In addition to yielding valuable information during the feasibility study, design sessions also help reduce later resistance to change by allowing managers to participate and have a say in the planning of the project. Psychologists tell us that participation has three beneficial effects. First, it helps the employee satisfy ego and self-fulfillment needs. Second, it gives the employee some degree of control over the change and thus contributes to a greater feeling of security. And finally, it removes the fear of the unknown. The participation of supervisors and informal group leaders may greatly reduce the level of resistance. But participation is not a gimmick to manipulate people. The employees who participate must be respected and treated with dignity because it should be recognized that their suggestions have merit.

3. *Use managerial evaluation.* Make the skill with which supervisors handle change one of the criteria for evaluating their managerial capability. Let the supervisors know that this criterion has been established.

4. *Consider the timing of the change.* Do not establish unrealistic conversion deadlines, and do not have several major changes taking place simultaneously. Give personnel time to get used to one major change before another is initiated.

stand above it all on the sidelines maintaining, with amusement, that the computer is merely another in a long line of blessings which began with the invention of the wheel.

SUMMARY

A number of technical preparation tasks must be accomplished before the conversion to the computer can be completed. The physical site for the equipment must be readied; programs must be written, documented, tested, and debugged; files must be changed so that they are in a form acceptable to the computer; and the actual changeover must be accomplished. Many months are required to perform these tasks.

However, executives and data processing specialists should not become so preoccupied with technical matters that they ignore the personnel and psychological aspects of the transition. Rather, personnel preparations should be carried out during and after the feasibility study so that employees accept the change with a minimum of resentment and opposition.

Resistance to the change to electronic data processing is the rule rather than the exception. This resistance may appear in many forms when employees perceive that the change threatens the satisfaction of certain personal needs. Resistance may come from all employee levels — from clerks to vice-presidents. But by following certain guidelines and suggestions with care, the changers may be able to reduce the level of opposition.

DISCUSSION QUESTIONS

1 What technical preparation matters must be considered before the arrival of the computer?

2 (a) What is meant by parallel running? (b) How does parallel running differ from pilot testing?

3 What assistance can computer vendors offer during the conversion period?

4 In what forms may resistance to change appear?

5 What are the needs which motivate human behavior?

6 Why do managers and employees resist change?

7 How may resistance to change be reduced?

SELECTED REFERENCES

James B. Bower and J. Bruce Sefert, "Human Factors in Systems Design," *Management Services*, November-December, 1964, pp. 39-50.

Richard G. Canning, "What to Expect from the Computer Manufacturer," *EDP Analyzer*, May, 1964.

Jamie Dennis, "Managing Change," *Personnel Administration*, September-October, 1965, pp. 6-11.

Bruce DeSpelder, "Designing the Participative Decision-making System," *Systems & Procedures Journal,* January-February, 1964, pp. 20-24.

Fred Gruenberger, "Vendor Relations," *Data Processing Digest,* July, 1966, pp. 1-7.

Walter A. Hill, "The Impact of EDP Systems on Office Employees: Some Empirical Conclusions," *Academy of Management Journal,* March, 1966, pp. 9-19.

Lloyd P. Smith,"Management Problems in a Changing Technological Environment," *Computers and Automation,* April, 1965, pp. 18-22.

Goodwin Watson and Edward M. Glaser, "What We Have Learned about Planning for Change," *Management Review,* November, 1965, pp. 34-46.

14. PREPARING FOR CHANGE: II

In the last chapter we saw that business managers could expect—and should make plans to reduce—employee resistance to the change to electronic data processing. The subject of personnel preparation is continued in this chapter. In the earlier pages we shall examine the staffing approaches used to *select* and *train* workers for *new jobs*; in the remaining pages we shall study the effects of electronic data processing on *existing occupations* and on the *number of workers employed*. The managerial function of planning is required both for staffing new positions and for alleviating hardships caused by the elimination of old jobs.

SELECTING WORKERS FOR NEW JOBS

It is extremely difficult to overemphasize the importance of selecting capable people and giving them the proper training to fill the new data processing jobs. After all, the quality of the information systems which are developed is directly dependent upon this staffing effort. In this section we shall look at the *selection* process by examining (1) the *new positions* which must be filled, (2) the *effects* which the computer is having *on skill levels*, (3) the *sources of job candidates*, and (4) the actual *selection procedures*. *Training* approaches are considered in the following section.

New positions created

You may remember that in Chapter 3 we classified data processing personnel according to the following occupational categories: (1) *data processing management*, (2) *systems analysis and design*, (3) *program preparation,* and (4) *computer operations.* Let us look again at each of these categories.

Data processing management It is particularly important that a competent data processing manager be appointed. This manager—like all managers—must perform the management functions of planning, organizing, staffing, and controlling. He must plan the activities of his department so that it provides a quality, timely, and economical product. Careful planning is required to schedule installation activities and to provide the basis for control of the installation project. To be able to plan effectively and then control the activities of his department, the manager should possess technical competence in addition to managerial ability. He should understand the company's business and its data processing procedures; he should be able to work with people; and he should possess the poise, stature, and maturity required to command the respect of other company executives.

The data processing manager must, of course, organize the human and physical resources of his department to achieve company objectives in a smooth and efficient manner. He must initially select and see to the training of competent employees; he must encourage these employees to keep up with the rapid new developments occurring in their specialties; he should develop quantity and quality job evaluation standards for control purposes; and he must attempt to retain good employees—a rather difficult task in these days when severe shortages exist in the more skilled categories.

Increasingly, people planning to seek a career in business computer management must first acquire a college degree. Courses in business administration, economics, data processing, and statistics are desirable. It was noted in Chapter 3 that there were an estimated 30,000 qualified managers in 1966—a figure which was 10,000 short of the need at that time.[1] It is further estimated that 85,000 managers will be needed in 1970. An approach sometimes used by businesses is to staff the manager's position with a good systems analyst. If the company has an analyst or other manager with the proper qualifications, it is fortunate; if it does not have such a person (and it is felt that no present manager should be trained to take the job), it is obvious from the above figures that it can expect to encounter spirited competition in its attempts to hire one from outside the organization. If one *is* hired from outside, he should be brought in far enough in advance to learn the business and to gain the respect of other managers before the conversion begins.

[1] These estimates and those which follow come from Dick H. Brandon, "Jobs and Careers in Data Processing," *Computers and Automation*, September, 1966, p. 25.

Systems analysis and design   There are frequently several grades of analysts, but the job basically consists of (1) gathering facts about, and analyzing the basic methods and procedures of, current business systems; (2) determining company information needs; and (3) modifying, redesigning, and integrating these existing procedures into new systems specifications as required to provide the needed information. In addition to making the most effective use of existing data processing equipment, the analyst may also (as in the case of the feasibility study) recommend justifiable equipment changes.

The systems analyst must be familiar with the specific firm—he must know its objectives, its products and services, its industry, and its special problems. Also, he must know the uses and limitations of computers as well as other types of data processing equipment. He must understand basic programming; he must be able to determine which jobs can be prepared for computer processing; he must have logical reasoning ability; he must have initiative and the ability to plan and organize his work, since he will frequently be working on his own without much direct supervision; and he must be able to communicate with, and secure the cooperation of, operating employees and supervisors.

Educational backgrounds vary, but a college degree or the equivalent is generally desired. Courses which have proven valuable to systems analysts are the same as those mentioned above for data processing managers. The good analyst is often a prime candidate for promotion to more responsible management positions both in and out of data processing because of his broad knowledge of the business. The estimated number of qualified systems analysts in 1966 was 60,000—a figure which fell 35,000 short of the need. The estimated number needed in 1970 is 190,000. (It is, of course, quite unlikely that the number of qualified analysts will more than triple in four years.)

Program preparation   To summarize briefly, the job of the programmer (as defined in this book) is to take the broad systems designs of the analyst and transform these specifications into workable coded machine instructions. As with analysts, there are different programmer categories. Also, the duties of programmers vary in different organizations. For example, in some companies a person with the title of "programmer" may perform *both* the systems analysis and programming functions.[2] In other firms, a programmer may carry the work from the

---

[2] The degree of separation of systems analysis and programming functions depends upon the size and complexity of the company and its data processing systems, the ability of data processing personnel, and the desire on the part of management to reduce communication problems and fix responsibility for each application on a single person.

broad systems specification stage through the program flow charting stage and then turn the task of writing the actual machine instructions over to a *coder.*

Opinions vary on the educational background required of business programmers. Such factors as the duties of the programmer, the degree of separation between the systems analysis and programming functions, the complexity of the data processing systems, and the industry in which the business operates should probably be considered by the company in establishing educational standards. As the programming job is defined here, a college degree is not necessarily a condition for employment in most organizations.

What is required, however, is that the programmer have (1) analytical reasoning ability, (2) the ability to remember and concentrate on small details, (3) the drive and motivation to complete programs without the need of direct supervision, (4) the patience and perseverance to search for small errors in the programs, (5) the accuracy to minimize the number of such errors, and (6) the creativeness to develop new problem-solving techniques.

In 1966, the estimated number of qualified programmers was set at 120,000 (about 50,000 short of the need!). It is further estimated that an *additional* 100,000 programmers will be needed by 1970.

Computer operations The duties of the *computer operator* (or console operator) include setting up the processor and related equipment, starting the program run, checking to ensure proper operation, and unloading the equipment at the end of the run. Some knowledge of programming is needed. A high school education is often acceptable, although additional educational levels may be specified.

Keypunch operators, a media *librarian* who maintains control over master tape and card files, and various other *clerks* and *operators of peripheral equipment* may be needed in the department. The staffing of these positions generally presents no problem. Manual dexterity, a sense of responsibility, and a high school education or the equivalent are the usual requirements.

Effects on average skill levels

What effect does the use of a computer have on the *average* skill levels of administrative employees? That is, does the use of a computer generally result in an average *upgrading* of (1) the content of those jobs which remain to be performed and of (2) the skills required to perform them?

Strangely enough, this is a matter of confusion and some controversy. A common assumption in the past has been that the jobs remaining after a firm begins to use a computer are more interesting and that greater skills are required to perform them. Although few would argue with the fact that most employees selected to be systems analysts and programmers have moved into positions requiring more skill than in their previous occupations, it is the *overall* effects on skill levels which are sometimes disputed. It is, of course, true that certain menial clerical tasks in one or more departments can be eliminated through the use of a computer. But this does not necessarily mean that the workers in the affected departments whose jobs are eliminated are the same ones who are upgraded to become programmers and systems analysts. The number of such vacancies is limited, and the employees who fill them should be typically chosen from the more able workers in a large number of departments. Thus, it may be that few, if any, employees in an affected organizational unit move into positions of analysts and programmers.

Many writers feel that computer usage does not have much (if any) upgrading effect on average skill levels. This is the conclusion which can be drawn from studies dealing with 19 large organizations in the San Francisco area,[3] 11 companies in the Minneapolis-St. Paul area,[4] 20 large firms in the East and Midwest,[5] 41 small businesses in Texas,[6] and two utilities.[7,8] In short, the bulk of actual research supports the following conclusion of Professors Mann and Williams:[9]

The least interesting and the most menial types of jobs had been eliminated, but so had a number of high-level non-supervisory jobs. . . . Nearly everyone, management and employees alike, had anticipated higher average job grades as a result of the change, but these higher job grades did not materialize.

[3]See Ida R. Hoos, *Automation in the Office* (Washington, D.C.: Public Affairs Press, 1961), p. 57.

[4]See Roger C. Vergin and Andrew J. Grimes, "Management Myths and EDP," *California Management Review*, vol. 7, Fall, 1964, p. 66.

[5]See *Adjustments to the Introduction of Office Automation* (U.S. Bureau of Labor Statistics Bulletin 1276), p. 5.

[6]See Donald H. Sanders, *Introducing Computers to Small Business* (Park Ridge, Ill.: Data Processing Management Association, 1966), pp. 143-144.

[7]See Walter A. Hill, "The Impact of EDP Systems on Office Employees: Some Empirical Conclusions," *Academy of Management Journal*, vol. 9, March, 1966, pp. 16-17.

[8]See F. C. Mann and L. K. Williams, "Observations on the Dynamics of a Change to Electronic Data Processing Equipment," *Administrative Sciences Quarterly*, vol. 5, September, 1960, pp. 246-247.

[9]*Ibid.*

Sources of job candidates

New jobs may be filled from the pool of present employees (the *internal* source of supply) or from candidates recruited from *external* sources. The data processing manager may sometimes be hired from an outside source to supervise an initial computer installation because it is assumed that there are no candidates with the necessary experience in the company. This is sometimes the case. But the big disadvantage of this approach is that the person hired has little knowledge of the firm or of the personnel with whom he must work. The preferable approach is to appoint someone in the company who has the managerial qualifications and give him the needed technical training. The alternative of hiring from outside is acceptable if enough time is available before the conversion to give the manager the proper company orientation.

In staffing other vacancies, too, most firms prefer to select suitable candidates internally and give them the necessary training. This approach is particularly valid in the case of systems analysts because of the requirement that analysts be familiar with company operations. Programmers may more likely be obtained from outside than analysts or other data processing employees. This may be especially true when the programming job is considered to be basically coding and includes little in the way of systems analysis. In staffing programming jobs requiring some degree of systems analysis (and as programming is defined here, this is the case), firms can either give computer training to people possessing a knowledge of the business or hire experienced programmers (or programmer trainees) and school them in company policies, problems, and operations. Businesses have usually found that *when suitable candidates are available*, the first approach is preferable. Harold Jarrett, Director of Educational Services for the National Cash Register Company, writes in this connection:[10]

The expert from outside who doesn't know the customer's business is likely to spend considerably more time in training than the non-technical person from within. When he finally gets to know the business, he may job-hop again, to a competitor; after all, he had no particular loyalty to begin with.

Firms have little difficulty in staffing other occupations such as computer operators and keypunch operators from internal sources.

There are several advantages associated with internal selection: (1) as we have seen, employees have a better understanding of the busi-

[10] Harold Jarrett, "Data Processing Careers Demand New Approaches," *Computers and Automation*, September, 1966, p. 16.

ness; (2) their work habits and personality traits are easier to appraise; and (3) having demonstrated some degree of company loyalty, they may be less inclined to leave the firm after they are trained. Also, internal selection can improve employee morale. In spite of the advantages of internal selection, however, it is quite possible that there are not enough qualified programmmer (or other) candidates available among employees. Hiring experienced programmers may help speed up the conversion process and reduce the time and expense involved in conducting a lengthy training program. Many organizations have found that programmers skilled in the use of the hardware ordered for the new system are a valuable complement to company trainees.

The particular circumstances faced by each company should, of course, determine its staffing plans. Such factors as the nature of the existing work force, the availability of needed skills in the labor market, company staffing policies, and possible union contract agreements must be considered.

Selection procedures

A prerequisite to sound staffing procedures is the preparation of job descriptions and job specifications for the new positions to be filled. A *job description* defines the duties which must be performed and the equipment which is used, indicates the degree of supervision which is given and received, and describes the working conditions associated with the position. A *job specification* identifies the qualifications which candidates for each job should possess. Job specifications include the levels of education, experience, and training considered necessary to perform each job adequately.[11] Also included is a statement outlining the necessary physical and communication skills needed as well as the personality traits desired. In summary, job descriptions deal with the work itself, while job specifications deal with the human qualifications needed by those who are to do the work.[12] Job descriptions and specifications are useful (1) for staffing purposes, since both the recruiter and the candidate know what is needed and expected; (2) for wage purposes in determining the relative worth of the new jobs; and (3) for manpower planning purposes (it is desirable to hire new

[11] Job specifications, of course, are based on managerial judgment. An error committed by some businesses in the past has been to require a college degree for many jobs which do not require this level of education.

[12] Brief job descriptions and specifications were outlined for the more important new jobs in preceding pages. It is not possible to set forth specific standards which apply in all cases.

employees with the potential to move up into more responsible positions).

Two general procedures have often been used by companies to assemble a list of possible candidates for the new jobs. One procedure is to review personnel records and supervisory recommendations (or application forms and references in the case of nonemployee candidates) to compile a selective list of people considered qualified. People on this screened list are then contacted to determine whether or not they might be interested. The main weakness of this approach is that qualified candidates are overlooked.

A second "reserve pool" procedure used to compile a list of candidates is to announce the openings to all employees and invite them to make applications if interested. Those applicants who appear to possess the necessary qualifications become the group from which initial and subsequent openings are filled. A newspaper advertisement can serve the same purpose in securing nonemployee applications. In addition to newspaper advertising, the company may use outside employment agencies, contacts made at professional association meetings, and the knowledge of vendor representatives to collect a list of experienced job candidates.

Once possible candidates have been identified, it is then necessary to balance and compare their qualifications with those listed in the job specifications. Sorting out the best applicants can be a difficult job. The screening process generally involves the use of such selection devices as *aptitude tests*, *personal interviews*, and careful examination of *records* indicating the candidate's educational background, experience, and work habits. A frequently used approach in the selection of analyst and programmer *trainees* is to give candidates an aptitude test [13] and then to follow up with interviews and careful record examinations on all who receive a satisfactory test score. In the selection of *experienced* programmers, personal interviews and personal or telephone contacts with parties familiar with the work of the applicant are of particular importance. Proficiency tests are sometimes used to check on the ability of a candidate to program a test problem.

A *programmer aptitude test*, as the name implies, is a form of general intelligence test which *attempts* to measure the ability of a person to acquire those skills needed to become a successful programmer. Although there is lack of agreement about the ability of these tests actually to measure what they claim to measure, when carefully used, they

[13] The IBM Programmer Aptitude Test is available to IBM customers and is by far the most widely used.

may give an indication of a person's ability to reason in arithmetic and abstract terms. Since this ability is an important characteristic of all the upper-level data processing jobs, the test may serve as a screening aid. But good test performance alone does not necessarily mean that the person will be a successful programmer. The tests do not measure motivation, and they may not begin to measure all the other qualities that may be required. In short, programmer aptitude tests may provide clues, but they should not be the only selection device employed. Tests are also used to aid in the selection of keypunch operators and operators of peripheral equipment. These tests measure manual dexterity, mechanical aptitude, clerical aptitude, etc., and generally yield satisfactory results.

Selection decisions follow the testing, interviewing, and background investigation phases. The chosen candidates must then receive the necessary training to prepare them for their new duties.

TRAINING WORKERS FOR NEW JOBS

Before looking at the methods used to train data processing personnel, it is appropriate to pause here just long enough to mention that *noncomputer personnel* should also receive some training prior to the arrival of the hardware. It is especially desirable that top executives, operating managers, and other key employees be exposed to basic computer concepts. By understanding the uses and limitations of the equipment, noncomputer personnel can see how their operating needs can be served. Such orientation may also serve to reduce resistance to the change. Equipment vendors offer training seminars for customer executives; similar training may be obtained from consultants, university workshops, and professional associations.

The most extensive training must be given to those selected to be the systems analysts and programmers. The first requirement of the systems analyst is that he have a thorough knowledge of the business and the industry. Many months (or years) of on-the-job experience is necessary to satisfy this requirement. The second requirement is that he understand the techniques of systems analysis and design. There is little uniformity in the methods used to train ("educate" is probably a better word here) analysts to meet this requirement. A good grounding in the "core" courses found in collegiate schools of business combined with further emphasis on accounting systems, communication skills, mathematics, and statistics are felt by many to be prerequisites to more specialized systems training. There are a number of universities which offer degree programs in computer science; courses in systems analysis are included in their curricula. Vendors teach machine-dependent skills to their customer trainees, but since systems analysis is independent of machines, they do not offer too much in the way of formal systems training.[14] (Their site representatives, of course, frequently provide on-the-job training in systems analysis techniques.) Consulting firms and organizations such as the American Management Association conduct systems analysis seminars on a limited basis. Correspondence courses in systems work are also offered by the Systems and Procedures Association and others.

A third requirement of the analyst is that he possess an understanding of computer hardware and software. Most of the formal training given to analysts during the computer preparation period is in this area; it is usual for this training to parallel or be identical with the formal training received by programmers.

The usual method employed to introduce analyst and programmer trainees to hardware and software concepts is first to enroll them in the vendor's programming courses. At no additional charge to the customer, these courses introduce the trainees to the hardware which has been ordered and to the programming languages which will be used. The emphasis is generally placed on coding. The courses vary in length from one to six weeks; they are usually offered at a vendor's training site. Following satisfactory completion of the vendor's course, the novice programmers—for at this stage they have only a rudimentary grasp of the subject of programming—receive additional on-the-job instruction from the vendor's site representative and from other experienced programmers who may be available.

Programmer training is a continuous, lengthy, and expensive process. To the surprise (and dismay) of many executives, it has been found that *at least* six months is generally required before programmers attain a minimum level of proficiency. Training costs per programmer may run into the thousands of dollars. In addition to vendor courses, consultants, professional organizations, colleges and universities, and vocational schools also teach programming skills. Companies with computer experience sometimes run their own training programs.

Equipment manufacturers and vocational schools offer brief courses to train operators of peripheral equipment. On-the-job training is often the only preparation required. Vendors also give formal training to computer operators. Because of their need to know some programming, computer operators are sometimes sent to the vendor's pro-

---

[14] Vendors, of course, train their own systems analysts. There is some indication that they plan to do more in this area for their customers.

gramming course. Qualified console operators are frequently promoted to programming positions.

PLANNING FOR DISPLACEMENT

Under the chapters entitled "Preparing for Change," we have looked at the technical preparations which must be made; we have seen that planning is needed to reduce personnel resistance to the change; and we have looked at the approaches which are commonly used to select and train workers for data processing jobs. But what about the workers whose jobs *disappear* when the computer arrives? In the final pages of this chapter let us briefly look at the impact which computers have on clerical employment.

Distinction between displacement and unemployment

There has been much discussion in books, magazines, and newspapers about whether or not computers cause wide-spread unemployment among white-collar workers. Printed sources could be cited to support the position that the computer (and technological change in general) provides increased job opportunities. But other printed sources could also be quoted which take an apparently opposite view. To some extent, the controversy is fed by a failure on the part of some writers to make a distinction between unemployment and displacement. Those who see the effects of computers on employment in an optimistic light are generally looking at the result of technological change on the *total employment* picture. In other words, they are looking at the effect on the *total number* of jobs in the labor market. Those who view the picture pessimistically are frequently looking at the short-run effects of *displacement* on *specific occupational categories*—i.e., they are looking at the reduction in the number of jobs in a specific segment of the labor market.

Unemployment and displacement are *not* the same. *Unemployment* is an *aggregate* term which refers to the total number of people involuntarily out of work. *Displacement* occurs when the jobs of individual workers are eliminated as a result of technological change. *If* these displaced workers cannot find similar jobs elsewhere and *if* they cannot find work in other occupations, then there is, indeed, an increase in the *unemployment* figures. But has the development of the computer caused a *larger* number of people to be unemployed than would otherwise have been the case? In other words, have computers reduced the total number of jobs available in the total labor market? Professor

Yale Brozen, University of Chicago economist, expresses the views of most authorities when he writes:[15]

> The reigning economic myth is that automation causes unemployment. It has only a slight element of truth — just enough to make the proposition plausible. Automation does cause displacement. A few become unemployed because of it. However, it does not create unemployment in the sense that a larger number are unemployed than would have been if no automation had occurred. . . . Many observers point to specific persons unemployed as a result of [automation]. What they fail to do is point to the unemployed who found jobs because of automation or to those who would have joined the jobless if new technology had not appeared.

It is beyond the scope of this book to go into the economic causes of unemployment. We may conclude this topic by mentioning that most economists are of the belief (1) that displacement must not be prevented and (2) that unemployment is best avoided by high levels of capital formation, unhampered mobility of capital and labor, and a continuing high level of technological progress. The alternative to technological progress is economic stagnation.

Although technological change is beneficial to the nation as a whole and in the long run, this does not mean that the short-run effects of displacement on particular individuals are not a matter of importance. A displaced worker may realize the long-run benefits; but he is likely to be in greater sympathy with the famous economist who noted that "in the long-run we are all dead." Or as business executive Don Mitchell has said: "It doesn't do much good to try to convince an individual worker that over a 25 years' span there is no such thing as technological unemployment. He doesn't care whether there is or not. All he is worried about is that he lost a job."[16] It is true that displacement must not be prevented; but leaders in business, government, and labor must make every effort to see that displacement does not lead to unemployment.

Business displacement experience

Displacement can affect large numbers of people. Several studies have shown that there have been substantial reductions in clerical jobs be-

---

[15] Yale Brozen, "Putting Economics and Automation in Perspective," *Automation*, vol. 11, April, 1964, p. 30.

[16] Quoted by Walter Buckingham, *Automation: Its Impact on Business and People* (New York: Harper & Row, Publishers, Incorporated, 1961), p. 120.

cause of the introduction of a computer. For example, the Bureau of Labor Statistics in a survey of 20 large organizations found that "employment in the affected units was about 25 percent lower."[17] However, *total* office employment in these organizations increased slightly during the study period. In a study of 32 companies, Ernest Dale found some substantial reductions in personnel. All except three of the 32 firms ". . .used fewer people for the same amount of work or found that the same number of people could do more work than before."[18] Dale reported reductions of 4,000 people in an insurance company and 1,000 people in an oil company.[19] And on the West Coast, Ida R. Hoos found that in one firm with 3,196 clerical employees ". . .286 jobs have already been dropped from the payroll, and it is estimated that 982, or about one-third of the workers, are being affected."[20] Although other examples could be given, the above serve to show that a number of jobs can be eliminated. This, of course, is not surprising; as you will remember, a reduction in clerical labor costs is often an objective sought by businesses.

But a number of other examples could be presented which would show little or no displacement. The extent to which displacement actually occurs, and the significance of the problem in particular cases, depends in large measure on the following factors:

1. *The rate of growth of the firm and economy.* If the company is growing rapidly and if demand for its output is increasing so that more work must be done to handle the expanding business, then there may be little or no effect on the number of clerical workers employed by the company. In many cases, as we saw in the Bureau of Labor Statistics study noted above, the total number of clerical workers may increase. The computer enables workers to be more productive; but the increase in consumer demand can prevent a displacement problem. Reassignment of surplus workers to different departments may, of course, be required. The impact on the worker who may be laid off is reduced if the economy is in a period of prosperity, because the worker has greater opportunity to find employment elsewhere. It is fortunate that most computer installations have occurred during relatively prosperous periods.

2. *The objectives sought.* Is the company acquiring the equipment for proc-

[17] *Adjustments to the Introduction of Office Automation* (U.S. Bureau of Labor Statistics Bulletin 1276), p. 31.

[18] Ernest Dale, *Management: Theory and Practice* (New York: McGraw-Hill Book Company, 1965), p. 678.

[19] *Ibid.*

[20] Ida R. Hoos, "When the Computer Takes over the Office," *Harvard Business Review*, vol. 38, July–August, 1960, p. 103.

essing purposes which could not otherwise be considered? Is the objective to do more work with existing workers? Or is it to save money by eliminating existing jobs? Objectives obviously play a part in determining the degree of displacement.

3. *The type of occupations threatened.* Up to the present time, most of the jobs which have been eliminated are (1) those which involve posting, filing, sorting, checking, and maintaining records; and (2) those which involve the operation of calculating, bookkeeping, and other computing and statistical office machines. These are the types of jobs which are typically held by young women — workers who can be transferred to other departments without too much difficulty. Also, turnover among these workers is usually high because of attrition, e.g., quitting to get married, and pregnancy. In the past, few clerical workers have been laid off in larger businesses when job reductions occur.[21] How is this possible? The workers who quit during the many months between the time the computer order is placed and the time the conversion is completed are *simply not replaced*. Thus, as far as the company is concerned, the displacement problem is solved.

However, from a broader viewpoint it must be recognized that the people who are most affected by technological unemployment are not the ones presently employed. Rather, they are the employables who have a minimum amount of training and who are now entering the labor force. There has been a pronounced leveling off in the rate of growth of clerical employment in the past several years. Future opportunities in the job categories mentioned above are not likely to be good. As Walter Buckingham writes: "For the most part overall economic growth will probably have to provide the economic environment in which new entrants to the work force and other victims of 'silent firing'. . . will be able to find opportunities for employment."[22]

Before we leave the subject of threatened occupations, it is important to emphasize that when the affected jobs are *not* of the clerical type described above, the displacement problem is likely to be much more severe. Attrition and turnover, may not, in these situations, be of much help. The affected workers may be older employees or lower-level managers whose skills are no longer needed. They are not likely to quit, but they may not be easy to retrain for jobs at an appropriate level. Such problems can be perplexing; and in the future, as computer applications become more sophisticated and move into more operating areas, they can be expected to occur with increasing frequency.

[21] Small companies have not been as successful in preventing layoffs, possibly because there may not have been other departments to which surplus workers could be reassigned. In a study, conducted by the author, of small firms in Texas, it was found that of 43 companies which reduced the number of jobs about half were forced to separate employees. See Donald H. Sanders, *op. cit.*, p. 163.

[22] Walter S. Buckingham, "The Human Side of Automation," *Business Horizons*, vol. 3, Spring, 1960, p. 28.

4. *The planning and preparation to reduce hardship.* Business executives should give careful and serious thought to the displacement problems which they are likely to encounter. It should be remembered that fear of displacement is one of the basic causes of resistance to change. If significant displacement is not expected, employees should be given this information. If jobs are to be eliminated, plans should be made to protect present employees as much as possible. In departments where reductions are expected, employees can be given the first chance to fill vacancies occurring elsewhere in the organization (including the new data processing jobs to be filled and including jobs at other geographic locations). Vacancies created by normal attrition in the affected areas can be left unfilled, they can be filled by new employees who have the ability to adjust quickly to different positions, or they can be filled with temporary outside help. Special training courses can be established to train soon-to-be-surplus workers in skills needed in other departments.

One final point should be mentioned. The business executive who is able to avoid layoffs is to be commended. But this is no reason for him to become complacent about personnel preparation matters. Workers whose jobs are eliminated, and who are to be reassigned to other departments, are likely to face adjustment problems and may be expected to resist the change. Planning is required to make this adjustment as painless as possible.

SUMMARY

Preparing personnel for the change to electronic data processing has been the general subject of this chapter. Workers must be selected and trained for new positions; plans must be made to reduce hardships brought about by the elimination of old jobs.

New jobs may be filled from the pool of present employees or from candidates recruited from external sources. Most businesses have found that it is preferable to select suitable candidates internally and give them the necessary training to qualify them for the new positions. However, when suitable candidates are not available internally, the company must resort to external sources. This situation occurs frequently in the case of programmers. Many companies have found that programmers skilled in the use of the hardware ordered for the new system are a valuable complement to company trainees. Workers are usually selected on the basis of aptitude test scores, personal interviews, and background records.

The most extensive training during the preparation period must be given to analysts and programmers. It is necessary that the analyst first have a thorough knowledge of the business and that he then understand the techniques of systems analysis and design. The first requirement calls for months (or years) of on-the-job experience; the second requirement is currently being met by a variety of methods including university preparation, special courses, and on-the-job training. Both analysts and programmers must understand computer hardware and software concepts. Formal training in the vendor's programming courses, on-the-job training, etc., provide the necessary skills. Training given for other positions may consist of short training classes combined with on-the-job training or just on-the-job training.

The company executives should plan at an early date and at frequent intervals to reduce the personnel hardships which can occur when jobs are eliminated. For the nation as a whole, and in the long run, technological change is desirable; but the effects of displacement on particular individuals as a result of the installation of computers can be serious. Although displacement must not be prevented, business, government, and labor leaders must make every effort to see that displacement does not cause an individual to be involuntarily thrown out of work.

DISCUSSION QUESTIONS

1 What are the duties and responsibilities of the new positions created by the acquisition of a computer?

2 From what sources may candidates for new jobs be obtained?

3 What are the advantages and limitations of staffing new data processing jobs with present employees?

4 Define the following terms:
(a) job description
(b) job specification
(c) aptitude tests

5 What procedures may be used to fill data processing positions?

6 What is the distinction between displacement and unemployment?

7 What factors affect the significance of the displacement problem when computers are introduced into businesses?

SELECTED REFERENCES

George J. Brabb, "Education for Systems Analysis: Part Two," *Systems & Procedures Journal*, March-April, 1966, pp. 38-43.

Frank Greenwood and Erwin M. Danziger, *Computer Systems Analysts* (New York: American Management Association, no. 90, 1967).

Frank Greenwood, "Education for Systems Analysis: Part One," *Systems & Procedures Journal*, January-February, 1966, pp. 13-15.

W. H. Griffin, "Staffing an EDP Installation," *Personnel*, May-June, 1965, pp. 60-66.

Roger C. Vergin, "Staffing of Computer Departments," *Personnel Administration*, July-August, 1965, pp. 6-12.

15. ORGANIZATION AND THE COMPUTER

Chapters 12 to 14 have emphasized the managerial function of *planning*. The *staffing* function has also been considered. In this chapter attention is turned to the *organizing* function and to the effects of computer usage on business organizations and on the managers who hold positions in these organizations. (In the following chapter we shall look at the *control* function.)

You will remember that the broad objective of this part of the book is to take note of the impact of computers on business managers and on the environment in which managers work. In Chapters 12 to 14, some of the managerial problems associated with the introduction of computers were indicated; some of the possible effects on managers were also mentioned. For example, we have seen (1) that there are numerous possible pitfalls in the acquisition process, (2) that managers are quite likely to resist the change because their departments may be adversely affected and/or their prestige may suffer, (3) that noncomputer managers should be trained in basic computer concepts to reduce their fear of the unknown and to show them how their operating needs can be served, and (4) that some managers are not immune from the threat of job displacement.

In this chapter we come to grips with the question of the present and potential consequences of computers on the environment in which managers work, i.e., with the impact of computers on the organizational structure of the business. Furthermore, since managers work in such an environment, it is clear that anything which affects the organizational structure is also of vital interest to them. Following the presentation of some *preliminary concepts*, the subjects to be introduced in this chapter include (1) *the organization of data processing activities* and (2) *the computer's impact on organization in the future*.

PRELIMINARY CONCEPTS

You will recall that the organizing function involves the grouping of work teams into logical and efficient units for the purpose of accomplishing goals and plans. As Ernest Dale points out, the organizing function includes:[1]

> ... first, dividing the work so that most jobs can be done by people with specialized skills and/or knowledge (and the specialization may be very narrow in the lower jobs) and, second, providing means of coordinating the jobs done by different people. In other words, the aim of organization is to enable a group of people, nearly all of whom are specializing in one particular task or field, to function as a unit, each doing his part without hampering the efforts of others.

If work units *are* to function efficiently, each unit member must know what his job includes and what position he occupies in the formal organizational structure. For this reason, it is customary for all but the smallest of firms to prepare, in graphical form, the formal organizational *or authority structure* of the business. An *organization chart* such as the one shown in Figure 15-1 indicates, by position titles, the place in the organization of each job, the lines of authority and reporting relationships among positions, and the assigned role of the work unit in the total structure. For example, in the hypothetical manufacturing company charted in Figure 15-1, we see that three vice-presidents report to the president. We also see that each of these vice-presidents is in a position of *authority* over several subordinates— i.e., each vice-president has the right to give orders to subordinates and the power to see that those orders are carried out to achieve company objectives. Lines of authority are extended downward in the marketing area to show some primary reporting relationships. A similar expansion may be made of other organizational elements. In addition to giving company personnel a better understanding of the formal organizational picture, charts can sometimes point out, and lead to the correction of, awkward authority relationships. You will note in our example that work units are grouped by *type of work* (finance, marketing, and production), by *geographic area* (regional and district sales offices), and by *product line* (products A, B, and C). But, of course, one logical and efficient means of organizing for one business may not be desirable for another.

---

[1] Ernest Dale, *Management: Theory and Practice* (New York: McGraw-Hill Book Company, 1965), pp. 225–226.

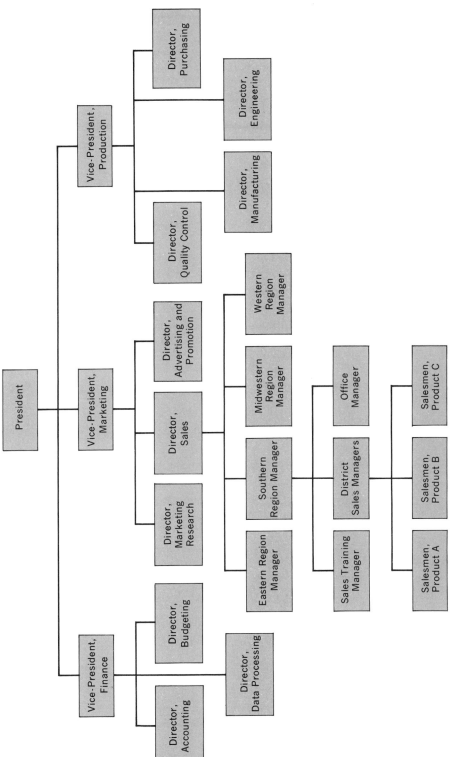

Figure 15-1. Organization Chart, Manufacturing Firm

An organizational structure does not remain static once it has been created. It must be flexible; it must be adapted to constantly changing conditions. For example, organizational changes may be required because of existing inadequacies, because of company growth, because of changes in markets and products, because of key personnel changes, and because of technological changes. When a computer is introduced into a business, it may take over a large part of the work of several organizational units. When there is no longer a valid reason for some units to continue to exist, changes should be made in the organization to avoid duplication and wasted effort.

It should be remembered, however, that when organizational changes are made or appear likely because of computer usage, the result may often be employee and managerial resistance to the change. Furthermore, changes in one organizational element may produce stress in other units, which can serve to work against improved efficiency. In short, since organizational changes affect social needs, they must be carefully planned if the full potential of the new system is to be realized.

Centralization or decentralization

If we are to avoid semantic difficulties in the pages which follow, it is necessary that we explain the concepts of centralization and decentralization at this point. *Centralization of authority* refers to a concentration of the important decision-making powers in the hands of a relatively small number of top executives. *Decentralization of authority*, on the other hand, refers to the extent to which significant decisions are made at *lower levels* in the organization structure. While in very small businesses *all* decision-making power is likely to be centralized in the hands of the owner-manager, in larger organizations the question of centralization or decentralization *is a matter of degree*—i.e., it is a question of *how much* authority is held at different managerial levels. The extent to which authority is delegated to lower levels depends, in part, on such factors as: (1) the managerial philosophy of top executives; (2) the growth, size, and complexity of the business; (3) the availability of qualified subordinates; and (4) the availability of adequate operating controls. Since change may occur in all the above factors, it is apparent that the degree of centralization of authority is also subject to constant revision.

In addition to centralization or decentralization of authority, it is also possible to refer to the centralization or decentralization of (1) company operations in a *geographic* sense and (2) *activities to be per-*

formed. For example, a manufacturing firm may centralize its production operations in a single geographic location to be near customers, workers, and raw material suppliers. And the data processing activities of a geographically decentralized company may be concentrated at a single point to make use of a large-scale computer system. It is important to remember that *an organization may be centralized in one sense of the term and not in others*. For example, data processing *activities* may be centralized; but this approach may have little or no effect on the degree of *authority* or *geographic* centralization. This distinction is occasionally overlooked. As Harold Koontz has pointed out, there has been ". . .confusion between centralization of activities—things to be done—and centralization of authorities—the power to make decisions. Centralization or decentralization of activities does not necessarily imply centralization or decentralization of authority."[2]

ORGANIZATION OF DATA PROCESSING ACTIVITIES

Before the introduction of computers, data processing activities tended to be decentralized in all but the smaller organizations. The functional areas of businesses, e.g., the manufacturing, marketing, and finance divisions, frequently maintained their own data processing operations when manual procedures were used. In many cases this approach was not significantly changed when electromechanical equipment was acquired.

However, a number of technological and systems developments of the last decade have made it possible to centralize data processing activities *if* company needs are best served by such action. Such developments include (1) rapid increases in processing speed and capacity; (2) the creation and improvement of random access mass storage devices; (3) the simultaneous processing of several tasks through the multiprogramming of large computers; (4) the direct connection of remote input/output stations to distant processors by means of high-speed data communication facilities; and (5) the designing of broader systems which cut horizontally across organizational lines to achieve greater integration of data processing activities. As a result of such developments, companies must now decide to what extent (if any) they wish to centralize their data processing operations. In other words, should smaller computers be acquired and operated by individual organizational units? Or should these units be required to furnish input

[2] Harold Koontz, "Top Management Takes a Second Look at Electronic Data Processing," *Business Horizons*, vol. 2, Spring, 1959, p. 83.

to one or more computer centers which are established for the purpose of processing data originating at many points?

The considerations *in favor* of the *centralized* approach are as follows:

1. *It permits economies of scale.* If we assume that satisfactory work loads are attained, operating costs should be reduced through the use of faster and more powerful large-scale equipment. Cost savings may be in the form of lower unit cost for each item processed, lower total equipment charges, and lower personnel costs, which are reduced by concentrating fewer skilled programmers at one site and using them more efficiently.

2. *It permits other economies.* Duplications in record storage, file updating, and program preparation may be eliminated; less-expensive standardized forms may be used; and site preparation costs may be reduced since only one site is involved.

3. *It facilitates necessary systems integration.* Systems integration is usually easier to accomplish when centralized processing is being used. For example, achieving companywide agreement on the matter of customer code numbers may be a first step in integrating the procedures required to process customer orders. Obtaining such agreement is easier if the approval of a number of operating managers (who may be reluctant to change their own coding methods) is not required. Also, having a corporate data bank available at one location makes it possible for top executives to obtain information which might not otherwise be available in time to be of use.

4. *It has certain personnel advantages.* In addition to possibly reducing the total number of data processing personnel, the centralization of data processing activities may "... enable the company to attract better, more professional personnel. This is because a sizable operation means increased responsibility for operating personnel and brings together enough volume of a particular type of work to justify the hiring of a man who is specially skilled in that area."[3] In addition, the advantages of having a professional group to help train new personnel should not be overlooked.

5. *It permits better utilization of processing capability.* With a centralized corporate computer center *companywide* priorities can be assigned to processing tasks. Those tasks which are of greatest importance are, of course, completed first. With a decentralized approach, however, low-priority work may be processed in one division with excess capacity, while in another division a higher priority application may be left unfinished because of inadequate processing capability.

[3] Victor Z. Brink, "Who Gets the Computer?," *Columbia Journal of World Business,* vol. 1, Fall, 1966, p. 72.

In view of these benefits, it might seem that a decision to follow a centralized approach would be automatic. Yet there are a number of limiting factors in centralization which may cause a company to follow a more decentralized path. Included among the *advantages of decentralization* of data processing activities are:

1. *Greater interest and motivation at division levels.* When division managers control their own computers, they are more likely to be interested in using the equipment in ways which best meet their particular operating needs. Such increased motivation, combined with greater knowledge of division conditions, may produce an information output of greater quality and value even though the processing costs may be higher. Division managers may also be more interested in maintaining the accuracy of input data when they have control over their own equipment.

2. *Better response to user needs.* With decentralization, programs can be specially prepared to meet the exact needs of the division. (The standardized information systems typically required for centralized processing may not be equally suitable for all divisions.) In addition, although a smaller machine will probably be slower than the centralized equipment, it should be remembered that central machine time must be allocated to a number of users. Information considered important to one division may be delayed because higher priority is given to other processing tasks. It is thus quite possible that the full attention to a job given by a smaller machine may lead to faster information processing at the division level. (It is also possible that some small-volume division applications may represent an inefficient use of large-scale equipment.)

3. *Reduced breakdown risks.* When there is a breakdown in the centralized equipment or in the communications links, the entire information processing system is likely to be inoperative. A similar breakdown in one division, however, does not affect other decentralized operations.

Trend toward hardware centralization

There is no general answer to the question of whether or not a company *should* centralize or decentralize its processing activities. A number of considerations are involved, and each firm must develop its own solution in a manner designed to serve its own unique requirements. In the final analysis, the decision involves a trade-off between motivational values and responsiveness to division needs, on the one hand, and operating costs, on the other. Centralization of hardware reduces operating costs, but often at the expense of being less responsive to user needs. The reverse is true in the case of decentralization.

Although it is impossible to generalize about the desirability of either centralization or decentralization for a particular company, it *is* possible to point out that the trend at the present time is toward the creation of central computer centers in the interest of reduced operating costs. Small firms have little choice in this matter, since their organizational units do not have sufficient volume to justify separate machines. Because of the complexities associated with such a task, very large organizations have not created single, huge, centralized installations. Rather, they often achieve a greater degree of centralization by establishing a number of regional data centers.

Data communications facilities and remote input/output stations, it is hoped, will give operating managers a sense of control over their information needs and will encourage them to take a proprietary interest in the data processing activities. Another approach to achieve these same results is to centralize the hardware and processing activities while maintaining systems analysis operations on a more decentralized basis. This is a particularly logical arrangement: (1) because a decentralized systems group should have a better understanding of the information needs of the division and (2) because operating managers can hardly be held accountable for the adequacy of their information systems if the design of those systems is beyond their control.

Organizational location of computer department

Just as each firm must develop its own solution to the question of whether or not to centralize its data processing, so, too, must it determine the proper organizational location for its data processing department. What is "proper" in any given case depends, in part, on the applications to be processed, on the degree of systems integration achieved and sought, and on the importance which is attached to the data processing function by top executives. Figure 15-2 shows a simplified version of the organization chart presented in Figure 15-1. Three alternate locations for the computer department are given. Let us look at each of these arrangements.

Location number one The computer department is found to be a part of the finance function in a majority of businesses. The reasons for the popularity of this location are not hard to understand. In many companies the accounting department is the first to see that a computer can easily and profitably be used to process large-volume accounting applications such as payroll and customer billing. The computer is regarded as a fast and accurate accounting machine which can, in many cases, be substituted for accounting department bookkeeping machines

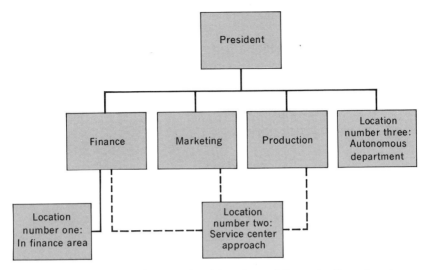

Figure 15-2. Alternative Organizational Locations of Computer Department

and punched card equipment. Since the bulk of the early business applications was of a financial nature, the computer was most often placed under the control of the financial managers. Of course, in those businesses engaged in large-scale engineering and scientific projects, it is often the research and engineering departments which are the first to see the advantages of acquiring a computer. Thus, the computer department is located in that area. To a large extent, then, the organizational location of the machine depends on its original sponsor.

As long as the processing requirements of the financial area are sufficiently large to keep the computer busy, and as long as no other areas of the business have the need or desire to use the computer, then location number one is satisfactory. However, it is unlikely that these conditions will be maintained in most businesses—i.e., it is unlikely that one area can utilize all the computing capacity, and it is also unlikely that the other nonfinancial departments of the business do not have a need for information which the computer can deliver. Therefore, the computer department is usually required to process nonfinancial applications.[4]

---

[4] In a few large companies, of course, *each* functional area may support one or more computers on a decentralized basis (although this tends to defeat systems integration objectives and is more expensive). But when a division of a large corporation is a relatively *self-contained* operating unit, e.g., when the division manager is responsible for finance, marketing, and production activities, and when a single computer is to serve the entire division, then the organizational situation may be comparable with that of the majority of computer-using firms.

Although the finance-area location is most common today, there are a number of disadvantages associated with this organizational position. A most important fault is that there is often a lack of objectivity in the setting of job priorities. Regardless of the good intentions of the computer department personnel, it is only natural that they tend to concentrate on the accounting applications at the expense of important nonfinancial tasks. The data processing manager may be excused if he gives more attention to the wishes of the top financial executive than he does to the heads of marketing or production. (After all, who controls the computer manager's promotion prospects and salary increases?)

Another fault of this location is that the computer department may continue to be staffed and managed by people whose viewpoint is limited primarily to the accounting area. In other words, a corporatewide orientation may be lacking. As John Diebold, a leading computer consultant, writes:[5]

Assistant controllers equipped with the best computers in the world are not going to make the vision of applied information technology a reality very often. They are buried too deep in one leg of the business. They lack status. They lack authority. . . . But most important of all, they lack the entrepreneur's view of the enterprise as a whole.

In addition to the fault of a limited viewpoint, Diebold points out another obstacle which is likely to prevent the company from realizing the computer's true potential. This obstacle is that organizational status and authority are lacking when an "assistant controller" manages the computer department. A firm can expect little in the way of needed systems integration when the data processing manager has little or no power to bring about interdepartmental changes and compromises.

Location number two   One approach which can avoid the lack of objectivity in setting job priorities is to establish a company service center to handle the various processing tasks. Each department is charged their proportionate share of the center costs. While the center manager may report to a neutral top-level executive or to an executive committee made up of users, the service center basically occupies a position which is on the periphery of, or outside, the main organizational structure. Occasionally such a service center is operated as an "open shop"—i.e., the using departments prepare and run their own applications with the assistance of center personnel.

[5] John Diebold, "ADP: The Still-Sleeping Giant," *Harvard Business Review*, vol. 42, September–October, 1964, p. 63.

The main limitation of this type of organizational arrangement as far as business data processing is concerned is that the center manager generally does not have any company status or authority outside his own department. Thus, little attempt is made to initiate systems improvements or to develop integrated systems; a fragmented, every-department-for-itself approach may be expected.

Location number three   It is the opinion of most information processing authorities that an independent computer department should be established as shown in location number three of Figure 15-2 if the full potential of the computer is to be realized. Such factors as the size of the firm, the extent of computer usage, the managerial personalities involved, and the existing spirit of cooperation make it impossible to state that location number three is best for all firms. But there are compelling reasons for thinking that this is the preferred location in the case of medium-sized and larger concerns which seek to develop desirable systems integration. Among the reasons which can be given in support of this conclusion are that:

1. *The scope of information processing is corporatewide.* Independent status is needed to give impartial service to all using organizational units. An interdepartmental viewpoint is required of data processing personnel.

2. *A stronger voice is needed.* The manager in charge of the information processing function should determine the suitability of new and existing applications, should set processing priorities, should study interdepartmental systems and procedures, and should make the necessary changes to achieve desirable integration. To perform these duties, the information processing manager must have the cooperation of executives at the highest operating levels. It is unlikely that such cooperation is forthcoming, in the event of significant change, unless the information manager occupies a position which is no lower in the organization than the highest using department. Furthermore, in the event of a dispute, the information manager should report to an executive who is at a higher organizational level than any of the parties of the dispute. Since the parties who resist significant systems integration changes may be vice-presidents, the information manager should generally report to the president (or his equivalent) or to an executive vice-president. One computer department head, with the title of Administrative Services Manager, told the author that when several changes were introduced in his company, there was a great amount of corporate politics involved as well as resistance from several vice-presidents. Fortunately, the Administrative Services Manager reported directly to the President, and the President backed the changes.

3. *There is greater willingness to innovate.* Personnel of an independent department may be more objective in evaluating the merit of user applications than would be possible if they were a part of the user organization. They can be encouraged to recommend improvement and change whenever

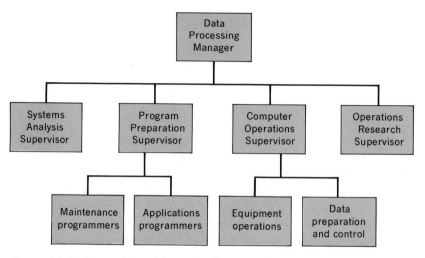

Figure 15-3. Composition of Computer Department

and wherever the opportunity arises; and they can be encouraged to introduce, for the greatest total benefit, fresh ideas which may upset certain conventional approaches.

Composition of computer department

The composition of the computer department depends on the size of the company, on the scope and number of data processing activities which must be performed, and on the extent to which these activities are carried out by the computer department. Since the work of the department deals with systems analysis and design, program preparation, and computer operations, it is usual to find these functional components in the departmental organization structure. Figure 15-3 presents one possible way of arranging these functions. Although a variety of *other arrangements might logically be made*—e.g., having one supervisor below the data processing manager in charge of both systems analysis and program preparation—Figure 15-3 serves as a framework from which combinations or further subdivisions of functions may be made as needed.

Systems analysis section   Because of the close cooperation which must exist between programmers and systems analysts,[6] it is generally desirable

---

[6] You will remember from the preceding chapter that companies differ on the point at which systems analysis ends and programming begins.

that both groups report to the same executive to minimize friction. The duties of systems analysts have been explained in Chapter 14, so we need not repeat them here. The systems analysis section acts as the vital interface between outside operating departments and the other sections in the computer organization. As noted earlier, it may be also desirable to maintain systems groups in the operating divisions of large firms with centralized computer centers because of the better understanding of division information needs which they can acquire and because of the desirability of having operating managers participate in the establishment of systems specifications.

Program preparation section   In smaller organizations, a single supervisor can be in charge of both systems analysis and program preparation. Or, perhaps, the data processing manager may also serve as the program preparation supervisor. In medium-sized and larger organizations, on the other hand, a separate supervisor is usually found. The programming function is sometimes subdivided into (1) the preparation of new applications and (2) the maintenance of existing programs. Authority may also be given to one or more individuals to make sure that proper documentation levels are maintained.

Computer operations section   The function of the computer operations section is to prepare the input data and produce the output information on a continuing production basis. Multiple shifts may be required. The control of equipment time and the scheduling of processing activities are an important part of the duties of the computer operations supervisor. Proper controls must also be established to make sure that input data are accurate.[7] Computer operators, operators of peripheral equipment, keypunch operators, and media librarians are found in this section. The total number of employees may be quite large, and the turnover is likely to be high among keypunch operators; thus, personnel management considerations may occupy a significant part of the operations supervisor's time.

Operations research section   This section may logically be assigned to some other corporate planning element concerned with the overall study of company operations. But since the use of computers is required to support many of the mathematical models which OR personnel create, there may be good reasons for assigning them to the computer department for coordination purposes. Certainly, the work of the OR and

[7]The subject of control will be considered in greater detail in Chap. 16.

systems analysis groups should be closely coordinated. As H. Warren White points out:[8]

Experience indicates that the design of mathematical models, for example, must be accomplished through close liaison with the systems specialist, as models can serve a useful purpose only if the systems provide the necessary data to fit in the model.

THE COMPUTER'S IMPACT ON ORGANIZATION IN THE FUTURE

It was pointed out earlier in the chapter that a company may centralize its data processing activities without at the same time changing the existing degree of centralization or decentralization of authority. Centralized processing is compatible with a decentralized authority structure. For example, a department manager with the authority to make a decision may not care whether the information to support that decision is processed in the next room or in the next state so long as it is timely, accurate, and complete. The definite trend in businesses today is toward the centralization of data processing *activities*. But a broader issue, and one which should be of particular interest to those management students whose careers lie before them, is what effect computer usage will have on the centralization or decentralization of managerial *authority*. It is this issue which will receive our attention for the remainder of the chapter.

Prior to the introduction of computers in business, the general trend was in the direction of *greater decentralization* of authority. To some managers this was a matter of necessity rather than of choice. Top-level executives often found themselves in a position where they could (1) wait for the necessary supporting facts to arrive from lower levels before making a decision (in which case corporate reaction time suffered and many opportunities were lost); (2) place their trust in experience, intuition, and their horoscope and make the decision without proper supporting information; or (3) delegate the authority to make the decision to a lower-level manager who was closer to the situation calling for the decision and who could thus be expected to react in a prompt and more informed manner. Given these alternatives, it is understandable that as businesses grew in complexity, the third path was frequently chosen.

With the introduction of fast-response computer systems, however, information may be processed and communicated to top executives at

[8]H. Warren White, "Electronic Data Processing: A 10-Year Perspective," *NAA Bulletin*, vol. 45, April, 1964, p. 13.

electronic speeds; reaction time may be sharply reduced; and thus the *need* for decentralization of authority may be lessened. But although the computer may make it possible for a company to reconcentrate, at the upper echelons, authority and control previously held at lower levels, there is no reason why the information output cannot be disseminated to lower-level managers to provide them with better support for decision-making purposes. Up to the present time, companies have demonstrated that computer usage can support either a centralized or a decentralized decision-making philosophy. Professor Glenn Gilman of Georgia Tech expresses this point succinctly when he writes:[9]

The computer can serve equally well to support a move toward greater decentralization as toward greater centralization. If change in either direction develops, it will be the result of managerial choice, as it always has been. The computer's role in this respect is neutral — except as it offers the possibility to do what ought to be done in any case.

Computer usage has thus far supported both a centralized and a decentralized organizational philosophy. But what will be the future effects on organizational structure as more sophisticated management information systems are developed? In making their "managerial choice," will it seem clear to top executives that one approach has definite advantages over the other? In other words, will the organizational preferences and philosophies which are valid and suitable today be equally valid and suitable tomorrow? Will firms with a decentralized organizational philosophy be prompted to switch to the greater-centralization-of-authority approach because of changing conditions? Will the reverse be true?

There cannot, of course, be any final answers to such questions at this time. Still, it is possible and desirable that we have an understanding of the conflicting viewpoints, speculations, and predictions which surround these questions. It is no understatement to say that the future career of every business student will be affected in some way by the ultimate answers.

Centralization or decentralization of authority?

There are three schools of thought on the question of the effect which computer usage will have on the centralization or decentralization of managerial authority. The first school believes that the computer *need*

[9]Glenn Gilman, "The Computer Revisited," *Business Horizons*, vol. 9, Winter, 1966, p. 89.

have little effect on the organizational structure; the second school believes that *greater decentralization* of authority may be encouraged; and the third group takes the position that *recentralization* of authority is inevitable. Let us examine each of these positions.

No-necessary-change school After looking at the effects of computer usage up to the present time and after observing that some firms have moved in the direction of authority centralization while others have not changed or have moved in the opposite direction, the proponents of this school conclude that the computer is essentially neutral with respect to the organizational structure.[10] It is their position that the computer can act as a catalyst to help a firm move in whatever direction it feels it must go. The factors which influence the direction include market changes, competitive changes, organizational flexibility, and managerial philosophy.

In the short run, and as long as the computer is used primarily for the purpose of processing more-or-less routine applications, the available evidence seems to indicate that the viewpoints of this school will remain correct. However, proponents of other views are assuming that more sophisticated uses of computers will be developed. These new systems, it is felt, will cause significant changes in competitive positions, in organizational environment, and in the philosophy of top executives; such changes, so the argument goes, will persuade top executives that it *is necessary* to move in a specific direction; and such changes, it is believed, will produce pronounced authority trends which do not now exist.

Decentralization school Some writers believe that the future trend may be toward decentralization of authority. It was mentioned earlier that the availability of adequate controls is a factor in determining the extent of authority delegation. Managers are more likely to delegate decision-making powers to subordinates when they can be reasonably sure that the delegated authority is properly handled. The computer makes it possible for systems to be designed which can quickly indicate to top executives when actual performance deviates from what was planned. Thus, by providing better control, the computer may make it possible to eliminate one important objection to decentralization. Furthermore, as the computer relieves them of certain routine aspects of

---

[10] Most authorities agree that the hardware itself is, indeed, neutral. The point of dispute, however, is that the *systems* in the *future* which can be supported by the computer *may not* be so neutral.

their jobs, the subordinate managers are able to concentrate on their more important duties. The net effect is that upper-echelon executives have greater confidence (1) in the ability of subordinates and (2) in their own ability to control subordinate performance properly. The conclusion is that the decentralization philosophy will be reinforced. In the words of John Burlingame:[11]

> Counter to many arguments, the anticipated advances in information technology, in my opinion, can strengthen decentralization in those businesses that have adopted it and will encourage more managements to experiment and to operate in accordance with the decentralization philosophy.

Centralization school　The centralization group believes that the computer makes it possible for those executives whose leanings are toward centralized management to bring back under their own jurisdiction the authority which they were forced to delegate as a matter of necessity.[12] Furthermore, it is felt that when *other* top executives realize that their new management reporting systems[13] can uncover problems at lower levels and can place at their fingertips vital decision-supporting data, they will be unable to resist making operating decisions even if it were not their original intention to do so when the systems were designed.[14] Subordinate managers will thus be effectively bypassed; not as many of them will be needed; and delegated authority will be recovered. Since the new systems will be capable of taking over various functions previously performed by subordinate managers, there will be a need to consolidate the remaining functions to produce new positions. The resulting reorganization will have the effect of producing a more *flattened* organizational structure—i.e., there will be fewer managerial

[11] John F. Burlingame, "Information Technology and Decentralization," *Harvard Business Review*, vol. 39, November-December, 1961, p. 124.

[12] There is little argument against this point.

[13] The types of reports included in these new systems may be: (1) periodic *monitoring reports* which compare actual performance with planned expectations; (2) non-scheduled *triggered reports* which are prepared only when actual performance deviates too much from plans; (3) *demand reports* which answer managerial probings (by means of, perhaps, online consoles and/or visual display stations) about the causes of triggered reports and about other special problems; and (4) *planning reports* which seek to identify trends, opportunities, and appropriate courses of action. See Richard G. Canning, "New Management Reporting Systems," *EDP Analyzer*, vol. 5, January, 1967, pp. 7-8.

[14] This point is disputed. If true, it could present problems if lower-level decisions absorbed too much top-executive time so that higher-level planning activities were slighted.

levels between the lowest supervisor and the top company executive. Auren Uris summarizes the opinion of many writers when he says:[15]

The trend will be away from decentralization, with more planning from a single headquarters. Even companies adding new units that previously would have been granted considerable autonomy will depend on a strong central control, not only in operational planning but in setting of operating and financial policy.

Effects on managers?

We have now briefly examined three schools of thought about the future effects of the computer on business organizations. Changes in the future on the organizational structure of a business will obviously have a direct bearing on the managers who occupy places in that structure. Since the reader may expect to be a manager in a computer-using organization in years to come, let us conclude this chapter with a look at some of the predictions which have been made of how new systems will affect tomorrow's managerial positions.

The bulk of speculation and argument has been centered around *middle management* positions,[16] because it is believed that the greatest impact will be felt at these levels. Top executives, of course, will be affected; they may reassume some of the decision-making powers previously delegated to subordinates (centralization school); or they may, with a greater feeling of confidence, delegate additional authority to subordinates (decentralization school). The primary role of top managers lies in formulating company objectives and policies and in planning and guiding overall company strategy. Computer systems should help to remove some of the uncertainties from the usually unique and ill-structured problems which top executives face. But substantial changes in this top management role are generally not expected.

If significant reductions are made in clerical and/or production

---

[15] Auren Uris, "What's Ahead for Middle Management?," *Chemical Engineering*, vol. 70, August 19, 1963, p. 178.

[16] *Middle managers* may be defined as those who are above the lowest level of supervision and below the top executive of a self-contained operating unit — i.e., they occupy positions between production foremen, keypunch supervisors, etc., on the one hand, and company presidents, executive vice-presidents, and division managers of large corporations, on the other. Therefore, the term "middle manager" is rather nebulous and is applied to a number of areas and levels. The difficulties of generalizing about such a wide range in many organizational structures should be recognized; it is not at all certain that the paths leading from all middle management levels will lead in the same general direction.

workers because of computer usage, it is to be expected that lower-level supervisory reductions will also occur. But because a primary role of the foreman is to provide face-to-face communication, direction, and leadership to production-oriented employees, it is generally not felt that this role will be revised, although the computer can relieve the foreman of many of his clerical duties.

And this brings us to the middle manager. Although there are some who believe that computer usage will have no major or lasting effect on middle managers, it is possible to classify the bulk of the comment into two categories: there are those who believe that middle management positions will be *more rewarding and challenging* in the future; and there are those who see the prospects in a much more *pessimistic* light.

The greater-challenge viewpoint Middle managers, like all managers, must perform the functions of planning, organizing, staffing, directing, and controlling. The writers who feel optimistic about the future role of middle managers point out that less time will have to be spent on the controlling function because the computer system can take over many of the clerical control activities—e.g., it can signal with a triggered (or exception) report whenever actual performance varies significantly from what has been planned. Time saved in controlling will enable middle managers to devote more attention to planning and to directing the work of their subordinates. More accurate and timely information supplied by the computer system will make it possible for these managers to spend more time identifying problems, recognizing opportunities, and planning alternate courses of action. In this respect, then, their jobs will more nearly resemble those of chief executives. With more time to devote to departmental employee matters, improved morale may be expected, and better communication will result. Furthermore, with more timely information at the middle managers' disposal, top managers will expect them to react more quickly. This may call for frequent face-to-face coordinating conferences between managers. Such meetings foster better interdepartmental communication. In summary then, a number of authorities agree with Professor Peter F. Drucker:[17]

The computer will force us to develop managers who are trained and tested in making the strategic decisions which determine business success or failure. I doubt that the computer will much reduce the number of middle manage-

[17] Peter F. Drucker, "What the Computers Will Be Telling You," *Nation's Business*, vol. 54, August, 1966, p. 89.

ment jobs. Instead the computer is restructuring these jobs, enabling us to organize work where it logically belongs and to free middle managers for more important duties.

An intermediate position Other writers agree with the viewpoint that in the future middle management jobs will be more rewarding and challenging, but they also believe that the number of such jobs will be *significantly reduced*. These writers are, in other words, occupying a middle position between optimism and pessimism. They are optimistic about the *job content* of the future middle management position; they feel that this job will be more intellectually demanding; they feel that the occupant will find more freedom and creativity in it; but they are pessimistic about the *number* of such managers who will be needed.

This is the consensus position taken in a report published by the American Foundation on Automation and Employment. The report, based on 35 extensive interviews with business, government, and academic leaders, states that computers have ". . .already cut deeply into the need for middle managers." And although there is as yet no evidence of widespread unemployment in their ranks, the report warns that "the middle manager's job stability. . .is subject to a far more serious threat and open to greater possibilities than past experience and expected trends in the immediate future would suggest."[18]

The pessimistic viewpoint The most pessimistic group takes the position (1) that middle management job content will be *less challenging* because of computer usage and (2) that the *number* of such managers will be substantially *reduced*. The argument of this group is as follows:

1. Many of the decisions made by middle managers are highly structured and repetitive and are thus programmable on a computer. (An example is the decision of an inventory control manager to reorder a basic part used in production.)

2. Therefore, many planning and decision activities will move from middle managers and will be handled by the data processing systems.

3. The need for managers will be greatly reduced; and the content of remaining jobs at the middle levels will be *less challenging*, more routine, and more formalized than before.

4. Why will remaining jobs be less challenging? Because the tasks of middle managers will be divided. Duties requiring less judgment and skill will

[18] From a report entitled *Automation and the Middle Manager, What Has Happened and What the Future Holds*, published by the American Foundation on Automation and Employment. Quotations appearing in *Administrative Management*, June, 1966, p. 54.

remain with middle managers; other tasks requiring the skilled interpretation of systems information will move toward the top management level.

5. Three organizational layers will be involved in future management information systems: There will be the production-oriented workers and their supervisors who will prepare the computer systems input; there will be an elite group of systems and computer specialists who will perform the required computer department activities; and there will be a small group of top executives who will analyze the facts and make the necessary decisions. There will be a minimum of personnel transfers between these layers.[19]

Those who are optimistic about job content and who also feel that the future trend will *not* lead to a reduction in middle management numbers frequently belong to the authority *decentralization school*. Those who foresee a trend toward *centralization* of authority *may or may not* agree about the outlook for middle management job content. But they *do* concur in the belief that the number of such jobs will be reduced. It seems fair to conclude, therefore, that a majority of the published predictions at least agree that the future middle manager will function in a setting which will be more intellectually demanding. He will certainly not become extinct although his numbers may be reduced. The manager of today must upgrade his abilities if he is to meet the sterner challenges of tomorrow. And the business student of today must acquire an understanding of business systems and of the uses and limitations of computers if he is to compete effectively in the future managerial environment. (The basic purpose of this book, of course, is to lay the foundation for the continuing study which will provide this understanding.)

SUMMARY

In this chapter we have looked at the present and potential consequences of computers on managers and on the environment in which managers work.

The data processing *activities* of a business may be centralized or decentralized. A number of variables must be considered by each individual company before it can decide if it should follow either path. The present trend, however, is toward the creation of centralized computer centers in the interest of reducing operating costs. Each firm must also decide, on the basis of its own requirements, where in the organizational structure the computer department should be located. A location within the finance function is

---

[19] Middle managers are aware of such predictions; they have also read of companies which have cut out a large number of middle positions. Is it any wonder, then, that they are likely to be apprehensive about their own future? Their resistance to the change to a computer system now becomes more understandable.

currently the most popular; however, for many companies a preferable alternative might be to create an independent department. Regardless of the organizational location, the department itself usually consists of systems analysis, program preparation, and computer operations sections. An operations research staff may also be included.

Although it is generally agreed that the present trend is toward centralization of data processing activities, there is no such agreement on the effects which computers will have on the centralization or decentralization of managerial authority. Thus far, the computer has supported a change in either direction; it is likely that it will continue to do so for the short-run future without the establishment of discernible trends in either direction. But speculation and controversy surround the unanswered question of what will happen to authority delegation when more sophisticated computer uses are perfected. Will any trends then be discernible? And if so, what will the direction be? Answers to these questions will obviously affect the future of managers at all levels. For the foreseeable future, it seems fair to conclude that middle managers will function in a setting which will become more challenging, more demanding, and more competitive.

DISCUSSION QUESTIONS

1 (a) What is an organization chart? (b) What value does such a chart have?

2 (a) What is meant by centralization of authority? (b) What determines the extent to which authority is delegated to lower managerial levels?

3 (a) What developments have made it possible to centralize data processing activities? (b) Why is the trend in the direction of centralization of data processing activities? (c) What possible advantages may there be in having data processing activities decentralized?

4 What reasons can be given to justify the establishment of an independent computer department?

5 (a) Why has the general trend in the past been in the direction of decentralization of authority? (b) Why can computer usage reduce the need for decentralization?

6 On the question of the effect which computer usage will have on the centralization or decentralization of authority, which school do you believe has the best argument?

7 How can computer usage affect your career as a manager?

SELECTED REFERENCES

Victor Z. Brink, "Who Gets the Computer?," *Columbia Journal of World Business*, Fall, 1966, pp. 69–77.

Glenn Gilman, "The Computer Revisited," *Business Horizons*, Winter, 1966, pp. 77-89.

William Heshka, "This Point Cannot Be Overemphasized," *Systems & Procedures Journal*, July-August, 1966, pp. 48-49.

Hak Chong Lee, *The Impact of Electronic Data Processing upon the Patterns of Business Organization and Administration* (Albany: State University of New York, School of Business, Bulletin No. 1).

Justin A. Perlman, "Centralization vs Decentralization." *Datamation*, September, 1965, pp. 24-28.

W. Thomas Porter, Jr., and Dennis E. Mulvihill, "Organization for Effective Information Flow," *Management Services*, November-December, 1965, pp. 13-20.

Donald R. Shaul, "What's Really Ahead for Middle Management?," *Personnel*, November-December, 1964, pp. 8-16

16. CONTROL AND THE COMPUTER

When we consider the subject of control and the computer, we must first clarify what we are controlling. There are at least two possibilities. *First*, it is possible for the subject to be the *managerial control of business operations* with the help of computer systems. If managers are to perform this function of the management process satisfactorily, they must have access to information of high quality. And *second*, the *processing techniques, procedures, and systems* which produce this information must also be controlled if error is to be minimized and if information quality is to remain high.

The subject of managerial control of business operations with the help of computer systems has been considered in a number of places throughout this text. For example, we saw in Chapter 1 that meaningful information provides managers with the means of operating and controlling a business; this same topic has been discussed in other chapters, e.g., Chapter 11, so we need not dwell at length here on this context of control and the computer. Rather, after a brief review of managerial control the remainder of this chapter will be devoted to a study of the control arrangements which have been established in many firms to assure managers that accurate and proper information is being produced by the computer.

With this brief introduction, we shall now move on to consider the following topics: (1) *a review* of the role which computer systems may play in *managerial control*; (2) *the properties of quality information*; (3) *the nature of internal control*; (4) *administrative controls*; and (5) *data controls*.

MANAGERIAL CONTROL: A REVIEW

The controlling function of the management process is a follow-up to planning activities—i.e., it is the check on current performance to determine if planned goals are being achieved. Thus, control activities are involved in the day-to-day administration of a business operation. You will recall that the general control procedure involves several steps: (1) predetermined goals or standards must be established; (2) performance must be measured; (3) actual performance must be compared with the standards; and (4) appropriate control decisions must be made.

The information output of the computer can help the manager carry out this procedure in many ways. First of all, better information about such things as the effectiveness of the firm's sales and distribution efforts, the quality and cost of the firm's products and services, and the strengths and weaknesses of the company's financial position can lead to better planning and to the creation of more realistic *standards*. Computer simulation can assist managers in setting goals by showing them the effects of various alternate decisions when certain conditions are assumed; and computer-based network models such as PERT and CPM can improve planning (and therefore control) by forcing managers to identify all project activities which must be performed.

Computer processing systems can also help managers control by gathering, classifying, calculating, and summarizing *actual performance* data promptly and accurately. Once performance data are read into the computer, it is possible for the machine to *compare* the actual performance with the established standards. Periodic reports showing this comparison can be prepared; in some systems, triggered reports may be furnished to the manager *only* when variations are outside certain specified limits.

It is also possible to program the computer so that it signals when predetermined *decisions* should be carried out. For example, a program may specify that when the inventory of a certain basic part falls below a given level an output message signals the need to reorder and indicates the reorder quantity. By thus relieving man of many of the routine operational control tasks, the computer frees him to devote more time (1) to planning future business moves and (2) to leading the all-important human resources of the organization. Such a man-machine relationship, in other words, makes it possible for man to concentrate more of his attention on the heuristic area of intellectual work—an area in which he is far superior to the machine—while the machine *is permitted* to take over the well-structured control tasks.

An assumption underlying everything said in the paragraphs of this section is that the *information produced* by the computer system *is of high quality.* If it is, total business operations may be well controlled; if it isn't, inadequate managerial performance may be expected.

THE PROPERTIES OF QUALITY INFORMATION

The information produced by a firm's data processing systems must be considered in terms of how *accurate* or reliable it is for decision-making purposes. The quality and usefulness of a report are, of course, directly related to its accuracy. Appropriate internal controls must be established in a business to keep information errors at an acceptable level. And in addition to being accurate, information must be *timely*, *complete*, and *pertinent* if it is to be of maximum value in helping managers make the decisions which lead to profitable business actions.

Accuracy

Accuracy may be defined as the ratio of correct information to the total amount of information produced over a period of time. Therefore, if 1,000 items of information are produced and if 950 of these items give a correct report of the actual situation, then the degree of accuracy is said to be 0.95. Whether or not this level of accuracy is *sufficient* depends on the particular type of information being produced. For example, 50 incorrect customer statements out of a total of 1,000 is hardly an acceptable level to either the customers or the business. On the other hand, if the physical inventory records kept on large quantities of low-value items are accurate 95 percent of the time, this may be quite acceptable. Greater accuracy can be obtained; but the *additional* value to managers of having more-accurate information may well be *less* than the *additional costs* required to obtain the higher accuracy. Determining the optimum level of accuracy generally involves at least an implicit comparison of these factors of information cost and management value. It is obviously foolish to pay more for greater accuracy if this is not needed.

What causes inaccuracies? Processed results may differ from actual results because of *human errors* and/or *machine malfunctions*. Human error in system design, in program preparation, in machine operation, in data input preparation, and in any number of manual processing operations is, of course, the primary cause of inaccuracy. "To err is human"; any data processing system confirms this fact.

Machine malfunctions occur only infrequently. The major portion of those equipment failures which occasionally *do* appear in computer systems may be traced to the input/output devices. This is understandable in view of the mechanical operations which these devices must perform. Fortunately, appropriate software and built-in error-detecting features (such as parity checks to identify the presence of invalid character codes and dual stations in card readers and punches to signal reading and punching discrepancies) may serve to locate input/output errors and malfunctions.[1]

It is appropriate to point out here that although computer systems are certainly capable of being more accurate than the manual or electromechanical systems which they replace, it may not *seem* that this is the case during and immediately after the conversion period. At that time many errors may crop up which were routinely caught and informally corrected by people in the old system. Since correcting these errors was not a part of their primary duties, however, this aspect of their work might be ignored when the new systems are designed. The errors may continue to appear, because the new system has not made provision for their correction. Also, in file conversion operations, numerous errors may be uncovered; but because of schedule pressures others may be allowed to slip through to plague the new systems. Additional discrepancies may become apparent, perhaps for the first time, when files are consolidated or combined for the new systems. In short, it often seems that a multitude of errors are revealed during the conversion period and that the tendency of some employees is to blame the new systems. Perhaps the new procedures are poorly designed; perhaps, as a result, programs do not make provision for all contingencies which may have previously been handled on an informal basis; but many of the errors which must be corrected are those which are being purged from the existing systems during the conversion.

Timeliness

In addition to being accurate, information produced by a firm's data processing system must be *timely* to be of value for decision-making purposes.[2] If a manager has a problem which requires a decision, the information to support that decision should be available within a reasonable time period. It obviously is of little consolation to the manager to know that the information which arrived too late to be of any use was accurate. Accuracy alone is not sufficient.

What is a "reasonable" time period? Unfortunately, it is again im-

[1] See Chap. 5 for a more detailed description of these error-detecting features.

[2] Just as there must often be a trade-off between the value of additional accuracy and the additional costs incurred, so also may there need to be a compromise on the question of accuracy and timeliness. Greater accuracy may require more data control points, and this may slow down the speed of processing and therefore the timeliness of output information. Computer usage has reduced the significance of this conflict between accuracy and processing speed.

possible to give a straightforward answer. We can rule out an immediate time period for *regular reports* because this would involve a steady outpouring of documents, each of which covered a very brief time interval and each of which was prepared with a minimum of delay. The result might well be an expensive avalanche of paper. The report contents could not possibly be digested by the manager (and even if they could be, the time periods would probably be too short to reveal any meaningful trends, although superficial events could be blown up out of proportion to their importance). In the case of regularly scheduled reports, then, managers generally prefer that the reporting periods be long enough to reduce the paper volume and to reveal meaningful information. But this reporting period cannot be stretched too far, or summarization may become too extensive—i.e., important trends signaling the need for action may be hidden in longer-run totals and averages. Although the length of the reporting period thus varies, it is important for the manager to receive the report with a minimum of delay after the cutoff date for the period has arrived.

In the case of quick-response systems, as we saw in Chapter 3, information contained in records may be accessible within a fraction of a second after inquiry. How current this information is depends upon the degree of quickness in updating the records. In some online processing systems, records may be updated periodically (perhaps daily); in the case of real time operations, they may be updated immediately. To summarize, for some information processing applications, timeliness may be achieved by batch processing methods involving reporting periods of various lengths; for other applications, the needs of managers are best met by online (but not real time) processing; and for still other applications, real time processing methods offer the best solution.

Completeness and pertinency

Few things may be more frustrating to a manager having to make a decision than to receive supporting information which is accurate, timely—and *incomplete*. Although it may not be possible to supply managers with all the information they would like to have, it is often possible, through better systems design and integration, to provide them with more complete information. If information available in bits and pieces and at scattered points had been integrated, the Japanese attack on Pearl Harbor might have been repulsed. And if the necessary integration of the facts available at scattered points in a business can be achieved, the manager will receive information which is more complete and more valuable for decision-making purposes.

But in striving to obtain information which is more complete, managers and systems analysts should be careful that they do not demand an excessive quantity of information. Information that is *pertinent* and of high quality is designed to meet the manager's needs; it also is limited to the ability of the manager to make use of it; but it is *not* a large, detailed, and unrefined mass from which relevant items must be sifted. Taken by themselves, output reports generally have little or no value to a business. They prove valuable only when they can be used to make decisions which lead to profitable business actions. It is folly to present a manager with excessive reports which add nothing to his decision-making capability but which may add many dollars to processing costs.

We have now seen that high-quality information is needed to operate and control a business. We have also seen that the quality and usefulness of information may be measured by how accurate, timely, complete, and pertinent it is for decision-making purposes. In the remainder of this chapter we shall look at the means of controlling the processing procedures internally so that an accurate information output is produced.[3]

THE NATURE OF INTERNAL CONTROL

Internal control, as the name implies, is the total of all the control arrangements adopted within an organization to (1) check on and maintain the accuracy of business data; (2) safeguard the company assets against fraud and other irregularities; (3) promote operating efficiency; and (4) encourage compliance with existing company policies and procedures.[4]

Need for internal control in computer systems

In noncomputer systems the data processing activities are typically separated into several departments with a number of employees being responsible for some portion of the total activity. For example, in the processing of a customer order, credit approval may come from one

[3] Accuracy levels may be verified, although the other attributes which combine with accuracy to produce high-quality information are of a more intangible nature. It is therefore not surprising that most of the formal control techniques are directed toward curbing inaccuracies, promoting efficiency, and disclosing irregularities.

[4] This definition is based on the one prepared by the American Institute of Certified Public Accountants. See *Auditing Standards and Procedures* (American Institute of Certified Public Accountants, Statements on Auditing Procedure, no. 33, 1963), p. 27.

location, control of the inventory of ordered items may be located in another department, customer billing may be in a third department, and receipt of payment for items shipped may be in a fourth location. Thus, the organizational structure separates those people who authorize and initiate the order from those who record and carry out the transaction. And both of these groups are separated from those who receive payment for the order. Such a division of data processing activities makes it difficult for fraud to go undetected, since a number of people from different departments would have to be a party to any deception. Also, personnel in each organizational unit can check on the accuracy of others in the course of their routine operations.

But as the preceding chapter pointed out, the tendency is for data processing *activities* to be *centralized* as a result of computer usage. Centralization of activities, along with greater integration of processing steps, may make it possible for a single department to perform all the activities required to process a customer order. In the past, internal control has been achieved by the reviews and cross-checks made by personnel at separate points in the organizational structure. In other words, internal control was *employee oriented*. With fewer departmental units involved, however, and with the likelihood that fewer people are cross-checking data, it *may appear* that, even though source documents originate outside the computer department, the use of computer systems results in a reduction of internal control.

Such a reduction *can* occur in an inadequately controlled centralized computer department. But there is *no reason* why a company *should* have less internal control because of computer usage. On the contrary, there is no reason why *systems-oriented* controls, in the form of computer programs, cannot be substituted for employee-oriented controls; and there is no reason why the separation of duties and responsibilities cannot be maintained *within* the computer department to safeguard the integrity of the systems-oriented controls. In fact, there is no reason why a company cannot achieve better control because of the computer's ability to follow policies and execute processing procedures uniformly, because of the difficulty of changing and manipulating, without detection, the programmed systems controls, and because of the inherent accuracy advantage when the computer is given correct input data.

Organizational considerations

Separation of activities *within* the computer department can help maintain the integrity of systems-oriented controls. One important control principle is that there should be an organizational separation between those who design and prepare the new systems (the analysts and programmers) and those who prepare the input data and operate the equipment. In other words, analysts and programmers should design, maintain, and make necessary changes (according to specified procedures) on programs, but they should *not* be involved with day-to-day production runs; equipment operators, on the other hand, should not have unrestricted access to completed computer programs, nor should they be involved with making changes in data or programs. Completed programs and their supporting documents should be kept and controlled by a librarian who is not engaged either in planning or maintaining programs or in operating processing equipment. These programs and documents should be issued to interested parties only upon proper authorization.

Internal control and auditing

Business information systems undergo periodic examinations or *audits* by *internal auditors* (employees of the firm) and by *external auditors* (independent certified public accountants employed by the board of directors or stockholders). The evaluation of internal control arrangements is the point of departure in auditing. Although no exact audit procedure is used, the auditors seek to determine, by observation, inquiry, and review of charts and manuals (1) whether a proper organizational separation of duties has been made and (2) whether adequate controls have been created to maintain accuracy, safeguard assets, etc.

During the course of the examination, attention is turned to the *audit trail* to determine if controls are effective and if reported procedures and policies are being followed. The audit trail begins with the recording of a transaction, winds through the processing steps and through any intermediate records which may exist and be affected, and ends with the production of output reports and records. By selecting a representative sample of previously processed source documents and by following the audit trail, the auditor can trace these documents through the data processing systems to their final report or record destinations as a means of testing the adequacy of systems procedures and controls. In a manual system, original transactions may be recorded in one or more books of original entry; from there they may be connected to the final output by means of ledgers, documents, and summary totals. A visual and readily traceable trail is thus created.

With the introduction of computer systems, however, the form of the trail has changed.⁵ Intermediate steps in the information systems which were previously visible have *seemed* to vanish into reels of magnetic tape, into magnetic disks, and into magnetic cards and strips. To those auditors not familiar with computer systems, a portion of the audit trail "disappeared" at the entrance to the computer site.⁶ Since a "lost" audit trail is naturally a serious control matter, accounting literature is full of articles on this subject. Most of these articles deal with the several methods which can be used to audit computer information processing procedures.

In a majority of the electronic systems audits which have been made, the "around-the-computer" approach has been used. In this approach, the assumption is that if the input data to the computer are correct and if the output is properly handled, then the intermediate processing must be correct. This approach owes much of its popularity to its simplicity and familiarity to the auditor, and to its minimization of the need to understand the operation of processing systems. An alternative is the "through-the-computer" approach,⁷ where the auditor verifies (1) that input data are correct and (2) that internal processing is properly conducted. He then assumes that output is correct. The around-the-computer approach may be suitable for audits made during the initial phases of a computer changeover and for some low-volume, uncomplicated systems; the through-the-computer method is frequently preferable for larger, more sophisticated procedures. Many auditing authorities recommend that a combination of approaches be employed.

To go further into the complex subject of auditing is beyond the scope of this text. The *function* of the auditor will probably not change in the future; but his *techniques* will certainly be subject to revision as a result of computer usage. One of the greatest challenges facing the systems designer and the auditor will be to devise ways of preserving an audit trail which (although it may seem to be nearly invisible) must be readily retraceable. Furthermore, this trail must be kept as simple

---

⁵ It cannot be *eliminated* because of desire for good internal control and because of tax and legal requirements. The Internal Revenue Service, in a 1964 report on the use of EDP equipment, said that ". . . the audit trail or the ability to trace a transaction from the general ledger back to its source document must not be eliminated." See Benton Warder, "An Auditor Looks at Data Processing," *Journal of Data Management*, vol. 5, February, 1967, p. 17.

⁶ The use of random access storage devices to hold additional intermediate data and the substitution of online processing for batch processing may result in an even greater decrease in the visible portion of the audit trail.

⁷ A number of different techniques have been developed for this approach.

as possible, and it must not require great masses of supporting printed detail. To perform their function properly, auditors will need to understand computer systems. A psychological barrier will be removed with understanding, and concern about an invisible audit trail will abate. As T. W. McRae writes:[8]

> The fact that the records are not visible is a psychological rather than a practical handicap. . . . The problem is not that the records are invisible but rather that the auditor is dependent on the computer room staff for translating coded tape into a printed format.

On the basis of the definition of internal control given earlier, we can separate the types of controls which should be developed into two categories. In the *first* category are those controls which are established for administrative purposes. These *administrative* controls are designed (1) to promote operating efficiency and (2) to encourage employees to comply with existing company policies and procedures. The *second* category of internal controls which should be developed is concerned with the accuracy and propriety of recording and processing data. In other words, *data or procedural* controls are those which are created to check and maintain the accuracy of business data. Prevention of fraud and other irregularities is controlled by organizational separation of duties and by administrative and data controls. In the remaining pages of this chapter we shall briefly survey some of the computer-related administrative and data controls which the auditor may look for during his examination.

ADMINISTRATIVE CONTROLS

In checking operational efficiency and procedural consistency, the auditor is interested in techniques which have a direct bearing on *systems design, programming*, and *computer operation*.

Systems design controls

In Chapter 9 it was emphasized that adequate systems and program documentation is needed to provide a means of recording, analyzing, and communicating information. Such documentation is generally required for efficient systems design, for effective preparation of initial programs, and for proper program maintenance. But in addition to

---

[8] T. W. McRae, *The Impact of Computers on Accounting* (New York: John Wiley & Sons, Inc., 1964), p. 165.

promoting operating efficiency, adequate documentation provides the *basis for* the *evaluation and control* of new and existing computer systems. *New* system specifications should be designed (and documented) with audit and control considerations in mind. (It is expensive to ignore control aspects and then to have to revise and rework a designed system. The participation of a knowledgeable auditor in the design phase, so that proper controls may be built in and so that the audit trail does not vanish in fact as well as in appearance, is thus a wise precaution.) Without good supporting documents and flowcharts on *existing* systems, managers and auditors will probably not know if system changes have been made or if other action should be taken. In other words, as one authority correctly notes, "poor documentation represents a fundamental weakness in internal control which is present, in varying degrees, in many installations."[9] Therefore, one of the most important controls which can be exercised over systems design is to assign authority to one or more individuals to make sure that systems and program flowcharts, decision tables, etc., are properly prepared and maintained. Specifically written control procedures should be established for this purpose, and standardized charting symbols and methods should be used.

Programming controls

The above comments on the importance of good documentation for control purposes extend, of course, into the program preparation activity. A detailed explanation of the purpose of each program together with copies of all related documents should be kept in a *program file.* A manual containing *standard programming procedures* should also be prepared and kept up to date.[10] The operating policies and approaches which are to be followed by personnel should be specified. Among the topics which might be covered should be program documentation methods and standards, program testing and modification procedures, magnetic tape labeling and retention policies, and the use of standardized symbolic names to describe company data. Such specified procedures promote consistency, reduce program maintenance problems, and make it easier for others to take over the work of a programmer who decides to leave the company.

[9] Maurice S. Newman, "Internal Control and Data Processing," *Financial Executive*, vol. 32, November, 1964, p. 45.

[10] For an in-depth treatment of the topic of data processing standards, see Dick H. Brandon, *Management Standards for Data Processing* (Princeton, N.J.: D. Van Nostrand Company, Inc., 1963).

A definite procedure should be formulated to handle *program changes*. Changes should be made only after written approval is given by someone in a position of authority, e.g., the manager of the affected department. It is sometimes a good policy to postpone making a number of minor changes until the end of an accounting cycle so that data handling remains consistent throughout the accounting period. Changes in programs should be made by programmers and not by computer-operating personnel. All changes should be carefully charted and explained in writing; when completed, they should be reviewed and cleared by someone other than a maintenance programmer. All documents related to the change should be made a part of the permanent program file.

Computer operation controls

Computer operation controls may be maintained in the following ways:

1. *By the use of appropriate manuals.* A standard *operating manual* should include an explanation of the procedures established to deal with such things as the issuance and return of program and data tapes and cards and the means of scheduling and keeping records of equipment operating time. A manual of *program operating instructions* should be available which tells the operator how each program should be run. These instructions can specify the peripheral equipment to use, the console switch settings to make, the action to take on all program halts, the exceptions to standard procedures and routines which may be needed, the input data to use, and the disposition of the output information obtained.

2. *By the creation of a data security program.* Definite controls should be established to safeguard programs and data from fire and water damage or destruction. Duplicate program and master file tapes may need to be kept at a location away from the computer site. A fireproof storage vault at the computer site is a wise precaution. The importance of proper identification of, and control over, library tapes, cards, disks, and blank forms cannot be overemphasized.

3. *By control over console intervention.* It is possible for the computer operator to by-pass program controls. He has the ability to interrupt a program run and introduce data manually into the processor through the console keyboard. With a proper organizational separation of program preparation and computer operation, it is unlikely that the operator has enough knowledge of the program details to manipulate them successfully for improper purposes. But the possibility of unauthorized intervention should be reduced in a number of ways. Since, for example, the console typewriter may be used to print out a manual intervention, the paper sheets in the typewriter can be prenumbered and periodically checked. Other approaches using locked recording devices may be employed. Ad-

ditional control techniques include rotating the duties of computer operators and having them account for operating time (manual intervention is
slow; manipulation can thus result in processing times that are longer
than necessary for affected runs).

DATA CONTROLS

Data controls are concerned with the accuracy and propriety of the
data flowing through a processing system; therefore, let us consider
these controls at the *input, processing,* and *output* stages.

Input controls

The purpose of input controls is to make sure (1) that *all* properly au-
thorized input transactions are identified, (2) that these transactions
are *accurately recorded* in a machine-usable form at the *right time,*
and (3) that *all* these transactions are then sent to the processing station. Among the control techniques which may be adopted are:

1. *The use of prenumbered forms.* Whenever possible, a simple and effective
   control is to use serially numbered forms so that documents may be accounted for. A missing number in the sequence signals a missing document.

2. *The use of control totals.* When batch processing is used, certain totals
   can be computed for each batch of source documents. For example, the
   total dollar-sales figure may be computed on a batch of sales invoices
   prior to, perhaps, key punching. The same calculation can be made after
   key punching to see if the figures compare. Control totals do not need to
   be expressed in dollars. They can be the totals obtained from adding figures in a data field which is included in all source documents being considered. A simple count of documents, cards, and other records is an
   effective control total. For example, the number of cards processed in the
   computer-operating department can be compared with the count of the
   number of cards which are delivered for processing. Similar comparisons
   between records read on magnetic tape and the number of input source
   documents may be possible. Of course, with control totals as with other
   data controls, the volume of transactions and the importance of the data
   should determine the degree of control and the amount of money which is
   spent to maintain that control.

3. *The use of transcription methods.* One means of controlling data transcription is to have knowledgeable clerks conduct a preaudit of source documents prior to recording the transactions in a machine-usable form. If input is by means of punched cards, the card verifier described in Chapter
   2 can be used.

4. *The use of programmed checks on input.* Program instructions can be
   written to check on the reasonableness and propriety of data as they enter

348

the processing operation. For example, program checks can be written to determine (1) if certain specified limits are exceeded, (2) if the input is complete, and (3) if a transaction code or identification number is active and reasonable. When online processing is used, lockwords or passwords may be required from remote stations before certain files can be *accessed*.

Processing controls

Processing controls are established (1) to determine when data are lost or not processed and (2) to check on the accuracy of arithmetic calculations. These controls may be classified into *hardware* and *software* categories. Important hardware controls include parity checks and the use of dual reading and writing heads. These controls were explained in Chapter 5. Although not a built-in hardware control, a definite program of *preventive maintenance* can pay big dividends by reducing the number of machine malfunctions.

Software or programmed controls include the input checks mentioned above. The number of possible programmed controls which may be used is limited only by the programmer's imagination.[11] Some of the possibilities include:

1. *The use of record count*. As a check against a predetermined total, the computer can be instructed to count the number of records which it handles in a program run.

2. *The use of tape labels*. The *external* labeling of magnetic tapes should, of course, be carefully controlled. These outside labels may give those interested such information as the tape contents, the program identification number, and the length of time the contents should be retained. *Internal* header and trailer control labels may also be recorded on the tapes themselves. The first (or *header*) record written on the tape gives the program identification number and other information. Before actual processing begins, then, a programmed comparison check may be made to make sure that the proper tape reel is being used. Since accidentally writing on a master file, of course, erases information previously recorded, this is an important precaution. The last (or *trailer*) record contains a count of the number of other records on the tape.

3. *The use of sequence check*. In batch processing, the records are in some kind of sequence, e.g., by employee number or by stock number. Programmed checks to detect out-of-sequence and missing cards and records prevent a file from being processed in an incorrect order.

[11] But the value of the controls must be weighed against the additional programming expense and the cost of additional computer running time.

Output controls

Output controls are established as final checks on the accuracy and propriety of the processed information. Among the output control methods which may be employed are:

1. *The use of control totals.* How do the control totals of processed information compare with the input control totals? For example, is there agreement between the number of records which were delivered for processing and the number of records which were actually processed? A basic output control technique is to obtain satisfactory answers to such questions.

2. *The review of interested parties.* Feedback on a regular basis from input-initiating and output-using departments points out errors which slip through in spite of all precautions. Follow-up action must be taken to correct file inaccuracies which are revealed.

3. *The use of systematic sampling.* Internal auditors can check on output by tracing randomly selected transactions from source documents through the processing system to the output destination. This should be done on a regular and systematic basis.

4. *The use of prenumbered forms.* Certain output forms should be prenumbered and accounted for in the same manner as input documents. Blank payroll check forms, for example, should be closely guarded.

SUMMARY

Managers must have access to information of high quality to control the total operation of the business successfully. The quality and usefulness of information are directly related to its accuracy. But in addition to being accurate, information must also be timely, complete, and pertinent if it is to be of maximum value in helping managers make the decisions which lead to profitable business actions.

Appropriate internal data controls must be established in a business to check on the accuracy and propriety of processed information. Administrative checks on the efficiency and consistency of processing procedures must also be made. In manual systems, employee-oriented controls are established. Processing efficiency is often low, but review and cross-checking of a number of workers at separate organization points have desirable internal control features. When computer processing is used, systems-oriented controls may be substituted for some of the employee checks. But when proper systems precautions are taken, improvements in overall internal control should result.

Internal and external auditors periodically check on the adequacy of the internal control arrangements which have been made. During their examinations, auditors trace transactions through the processing systems as a means of testing the accuracy of information and the adequacy of procedures and controls. Computer usage has changed the form of this audit trail; its visibility has been reduced by the elimination of paper documents. New techniques have been developed because of audit trail changes; additional changes in audit methodology will be required in the future.

During the audit, the auditor checks to see if a proper organizational separation of duties has been made. He also wants to know if adequate administrative and data controls have been created. A number of administrative and data control methods are presented in the latter pages of the chapter.

DISCUSSION QUESTIONS

1 How can computer usage help a manager control total business operations?

2 Identify and discuss the properties which determine the quality and usefulness of business information.

3 (a) What is internal control? (b) Why is it needed?

4 What is the difference between employee-oriented and systems-oriented controls?

5 Of what significance is organizational structure in maintaining internal control?

6 (a) Distinguish between internal and external auditors. (b) What is the function of the auditor?

7 (a) Define the audit trail. (b) Why is the audit trail important?

8 Explain the methods which can be used to audit computer information processing procedures.

9 (a) What are administrative controls? (b) Give some examples of such controls.

10 (a) What are data controls? (b) Give some examples of such controls.

SELECTED REFERENCES

Dick H. Brandon, *Management Standards for Data Processing* (Princeton, N.J.: D. Van Nostrand Company, Inc., 1963).

H. Bruce Joplin, "An Internal Control Checklist for EDP," *Management Services*, July–August, 1964, pp. 32–37.

Maurice S. Newman, "Internal Control and Data Processing," *Financial Executive*, November, 1964, pp. 42–52.

W. Thomas Porter, Jr., "A Control Framework for Electronic Systems," *The Journal of Accountancy*, October, 1965, pp. 56–63.

Robert E. Schlosser and Donald C. Bruegman, "The Effect of EDP on Internal Control," *Management Services*, March–April, 1964, pp. 44–51.

Benton Warder, "An Auditor Looks at Data Processing," *Journal of Data Management*, February, 1967, pp. 16–19.

17. TOMORROW'S OUTLOOK

A brief survey of computer books and of articles in computer magazines reveals an interesting fact: a large amount of space is devoted to the prediction of things to come. Writers in this field, it seems, are drawn to prognostication as the moth is drawn to the flame—and, like the moth, they are often singed for their presumptuousness!

In this final chapter, the discussion devoted to the subject of tomorrow's outlook is limited for two reasons: (1) in earlier chapters speculation about future trends was presented as particular subjects were discussed; and (2) the time period involved is, for the most part, "tomorrow," i.e., for the next five years or so, rather than the "day after tomorrow."[1] Thus, this final chapter attempts to summarize some of the developments which may logically be expected in the next few years based on the current state of the art in the electronic data processing field. The topics to be considered can be classified as (1) the *hardware outlook*, (2) the *software outlook*, (3) the *outlook for business information systems*, and (4) the *outlook for managers*.

THE HARDWARE OUTLOOK

Trends in input/output devices

It is likely that considerable progress will be made in data *input* methods. Since input has generally been a limiting factor in business data processing, a great deal of attention has been, and will continue to be, focused on improved input performance. The bulk of the computer input in the next five years will continue to be in the form of punched cards or magnetic tape. Tape-recording densities will increase in the

---

[1] The literature is not lacking in guesses about the effects which computers will have on business twenty or more years in the future. When appropriate, sources of longer-range predictions are footnoted for the benefit of the interested reader.

future, and storage costs will thus be reduced. But there will be a trend toward recording data in machine-usable form at the point of origin through the greater use of online terminals. Remote I/O consoles, transaction recorders, input tablets and light pens, CRT-equipped display stations—all these online instruments will become less expensive and will be used more often in the future. When such a direct man-machine interface is possible, the need for a data-recording medium may not be required. The direct input techniques, then, will help to reduce the key punching of cards from source documents— a laborious translating operation.

Optical character recognition of machine-printed characters and hand-printed marks and numbers will also increase in importance at the expense of manual key punching. The cost of using OCR will decline, and reliability will be improved by a movement toward standardization of paper, inks, and type fonts. Research will continue on the development of machines which will read handwritten letters and on machines which will accept voice input. Such equipment will not be in wide-spread use in the next five years, but could become important at a later date.

The high-speed printer will continue to be the primary *output* device when information is to be used directly by man. Dramatic improvements in impact printers will not be forthcoming; however, they will become more reliable and somewhat less expensive. There will be a trend in the direction of lessening the role of the printer. It will be by-passed by the use of online stations which will give the information requested directly to the user. Of course, if the remote station is equipped with a typewriter, a printed document will be produced; but if the station has a CRT, no printed document may be prepared. Better systems design and the utilization of the "management-by-exception" principle may also result in fewer and more concise reports. The use of voice output will grow in those specialized situations where an audio response can be given to predictable queries.

Trends in the central processor

Rapid changes may be expected in the next five years in the *size*, *speed*, *cost*, and *storage capacity* of the central processor. The basic components will be further reduced in size through integrated circuit technology. This size reduction will mean shorter distances for electrical pulses to travel, and thus processor speed will be increased. Probably the most dramatic changes will be in the area of costs. In the past, there have been substantial cost reductions for a given level of computing power; this trend will continue in the future. For example, we saw in Chapter 3 that in 1965 it cost about 20 cents to provide internal storage capacity for one bit (down from $2.61 in 1950 and 85 cents in 1960). The comparable cost in 1970 is estimated to be from 5 cents to 10 cents, while the 1975 figure is predicted to be $1/2$ cent! The result of such cost reduction will be a further acceleration in the use of computers. Nor is the cost reduction limited to internal storage circuitry. Roger L. Sisson notes that an arithmetic-logic circuit ". . .which cost several dollars in 1955 and is now 50 cents or so will go to 3 to 5 cents [in five to ten years]."[2] In the opinion of Dr. David C. Evans, Director of Computer Science at the University of Utah:[3]

It now seems clear that integrated-circuit technology will soon produce circuits of great complexity at very low cost. . . . It is my personal opinion that computer designers will be hard-pressed to develop concepts to exploit the rapid advances in components.

Integrated circuits have also helped in the development of the *distributed computer* concept—i.e., they have helped shift some of the processing functions previously handled by the CPU to peripheral equipment. For example, with appropriate built-in circuitry, an on-line station may make some of the programmed input checks described in the preceding chapter before transmitting the data to the central processor. The distributed computer approach is likely to be developed more fully in the future.

In addition to being smaller, somewhat faster, and much less expensive, computer storage devices will have larger storage capability. Equipment will be available with the number of bytes of *internal* storage measured in the tens of millions. Much of the equipment produced in the next five years will use magnetic core storage techniques. But the trend will be in the direction of such noncore storage forms as thin film, plated wire, and sheet ferrite—all of which hold out the promise of being easier to fabricate than magnetic core planes.

External online storage devices will continue to be primarily magnetic cores, drums, disks, and cards or strips. The use of replaceable cartridges gives an openended storage capability to magnetic disks and cards or strips at the present time. But in the future the use of

[2] Roger L. Sisson, "Planning for Computer Hardware Innovations," *Data Processing Digest*, vol. 13, January, 1967, p. 5. For predictions on computer hardware beyond 1975, see page 11 of this source.

[3] David C. Evans, "Computer Logic and Memory," *Scientific American*, vol. 215, September, 1966, p. 84.

higher recording densities will make it possible for each disk, strip, or card to hold more data. Online storage capacity will therefore be expanded, and random access times will also be improved. There will be a continuation of the inverse relationship which currently exists between random access time and storage capacity—e.g., strips or cards will have the slowest random access time along with the largest storage capability.

The future of smaller, free-standing computers is a matter of some dispute. Although these machines represent the bulk of the present installations, there are some who believe that the future will see a decline in their *number* in favor of large time sharing equipment. In other words, it is felt that remote terminals connected to time sharing facilities will *replace* smaller computer installations. Although a number of individual organizations will follow this route in the next five years, there will not, during this period, be a discernible trend in this direction. It was pointed out in Chapter 2 that 85,000 computers are expected to be installed by 1975 (about double the number installed in 1967). Obviously, most of these machines will *not* be large time sharing systems. However, we should keep the distinction between the *number* of machines and the computing capability and value of each installation clearly in mind. Most of the computers installed in the 1970s will be small, just as most of today's computers are small. But the number of time sharing installations will grow rapidly; each of these installations will have the computing capability of a number of smaller machines; and it has been predicted that the dollar value of the time-shared machines installed in 1970 will account for nearly half of industry sales at that time.

For at least the next ten years there will be an increase in the number of both large and small hardware systems. There will be *increasing compatibility* between smaller machines and larger time-shared ones. This compatibility will eventually (the Swami is now looking further into the future than five years) help bring about a size polarization: On the one hand, there will be large centralized computing facilities used on a time-shared basis; and on the other hand, there will be large numbers of small and relatively inexpensive computers used independently to satisfy the particular special requirements of the user. Furthermore, many of these small free-standing computers will be compatible with, will be connected to, and will communicate with, the larger time-shared facilities. Such communication among computers will not be limited to single organizations; rather, it will cut across company boundaries.

Trends in data communications

With increased emphasis being placed on time sharing, the trend will obviously be toward greater use of data communications facilities. The American Telephone and Telegraph Company predicts that by 1970 its revenue from long-distance data transmission will exceed the revenue received from long-distance voice communication. Also, Western Union has predicted that 60 percent of the computers sold by 1975 will be linked in some way to a data communications network.

Improved technology and greater usage of data transmission facilities will combine to reduce gradually the cost of long-distance data communications. Such reductions will probably not be substantial. Laser research and the use of communications satellites may eventually result in more economical transmission, but not in the next five years. It is quite possible, in fact, that most of the costs associated with processing a task originating at a remote station will be directly attributable to communications charges. Such charges will result in the construction of more company-owned communication systems. But most of the data transmission facilities will, of course, be furnished by telephone and telegraph companies. Teletype and voice-grade telephone channels will continue to transmit most of the data. Touch-Tone telephones, with push-button input and audio output, will become a common low-cost I/O device in the next five years. Data will be transmitted directly to a computer by "keying" the Touch-Tone buttons.

THE SOFTWARE OUTLOOK

Language trends

Procedure oriented languages designed to fit a general class of processing applications, e.g., mathematic-scientific and commercial, will continue to be the dominant programming languages for the next few years. Compilers will be further improved, and machine oriented symbolic languages will continue to decline in use. Because of the huge investment in such languages as FORTRAN and COBOL, they will be maintained and updated. As the use of decision tables becomes more wide-spread, decision-table programming languages will receive greater attention. Increased emphasis will certainly be placed on PL/I. But these languages will not, of course, be the final solution to the laborious and expensive task of program preparation. There is lack of agreement among computer authorities about the language trend in the more distant future. "The extreme predictions are on one hand of one language (PL/XII?) for all applications on all machines, and on the other of a different language for every application in every shop."[4] It may well be that two advanced universal languages will evolve from current experience—one to be used for mathematical applications and one to be used for business purposes.

Eventually, the use of *conversational programming* is likely to become common. When such a programming approach is used (time-shared terminals are needed), the computer itself keeps track of the acceptable vocabulary of the language and displays permissible alternate terms and statements to the user until the problem is satisfactorily formulated. The machine then computes the answer to the problem. In short, the user's major skill will lie in his ability to state problems. He will be assisted by a "dialogue" with the computer as it attempts to find out what he wants to say. "Under the tutelage of the computer (for here the machine will be part teacher, part learner), the problem will be formulated until it is in a form for which a useful solution can be 'programmed' by the computer itself."[5]

Trends in applications packages

Packaged programs for common applications will be improved; and applications packages for more specific tasks will be developed by computer manufacturers, by user groups, by computer centers, and by software specialty organizations. Generalized file-processing systems which can be modified by the user to meet unique requirements will reduce the time and costs involved in systems analysis and programming in an increasing number of cases. The number and versatility of subroutines in the libraries of manufacturers, user groups, etc., will expand. Computer centers will provide low-cost processing services to a rapidly growing number of small organizations through the use of these packaged programs.

Growth of software specialists

Independent software specialty companies will do a rapidly expanding volume of business in the future. The growth of the better organizations in this field will be dramatic. In addition to providing consult-

[4] Stanley M. Naftaly, "How to Pick a Programming Language," *Data Processing Digest*, vol. 12, November, 1966, p. 13.

[5] John W. Carr, III, "Programming in the 1970's," in *Data Processing* (Park Ridge, Ill.: Data Processing Management Association, 1965), VIII, p. 151.

ing services and designing and preparing software to special customer order,[6] they will also develop proprietary software systems which they will offer for sale.[7] Why would anyone buy software when computer manufacturers furnish it at no additional charge? An obvious reason, of course, is that what is needed might not be available from the manufacturer and would cost less to buy than prepare. Another reason is that the software might be more efficient than that provided by the manufacturer. (Manufacturers write software for a general audience, while the independent firms can offer more specialized—and thus generally more efficient—programs.)

The question of software pricing will receive much greater attention in the next few years.[8] At this writing, equipment vendors place sale or lease prices on the hardware, but no explicit additional charges are made for the furnished software. In the installation of tomorrow, however, total software costs will exceed total hardware costs. Thus, present pricing policies will become unrealistic in the future. From the user's point of view, it will then be desirable for hardware and software prices to be *separated*. The best software to meet the needs of a particular user may well be prepared by the manufacturer of the selected equipment. But with compatible equipment being produced by several vendors it may be that another vendor's software will be preferable. Or it is possible that an independent software firm (or even another computer-using organization) will have the best software value. The user will possibly choose to acquire software from a number of sources. A separation in hardware and software pricing will, of course, enhance the growth potential of software specialty organizations.

THE OUTLOOK FOR BUSINESS INFORMATION SYSTEMS

Trend toward quick-response systems

There is a trend in the direction of the judicious use of quick-response systems. As pointed out in previous chapters, however, the degree of quickness needed will vary; therefore, the needs of each business will

[6] Many of these firms will be engaged to help with the preparation of the formidable multiprogramming software required for new time-shared installations.

[7] Their proprietary rights may be protected by contractual arrangements, by copyrights, and, perhaps, by future patents. Much more attention will be given in the future to the protection of software property rights.

[8] For an excellent, and more-detailed discussion of this topic, see Richard G. Canning, "Coming Changes in the Software Market," *EDP Analyzer*, vol. 4, July, 1966, pp. 7–12.

determine the speed with which records are updated. Real time processing will be increasingly common in those applications where immediate updating of records is justifiable.

When the time limitations are not so severe, online processing, with periodic updating of records, will be frequently used in place of traditional batch processing methods. Source document data will be keyed directly into the computer; thus, the use of intermediate cards or tapes will be eliminated, and the computer can be programmed to check input and develop control totals. The source documents which may be required will, of course, be accumulated for short periods of time, but sorting can be eliminated, batch sizes can be smaller, and data flow can be steadier.

The advantages of quick-response systems—e.g., they allow managers to react more quickly to changes in the external environment, and they give managers quicker answers to inquiries—are responsible for the growing interest in their use. But in spite of such possible advantages, batch processing is economical, is suited to many types of applications, and will continue to account for the bulk of the work done for some time to come.

Movement toward broader systems

In the next five years companies will increase their efforts to find ways and means of consolidating data processing activities into broader and more-integrated systems. A large number of organizations will be moving in this direction, but because of the complexities involved the movement will be gradual. Firms will increasingly seek to define and classify certain types of basic data commonly so that better integration will be possible. Developmental work on corporate data banks, which will replace a multitude of the independent files maintained at the present time, will receive greater attention. The purchase of financial and marketing information in the form of cards or magnetic tape will grow; as a result, agreement in data-coding methods between information supplier and customer will become more important and will, in some cases, lead to standardized data descriptions.

Eventually, it is likely that many data systems which cross company lines will be linked together by compatible computer networks. Buyers and sellers may integrate their systems; and firms which perform similar services (in addition to airlines) may be connected by intercompany networks.[9] In the realm of account billing and payment there

[9] For thoughts on these longer-range possibilities, see Felix Kaufman, "Data Systems That Cross Company Boundaries," *Harvard Business Review*, vol. 44, January–February, 1966, pp. 141-155.

may eventually be a virtual elimination of the use of checks drawn on banks. The "checkless society" might operate in an individual's case as follows: (1) his pay would be credited to his account in the banking system automatically on authorization by his employer; (2) at the end of the month, the bills he owed would be entered (in the form of claims) into a banking central-clearing operation by his creditors; (3) he would approve the valid claims and authorize the banking system to make payment (perhaps by using a Touch-Tone telephone); (4) payment would be handled automatically by the banking-system computers. The need to prepare and mail checks would thus be largely eliminated. If all this sounds pretty far-fetched to you, consider this fact: a special committee has been organized by the American Bankers Association (a sober group of individuals) to give serious thought and study to this very concept. The committee plans to select a number of cities for checkless-society pilot projects.[10]

The growth of time sharing

Time-shared computers will not bring about a decline in the number of small free-standing machines in the next decade. But there will be substantial and accelerating growth in the number of large time sharing facilities; and these facilities will represent an increasing proportion of the total computer investment. The reader should not be surprised at this conclusion. Many of the predictions made in this final chapter depend in whole or in part on the use of time sharing equipment. A number of future trends—e.g., (1) the greater use of online I/O devices to provide a direct man-machine interface, (2) the greater communication between large machines and multitudes of smaller compatible ones, (3) the rapid increase in the use of data communications facilities, (4) the growth of conversational programming, (5) the trend toward quick-response systems, and (6) the development of broader intracompany and intercompany data systems—are all intimately associated with, and generally based upon, the growth of time sharing systems.

The majority of the time-shared systems installed in the next five years will be for the use of a single organization. But more "information utilities" will be established and will prove to be economical and

---

[10] For additional material on the checkless society, see *ibid.*, pp. 150-152; Robert V. Head, "Banking Automation: A Critical Appraisal," *Datamation*, vol. 11, July, 1965; and Dale L. Reistad, "Banking Automation: 1975," *Banking*, July, 1964, pp. 45-47.

successful.[11] Beyond the five-year period, the size polarization of computing equipment mentioned earlier in this chapter will begin to take shape. The speed with which information utilities appear on the scene will depend upon the speed with which formidable software obstacles can be overcome.

THE OUTLOOK FOR MANAGERS

In the operation of their businesses, managers must contend with the rapid scientific, social, and economic movements which are taking place in this nation and in the world. Scientific advances will result in the development of new products and the appearance of new processes; and population advances will result in more people to feed, clothe, house, educate, employ, and transport. Markets will change to accommodate changing tastes, the greater mobility of the population, and the changes in age composition.

The managerial implications of such changes are clear—the manager must be prepared to make continuous readjustments in his plans. He must make decisions about new and existing products and services; he must make decisions about new markets and about the channels of distribution to use; and he must determine how a more-flexible capital investment structure can best be acquired. Furthermore, he must make these decisions within the limits of a reaction time period which is constantly shrinking![12] If he is to compete effectively in the future, he must receive information which is accurate, timely, complete, and pertinent. Because of difficulties experienced with traditional information systems, businesses have developed quicker-reacting and more-integrated systems as a means of meeting their informational needs. Much more will be done along these lines in the future.

The computer is the tool which will provide needed information for managers of the future. It ". . .will help open as many new business opportunities tomorrow as past technology has occasioned today. And

---

[11] It is impossible to list all the sources of predictions about the bright future of information utilities. Some representative articles are Martin Greenberger, "The Two Sides of Time-sharing," *Datamation*, November, 1965, pp. 33−36; R. M. Fano and F. J. Corbato, "Time-sharing on Computers," *Scientific American*, vol. 215, September, 1966, pp. 129−140; and Richard E. Sprague, "The Information Utilities," *Business Automation*, March, 1965, pp. 42−47.

[12] President Thomas J. Ready, Jr., of Kaiser Aluminum and Chemical Corporation has stated in this connection: "A major change now that could take place over a three-year period could occur in a year or less, five years hence." (Quoted by Jack B. Weiner in "What's Ahead in Management?," *Dun's Review and Modern Industry*, January, 1965, p. 32.)

it will reap obsolescence in the same fashion for many businesses that are alive today."[13] If present and future managers want to prevent their firms from possibly being numbered among the obsolescent businesses, they will have to prepare for a successful working relationship with computerized information processing. And they will have to learn to adapt their operations to include the use of computer-dependent decision-making techniques. The middle manager who is able to apply the coming technological and systems developments in his job should have no fear about his future. He will not become extinct; rather, he will be in demand and will function in a setting which will be more challenging and stimulating.

The computer cannot and will not make difficult managerial decisions. "But it will greatly multiply the ability, the effectiveness and the impact of those people of intelligence and judgment who take the trouble to find out what the computer is all about."[14] And that is the message with which we began this book. You now have found out something about what a computer is, what it can and cannot do, and how it operates; and you now have an idea of the broad impact which computers have (and will have) on businesses and on the people who manage them. By continuing to build upon this foundation, you will be preparing for the challenging and competitive business environment of tomorrow.

SUMMARY

Significant advances will be made in hardware in the next five years. The bulk of computer input will continue to be in the form of punched cards and magnetic tape, but with increasing emphasis being placed on time sharing there will be greater use made of online I/O terminals. The use of optical character readers will grow.

Improvements in integrated circuit technology will result in smaller and faster central processors. Substantial cost reductions for a given level of computing power will be forthcoming, and storage devices will have larger storage capability. Higher recording densities will improve the performance of tapes, disks, cards, and strips. The number of small computers will grow as will the number of large time-shared machines. With the growth in time sharing will come greater communication between large machines and compatible smaller ones and increased use of data transmission facilities.

[13] James H. Binger, "The Computer: Engine of the Eighties," *Advanced Management Journal*, January, 1967, p. 27. This article, written by the Chairman of the Board of Honeywell, Inc., delves into some of the broader social changes which may appear in the 1980s.

[14] Peter F. Drucker, "What the Computer Will Be Telling You," *Nation's Business*, vol. 54, August, 1966, p. 90.

Procedure oriented languages will become more dominant. Compilers will be improved, and machine oriented symbolic languages will continue to decline in use. Applications packages will grow in popularity as will the use of services provided by software specialty organizations. Present hardware and software pricing policies will become unrealistic as hardware costs represent less and less of the total installation investment.

Although batch processing will continue to account for the bulk of the work done for some time to come, more systems with quick-response features will be designed and implemented in the next five years. Companies will increase their efforts to find ways of consolidating data processing activities into broader and more-integrated systems. These trends are developing because of dissatisfaction with the traditional ways of processing information.

Managers will face a rewarding and challenging future — *if* they plan and prepare for it. They will have to make decisions in a more complex and dynamic setting, and they will have less time to react to problem situations. But they can have access to higher-quality information upon which to base their decisions.

DISCUSSION QUESTIONS

1 What is a distributed computer?

2 How may Touch-Tone telephones be used as an I/O device?

3 What is conversational programming?

4 (*a*) Why may it be desirable, from the user's point of view, to have separate prices for hardware and software? (*b*) Why may computer manufacturers object to such a pricing policy?

5 (*a*) What is meant by the checkless society? (*b*) How might we also have a cashless society?

SELECTED REFERENCES

In addition to the references suggested in the chapter footnotes, the interested reader might examine the following sources:

H. Igor Ansoff, "The Firm of the Future," *Harvard Business Review*, September-October, 1965, pp. 162-163ff.

George Berkwitt, "Middle Managers vs. the Computer," *Dun's Review and Modern Industry*, November, 1966, pp. 40-42ff.

Richard G. Canning, "Trends in Corporate Data Systems," *EDP Analyzer*, August, 1966.

John Diebold, "What's Ahead in Information Technology," *Harvard Business Review*, September-October, 1965, pp. 76-82.

Thomas L. Whisler, "The Manager and the Computer," *The Journal of Accountancy*, January, 1965, pp. 27-32.

GLOSSARY

The communication of facts and ideas in the dynamic field of information processing is dependent on a mutual understanding of the technical terms used. Recognizing the need for a common information processing vocabulary, the USA Standard Committee, X3, on Computer and Information Processing, working under the Operating Procedures of the United States of America Standards Institute, prepared the "USA Standard Vocabulary for Information Processing." The Standards Institute approved and published this standard in 1966. The abridged glossary of terms which follows has been excerpted from this most authoritative of sources. Those words which are printed in *italics* are also defined elsewhere in this abridged vocabulary.

This material from "USA Standard Vocabulary for Information Processing," X3.12-1966, has been reprinted by permission of the United States of America Standards Institute. Copies of this standard may be purchased from the United States of America Standards Institute, 10 East 40th Street, New York, New York 10016.

Absolute Address (1) An *address* that is permanently assigned by the machine designer to a storage location. (2) A pattern of *characters* that identifies a unique storage location without further modification. (3) Synonymous with Machine Address.

Absolute Error (1) The amount of *error* expressed in the same units as the quantity containing the error. (2) Loosely, the absolute value of the error, i.e., the magnitude of the error without regard to its algebraic sign.

Access See *Random Access, Serial Access.*

Access Time (1) The time interval between the instant at which data are called for from a storage device and the instant delivery is completed, i.e., the read time. (2) The time interval between the instant at which data are requested to be stored and the instant at which storage is completed, i.e., the write time.

Accounting Machine   (1) A keyboard actuated machine that prepares accounting records. (2) A machine that reads data from external storage media, such as cards or tapes, and automatically produces accounting records or tabulations, usually on continuous forms.

Accumulator   A *register* in which the result of an arithmetic or logic operation is formed.

Accuracy   The degree of freedom from *error*, that is, the degree of conformity to truth or to a rule. Accuracy is contrasted with *precision*, e.g., four-place numerals are less precise than six-place numerals; nevertheless a properly computed four-place numeral might be more accurate than an improperly computed six-place numeral.

Adapting   See *Self-Adapting*.

Adder   (1) A device whose output is a representation of the sum of the quantities represented by its inputs. (2) See *Half-Adder*.

Address   (1) An identification, as represented by a name, label, or number, for a *register*, location in storage, or any other data source or destination such as the location of a station in a communication network. (2) Loosely, any part of an *instruction* that specifies the location of an *operand* for the instruction. (3) See *Absolute Address, Base Address, Direct Address, Indirect Address, Machine Address, Relative Address, Symbolic Address*.

Address Format   The arrangement of the *address* parts of an *instruction*. The expression "Plus-One" is frequently used to indicate that one of the addresses specifies the location of the next instruction to be executed, such as one-plus-one, two-plus-one, three-plus-one, four-plus-one.

Address Part   A part of an *instruction* word that specifies the *address* of an *operand*.

Address Register   A *register* in which an *address* is stored.

ADP (Automatic Data Processing)   Pertaining to data processing equipment such as *EAM* and *EDP* equipment.

ALGOL (Algorithmic Oriented Language)   An international procedure oriented language.

Algorithm   A prescribed set of well-defined rules or processes for the solution of a problem in a finite number of steps, e.g., a full statement of an arithmetic procedure for evaluating sin x to a stated precision. Contrast with *Heuristic*.

Algorithmic Language   A *language* designed for expressing *algorithms*.

Allocation   See *Storage Allocation*.

Alphabet   An ordered set of unique representations called characters, e.g., the 26 letters of the Roman alphabet, 0 and 1.

Alphameric   Same as *Alphanumeric*.

Alphanumeric   Pertaining to a character set that contains both letters and numerals, and usually other characters. Synonymous with Alphameric.

Analog   Pertaining to *data* in the form of continuously variable physical quantities. Contrast with *Digital*.

Analog Computer   A *computer* that operates on analog data by performing physical processes on these data. Contrast with *Digital Computer*.

Analysis   (1) The methodical investigation of a problem, and the separation of the problem into smaller related units for further detailed study. (2) See *Numerical Analysis*.

Analyst   A person who defines problems and develops algorithms and procedures for their solution.

Annotation   An added descriptive comment or explanatory note.

Arithmetic Unit   The unit of a computing system that contains the circuits that perform arithmetic operations.

Artificial Intelligence   The capability of a device to perform functions that are normally associated with human intelligence, such as reasoning, learning, and self-improvement. Related to *Machine Learning*.

Artificial Language   A *language* based on a set of prescribed rules that are established prior to its usage. Contrast with *Natural Language*.

ASCII   American Standard Code for Information Interchange, X3.4. *

Assemble   To prepare a machine language program from a symbolic language program by substituting absolute operation codes for symbolic operation codes and absolute or relocatable addresses for symbolic addresses.

Assembler   A program that *assembles*.

Associative Storage   A storage device in which storage locations are identified by their contents, not by names or positions. Synonymous with Content Addressed Storage, Parallel Search Storage.

Asynchronous Computer   A *computer* in which each event or the performance of each *operation* starts as a result of a signal generated by the completion of the previous event or operation, or by the availability of the parts of the computer required for the next event or operation.

Automatic Check   A *check* performed by equipment built in specifically for checking purposes. Synonymous with Built-In Check. Contrast with *Programmed Check*.

Automatic Coding   The machine-assisted preparation of *machine language* routines.

Automatic Computer   A computer that can perform a sequence of operations without intervention by a human operator.

Automatic Data Processing   See *ADP*.

Automatic Programming   The process of using a computer to perform some stages of the work involved in preparing a *program*.

*All American Standards are now designated USA Standards.

Automation (1) The implementation of processes by automatic means. (2) The theory, art, or technique of making a process more automatic. (3) The investigation, design, development, and application of methods of rendering processes automatic, self-moving, or self-controlling.

Auxiliary Operation An *operation* performed by equipment not under continuous control of the *central processing unit*.

Auxiliary Storage A *storage* that supplements another storage.

Band A group of circular recording *tracks* on a storage device such as a drum or disc.

Base (1) A reference value. (2) Same as *Radix*.

Base Address A given address from which an *absolute address* is derived by combination with a *relative address*.

Benchmark Problem A problem used to evaluate the performance of computers relative to each other.

Bias The amount by which the average of a set of values departs from a reference value.

Binary (1) Pertaining to a characteristic or property involving a selection, choice, or condition in which there are two possibilities. (2) Pertaining to the numeration system with a *radix* of two.

Binary Cell A *storage cell* of one binary digit capacity, e.g., a single bit *register*.

Binary Code A *code* that makes use of exactly two distinct characters, usually 0 and 1.

Binary Coded Decimal Pertaining to a decimal notation in which the individual decimal digits are each represented by a group of binary digits; e.g., in the 8-4-2-1 binary coded decimal notation, the number twenty-three is represented as 0010 0011 whereas in binary notation, twenty-three is represented as 10111.

Binary Digit A character used to represent one of the two digits in the *numeration system* with a *radix* of two. Abbreviated "Bit."

Binary Number Loosely, a *binary numeral*.

Binary Numeral The binary representation of a number; e.g., "101" is the binary numeral and "V" is the Roman numeral of the number of fingers on one hand.

Binary Search A search in which a set of items is divided into two parts, one part is rejected, and the process is repeated on the accepted part until those items with the desired property are found. Synonymous with Dichotomizing Search.

Bionics A branch of technology relating the functions, characteristics, and phenomena of living systems to the development of hardware systems.

Bistable Pertaining to a device capable of assuming either one of two stable states.

Bit (1) A binary digit. (2) See *Check Bit, Parity Bit*.

Blank Character A *character* used to produce a character space on an output medium.

Block A set of things, such as words, characters, or digits, handled as a unit.

Block Diagram A diagram of a system, instrument, computer, or program in which selected portions are represented by annotated boxes and interconnecting lines.

Boolean (1) Pertaining to the processes used in the algebra formulated by George Boole. (2) Pertaining to the operations of formal logic.

Branch (1) A set of instructions that is executed between two successive *decision instructions*. (2) To select a branch as in (1). (3) Loosely, a *conditional jump*.

Branchpoint A place in a routine where a *branch* is selected.

Buffer (1) A *storage device* used to compensate for a difference in rate of flow of data, or time of occurrence of events, when transmitting data from one device to another. (2) An isolating circuit used to prevent a driven circuit from influencing the driving circuit.

Built-In Check Same as *Automatic Check*.

Business Data Processing Data processing for business purposes, e.g., recording and summarizing the financial transactions of a business.

Byte A sequence of adjacent *binary digits* operated upon as a unit and usually shorter than a word.

Calculator (1) A device capable of performing arithmetic. (2) A calculator as in (1) that requires frequent manual intervention. (3) Generally and historically, a device for carrying out logic and arithmetic digital operations of any kind.

Call (1) To transfer control to a specified *closed subroutine*. (2) In communications, the action performed by the calling party, or the operations necessary in making a call, or the effective use made of a connection between two stations.

Calling Sequence A specified arrangement of instructions and data necessary to set up and call a given *subroutine*.

Card Hopper A device that holds cards and makes them available to a card feed mechanism. Synonymous with Input Magazine. Contrast with *Card Stacker*.

Card Stacker An output device that accumulates *punched cards* in a deck. Contrast with *Card Hopper*.

Carriage Return The operation that causes the next character to be printed at the left margin.

Central Processing Unit The unit of a computing system that includes the circuits controlling the interpretation and execution of *instructions*.

Chad The piece of material removed when forming a hole or notch in a storage medium such as *punched tape* or *punched cards*.

Chadless Pertaining to the punching of tape in which *chad* does not result.

Channel (1) A path along which signals can be sent, e.g., data channel, output channel. (2) The portion of a storage medium that is accessible to a given reading station, e.g., *track, band*. (3) In communication, a means of one-way transmission. Contrast with *Circuit*.

Character (1) An elementary mark or event that is used to represent *data*. A character is often in the form of a graphic spatial arrangement of connected or adjacent strokes. (2) See *Blank Character, Check Character, Control Character, Special Character*.

Character Recognition The identification of graphic, phonic, or other *characters* by automatic means. See *Magnetic Ink Character Recognition, Optical Character Recognition*.

Check See *Automatic Check, Built-In Check, Duplication Check, Echo Check, Odd-Even Check, Parity Check, Programmed Check, Summation Check, Transfer Check*.

Check Bit A binary *check digit*.

Check Character A *character* used for the purpose of performing a *check*.

Check Digit A *digit* used for the purpose of performing a *check*.

Checkpoint A place in a *routine* where a *check*, or a recording of data for restart purposes, is performed.

Circuit In communications, a means of two-way communication between two points, comprising associated "Go" and "Return" channels. Contrast with *Channel*.

Clear (1) To place a storage device into a prescribed state, usually that denoting zero or blank. (2) To place a *binary cell* into the zero state.

Clock (1) A device that generates periodic signals used for synchronization. (2) A device that measures and indicates time.

Closed Subroutine A *subroutine* that can be stored at one place and can be connected to a routine by linkages at one or more locations. Contrast with *Open Subroutine*.

COBOL (Common Business Oriented Language) A business data processing language.

Code (1) A set of rules that is used to convert data from one representation to another, e.g., the set of correspondences in the American Standard Code for Information Interchange, X3.4. (2) The set of representations defined by the set of rules as in (1), e.g., a coded character set as in the above American Standard Code or the repertory of instructions for a particular computer. (3) Same as *Encode*. (4) See *Binary Code, Computer Code, Excess Three Code, Machine Code, Operation Code*.

Collate To compare and *merge* two or more similarly ordered sets of items into one ordered set.

Collating Sequence   An ordering assigned to a set of items, such that any two sets in that assigned order can be collated.

Collator   A device to *collate* sets of *punched cards* or other documents into a sequence.

Column   (1) A vertical arrangement of characters or other expressions. (2) Loosely, a digit place.

Command   (1) A control signal. (2) Loosely, an instruction in *machine language.* (3) Loosely, a mathematical or logic operator.

Communication Link   The physical means of connecting one location to another for the purpose of transmitting and receiving information.

Compile   To prepare a *machine language* program from a computer program written in another programming language by making use of the overall logic structure of the program, or generating more than one machine instruction for each symbolic statement, or both, as well as performing the function of an *assembler.*

Compiler   A program that *compiles.*

Computer   (1) A device capable of solving problems by accepting data, performing prescribed operations on the data, and supplying the results of these operations. Various types of computers are *calculators, digital computers,* and *analog computers.* (2) In information processing, usually an automatic *stored program computer.* (3) See *Analog Computer, Asynchronous Computer, Automatic Computer, Digital Computer, General Purpose Computer, Special Purpose Computer, Stored Program Computer, Synchronous Computer.*

Computer Code   A *machine code* for a specific computer.

Computer Instruction   A *machine instruction* for a specific computer.

Computer Network   A complex consisting of two or more interconnected computing units.

Computer Program   A plan or *routine* for solving a problem on a computer, as contrasted with such terms as fiscal program, military program, and development program.

Computer Word   A sequence of bits or characters treated as a unit and capable of being stored in one computer *location.* Synonymous with Machine Word.

Conditional Jump   A *jump* that occurs if specified criteria are met.

Connector   In *flowcharting* the means of representing the convergence of more than one *flowline* into one, or the divergence of one flowline into more than one. It may also represent a break in a single flowline for continuation in another area.

Console   That part of a computer used for communication between the operator or maintenance engineer and the computer.

Control See *Numerical Control, Sequential Control.*

Control Character A character whose occurrence in a particular context initiates, modifies, or stops a control operation, e.g., a character to control *carriage return.*

Control Panel (1) A part of a computer *console* that contains manual controls. (2) Same as *Plugboard.*

Control Unit In a digital computer, those parts that effect the retrieval of instructions in proper sequence, the interpretation of each instruction, and the application of the proper signals to the arithmetic unit and other parts in accordance with this interpretation.

Convert To change the representation of data from one form to another, e.g., to change numerical data from binary to decimal or from cards to tape.

Copy To reproduce data leaving the original data unchanged. Synonymous with Duplicate.

Core See *Magnetic Core.*

Counter (1) A device such as a *register* or storage location used to represent the number of occurrences of an event. (2) See *Instruction Counter.*

Crosstalk The unwanted energy transferred from one circuit, called the "disturbing" circuit, to another circuit, call the "disturbed" circuit.

Cryogenics The study and use of devices utilizing properties of materials near absolute zero in temperature.

Cybernetics The theory of control and communication in the machine and the animal.

Cycle (1) An interval of space or time in which one set of events or phenomena is completed. (2) Any set of operations that is repeated regularly in the same sequence. The operations may be subject to variations on each repetition.

Data Any representations such as *characters* or *analog* quantities to which meaning might be assigned.

Data Processing Pertaining to any *operation* or combination of operations on data.

Data Processor Any device capable of performing *operations* on data, e.g., a desk *calculator*, a tape recorder, an *analog computer*, a *digital computer.*

Data Reduction The transformation of raw data into a more useful form, e.g., smoothing to reduce noise.

Debug To detect, locate, and remove mistakes from a routine or malfunctions from a computer. Synonymous with Troubleshoot.

Decimal (1) Pertaining to a characteristic or property involving a selection, choice, or condition in which there are ten possibilities. (2) Pertaining to the *numeration system* with a *radix* of ten. (3) See *Binary Coded Decimal.*

Decision A determination of future action.

Decision Instruction An instruction that effects the selection of a *branch* of program, e.g., a *conditional jump instruction*.

Decision Table A table of all contingencies that are to be considered in the description of a problem, together with the actions to be taken. Decision tables are sometimes used in place of *flowcharts* for problem description and documentation.

Deck A collection of *punched cards*.

Decode To apply a *code* so as to reverse some previous *encoding*.

Decoder (1) A device that *decodes*. (2) A matrix of logic elements that selects one or more output channels according to the combination of input signals present.

Delay The amount of time by which an event is retarded.

Density See *Packing Density*.

Destructive Read A *read* process that also erases the data in the source.

Diagnostic Pertaining to the detection and isolation of a malfunction or mistake.

Diagram See *Block Diagram, Functional Diagram, Logic Diagram, Venn Diagram*.

Digit (1) A *character* used to represent one of the non-negative integers smaller than the radix, e.g., in decimal notation, one of the characters 0 to 9. (2) See *Binary Digit, Check Digit, Significant Digit*.

Digital Pertaining to data in the form of *digits*. Contrast with *Analog*.

Digital Computer A computer that operates on discrete data by performing arithmetic and logic processes on these data. Contrast with *Analog Computer*.

Digitize To express data in a *digital* form.

Direct Address An *address* that specifies the location of an operand. Synonymous with One-Level Address.

Disc See *Magnetic Disc*.

Display A visual presentation of data.

Display Tube A tube, usually a cathode ray tube, used to display data.

Document (1) A medium and the data recorded on it for human use, e.g., a report sheet, a book. (2) By extension, any record that has permanence and that can be read by man or machine.

Documentation The collecting, organizing, storing, citing, and disseminating of documents or the information recorded in documents.

Double Precision Pertaining to the use of two *computer words* to represent a number.

Downtime The time interval during which a device is malfunctioning.

Drive See *Tape Drive*.

Drum   See *Magnetic Drum.*

Dump   (1) To copy the contents of all or part of a storage, usually from an internal storage into an external storage. (2) A process as in (1). (3) The data resulting from the process as in (1) (4) See *Dynamic Dump, Postmortem Dump, Selective Dump, Snapshot Dump, Static Dump.*

Duodecimal   (1) Pertaining to a characteristic or property involving a selection, choice, or condition in which there are twelve possibilities. (2) Pertaining to the *numeration system* with a *radix* of twelve.

Duplex   In communications, pertaining to a simultaneous two-way independent transmission in both directions. Contrast with *Half Duplex.* Synonymous with Full Duplex.

Duplication Check   A *check* based on the consistency of two independent performances of the same task.

Dynamic Dump   A *dump* that is performed during the execution of a program.

EAM (Electrical Accounting Machine)   Pertaining to data processing equipment that is predominantly electromechanical such as a *keypunch*, mechanical *sorter, collator,* and tabulator.

Echo Check   A method of checking the accuracy of transmission of data in which the received data are returned to the sending end for comparison with the original data.

Edit   To modify the form or format of data, e.g., to insert or delete characters such as page numbers or decimal points.

EDP (Electronic Data Processing)   Pertaining to data processing equipment that is predominantly electronic such as an electronic digital computer.

Electronic Data Processing   See *EDP.*

Electrostatic Storage   A *storage device* that stores data as electrostatically charged areas on a dielectric surface.

Encode   To apply the rules of a *code.* Synonymous with Code (3).

End-Around Carry   A carry from the most significant digit place to the least significant digit place.

Entry Point   In a *routine*, any place to which control can be passed.

Error   (1) Any discrepancy between a computed, observed, or measured quantity and the true, specified, or theoretically correct value or condition. (2) See *Absolute Error, Inherited Error.*

Error Range   The difference between the highest and lowest *error* values.

Excess Three Code   A *binary coded decimal* representation in which each decimal digit N is represented by the binary equivalent of N plus 3.

Executive Routine   A *routine* that controls the execution of other routines. Synonymous with Supervisory Routine.

Fault   A physical condition that causes a device, a component, or an element to fail to perform in a required manner, e.g., a short circuit, a broken wire, an intermittent connection.

Field   In a *record*, a specified area used for a particular category of data, e.g., a group of card columns used to represent a wage rate or a set of bit locations in a computer word used to express the address of the operand.

File   A collection of related *records* treated as a unit. Thus in inventory control, one line of an invoice forms an *item*, a complete invoice forms a record, and the complete set of such records forms a file.

File Gap   An area on a storage medium, such as tape, used to indicate the end of a file.

File Maintenance   The activity of keeping a file up to date by adding, changing, or deleting data.

Fixed-Cycle Operation   An operation that is completed in a specified number of regularly timed execution cycles.

Fixed Point   Pertaining to a *numeration system* in which the position of the point is fixed with respect to one end of the numerals, according to some convention.

Fixed Storage   A storage device that stores data not alterable by computer instructions, e.g., *magnetic core* storage with a lockout feature, or punched paper tape. Synonymous with Nonerasable Storage, Permanent Storage, Read-Only Storage.

Flag   (1) Any of various types of indicators used for identification, e.g., a wordmark. (2) A character that signals the occurrence of some condition, such as the end of a word. (3) Synonymous with Mark, Sentinel, Tag.

Flip-Flop   A circuit or device containing active elements, capable of assuming either one of two stable states at a given time. Synonymous with Toggle (1).

Floating Point   Pertaining to a *numeration system* in which the position of the point does not remain fixed with respect to one end of the numerals.

Flow Direction   In flowcharting, the antecedent-to-successor relation, indicated by arrows or other conventions, between operations on a *flowchart*.

Flowchart   A graphical representation for the definition, analysis, or solution of a problem, in which symbols are used to represent operations, data, flow, and equipment.

Flowchart Symbol   A symbol used to represent operations, data, flow, or equipment in problem description.

Flowline   In flowcharting, a line representing a connecting path between symbols on a *flowchart*.

Flying Spot Scanner   In *OCR*, a device employing a moving spot of light to scan a sample space, the intensity of the transmitted or reflected light being sensed by a photoelectric transducer.

Font   (1) A family or assortment of characters of a given size and style. (2) See *Type Font.*

Formal Logic   The study of the structure and form of valid argument without regard to the meaning of the terms in the argument.

Format   (1) The arrangement of data. (2) See *Address Format.*

FORTRAN (Formula Translating System)   Any of several specific procedure oriented languages.

Function   A specific purpose of an entity or its characteristic action.

Functional Design   The specification of the working relations between the parts of a system in terms of their characteristic actions.

Functional Diagram   A diagram that represents the functional relationships among the parts of a system.

General Purpose Computer   A computer that is designed to solve a wide class of problems.

Generate   To produce a program by selection of subsets from a set of skeletal coding under the control of *parameters.*

Generator   A controlling routine that performs a *generate* function, e.g., Report Generator, I/O Generator.

Half-Adder   A combinational logic element having two outputs, S and C, and two inputs, A and B, such that the outputs are related to the inputs according to the following table.

Input		Output	
A	B	S	C
0	0	0	0
0	1	1	0
1	0	1	0
1	1	0	1

S denotes "Sum Without Carry," C denotes "Carry." Two Half-Adders may be used for performing binary addition.

Half Duplex   In communications, pertaining to an alternate, one way at a time, independent transmission. Contrast with *Duplex.*

Hardware   Physical equipment, e.g., mechanical, magnetic, electrical, or electronic devices. Contrast with *Software.*

Head   A device that reads, records, or erases data on a storage medium, e.g., a small electromagnet used to read, write, or erase data on a magnetic drum or tape, or the set of perforating, reading, or marking devices used for punching, reading, or printing on paper tape.

Heuristic Pertaining to exploratory methods of problem solving in which solutions are discovered by evaluation of the progress made toward the final result. Contrast with *Algorithm*.

Hexadecimal Same as *Sexadecimal*.

I/O (Input/Output) Input or output or both.

Identifier A symbol whose purpose is to identify, indicate, or name a body of data.

Indirect Address An address that specifies a storage location that contains either a *direct address* or another indirect address. Synonymous with Multilevel Address.

Information The meaning assigned to data by known conventions.

Information Processing (1) The processing of data that represents *information*. (2) Loosely, *automatic data processing*.

Information Retrieval The methods and procedures for recovering specific information from stored data.

Information Theory A branch of mathematics that is concerned with the properties of transmitted messages. The messages are subject to certain probabilities of transmission failure, distortion, and noise.

Inherited Error The *error* in the value of quantities that serve as the initial conditions at the beginning of a step in a step-by-step calculation.

Initialize To set counters, switches, and addresses to zero or other starting values at the beginning of, or at prescribed points in, a computer routine.

Input (1) The data to be processed. (2) The state or sequence of states occurring on a specified input channel. (3) The device or collective set of devices used for bringing data into another device. (4) A *channel* for impressing a state on a device or logic element. (5) The process of transferring data from an external storage to an internal storage. (6) See *Manual Input*.

Instruction (1) A statement that specifies an *operation* and the values or locations of its *operands*. In this context, the term instruction is preferable to the terms command or order which are sometimes used synonymously. Command should be reserved for electronic signals, and order should be reserved for sequence, interpolation, and related usage. (2) See *Computer Instruction, Decision Instruction, Machine Instruction, Macro Instruction, Repetition Instruction*.

Instruction Counter A counter that indicates the location of the next computer instruction to be interpreted.

Instruction Register A *register* that stores an instruction for execution.

Instruction Repertory The set of *operations* that can be represented in a given *operation code*.

Interface   A shared boundary.

Interleave   To arrange parts of one sequence of things or events so that they alternate with parts of one or more other sequences of things or events and so that each sequence retains its identity.

Interpreter   (1) A program that translates and executes each *source language* expression before translating and executing the next one. (2) A device that prints on a punched card the data already punched in the card.

Interrupt   To stop a process in such a way that it can be resumed.

Item   A collection of related characters, treated as a unit. Contrast with *File*.

Jump   (1) A departure from the normal sequence of executing instructions in a computer. Synonymous with Transfer (1). (2) See *Conditional Jump*.

Keypunch   A keyboard actuated device that punches holes in a card to represent data.

Label   A key attached to the item of data that it identifies.

Language   (1) A set of representations, conventions, and rules used to convey information. (2) See *Algorithmic Language, Artificial Language, Machine Language, Natural Language, Object Language, Problem Oriented Language, Procedure Oriented Language, Programming Language, Source Language, Target Language*.

Latency   The time between the completion of the interpretation of an *address* and the start of the actual transfer from the addressed location.

Leader   The blank section of tape at the beginning of a reel of tape.

Library   (1) A collection of organized information used for study and reference. (2) See *Program Library*.

Library Routine   A proven *routine* that is maintained in a program library.

Line Printing   The printing of an entire line of characters as a unit.

Linear Programming   The analysis or solution of problems in which linear function of a number of variables is to be maximized or minimized when those variables are subject to a number of constraints in the form of linear inequalities.

Linkage   In programming, coding that connects two separately coded routines.

Load   In programming, to place data into internal storage.

Load-And-Go   An operating technique in which there are no stops between the loading and execution phases of a program, and which may include *assembling* or *compiling*.

Location   (1) Loosely, any place in which data may be stored. (2) See *Protected Location*.

Logic   See *Formal Logic, Symbolic Logic*.

Logic Design The specification of the working relations between the parts of a system in terms of *symbolic logic* and without primary regard for hardware implementation.

Logic Diagram A diagram that represents a *logic design* and sometimes the hardware implementation.

Loop A sequence of instructions that is executed repeatedly until a terminal condition prevails.

Machine Address Same as *Absolute Address*.

Machine Code An *operation code* that a machine is designed to recognize.

Machine Instruction An *instruction* that a machine can recognize and execute.

Machine Language A *language* that is used directly by a machine.

Machine Learning Pertaining to the ability of a device to improve its performance based on its past performance. Related to *Artificial Intelligence*.

Machine Word Same as *Computer Word*.

Macro Instruction An instruction in a *source language* that is equivalent to a specified sequence of *machine instructions*.

Magnetic Card A card with a magnetic surface on which data can be stored by selective magnetization of portions of the flat surface.

Magnetic Core A configuration of magnetic material that is, or is intended to be, placed in a spatial relationship to current-carrying conductors and whose magnetic properties are essential to its use. It may be used to concentrate an induced magnetic field as in a transformer, induction coil, or armature, to retain a magnetic polarization for the purpose of storing data, or for its non-linear properties as in a logic element. It may be made of such material as iron, iron oxide, or ferrite and in such shapes as wires, tapes, toroids, or thin film.

Magnetic Disc A flat circular plate with a magnetic surface on which data can be stored by selective magnetization of portions of the flat surface.

Magnetic Drum A right circular cylinder with a magnetic surface on which data can be stored by selective magnetization of portions of the curved surface.

Magnetic Ink An ink that contains particles of a magnetic substance whose presence can be detected by magnetic sensors.

Magnetic Ink Character Recognition See *MICR*.

Magnetic Storage A *storage device* that utilizes the magnetic properties of materials to store data, e.g., magnetic cores, tapes, and films.

Magnetic Tape (1) A tape with a magnetic surface on which data can be stored by selective polarization of portions of the surface. (2) A tape of magnetic material used as the constituent in some forms of magnetic cores.

Magnetic Thin Film A layer of magnetic material, usually less than one micron thick, often used for logic or storage elements.

Maintenance (1) Any activity intended to keep equipment or programs in satisfactory working condition, including tests, measurements, replacements, adjustments, and repairs. (2) See *File Maintenance*.

Malfunction The effect of a *fault*.

Manual Input (1) The entry of data by hand into a device at the time of processing. (2) The data entered as in (1).

Mathematical Model A mathematical representation of a process, device, or concept.

Matrix (1) In mathematics, a two-dimensional rectangular array of quantities. Matrices are manipulated in accordance with the rules of matrix algebra. (2) In computers, a logic network in the form of an array of input leads and output leads with logic elements connected at some of their intersections. (3) By extension, an array of any number of dimensions.

Medium The material, or configuration thereof, on which data are recorded, e.g., paper tape, cards, magnetic tape.

Memory Same as *Storage*.

Merge To combine two or more sets of items into one, usually in a specified sequence.

Message An arbitrary amount of information whose beginning and end are defined or implied.

MICR (Magnetic Ink Character Recognition) The machine recognition of characters printed with magnetic ink. Contrast with *OCR*.

Mistake A human action that produces an unintended result.

Multiplex To *interleave* or simultaneously transmit two or more messages on a single *channel*.

Multiprocessing Pertaining to the simultaneous or *interleaved* execution of two or more programs or sequences of instructions by a computer or computer network. Multiprocessing may be accomplished by *multiprogramming, parallel processing*, or both.

Multiprocessor A computer capable of multiprocessing.

Multiprogramming Pertaining to the *interleaved* execution of two or more programs by a computer. Contrast with *Parallel Processing*.

Natural Language A *language* whose rules reflect and describe current usage rather than prescribe usage. Contrast with *Artificial Language*.

Noise (1) Random variations of one or more characteristics of any entity such as voltage, current, or data. (2) Loosely, any disturbance tending to interfere with the normal operation of a device or system.

Nondestructive Read A *read* process that does not erase the data in the source.

Normal Direction Flow In *flowcharting*, a flow in a direction from left to right or top to bottom.

Normalize To adjust the representation of a quantity so that the representation lies in a prescribed range.

Number (1) A mathematical entity that may indicate quantity or amount of units. (2) Loosely, a *numeral*. (3) See *Binary Number*.

Number System Loosely, a numeration system.

Numeral (1) A representation of a *number*. (2) See *Binary Numeral*.

Numeral System Same as *Numeration System*.

Numeration System A system for the representation of numbers, e.g., the decimal system, the Roman numeral system, the binary system. Synonymous with Numeral System.

Numerical Analysis The study of methods of obtaining useful quantitative solutions to problems that have been expressed mathematically, including the study of the errors and bounds on errors in obtaining such solutions.

Numerical Control Pertaining to the automatic control of processes by the proper interpretation of numerical data.

Object Language Same as *Target Language*.

Object Program Same as *Target Program*.

OCR (Optical Character Recognition) Machine identification of printed characters through use of light-sensitive devices. Contrast with *MICR*.

Octal (1) Pertaining to a characteristic or property involving a selection, choice, or condition in which there are eight possibilities. (2) Pertaining to the *numeration system* with a *radix* of eight.

Odd-Even Check Same as *Parity Check*.

Offline Pertaining to equipment or devices not under direct control of the *central processing unit*.

Online Pertaining to equipment or devices under direct control of the *central processing unit*.

Open Subroutine A *subroutine* that must be relocated and inserted into a routine at each place it is used. Synonymous with Direct Insert Subroutine. Contrast with *Closed Subroutine*.

Openended Pertaining to a process or system that can be augmented.

Operand   That which is operated upon. An operand is usually identified by an *address part* of an instruction.

Operating System   An organized collection of techniques and procedures for operating a computer.

Operation   (1) A defined action, namely, the act of obtaining a result from one or more *operands* in accordance with a rule that completely specifies the result for any permissible combination of operands. (2) The set of such acts specified by such a rule, or the rule itself. (3) The act specified by a single computer instruction. (4) A program step undertaken or executed by a computer, e.g., addition, multiplication, extraction, comparison, shift, transfer. The operation is usually specified by the operator part of an instruction. (5) The event or specific action performed by a logic element. (6) See *Auxiliary Operation, Fixed-Cycle Operation, Sequential Operation, Serial Operation.*

Operation Code   A *code* that represents specific operations. Synonymous with Instruction Code.

Operator   (1) In the description of a process, that which indicates the action to be performed on *operands*. (2) A person who operates a machine.

Optical Character Recognition   See *OCR.*

Optical Scanner   (1) A device that scans optically and usually generates an *analog* or *digital* signal. (2) A device that optically scans printed or written data and generates their digital representations. (3) Synonymous with Visual Scanner.

Output   (1) Data that has been processed. (2) The state or sequence of states occurring on a specified output channel. (3) The device or collective set of devices used for taking data out of a device. (4) A *channel* for expressing a state of a device or logic element. (5) The process of transferring data from an internal storage to an external storage.

Overflow   (1) That portion of the result of an operation that exceeds the capacity of the intended unit of storage. (2) Pertaining to the generation of overflow as in (1).

Overlay   The technique of repeatedly using the same blocks of internal storage during different stages of a problem. When one routine is no longer needed in storage, another routine can replace all or part of it.

Pack   To compress several items of data in a storage medium in such a way that the individual items can later be recovered.

Packing Density   The number of useful *storage cells* per unit of dimension, e.g., the number of bits per inch stored on a magnetic tape or drum track.

Parallel   (1) Pertaining to the simultaneity of two or more processes. (2) Pertaining to the simultaneity of two or more similar or identical processes. (3) Pertaining to the simultaneous processing of the individual parts of a whole, such as the bits of a character and the characters of a word, using separate facilities for the various parts.

Parallel Processing   Pertaining to the simultaneous execution of two or more sequences of instructions by a computer having multiple arithmetic or logic units. Contrast with *Multiprogramming*.

Parameter   A variable that is given a constant value for a specific purpose or process.

Parity Bit   A *binary digit* appended to an array of bits to make the sum of all the bits always odd or always even.

Parity Check   A *check* that tests whether the number of ones (or zeros) in an array of binary digits is odd or even. Synonymous with Odd-Even Check.

Patch   (1) To modify a *routine* in a rough or expedient way. (2) A temporary electrical connection.

Plugboard   A perforated board that accepts manually inserted plugs to control the operation of equipment. Synonymous with Control Panel (2).

Point   (1) In *positional notation*, the character or implied character that separates the integral part of a numerical expression from the fractional part, e.g., a decimal point, binary point. (2) See *Branchpoint, Checkpoint, Entry Point, Fixed Point, Floating Point*.

Positional Notation   A number representation that makes use of an ordered set of digits, such that the value contributed by each digit depends on its position as well as on the digit value.

Postmortem   Pertaining to the analysis of an operation after its completion.

Postmortem Dump   A *static dump* used for *debugging* purposes that is performed at the end of a machine *run*.

Precision   (1) The degree of discrimination with which a quantity is stated, e.g., a three-digit numeral discriminates among 1000 possibilities. (2) See *Double Precision*.

Predefined Process   A process that is identified only by name and that is defined elsewhere.

Preset   To establish an initial condition, such as the control values of a loop.

Problem Description   A statement of a problem. The statement may also include a description of the method of solution, the solution itself, the transformations of data, and the relationship of procedures, data, constraints, and environments.

Problem Oriented Language   A *programming language* designed for the convenient expression of a given class of problems.

Procedure   The course of action taken for the solution of a problem.

Procedure Oriented Language   A *programming language* designed for the convenient expression of procedures used in the solution of a wide class of problems.

Processing   See *Automatic Data Processing, Business Data Processing, Data Processing, Electronic Data Processing, Information Processing, Multiprocessing, Parallel Processing.*

Processor   (1) In *hardware*, a data processor. (2) In *software*, a computer program that includes the *compiling, assembling,* translating, and related functions for a specific programming language, e.g., *COBOL* processor, *FORTRAN* processor. (3) See *Data Processor, Multiprocessor.*

Program   (1) A plan for solving a problem. (2) Loosely, a *routine.* (3) To devise a plan for solving a problem. (4) Loosely, to write a routine. (5) See *Computer Program, Object Program, Source Program, Target Program.*

Program Library   A collection of available computer *programs* and *routines.*

Programmed Check   A *check* procedure designed by the programmer and implemented specifically as a part of his program. Contrast with *Automatic Check.*

Programming   See *Automatic Programming, Linear Programming, Multiprogramming.*

Programming Language   A *language* used to prepare computer *programs.*

Protected Location   A *storage* location reserved for special purposes in which data cannot be stored without undergoing a screening procedure to establish suitability for storage therein.

Punched Card   (1) A card punched with a pattern of holes to represent data. (2) A card as in (1) before being punched.

Punched Tape   A tape on which a pattern of holes or cuts is used to represent data.

Radix   A quantity whose successive integral powers are the implicit multipliers of the sequence of digits that represent a number. For example, if the radix is five, then 143.2 means 1 times 5 to the second power, plus 4 times 5 to the first power, plus 3 times 5 to the zero power, plus 2 times 5 to the minus one power. Synonymous with Base.

Random Access   (1) Pertaining to the process of obtaining data from, or placing data into, storage where the time required for such access is independent of the location of the data most recently obtained or placed in storage. (2) Pertaining to a storage device in which the *access time* is effectively independent of the location of the data.

Range   (1) The set of values that a quantity or function may assume. (2) The difference between the highest and lowest value that a quantity or function may assume. (3) See *Error Range.*

Read   (1) To acquire data from a source. (2) See *Destructive Read, Nondestructive Read.*

Real Time (1) Pertaining to the actual time during which a physical process transpires. (2) Pertaining to the performance of a computation during the actual time that the related physical process transpires in order that results of the computation can be used in guiding the physical process.

Record A collection of related items of data, treated as a unit. Contrast with *File*.

Record Gap On a storage medium, an area used to indicate the end of a *record*.

Register (1) A device capable of storing a specified amount of data, such as one word. (2) See *Address Register, Instruction Register, Shift Register*.

Relative Address The number that specifies the difference between the *absolute address* and the *base address*.

Reliability The probability that a device will function without failure over a specified time period or amount of usage.

Relocate In programming, to move a routine from one portion of storage to another and to adjust the necessary address references so that the routine, in its new location, can be executed.

Repetition Instruction An *instruction* that causes one or more instructions to be executed an indicated number of times.

Reset (1) To restore a *storage device* to a prescribed initial state, not necessarily that denoting zero. (2) To place a *binary cell* into the state denoting zero.

Restart To reestablish the execution of a routine, using the data recorded at a *checkpoint*.

Retrieval See *Information Retrieval*.

Reverse Direction Flow In *flowcharting*, a flow in a direction other than left to right or top to bottom.

Roundoff To delete the least significant digit or digits of a numeral and to adjust the part retained in accordance with some rule.

Routine (1) A set of instructions arranged in proper sequence to cause a computer to perform a desired task. (2) See *Executive Routine, Library Routine, Service Routine, Subroutine, Supervisory Routine, Tracing Routine, Utility Routine*.

Run A single, continuous performance of a computer *routine*.

Sampling Obtaining a value of a variable at regular or intermittent intervals.

Scan To examine sequentially part by part.

Scanner See *Flying Spot Scanner, Optical Scanner*.

Search (1) To examine a set of items for those that have a desired property. (2) See *Binary Search*.

Selective Dump A *dump* of a selected area of storage.

Self-Adapting Pertaining to the ability of a system to change its performance characteristics in response to its environment.

Sequential Control A mode of computer operation in which instructions are executed consecutively unless specified otherwise by a *jump.*

Sequential Operation Pertaining to the performance of operations one after the other.

Serial (1) Pertaining to the time-sequencing of two or more processes. (2) Pertaining to the time-sequencing of two or more similar or identical processes, using the same facilities for the successive processes. (3) Pertaining to the time-sequential processing of the individual parts of a whole, such as the bits of a character or the characters of a word, using the same facilities for successive parts.

Serial Access Pertaining to the process of obtaining data from, or placing data into, storage when there is a sequential relation governing the access time to successive storage locations.

Serial Operation An *operation* whose processes are performed in a time sequence.

Service Routine A *routine* in general support of the operation of a computer, e.g., an input-output, diagnostic, tracing, or monitoring routine. Synonymous with Utility Routine.

Servomechanism (1) A feedback control system in which at least one of the system signals represents mechanical motion. (2) Any feedback control system.

Sexadecimal (1) Pertaining to a characteristic or property involving a selection, choice, or condition in which there are sixteen possibilities. (2) Pertaining to the *numeration system* with a *radix* of sixteen. (3) Synonymous with Hexadecimal.

Shift Register A *register* in which the stored data can be moved to the right or left.

Sign Position The position at which the sign of a number is located.

Signal The event or phenomenon that conveys data from one point to another.

Significant Digit A digit that contributes to the accuracy or precision of a *numeral.* The number of significant digits is counted beginning with the digit contributing the most value, called the most significant digit, and ending with the one contributing the least value, called the least significant digit.

Simulate To represent the functioning of one system by another, e.g., to represent one computer by another, to represent a physical system by the execution of a computer program, to represent a biological system by a mathematical model.

Simulator A device or computer program that performs simulation.

Skew The angular displacement of an individual printed character, group of characters, or other data, from the intended or ideal placement.

Skip To ignore one or more instructions in a sequence of instructions.

Smooth To apply procedures that decrease or eliminate rapid fluctuations in data.

Snapshot Dump A *selective dynamic dump* performed at various points in a machine *run*.

Software (1) The collection of *programs* and *routines* associated with a computer, e.g., *compilers, library routines*. (2) All the documents associated with a computer, e.g., manuals, circuit diagrams. (3) Contrast with *Hardware*.

Solid State Component A component whose operation depends on the control of electric or magnetic phenomena in solids, e.g., a transistor, crystal diode, ferrite core.

Sort To arrange data or items in an ordered sequence by applying specific rules.

Sorter A person, device, or computer routine that *sorts*.

Source Language A *language* that is an input to a given translation process.

Source Program A program written in a *source language*.

Space (1) A place intended for the storage of data, e.g., a place on a printed page or a location in a storage medium. (2) A basic unit of area on a record, i.e., an area that may contain no more than one printed character. (3) One or more blanks. (4) To move from one place to another according to a prescribed format, e.g., to move horizontally to the right on a printed page or vertically down a page.

Special Character In a character set, a character that is neither a numeral, a letter, nor a blank, e.g., virgule, asterisk, dollar sign, equals sign, comma, period.

Special Purpose Computer A *computer* that is designed to solve a restricted class of problems.

Statement In computer programming, a meaningful expression or generalized instruction in a *source language*.

Static Dump A *dump* that is performed at a particular point in time with respect to a machine *run*, frequently at the end of a run.

Storage (1) Pertaining to a device into which data can be entered, in which it can be held, and from which it can be retrieved at a later time. (2) Loosely, any device that can store data. (3) Synonymous with Memory. (4) See *Associative Storage, Auxiliary Storage, Electrostatic Storage, Fixed Storage, Magnetic Storage, Temporary Storage, Volatile Storage, Working Storage*.

Storage Allocation The assignment of blocks of data to specified blocks of storage.

Storage Capacity The amount of data that can be contained in a storage device.

Storage Cell An elementary unit of storage, e.g., a binary cell, a decimal cell.

Storage Device A device into which data can be inserted, in which it can be retained, and from which it can be retrieved.

Store (1) To enter data into a *storage device*. (2) To retain data in a storage device. (3) A storage device.

Stored Program Computer A digital computer that, under control of internally stored instructions, can synthesize, alter, and store instructions as though they were data and can subsequently execute these new instructions.

Subroutine (1) A *routine* that can be part of another routine. (2) See *Closed Subroutine, Open Subroutine*.

Summation Check A *check* based on the formation of the sum of the digits of a *numeral*. The sum of the individual digits is usually compared with a previously computed value.

Supervisor Routine Same as *Executive Routine*.

Switch A device or programming technique for making a selection, e.g., a toggle, a *conditional jump*.

Symbol (1) A representation of something by reason of relationship, association, or convention. (2) See *Flowchart Symbol*.

Symbolic Address An *address* expressed in symbols convenient to the programmer.

Symbolic Coding *Coding* that uses *machine instructions* with *symbolic addresses*.

Symbolic Logic The discipline that treats *formal logic* by means of a formalized *artificial language* or symbolic calculus whose purpose is to avoid the ambiguities and logical inadequacies of *natural languages*.

Synchronous Computer A *computer* in which each event, or the performance of each operation, starts as a result of a signal generated by a clock.

Syntax (1) The structure of expressions in a *language*. (2) The rules governing the structure of a language.

System (1) An organized collection of parts united by regulated interaction. (2) An organized collection of men, machines and methods required to accomplish a specific objective. (3) See *Number System, Numeral System, Numeration System, Operating System*.

Tabulate (1) To form data into a table. (2) To print totals.

Tape Drive A device that moves tape past a *head*. Synonymous with Tape Transport.

Tape To Card Pertaining to equipment or methods that transmit data from either *magnetic tape* or *punched tape* to *punched cards*.

Tape Unit A device containing a *tape drive*, together with reading and writing *heads* and associated controls. Synonymous with Tape Station.

Target Language A *language* that is an output from a given translation process. Synonymous with Object Language.

Target Program A program written in a *target language*. Synonymous with Object Program.

Telecommunications Pertaining to the transmission of signals over long distances, such as by telegraph, radio, or television.

Temporary Storage In programming, storage locations reserved for intermediate results. Synonymous with Working Storage.

Terminal A point in a system or communication network at which data can either enter or leave.

Thin Film Loosely, *magnetic thin film*.

Time Sharing Pertaining to the *interleaved* use of the time of a device.

Timeshare To use a device for two or more interleaved purposes.

Toggle (1) Same as *Flip-Flop*. (2) Pertaining to any device having two stable states.

Tracing Routine A *routine* that provides a historical record of specified events in the execution of a program.

Track The portion of a moving storage medium, such as a drum, tape, or disc, that is accessible to a given reading *head* position.

Transducer A device for converting energy from one form to another.

Transfer (1) Same as *Jump*. (2) Same as *Transmit*.

Transfer Check A *check* on the accuracy of a data transfer.

Transmit To move data from one location to another location. Synonymous with Transfer (2).

Type Font A type face of a given size, e.g., 10-point Bodoni Gothic.

Unit (1) A device having a special function. (2) A basic element. (3) See *Arithmetic Unit, Central Processing Unit, Control Unit, Tape Unit*.

Utility Routine Same as *Service Routine*.

Variable A quantity that can assume any of a given set of values.

Venn Diagram A diagram in which sets are represented by closed regions.

Verify (1) To determine whether a transcription of data or other operation has been accomplished accurately. (2) To check the results of *keypunching*.

Volatile Storage A *storage device* in which stored data are lost when the applied power is removed, e.g., an acoustic delay line.

Word Length The number of *bits* or other characters in a word.

Working Storage Same as *Temporary Storage*.

Write To deliver data to a medium such as *storage*.

X-Punch A punch in the second row, one row above the zero row, on a Hollerith punched card.

Y-Punch A punch in the top row, two rows above the zero row, on a Hollerith punched card.

Zero Suppression The elimination of nonsignificant zeros in a *numeral*.

Zone Punch A punch in the 0, X, or Y row on a Hollerith punched card.

INDEX

INDEX

Access time, 156
Accounting machines, 15-17, 24
Accumulator, 180-183
Acronyms, 3
Adder, 180-182
Address, 125-127, 179-185
Address register, 183-184
Administrative controls, 344-347
Aiken, Howard, 26
ALGOL (algorithmic language), 218
American Bankers Association, 96-97, 359
American Foundation on Automation and
    Employment, 330
American Institute of Certified Public
    Accountants, 340n.
Analog computer, 56-57
Analytical Engine, 25
Ansoff, H. Igor, 362
Anthony, Robert N., 271n.
Application packages, 39-40, 234-235, 356
Arithmetic-logic unit, 179-182
Arnoff, E. Leonard, 252
ASCII (American Standard Code for Informa-
    tion Interchange), 150n.
Assembly program, 214-215, 217, 234
Audit trail, 342-344
Auditors, 342-344
    external, 342
    function of, 342-344
    internal, 342

Babbage, Charles, 25-26
Barnes, V. Lee, 254n.
Barnett, Joseph I., 267n., 278
Bartee, Thomas C., 69, 93, 136n., 154, 186
Batch processing, 44-45, 73, 75, 358
Bello, Francis, 34n.
Berkwitt, George, 287n., 362
Berton, Lee, 61n.
Binary arithmetic, 142-144
Binary Coded Decimal system, 146-149
    extended versions of, 149-153
Binary numbering system, 135, 138-144
Binger, James H., 361n.
Boutell, Wayne S., 236
Bower, James B., 292

Brabb, George J., 310
Branchpoint, 131-132
Brandon, Dick H., 50n., 53, 254n., 296n., 345n.,
    350
Brink, Victor Z., 316n., 332
Broader systems, 48-50, 358-359
Brozen, Yale, 306
Bruegman, Donald C., 350
Buckingham, Walter, 307n., 308
Buffer storage, 119-120
Burlingame, John, 327
Business information systems, 41-50, 357-360
    broader, 48-50, 358-359
    quick-response, 43-48, 357-358
Business processing applications, characteris-
    tics of, 58-59
Byte, 149, 156-157, 173-174, 177

Calculating, 7
Campise, James A., 69
Canning, Richard G., 31, 38n., 53, 122, 206,
    278, 292, 327n., 357n., 362
Card punch, 78-80
Card read punch, 79
Card reader, 76-78
Carr, John W., III, 356n.
Cathode ray tube, 111-113
Central processing unit (CPU), 123, 352-354
    (See also Arithmetic-logic unit; Control
    unit; Storage, internal)
Centralization concepts, 314-315, 324-331, 341
Channels, data transmission, 115-118
    broadband, 117
    telephone, 115
    teletype, 115
Character addressable storage, 132-135, 156
"Checkless society" concept, 359
Classifying, 6
COBOL (common business oriented language),
    205, 212n., 218-233
    coding sheets, 221-224
    DATA DIVISION, 221-223, 227-230
    FILE SECTION, 221-222, 227-229
    PICTURE clause in, 228
    WORKING STORAGE SECTION,
    222-223, 227, 229-230

COBOL (common business oriented language), development of, 218
  ENVIRONMENT DIVISION, 221, 226
    CONFIGURATION SECTION, 221, 226
    INPUT/OUTPUT SECTION, 221, 226
  IDENTIFICATION DIVISION, 221, 225
  literal constant used in, 230n., 233n.
  PROCEDURE DIVISION, 223-224, 231-233
  reserved words in, 225
  supplied words in, 225
Cole, Kenneth C., 278
Collator, 24
Command code, 207-208
Communicating, 8
Comparer, 182
Compatability, 40-41, 67, 354
Compiler, 217, 219, 234
Computer acquisition methods, 269, 273-275
  long-term leasing, 273-275
  purchasing, 273-275
  rental, 273-275
Computer centers, 29
Computer conversion, 279-285
  parallel running, 283
  personnel preparations for, 285-291, 300-309
  program preparation for, 282-284
  site preparation for, 280-282
  vendor assistance, 284-285
Computer data processing, desirable characteristics for, 9-10
  history of, 25-28
  objectives and benefits of, 10-11
Computer data representation, 148-153
Computer hardware (see Hardware)
Computer operation controls, 346-347
Computer operators, 52, 298, 304-305
Computer software (see Software)
Computer user groups, 235
Computers, capabilities of, 59-61
  classifications of, 55-59
  evaluation and selection of, 269-271
  functional organization of, 63-67
    arithmetic-logic function, 66
    control function, 64, 66
    input function, 63-65
    output function, 64, 66-67
    storage function, 64-66
  limitations of, 61-62
  markets for, 28-29
Control totals, 347, 349
Control unit, 182-185
Corbato, F. J., 360n.

Dale, Ernest, 252, 307, 312
Danziger, Erwin M., 310
Data, demand for, 4
  need for, 3-4
  sources of, 4
Data banks, 49
Data buffering, 119-120
Data controls, 347-349

Data-Phone service, 115-117
Data processing, 4-9
  computer (see Computer data processing)
  employment oportunities in, 50-52, 295-298
    (See also specific occupations)
  factors behind need for improvement of, 8-9
  management of, 50, 295-296
  manual, 13-14
  mechanical, 14-17
  punched card (see Punched card data processing)
  steps in, 5-8
Data transmission, 114-118, 355
  channels, 115-117, 355
  equipment, 115-117
  services, 115-118
  trends in, 355
Data word, 134
Davis, Gordon B., 236
Dean, Neal J., 245n., 252, 272n.
Dearden, John, 249n., 257n.
Decentralization concepts, 314-315, 324-331
Decimal numbering system, 136-137
Decision tables, 188-189, 202-205
  benefits of, 204-205
  format of, 202-203
Decoder, 183-184
Dennis, Jamie, 292
DeSpelder, Bruce, 293
DETAB/65 (decision table 1965), 205
Diebold, John, 320, 362
Digital computer, 56-57
Display stations, 112-113
Distributed computer concept, 353
Driebeek, Norman J., 252
Drucker, Peter F., 59n., 329, 361n.
Dual purpose medium, 75, 81

EBCDIC (Extended Binary Coded Decimal Interchange Code), 149-153
Eckert, J. Presper, Jr., 26-27
EDVAC (Electronic Discrete Variable Automatic Computer), 27
Ehlers, Marvin W., 260n.
ENIAC (Electronic Numerical Integrator and Calculator), 26, 158
Evans, David C., 186, 353
Execution cycle, 183

Fano, R. M., 360n.
Feasibility study, 250, 253-277
  benefits of, 253-254, 257
  charter for, 260-261
  design sessions in, 259-260, 265
  determination of scope and objectives of, 257-259
  essential nature of, 253-257
  pitfalls associated with poor studies, 254-256
  prerequisites to, 257-261
  steps in study approach, 261-277
    data analysis and determination of alternatives, 264-268

Feasibility study, steps in study approach,
  data gathering, 262-264
  decision follow up, 276-277
  decision making (study team), 268-275
  final decision making (top managers), 276
  identification of problem, 261
  presentation of study recommendations,
    274, 276
  use of return-on-investment analysis in, 262,
    268-269, 271-272
Fergus, Raymond M., 12
Files, 45, 71-75
  master, 72-73
  randomly organized, 73-74
  sequentially organized, 73-75
  transaction, 71-72
Fisketjon, Kenneth O., 53
Fixed word-length storage, 132-135, 156-157,
  180
Flowcharting, 188-205
  benefits and limitations of, 199-200
  conventions of, 189, 193-194, 196-199
  program, 189, 194-200
  system, 188-189, 192-194, 262-265
  USA Standards Institute symbols for, 189,
    192-193, 195
FLOW-MATIC, 217
FORTRAN (formula translation), 217-219
Future outlook, 324-331, 351-362
  for application packages, 356
  for broader systems, 358-359
  for business information systems, 357-360
  for central processors, 352-354
  for data communications, 355
  for input/output devices, 351-352
  for managerial authority, 325-331
  for managers, 328-331, 360-361
  for organizational structure, 324-328, 331
  for programming languages, 355-356
  for quick-response systems, 357-358
  for software consultants, 356-357
  for time sharing, 359-360

Garrett, L. J., 49*n.*
Garrity, John T., 243*n.*, 254*n.*
General purpose computers, 57
Gilman, Glenn, 325, 333
Glaser, Edward M., 293
Greenberger, Martin, 360*n.*
Greenwood, Frank, 310
Grid chart (input/output chart), 265, 267
Griffin, W. H., 310
Grimes, Andrew J., 252, 299*n.*
Gruenberger, Fred, 12, 293

Hardware, development in, 35-39
  future trends in, 351-355
Head, Robert V., 359*n.*
Heckmann, I. L., Jr., 286, 288*n.*
Heilborn, George H., 278
Heshka, William, 333
Heuristic capability, 63

Hill, Richard H., 12, 261, 268
Hill, Walter A., 293, 299*n.*
Hillegass, John, 93, 122
Hodskins, J. A., 93
Hollerith. Herman. 18-19
Hoos, Ida R., 299*n.*, 307
Huneryager, S. G., 286, 288*n.*

IBM 650, 27*n.*, 57, 158, 217
IBM System/360, 36*n.* 40*n.*, 75, 134*n.*, 150,
  177, 226
Information quality, 337-340
  properties of, 337-340
    accuracy, 337-338
    completeness, 339-340
    pertinency, 339-340
    timeliness, 338-339
Information utilities, 47, 359-360
Input controls, 347-348
Input/output, future trends in, 351-352
  hardware and media alternatives, 68, 73,
    75-93, 95-114
    high-speed printers, 103-106
    magnetic ink character recognition, 95-99
    magnetic tape, 85-92
    online terminals, 106-110
    optical character recognition, 99-103
    punched cards, 75-81
    punched paper tape, 81-85
    visual communication, 110-113
    voice communication, 113-114
Input/output chart, 265, 267
Input tablet, 110
Instruction cycle, 183
Instruction register, 183-184
Instruction word, 134
Instructions, 127-128, 131, 182, 207-210
  repertoire of, 130, 208-210
  single-address, 208-209
  three-address, 208-209
  two-address, 208-209
  types of, 208-211
    arithmetic, 208, 211
    control, 210-211
    data movement, 209-211
    logic, 208-209, 211
Integrated circuits, 36-37
Integrated systems, 48
Internal control, 340-349
  administrative controls, 344-347
  auditing in, 342-344
  data controls, 347-349
  nature of, 340
  need for, 340-341
  organizational considerations in, 341-
    342
Interpreter, 24-25

Jarrett, Harold, 300
Job descriptions, 301
Job specifications, 301
Joplin, H. Bruce, 350

Karplus, Walter J., 53
Kaufman, Felix, 358n.
Keypunch, 21-22
Koontz, Harold, 241n., 252, 315

Languages, 210, 212-220
  machine, 212, 215
  procedure oriented, 212, 216-220
    development of, 217-219
    (See also ALGOL; COBOL; FORTRAN;
      PL/I)
  selection of, 219-220
  symbolic, 212-216
  trends in, 355-356
Law of trichotomy, 60n.
Learning experiments, 62-63
Lee, Hak Chong, 333
Leeds. Herbert D.. 214n., 237
Leibniz, Gottfried, 139n.
Licklider, J. C. R., 69
Light pen, 112
Lindsay, Franklin A., 248
Linear programming, 247
Looping, 131-132, 197

McCameron, Fritz A., 237
McDonough, A. M., 49n.
McFarlan, F. Warren, 257n.
McGill, D. A. C., 244.
McGregor, Douglas, 288n.
McIsaac, George S., 286
MacLean, John D., 283
McRae, T. W., 344
Macro instruction, 216
Magnetic card and strip storage, 174-179
Magnetic disk storage, 171-174
Magnetic drum storage, 158, 168-171
Magnetic ink character reader-sorter, 97-98
Magnetic ink character recognition (MICR),
  95-99
  advantages and limitations of, 98-99
  equipment, 97-98
  use and development of, 95-97
Magnetic tape, 85-92
  advantages and limitations of, 91-92
  blocks, 88-89
  coding of, 87-88
  data density of, 86-89, 91
  end-of-reel marker, 88-89
  equipment, 89-91
  interrecord gaps, 88-89
  labels, 348
  load-point marker, 88-89
  transfer rate of, 85-86
Management, 239-242
  functions of, 240-242
    controlling, 241-242, 335-336
    organizing, 241, 312-314
    planning, 240
    staffing, 241
Managerial control, 335-336
  (See also Management, functions of)
Managerial implications of computers, 242-
  249

Managerial implications of computers,
  decision-making implications, 246-248
    linear programming, 247
    PERT-CPM, 246-247
    simulation, 247-248
  economic implications, 245
  organizational implications, 244
  planning and control implications, 243-244
  staffing implications, 245
  systems implications, 248-249
Mann, F. C., 299
Manual data processing, 13-14
MARK-I, 26
Mark sensing, 23
Martin, W. W., 206
MATH-MATIC, 217
Mauchly, John W., 26-27
Mechanical data processing, 14-17
Methods, 41
Microsecond, 37
Miller, Ben, 290n.
Millisecond, 37
Mitchell, Don, 306
Mnemonic command code, 213-214
Modularity, 67
Morgan, James I., 206
Multiprogramming, 40, 85n.
Mulvihill, Dennis E., 333

Naftaly, Stanley M., 237, 356n.
Nanosecond, 37
Netzorg, M. J., 252
Neuschel, Richard F., 43n., 277n.
Newman, Maurice S., 345n., 350
Numbering systems, additive, 136
  positional, 136
  (See also Binary numbering system; Decimal
    numbering system; Octal numbering system

Object program, 214-215, 217
Octal numbering system, 138, 144-146
O'Donnell, Cyril, 241n., 252
Oersted, Hans Christian, 159
Online processing, 44-46, 358
Online terminals, 106-110
  console typewriter, 106-107
  data collection stations, 109-110
  inquiry stations, 107-109
  transaction recorders, 109-110
Open shop, 320
Operand, 207-208
Operation code, 207-208
Operations research (OR), 246
Optical character recognition (OCR), 99-103
  advantages and limitations of, 102-103
  equipment, 101-102
  uses of, 99-101
Optical readers, 101-102
Organization, of computer department, 322-
  324
  of data processing activities, 315-324
    alternative organizational locations, 318-
      322
    factors favoring centralization of, 316

Organization, of data processing activities
  factors favoring decentralization of, 317
  hardware centralization trend in, 317-318
Organization chart, 312-313
Originating-recording, 5-6
Output controls, 349

Packaged programs (*see* Application packages)
Paper tape punch, 84-85
Paper tape reader, 83-84
Parity checking, 60-61, 83, 88
Pascal, Blaise, 15
Perlman, Justin A., 333
Personnel displacement, 305-309
  business experience with, 306-309
  distinction between displacement and un-
    employment, 305-306
  factors affecting extent of, 307-309
Personnel resistance to change, 285-291
  employees who resist, 290
  forms of, 286-287
  reasons for, 287-290
  means of reducing, 291
PERT-CPM, 246-247, 276n., 336
Pfeiffer, John, 212n.
Pierce, John R., 122
PL/I (Programming Language I), 218-219
Porter, W. Thomas, Jr., 333, 350
Powers, James, 19
Printers, 103-105
  character-at-a-time, 103-104
  drum, 105
  impact, 104n.
  line-at-a-time, 104-105
  nonimpact, 105n.
  print chain, 105
Procedures, 41
Processing controls, 348
Programmers, 51, 297-298, 300-305
  aptitude tests for selection of, 302
Programming, aids in, 233-235, 285, 356
  analysis for, 187-206, 282
  controls, 345-346
  conversational, 354
  defined, 188
  documentation for, 199-200, 283, 345
  program coding in, 220-233, 279, 283-284
  program debugging and maintenance in,
    233, 268, 279, 283-285
Punched card data processing, 18-25, 75-81
  cards and the code, 19-20
  equipment   21-25, 76-80
  fields, 19-21
Punched cards, advantages and limitations of,
  80-81
Punched paper tape, 81-85
  advantages and limitations of, 85
  coding of, 82-83
  equipment, 83-85

Quick-response systems, 43-48, 357-358

Rabinow, Jacob, 122
Random access processing, 73-74

Random access time, 170
Ready, Thomas J., Jr., 360n.
Reagan, F. H., Jr., 122
Real time processing, 46-47, 358
Registers, 179-185
Reistad, Dale L., 359n.
Reproducing, 7-8, 23
Retrieving, 7
Rudolph, Harley H., Jr., 206

Sanders, Donald H., 29n., 31, 268n., 299n.,
  308n.
Saxon, James A., 237
SCERT (Systems and Computers Evaluation
  and Review Technique), 271
Schlosser, Robert E., 350
Schussel, George, 31
Scientific processing applications, character-
  istics of, 58-59
Second generation computers, 28
Sefert, J. Bruce, 292
Selection of computer personnel, 295-303
  new positions created, 295-298
  procedures in, 301-303
  sources of candidates, 300-301
Sequence register, 183-184
Sequential (batch) processing, 44-45, 73, 75,
  358
Shaul, Donald R., 333
Simulation, 247-248
Single flow systems, 48
Sisson, Roger L., 353
Smith, Lloyd P., 293
Software, 35
  consultants, 235, 356-357
  development in, 39-40
  future outlook, for, 355-357
Solid state components, 28
Solomon, Irving I., 273n.
Sorter, 23
Sorting, 6-7
Source program, 214-215, 217
Special purpose computers, 57
Sprague, Richard E., 53, 360n.
Statland, Norman, 93, 122
Storage, external offline, 73, 156, 167
  external online (random access), 45, 73-74
    155-158, 167-179, 353-354
    magnetic card and strip, 174-179
    magnetic disk, 171-174
    magnetic drum, 158, 168-171
  internal, 155-166, 353
    capacity of locations in, 132-135
    character addressable, 132-135, 156
    conceptual areas of, 123-125
    early types of, 158
    fixed word-length, 132-135, 156-157, 180
    locations in (*see* Address)

Storage, internal, magnetic core, 159-163
    memory rod, 165-167
    thin film, 163-166
    variable word-length, 132-135, 156-157,
        180, 208
    word addressable, 132-135, 156-157
Storing, 7
Subroutines, 188-189, 234
Summarizing, 7
Sutherland, Ivan E., 110n., 122
Symbolic addressing, 213
Synchronous computer, 185
Systems analysts, 51, 297-298, 300, 303-304
Systems-oriented control, 341, 344-345

Tabulating Machine Company, 19
Tape librarians, 87, 298
Taylor, James W., 245n., 252, 272n.
Telpak service, 117n.
Third generation computers, 36
Time sharing, 40, 47, 354, 359-360
Toan, A. B., Jr., 14n.
Total systems, 48-49
Touch-Tone telephones, 355, 359
Training of computer personnel, 303-305
Tuthill, Oliver W., 53

UNIVAC-I, 27
Uris, Auren, 328

Variable word-length storage, 132-135, 156-
    157, 180, 208
Vergin, Roger C., 252, 299n., 310
Verifier, 23
Visual input/output, 110-113
    display stations, 112-113
    use of, cathode ray tube in, 111-113
        input tablet in, 110
        light pen in, 112
Voice input/output, 113-114
Von Neumann, John, 27, 139

Wagoner, Max L., 69
Warder, Benton, 343n., 350
Watson, Goodwin, 293
Weinberg, Gerald M., 214n., 237
Weiner, Jack B., 360n.
Weingart, Laurence O., 273n.
Whisler, Thomas L., 290, 362
White, H. Warren, 324
Williams, L. K., 299
Word addressable storage, 132-135, 156-157
Wordmark, 133-134

Zone punching positions, 19-20